HANDBOOK OF RURAL DEVELOPMENT

Handbook of Rural Development

Edited by

Gary Paul Green

University of Wisconsin–Madison, USA

Edward Elgar

Cheltenham, UK • Northampton, MA, USA

Published by
Edward Elgar Publishing Limited
The Lypiatts
15 Lansdown Road
Cheltenham
Glos GL50 2JA
UK

Edward Elgar Publishing, Inc.
William Pratt House
9 Dewey Court
Northampton
Massachusetts 01060
USA

A catalogue record for this book
is available from the British Library

Library of Congress Control Number: 2013943225

This book is available electronically in the ElgarOnline.com Economics Subject Collection, E-ISBN 978 1 78100 671 9

Printed on elemental chlorine free (ECF)
recycled paper containing 30% Post-Consumer Waste

ISBN 978 1 78100 670 2

Typeset by Columns Design XML Ltd, Reading
Printed and bound in the USA

Contents

PART III   REGIONAL

Figures

Tables

Contributors

Alessandro Bonanno is Sam Houston State University Distinguished Professor, USA, and a Texas State University System Professor, of Sociology, USA. He served as the President of the International Rural Sociological Association from 2004 to 2008. Bonanno is currently the editor of *Rural Sociology*.

Ian Carrillo is a graduate student in the Department of Sociology at the University of Wisconsin–Madison, USA. He has a Master of Arts in Latin American Studies from the Center for Latin American Studies at the University of Kansas, USA. His interests are related to comparative macro- and micro-level development strategies and the political economy of development, primarily in Latin America.

Katherine J. Curtis is Associate Professor in the University of Wisconsin–Madison's Department of Community and Environmental Sociology, USA. Her research primarily concerns demographic dynamics and events that contribute to population and spatial inequality. Specifically, her work addresses the causes and consequences of migration and population redistribution, population and environment, and economic vulnerability and inequality, with attention to the underlying spatial and temporal dimensions. Her work consistently engages multiple literatures across disciplines to gain greater substantive and technical insight.

Michael L. Dougherty is an Assistant Professor in the Department of Sociology at Illinois State University, USA. His teaching and research center, broadly, on the sociology of the environment, development, and rural livelihoods. His current research examines the social dynamics around resistance to gold mining in Central America. Dougherty received his PhD from the University of Wisconsin–Madison, USA.

Stephen P. Gasteyer is an Assistant Professor of Sociology at Michigan State University, USA. Dr Gasteyer's research focuses on the nexus between water, land and community development. Before coming to Michigan State University, Dr Gasteyer was on faculty in the Department of Human and Community Development at the University of Illinois, USA. Prior to that, he was Research and Policy Director at the Rural Community Assistance Partnership in Washington, DC, USA and a research consultant on issues of global water governance.

W. Richard Goe is Professor of Sociology and Coordinator of the Sociology Program at Kansas State University, Manhattan, USA. His research focuses on development issues facing rural and urban communities and regions. His published research has appeared in *Social Forces*, *Rural Sociology*, *Urban Affairs Review* and *Regional Studies*, among other journals.

Stephan J. Goetz is the Director of the Northeast Regional Center for Rural Development and Professor of Agricultural and Regional Economics at the Pennsylvania State University, USA. Dr Goetz has published or presented over 200 professional papers and is the senior co-editor of four books, including *Targeting Regional Economic Development* (Routledge, 2009). He is the principal investigator on external grants valued at over $10 million.

Shaun A. Golding is Visiting Assistant Professor of Sociology at Bowdoin College in Brunswick, Maine, USA. His research focuses on rural development and social change through the lenses of demography and environmental sociology. He is primarily interested in the relationships between globalization, economic inequality, identity and politics, and in how those relationships impact both well-being and natural resource planning and decision-making in rural communities.

Gary Paul Green is a Professor in the Department of Community and Environmental Sociology at the University of Wisconsin–Madison, USA. His research and teaching focuses on community and economic development. His recent books include *Mobilizing Communities: Asset Building as Community Development* (Temple University Press, 2010), *Asset Building and Community Development* (Sage Publications, 2012) and *Local Food and Community Development* (Routledge, 2013).

Cameron (Khalfani) Herman is a graduate student in the Department of Sociology at Michigan State University, USA.

Thomas G. Johnson is the Frank Miller Professor of Agricultural and Applied Economics at the University of Missouri–Columbia, USA.

David Kraybill is Professor in the Department of Agricultural, Environmental, and Development Economics at the Ohio State University, USA.

Linda Lobao is Professor of Rural Sociology, Sociology, and Geography at the Ohio State University, USA. Her research focuses on spatial inequality or socio-economic well-being across communities and how this is affected by economic structure, including farming and by government. She has published numerous articles and three books, including an edited volume with Gregory Hooks and Ann Tickamyer, *The Sociology of Spatial Inequality* (State University of New York Press, 2007). Lobao is a past President of the Rural Sociological Society, a Fellow of the American Association for the Advancement of Science, and currently a co-editor of the *Cambridge Journal of Regions, Economy, and Society.*

David Marcouiller is a Professor of Urban and Regional Planning at the University of Wisconsin–Madison, USA, where he serves as Department Chair and State Extension Specialist. A resource economist by training, his work focuses on the linkages between natural resources and community economic development with a particular interest in multi-functional rural landscapes, the production of natural amenities, and the recreational home phenomenon. He has published over 160 manuscripts in a variety of outlets that span tourism and forest economics, outdoor recreation planning and rural development. His most recent book project was published by Ashgate Press in 2011 and is entitled *Rural Housing, Exurbanization, and Amenity Drive Development*, which he co-edited with Mark Lapping and Owen Furuseth.

Anirban Mukherjee is a recent PhD graduate in Sociology from Kansas State University, USA. His dissertation research focused on identifying factors influencing the migration and locational decisions of Indian professional workers employed in the Kansas City metropolitan area.

Carolyn Sachs is a Professor in the Department of Agricultural Economics, Sociology, and Education at Pennsylvania State University, USA.

Jeff Sharp is a Professor in the School of Environment and Natural Resources at the Ohio State University, USA. His areas of expertise include agriculture and community change at the rural–urban interface. He has published on such topics as the importance of social capital to reducing farmer–nonfarmer conflict, the agro-environmental attitudes of exurbanites, and the association of community policies and agricultural change and development.

Richard C. Stedman is an Associate Professor and Associate Director of the Human Dimensions Research Unit in the Department of Natural Resources at Cornell University, USA. His research and teaching focuses on the well-being of coupled social–ecological systems; he is especially interested in the well-being of resource-dependent communities and how they are affected by social change; and human elements such as place attachment and environmental attitudes in fostering the sustainability and resilience of such systems.

Elisa Da Già is a PhD candidate in the Department of Development Sociology, Cornell University, USA. Her research focuses on the political economy and ecology of rural development and agrarian change. Her dissertation examines the emergence of networks of seed saving and exchange in Southern Europe, with special emphasis on the role played by farm-saved seeds, peasant-led research and agro-ecological farming methods in contemporary struggles for food sovereignty and environmental sustainability.

Li Zhang is an Assistant Professor of Sociology at Virginia Commonwealth University, USA. Her research and teaching interests include demography, urban sociology, health and Chinese studies. Her research has turned into a sole-authored book, *Male Fertility Patterns and Determinants* (Springer, 2010) and a number of peer-reviewed journal articles published by *Social Science Research, Population Research and Policy Review* and *Demographic Research*.

John Aloysius Zinda is a post-doctoral fellow at Brown University. His PhD is from the University of Wisconsin–Madison, USA. He has a Master's degree in Natural Resources from the University of Michigan, Ann Arbor, USA. His research concerns efforts to reshape conservation and tourism practices in China's protected areas, the politics behind them, and their social, economic and ecological consequences.

Preface

Why should we care about rural regions today? Most countries are rapidly urbanizing. Rural-to-urban migration is often viewed as a path to improve economic and social opportunities for rural residents. Rural areas have an especially difficult time retaining youth because they often move to urban areas for social and cultural reasons as well. Technological advancements in agriculture have enabled farmers to grow more food and fiber, which has ultimately led to lower prices for urban consumers. This technological treadmill means that fewer farmers are needed to grow more food. The decline in population and employment in rural areas seems to be part of a natural process of national development. A basic premise of this book, however, is that it is not 'natural' and there are many critical reasons to be concerned with conditions for rural people and places today.

The majority of people, especially the poor, in the world continue to live in rural areas. The World Bank recognizes that rural development is essential to improving the quality of life in most developing countries in Africa, Asia and Latin America. Many of the World Bank programs now focus on improving technology transfer, access to services and economic conditions in rural areas. The economies of most developing countries are still rooted in the exploitation of natural resources, both renewable (land, water and forests) and non-renewable (oil and minerals). Rural people are the stewards of most of these natural resources and play a critical role in environmental protection. There is a growing recognition of the complex relationship between conservation and development: the two are often mutually dependent.

In the past, rural development programs and policies have focused primarily on increasing agricultural productivity. The assumption behind these efforts has been that increasing productivity will improve farmers' income and ultimately expand economic opportunities in rural areas. Many analysts have argued that we need to take a broader approach to rural development (Browne et al. 1992). In most developed countries, farming is no longer the major industry in rural areas. Another most important reason for broadening rural development programs is the strengthening of linkages between rural areas and the global economy. Cotton farmers in Africa, for example, are now competing with growers in the United States. This integration into the global economy generates new winners and losers, as well as constraints and opportunities for rural residents. Globalization may lead to greater specialization by region and influence more broadly how farmers interact with commodity markets.

Rural areas typically face obstacles to development due to their low population size and density. In particular, transportation, health care, education and access to technology are limited in many rural regions. It is very costly to provide these services to small communities because of economies of scale. For example, large schools can offer a broader curriculum than small schools. Other services may be more expensive in smaller communities as well. The distance to larger markets also adds transportation costs to economic activities in rural areas. Improved communication and technological systems have helped alleviate some, but not all, of the obstacles faced by rural communities. Many rural residents in Africa, for example, have access to cellphone service now, but they continue to have difficulty transporting goods to markets because of poor roads.

Rural areas, however, also have key assets that are frequently underutilized. Increasingly, the natural and cultural amenities of rural areas form the basis of consumption rather than production activities. This dependence on consumption economies is most often the case through tourism and recreation. Natural resources are, therefore, multi-functional – serving both production and consumption functions. Production activities, such as mining and forestry, can promote development in rural areas, but they also may contribute to environmental degradation and marginalization of indigenous populations. Globalization has increased the opportunities for amenity-based development as interest in international tourism has soared. Ecotourism is one of the fastest-growing sources of revenue and foreign exchange in many developing countries. There continues to be pressure from governments and corporations, however, to continue to extract natural resources (especially in forested and mining areas).

This *Handbook* is divided into three parts: Part I, rural development concepts and theories; Part II, common themes and issues; and Part III, regional trends and outlooks. Many people today reject the idea that development can be measured by a single indicator, such as gross national production (GNP). Such an approach is especially problematic for understanding the nature of rural development. The introductory chapter (Green and Zinda, Chapter 1) examines some of the issues in defining rural development and proposes that the concept should include not only economic indicators, but social and environmental dimensions as well. In addition, rural development programs must find meaningful ways of engaging rural residents in policies that build community capacity.

We focus our discussion of rural development on three broad levels: global forces, national policy, and grassroots movements. It is increasingly difficult to separate rural areas from the global economy, so it is important to examine how international forces influence rural households and communities. In Chapter 2 Bonanno argues that globalization encompasses a broad set of economic and cultural forces that impinge on rural areas. There are several key international organizations and institutions, such as the World Trade Organization and the World Bank, that are actively shaping opportunities and constraints in rural areas. Due to this fundamental transformation in social relationships, Bonanno calls for a global approach to address rural development issues.

Although globalization has been a critical factor shaping development, national rural development policy continues to influence rural livelihoods (Chapter 3). Subsidies for agricultural producers and social programs are under attack from international organizations, but there continues to be political pressure to maintain these programs in many countries. Johnson argues that many governments are now emphasizing institutional innovations as a means of promoting rural development.

Increasingly, grassroots organizations (especially nongovernmental organizations) are resisting globalization and state policies by generating alternatives that provide residents with new opportunities and strategies. Chapter 4 (Gasteyer and Herman) describes how grassroots organizations are active in a wide range of activities, such as health, environmental protection, education and credit programs. Many of these grassroots organizations actively promote community participation, while others focus primarily on providing technical assistance and services.

In Part II we explore several issues that are currently discussed among rural development practitioners and policy makers. One of the critical themes is the role of natural resources and the environment. Stedman (Chapter 5) argues that this relationship to the natural environment has often led to periods of bust and boom for many rural communities. Stedman reviews the literature on resource dependency and provides a more nuanced interpretation of the impacts of dependency on well-being in rural communities.

Rapid urbanization has created social problems in many developing countries. Urbanization creates pressures on the environment, social services and the economy. In Chapter 6, Golding and Curtis argue that many rural development policies focus on programs that are intended to reduce the migration flow to urban areas. In developed countries, migration has become a major factor shaping rural development. Golding and Curtis focus on some of the emerging issues related to migration into and from rural areas, both in developing and developed countries.

Agricultural production has historically been the economic base for most rural communities. The primary objective of rural development policy has been to increase the income of ranchers and farmers, primarily through increasing productivity. Increased productivity has increased the average size of farms and led to a decline in the number of farms, which has had significant impacts on rural communities through population and employment loss. There is a rather large body of literature that has documented the impacts of the changing structure of agriculture on rural communities. In Chapter 7, Lobao and Sharp review this literature and point to some of the unresolved issues in this research. Lobao and Sharp also discuss the potential and limits of promoting local food systems and urban agriculture in response to these structural changes in agricultural production.

Although the self-employment rates are higher in rural than urban areas, entrepreneurs in rural regions tend to face numerous obstacles. Rural areas are unlikely to attract much capital investment from urban areas, and as a result their economy is more dependent on creating new businesses. Entrepreneurs face numerous obstacles, but the most important appear to be financing, information and technical assistance. Chapter 8 (Goetz) discusses many of the benefits of promoting small businesses and self-employment for rural areas. He raises important questions about the relative low returns to investment among entrepreneurs and whether public policy should be supporting this type of activity. He does, however, point to a growing body of literature that suggests that self-employment and small business development have broad impacts on rural economies.

Tourism has become one of the most important industries in rural areas. Recreation and natural resources are key attractions in these areas. Although tourism creates new jobs and injects income into rural communities, it also raises a variety of concerns among residents. Research on tourism suggests that it often creates low-paying jobs with few benefits, and the jobs are often seasonal and part-time. It also creates excessive demands on the local infrastructure. In Chapter 9, Marcouiller discusses some of the many ways tourism can benefit rural community development. He provides a conceptual approach that links tourism to co-production and joint public–private processes in rural areas.

The role of women is probably one of the most understudied topics in rural development. Yet, women play a critical role in agricultural production and off-farm activities in rural areas. Rural development policies and programs often have unintended effects on women, especially for programs encouraging rural families to become more dependent on cash economies. In Chapter 10, Sachs examines the role of women in rural development programs and focuses on the growing important of gender mainstreaming in rural policy.

One of the most widespread innovations to help entrepreneurs in rural areas has been microenterprise loan funds. These programs make very small loans to help entrepreneurs who are too poor to gain access to traditional capital markets. The Grameen Bank in Bangladesh is often credited with establishing the development of these loan funds. Today, microenterprise loan funds are used in most developing countries. There are increasing concerns, however, that these programs charge excessively high interest rates and do not reach the poorest of the poor. In Chapter 11, Carrillo weighs some of the benefits and costs to microenterprise loan programs in rural areas.

Over the past decade, there has been growing interest in the potential of biofuels as a mechanism to promote rural development. Biofuels can improve environmental quality by reducing dependency on fossil fuels, as well as produce new jobs in rural communities. Biofuels have increased the demand for many crops, especially corn, and as a result, prices for many agricultural commodities have risen. Chapter 12 by Goe and Mukherjee explores the locational decisions of ethanol plants in the US Midwest. They find that these plants tend to be located in more urbanized areas of the rural Midwest and in regions that have lower earnings.

Land grabbing refers to the process of land transactions conducted in developing countries by transnational and foreign companies and governments for the production of biofuels and feedstock for export. This process is leading to increased concerns with food security, environmental degradation and the displacement of peasants in developing countries. The opening chapter in Part III, Chapter 13 by da Vià, focuses on how states and international institutions and organizations are engaged in strategies to promote land grabbing in the name of development.

Although there are some common themes to rural development, there is a considerable amount of variation in the obstacles and resources across different regions in the world. The rural population is proportionately large in Africa and Asia, and small in Europe, Latin America and North America. Latin American countries have the smallest percentage of rural residents – about one-fifth. The vast majority of rural workers in Africa and Asia continue to work in the agricultural sector (broadly defined as agriculture, hunting, fishing and forestry). Most African countries have relatively few rural residents in the non-farm sector. Several countries (e.g., Mali, Malawi and Rwanda) have less than 10 percent of their rural population in nonfarm activities. Although it has a relatively small rural population, Latin America has a relatively high proportion of rural residents working in the agricultural sector as well.

International development agencies, such as the World Bank, have focused many of their programs on supporting the rural nonfarm sector as a means of alleviating rural poverty. Investments in this sector, especially financial support for entrepreneurs, can be an effective strategy for providing economic opportunities for the poor who may not have access to land in rural areas. Although there are concerns with the low productivity of the rural nonfarm sector, the experience in many developing countries is that promoting the nonfarm sector reduces income inequality and promotes growth in rural areas. Given the relative size of the rural population in most developing countries, this strategy may help reduce out-migration to urban areas. In Part III in the *Handbook*, we examine some of the key rural development issues in Africa, China, and Latin America. These regions should provide interesting contrasts in rural development opportunities and constraints in these different contexts.

In Chapter 14, Kraybill discusses some of the key obstacles and opportunities to rural development in sub-Saharan Africa. This region is one of the poorest in the world. Although there is growing optimism for the region, much of the development is uneven and somewhat precarious. Kraybill reviews the current state of development in this region and examines some of the key trends.

In Chapter 15, Li Zhang provides a historical account of rural development policies in China. One of the most difficult obstacles to managing the growth in China over the past several decades has been the uneven regional development. This uneven development has been accompanied by rapid urbanization that has taken much of the pressure off the government to increase livelihoods in rural areas.

Finally, in Chapter 16, Dougherty discusses the efforts to promote rural development, especially through investments in extractive industries such as mining, in Latin America. He points to a significant transformation in the class structure of rural Latin America. More specifically, there has been a declining importance of the traditional peasant class and the rise of a semi-proletariat class that is employed by international capital. These changes have led to increased levels of income inequality, as well as environmental degradation in many regions. Grassroots opposition to these changes has erupted and Dougherty focuses on the need for civil society strategies to address these problems.

Even in the context of rapid globalization and urbanization, development of rural people and places continues to be a critical issue for most countries. Rural development touches on a wide variety of issues of concern today, including social and environmental justice. Rural development has become more complex, however, because of the interaction between global, national and grassroots forces. This *Handbook* reviews the literature on these key issues and attempts to identify some of the important strategies for improving the quality of life for rural people around the globe.

Gary Paul Green

REFERENCE

Browne, William P., Jerry R. Skees, Louis E. Swanson, Paul B. Thompson and Laurian J. Unnevehr (1992), *Sacred Cows and Hot Potatoes: Agrarian Myths in Agricultural Policy*, Boulder, CO: Westview Press.

PART I

THEORY

1. Rural development theory
Gary Paul Green and John Aloysius Zinda

INTRODUCTION

Rural development continues to be a high priority in both developed and developing countries. Inadequate living standards in rural areas can threaten a nation's food supply. Rural residents are often the caretakers of a nation's natural resources and lack of development can lead to the destruction of those resources. Urban social problems can be exacerbated by high levels of rural-to-urban migration. Uneven development between rural and urban areas presents social and environmental justice issues for officials and has the potential of generating social unrest as well. Thus, rural development continues to be a critical policy arena because it extends to so many issues that affect the quality of life for both urban and rural residents.

Rural development practitioners and policy makers face some common obstacles in addressing these issues. Low population density and distance to markets are often cited as major constraints to rural development because it is more difficult to provide services and to access markets. These same factors also typically translate into the lower political power of rural people. The small scale of rural communities limits access to key resources, such as education, health care, cultural activities and employment. Rural communities also tend to be dependent on single industries, especially those in the extractive sector (for example, forestry, mining and fishing). This dependency creates additional challenges to improving the quality of life in rural communities because residents are vulnerable to major shifts in markets and technology.

In this chapter, we review some of the key issues in defining rural development and examine a variety of strategies that are being used today to address the changing context in the global economy. We argue that it is essential to recognize the important roles that markets, states and communities play in rural development.

DEFINING DEVELOPMENT

Development is one of the most controversial concepts in the social sciences. It remains mired in numerous debates and controversies. One of the most hotly contested issues is the relationship between development and growth. The two concepts are often treated as if they were synonymous, but there are several critical differences between the two. Growth usually refers to increased levels of population, employment, income or gross domestic product (GDP). There is a general acknowledgement by researchers that these indicators are inadequate, but they are the most readily available. One of the problems is that these indicators reduce our understanding of development to only material benefits. For example, using income as a measure of development assumes that individuals maximize their preferences through increasing their earnings. Additional earnings provide individuals with the resources to purchase a new car or have more leisure time, whichever they prefer. Income is considered the essential means by which individuals satisfy their preferences. Similarly, population growth in a community is considered as a precursor to development because it provides local governments with additional tax revenues to improve services and possibly reduce the overall tax rate to the local residents. The assumption is that residents will move to communities that provide them with the mix of taxes and services they desire (Peterson 1981). This view of development, however, ignores the social, environmental and fiscal costs that communities face with population growth (McKibben 2007). Much of the residential preference literature suggests that most people would prefer to live in smaller communities. Finally, this approach to measuring development assumes that individuals (and city governments) are always rational actors and they tend to maximize individual interests. There is a growing movement to go beyond measures of development that rely entirely on growth indicators. In some cases, measures of happiness or satisfaction are preferred.

A second controversy surrounding the concept of development concerns the perceived beneficiaries and/or the outcomes. Development is often viewed as disproportionately benefitting the rich, large corporations, or wealthy nations. Generating more economic activity may provide new jobs to a community, but it also tends to reward investors and business owners more than workers, and thus generates more income inequality. In poorer countries, development is frequently viewed by residents as a process that extracts profits and value from the local population. Over the last few decades, there has been criticism of international financial institutions, such as the International Monetary Fund (IMF), for promoting policies that have increased the gap between the poor and wealthy countries in the name of development (Stiglitz et al. 2006). In our view, however, development should increase the opportunities for the broader population and in many cases will lead to a change in the distribution of income or wealth (reduce inequality).

A third issue regarding development is that growth promotion often takes a short-term perspective or focuses solely on the benefits rather than also considering costs associated with growth. For example, many environmentalists see job and income growth as inevitably leading to environmental degradation. Growth ultimately leads to more consumption that comes at the expense of natural resources, which are often non-renewable. Communities that grow rapidly do see benefits in terms of jobs and tax revenue, but it also may be associated with additional costs, such as demands for new infrastructure, schools and additional services (Logan and Molotch 1987). Indicators of development should reflect the actual environmental and social costs, both short and long term. It is much more difficult to construct indicators that internalize these costs.

Finally, for some, the concept of development is inherently embedded in Western, and especially American (United States), culture. It is rejected in many developing countries as contributing to the loss of traditional values and culture. The assumption is that development requires the adoption of modern values and behaviors: Western culture. A broader view of development does not impose any particular values or cultural perspective, but acknowledges that development enables individuals to pursue multiple objectives and goals. Thus, it should be possible to enhance the quality of life without sacrificing the core values that individuals may hold.

Based on the discussion above, we believe development involves institutional change that enables individuals to improve their quality of life. A consequence of development is that individuals are better able to maximize their preferences and capacities, whatever they are. This definition is sufficiently broad enough to avoid many of the problems raised by efforts to measure development exclusively through material conditions, such as income and wealth. In other words, preferences can be achieved through both material and non-material means. If individuals prefer to maintain a lifestyle based on traditional values and beliefs, development would enable them to achieve that goal. Development also should not limit the development opportunities for future generations by maximizing benefits for the current generation.

There are other dimensions to development that may be included in the definition. Amartya Sen, the Nobel Prize winner economist, defined development as freedom (Sen 1999). From his perspective, high levels of social and economic inequality present obstacles to development because the poor do not have the same opportunities to develop their capacity. Sen argued that development should encompass five different dimensions of freedom: (1) political freedoms; (2) economic facilities; (3) social opportunities; (4) transparency guarantees; and (5) protective security. Political freedoms refer primarily to civil liberties. Economic facilities are resources that families hold to produce, consume or exchange in the marketplace. Social opportunities are the societal arrangements for the conditions to improve quality of life, such as education and health care. Transparency guarantees can be defined as the level of trust that exists among individuals and between individuals and their government. Finally, protective security includes institutional arrangements that 'provide a social safety net for preventing the affected population from being reduced to abject misery, and in some cases even starvation and death' (Sen 1999, p. 40). Although Sen's analysis focuses on national and global development, many of these elements can be applied to rural areas as well. Sen's definition places much more emphasis on overcoming a wider variety of obstacles than just material or economic issues. It also recognizes that many rural areas are constrained by non-economic factors that limit the capacity of individuals.

What are the implications of this discussion of conceptualizing development for rural regions? Rural areas generally lag behind urban areas in most indicators of development. Population density and distance from urban populations are two especially difficult obstacles to overcome. Population density is strongly related to the availability of resources. Schools in rural areas, for example, may not be able to offer the same wide array of programs that are offered in urban areas. Health care programs in rural areas may be more limited than in urban areas. Distance to urban markets may add additional costs for producers and make it more difficult to market commodities. Civil liberties and social opportunities are sometimes more limited in many rural areas due to more traditional values. These differences raise important questions about social justice and fairness to rural residents.

Rural areas, however, offer benefits or advantages to residents that are often overlooked in comparisons with urban areas. Access to wildlife and recreation (hunting, fishing, and so on) is often valued more by rural than urban residents. Social relationships with neighbors and friends are much stronger in rural than in urban areas, and these social ties provide resources and other forms of support that keep residents from moving to cities. Rural communities may provide additional benefits, such as close proximity to nature and natural amenities (Green et al. 2005). It is difficult to quantify these benefits, but there is general support for the idea that these attributes of rural areas enhance the quality of life of residents (Marans and Wellman 1978).

Economic theory suggests that rural residents may make a trade-off between economic and non-economic benefits. In other words, they may sacrifice higher wages or other employment benefits for non-economic values. For example, rural residents may decide to stay in their community due to these non-material benefits, even though they could obtain higher earnings by migrating to an urban area. Thus, focusing exclusively on wages tends to miss the important role that non-economic factors play in household migration decisions or residential preferences. This thesis about trade-offs between material and non-material benefits is difficult to test, however. To what extent are these decisions and preferences a result of limited opportunities or limited knowledge of other opportunities? This argument also does not take into consideration equity issues. Do rural residents have the right to equal access to health care and education, or wages similar to urban workers? One of the problems in assuming that rural residents trade off these services too is that children are often the most affected by these decisions and they may not be involved in the decision-making process about where the family should live. Also, this view of trade-offs seems to ignore some of the structural constraints to residential mobility. Some rural residents may lack the economic or social resources, as well as information, to move somewhere else. Thus, it would be difficult to conclude that rural residents are necessarily more likely to make these sacrifices for some of the benefits of living in a rural area.

RURAL REGIONS AND DEVELOPMENT

Much of the conceptual work on rural development has been informed or shaped by the theory of the rural–urban continuum (Newby 1980). This theory was popular in the 1960s, and continues to influence in many ways rural development theory, policy and practice today. The rural–urban continuum thesis assumes that there are geographic differences in values, attitudes and social relationships that lead to differences in the quality of life between rural and urban regions. These differences are alleged to be due largely to the lower levels of population density and distance from large cities.

This rural–urban continuum thesis was most often rooted in a broader social theory referred to as modernization theory (Long 1987). Modernization theory made several key propositions about rural development. First, it assumed that development is a linear process and is essentially progressive. In other words, there is a single path of development that rural regions must follow in order to achieve development. In addition, the assumption was that as rural areas develop they look more like urban areas in terms of attitudes, values and behavior.

Second, development is presumed to be gradual and a result of internal, rather than external, factors. According to the theory, external organizations and institutions have a minimal role in facilitating development. This does raise the difficult question, however, about the source of social change in rural areas. Much of the emphasis in the literature has been on the role of improved technology and communication as a critical component of modernization (Rogers 1995).

Finally, modernization theory holds that as rural regions develop, social classes would become less important. This issue is important because it means that opportunities for social and economic mobility improve for rural residents as these class distinctions diminish. In addition, these economic changes result in increased democracy and civil rights in rural regions.

In direct opposition to the modernization thesis is dependency theory. Dependency theorists argued that rural–urban differences are not due to dissimilarities in values, behavior or social relationships. Development and underdevelopment are not two stages, but are part of the same economic process. In other words, urban areas have developed at the expense of rural areas. Rural areas are often the source of resource extraction and low-cost labor for the larger society. There is a high level of absentee ownership of key businesses and institutions that often limits the potential for development. This theory does not assume that rural areas will necessarily follow the same path of development as urban areas, but instead must reduce their dependency on external organizations and institutions in order to develop. Change, therefore, results from breaking the dependency relationships with urban institutions and organizations.

Although modernization and dependency theories provide much different explanations of rural development, they both tend to focus on the nation-state as the fundamental unit of analysis. For modernization theorists, rural residents are exposed to urban influences and become more integrated into the larger society. This integration leads to attitudinal and behavioral, as well as institutional, change that results in progress. For dependency theorists, the primary dynamic occurs through the interaction between urban and rural areas within the nation-state.

An alternative to these approaches focuses on the link between rural areas and the global economy. McMichael (2004, p. xviii) refers to the rise of developmentism on a global scale as the 'globalization project'. This concept suggests that post-World War II governments and multilateral agencies institutionalized development as the principal organizing principle for this era. A key component of this globalization project has been the tight integration of commodity markets, the rise of financialization and increasing dominance of large corporations. For example, global commodity markets now shape the fate of communities based in extractive industries. Thus, globalization rather than government policy may be the primary determinant of development in many rural areas. This project has sparked numerous social movements and counter trends that challenge this principle (McMichael 2010).

In the past, rural areas were often viewed as providing low-cost labor for production (Galston and Baehler 1995). Today, however, rural regions may not provide as much of a cost advantage as other regions around the world. As capital and labor have become more mobile, there is constant pressure to increase the profit rate among businesses. Increased global integration and competition, therefore, may be advantageous for some rural areas and disadvantageous for others. It also means that there is no single path to development and that it is much more contingent on how local conditions link to the global economy.

Modernization and dependency theories provide polar opposite prescriptions for rural development strategies. Modernization theory suggests that the more integrated rural regions are into the broader economic and social systems, the more they are likely to develop. Conversely, dependency theory implies that the most appropriate strategy for rural areas is to break their relationship with the broader economic and social systems and become more autonomous. Globalization theory, however, provides more concrete guidance for rural development policies. Rural areas are unlikely to be able to break their relationship with the larger economy; nor should they. Instead, they need to enhance their assets and build on competitive strategies that manage their relationship with the global economy (Green and Haines 2012). In the following, we briefly discuss some of the key strategies that help rural regions become more competitive in the global economy.

RURAL DEVELOPMENT STRATEGIES

We now turn to a discussion of some key rural development strategies that have been adopted by policy makers and practitioners. Most rural communities continue to focus on traditional economic development strategies, such as industrial recruitment or business expansion and retention (Sears and Reid 1995). Much of the evidence suggests that these strategies may have little pay-off in the global context for rural areas. We examine, however, some of the leading alternative strategies that are being promoted by policy makers and practitioners today. The most successful strategies tend to focus on identifying competitive niches in markets, building public policies that help overcome obstacles in rural areas, and involving broad support within the community. In particular, we look at amenity-based development, entrepreneurship, industrial clusters and regionalism.

Amenity-Based Development

Historically, rural areas have been dependent on industries involved in extracting natural resources (for example, agriculture, forestry, fishing and mining). These local economies rely on the production of commodities for external markets as a means of creating jobs and generating income. A good illustration is forest products industries located in many rural regions. Forest products are extracted and often processed regionally for external markets. This income not only supports workers in these industries, but it has a multiplying effect throughout the region.

Natural resources, however, are viewed increasingly in terms of their consumptive rather than their production value (Marsden et al. 1993). In other words, environmental protection of natural resources can potentially add more value to the rural communities than extraction of the resources. Recreation or tourist destinations especially offer the potential for generating economic opportunities in rural areas (often referred to as use value). The general public may also place a value on protecting natural amenities for potential use in the future (option value) or simply to know that such places will continue to exist in the future (existence value). For example, the public may be willing to use tax dollars to invest in conservation, such as national parks or wildlife areas, without directly using or benefitting from those investments. This shift in how natural resources are viewed also provides the potential for increasing non-material benefits for both residents and non-residents of the region. Strategies focusing on the consumptive aspects of natural resources tend to be referred to as amenity-based development. This strategy not only provides new opportunities, it also protects the natural environment that is so critical to the quality of life in rural communities.

There are several potential relationships between natural amenities and rural development (Green 2001) (see Figure 1.1). Probably the most common relationship is that development can lead to the destruction of natural amenities. Strip mining in Appalachia is an example of how natural amenities can be destroyed through extracting natural resources in the name of development. The trade-off between jobs and the environment is most evident in this case. Extracting natural resources in this manner restricts both short- and long-term development efforts in these communities. In many instances, it may be impossible to replenish or renew the natural amenities that are destroyed through the extraction process. It also may limit other economic activities in the region because complementary forms of economic activity, such as tourism, may not be possible in these regions. In addition, strip mining is usually conducted by firms that are not locally owned, and thus many of the profits are extracted from rural areas.

The opposite relationship between amenities and development, however, is also possible. Preservation of natural amenities can lead to a lack of development. Restricting any economic activity sometimes limits the development options for rural residents in nearby areas. This relationship is

| Development destroys natural amenities | Preservation of natural amenities restricts development |
| Development enhances natural amenities | Preservation of natural amenities increases development |

Figure 1.1   Relationships between natural amenities and development

frequently cited when proximity to protected areas places limits on how residents may use their land. In addition, public land devoted to protecting natural resources often takes land off the tax rolls in a region, which reduces the fiscal capacity of local governments. An example would be rural regions in the western US where there are vast amounts of public land. In many of these rural communities there are very limited resources for health, education and social programs.

In some cases development may be necessary for the conservation and/or preservation of natural resources. Establishing a conservation easement in a rural area, for example, typically requires financial resources. Conservation programs can be very costly and many of these costs may be forced on local communities. Thus, it may be more difficult for a very poor area to conserve its natural amenities. There is a large body of literature suggesting that the poor are likely to exploit their natural environment if there are no other opportunities to improve their livelihoods (Cernea and Schmidt-Soltau 2006). Thus, many conservation programs today understand the need to provide economic opportunities for rural residents in order to build a successful conservation program. In this instance, there is a mutual relationship between the environment and jobs.

Finally, efforts to preserve natural amenities can contribute to increased rural development in a region. Tourism and recreation areas are examples of this relationship. These activities contribute to development through injecting additional external resources into the local economy, providing jobs and creating new opportunities for income mobility. Tourism may also lead to greater efforts to protect the natural resources and environment that are so critical to the economic base of the community. Again, this example assumes there is not a necessary trade-off between jobs and the environment.

Much of the literature suggests, however, that employment in tourism and recreational destinations tends to be low-wage and part-time. In addition, jobs in these sectors tend to provide few benefits (such as health care or retirement) or opportunities for income mobility. Although recreation and tourism may inject income into communities, it also is accompanied by additional fiscal costs for local governments, especially in terms of increased infrastructure costs.

Tourism and recreation destinations can address some of these obstacles by diversifying their economy. Many retirement destinations have seen their service sector grow, especially the health care industry. Rural communities have found ways of supporting extractive industries without destroying their natural amenities that are such key assets.

Overall, amenity-based development offers important opportunities for many rural areas. One of the policy issues that must be addressed, however, is the free-rider problem. Many of the beneficiaries of amenity-based development may not be residents, while the costs are almost entirely borne by locals. Policy makers must recognize that these amenities are often public goods and that sources of financial support may be needed from the broader region. Another potential policy issue is how to avoid the gentrifying impact of amenity-based development on the local workforce. Often workers are unable to live in the area because of the rising housing costs associated with development.

Amenity-based development provides a more holistic approach than do traditional rural development strategies by recognizing the integral linkages between the environment and the economy. In many instances protecting and enhancing environmental quality can be a key to economic development. It also can be a basis for improved access to health care and education. Retirement destinations in amenity-rich areas may require investments in improved health care as a way to attract more retirees. These investments in health care have broader benefits to the population. Yet, research suggests that social conflicts between local residents and tourists (and seasonal residents) over growth and development is typical in these settings (Green et al. 1996). Local residents tend to prefer to see more job and income growth, while tourists and seasonal residents may place a higher priority on environmental quality. These differences may be difficult to overcome, but some form of consensus may be necessary to overcome the perceived trade-off between jobs and the environment.

Entrepreneurship

Rural areas generally have higher levels of entrepreneurship than do urban areas (Lin et al. 1990). Research on entrepreneurship has emphasized two broad approaches – supply-side and demand-side perspectives – that explain the differential patterns in rural and urban areas (Thornton 1999). The supply side is usually characterized by its focus on the importance of the individual characteristics of entrepreneurs. For example, much of the research in this approach has examined how culture and ethnicity produces entrepreneurial behavior (Aldrich and Waldinger 1990; Light and Bonacich 1988). Additional research has emphasized the importance of values and motivation as important determinants of innovation. This research assumes it is the individual values and attitudes that explain the differential rate of entrepreneurship among groups. From this perspective, the cultural emphasis on independence and self-sufficiency must play a role in explaining the higher levels of entrepreneurship in rural regions.

Research on the demand side focuses on the role of social and economic context in shaping entrepreneurship. Much of this research has examined the role of firms and markets in influencing rates of entrepreneurship. Some of this research looks at how entrepreneurs spin off from existing firms and are shaped by market opportunities. There is some debate whether new firms are more likely to be created by large, core firms or small, peripheral firms. Many of the high-tech establishments tend to be related to large firms and universities, while other establishments may be more autonomous. Bruno and Tyebjee (1982) suggest other environmental factors influence entrepreneurship, including access to venture capital, technical support, skilled labor, restricted regulations, low taxes and access to new markets. There is considerable debate over the effects of these contextual influences on economic development in general, and entrepreneurship more specifically (Bartik 1991). The debate in the economic development literature generally discusses whether employing these as incentives actually influences firm decision making or simply subsidizes firms (Mokry 1988). For rural areas, the lack of large firms investing in these regions may provide incentives and market opportunities for entrepreneurs.

Beyond these political and economic factors, there has been an increasing amount of attention given to the role social factors might play in entrepreneurship. Much of this work has focused on racial and ethnic differences in entrepreneur networks (Aldrich et al. 1990; Boyd 1990, 1991). This research has examined why some racial and ethnic groups have different types of social networks (in terms of size and density) and the impact this has on the rates of entrepreneurship.

Another important issue in this research is how the social and economic context may influence the effectiveness of these networks. Burt (1992) has shown how the structure of networks, especially the level of redundancy among actors, may influence the likelihood of success among entrepreneurs. Social networks may improve the breadth and depth of information available to entrepreneurs. Information about available resources, markets and sources of information can play a critical role in the success of entrepreneurs. Social networks may play a role in stimulating and developing innovations and new ideas.

Network resources are often considered as a form of social capital (Putnam 2000). This concept has been criticized because it has been viewed as implying that social capital can compensate for the lack of financial and human capital available to entrepreneurs (Tigges and Green 1994). Another way to conceptualize the role of social networks, however, is to view them as mediating influences on access to financial and human capital. Stronger and broader networks may increase the likelihood that entrepreneurs can access different forms of financial capital markets, as well as improve their own human capital.

Social networks may be more critical to the success of entrepreneurs in rural than in urban areas. The smaller population and organizational density makes communication much more difficult. Rural areas generally have a lower level of specialized service firms to support entrepreneurs. Access to public and non-profit agencies offering support to businesses is a greater challenge outside of metropolitan areas as well. Most high-tech start-up firms will locate in urban areas where they have greater access to professional services and contacts with similar needs. Rural areas also tend to lack access to venture capital. Venture capital firms tend to locate in urban settings because they prefer to lend to entrepreneurs in close proximity. Given the structure of opportunities in urban areas, social networks may be critically important to the community support for entrepreneurs in rural areas.

One concrete example of using a network strategy to promote entrepreneurship in rural areas is entrepreneurial clubs (Green et al. 2007). In many communities, these organizations bring together potential entrepreneurs to discuss business plans, financing and other relevant issues. In addition, entrepreneurial clubs provide opportunities to network with others who may have potential resources and support for participants.

Although rural communities face some serious challenges in supporting entrepreneurs, they also offer some unique opportunities. Local public policies are needed, however, to help potential entrepreneurs overcome the lack of resources. Promoting entrepreneurship is considered an important rural development strategy because it opens up opportunities for residents and builds on local assets and resources. In many cases, entrepreneurship opportunities can fit into the local cultural context rather than imposing on the community from the outside. Research suggests, for example, that entrepreneurship is an especially valuable strategy for enhancing the opportunities for minorities. Entrepreneurship provides minorities with new means of expressing their values and for residents to support those values. In addition, establishing an entrepreneurial climate can also contribute to the success of non-profit and community-based organizations.

Cluster Development

Many states, regions and municipalities have recently adopted cluster strategies in order to promote rural development. Clusters refer to closely associated businesses and institutions that are linked by commonalities and complementarities. Michael Porter (2000) has been one of the chief architects and proponents of cluster development. According to Porter, clusters are a more effective strategy than traditional approaches for regions to compete in a global economy. Rather than viewing each business or industry in competition with one another, clusters cultivate cooperative arrangements among economic actors in a region. The most famous examples of cluster development are the high-tech industries in Silicon Valley and the film industry in Hollywood. Both examples involve many local firms that are intimately tied to one another to produce a set of products or services.

Clusters are conceptualized as larger than industries and include suppliers of specialized inputs and services as well. They also may include institutions that provide specialized training and technical support, as well as trade associations and other organizations that may include cluster firms. In the case of Silicon Valley, Stanford University and the University of California–Berkeley have provided an important source of innovation and labor for the high-tech industries in the region. It is difficult to define the exact boundaries of a cluster because it may vary by region, product or service.

The central thesis of the cluster development strategy is that a location's competitiveness is not based on the industries, but on how the cluster as a whole competes in the global economy. Clusters shape innovation and productivity growth through several different means. For example, clusters will be able to more easily identify common training needs across firms and develop programs that meet their needs. Similarly, suppliers in a cluster should be able to perceive better the needs of customers because of their long-term relationships.

Rural regions face some difficult challenges in implementing cluster development strategies, but these obstacles are not formidable. Distance and density may make it more difficult to coordinate clusters. For example, job training may be delivered through several different educational institutions. Fragmentation of local governments also adds hurdles to implanting cluster strategies. It is difficult to coordinate land use and other policies across numerous local government entities. Industry associations and organizations can play an important role in overcoming some of these problems. Rural clusters also may have more difficulty in transitioning from low-wage employment because many firms are within natural resource extraction industries.

There are many success stories, however, of rural regions that have employed a cluster strategy. Limited resources in many rural areas may promote greater collaboration and partnerships across communities. Because rural areas may have more experience with collaboration, they may have some key advantages in adopting cluster strategies. Similarly, cluster strategies can generate other opportunities for rural communities to collaborate on service provision that may bring additional benefits to rural residents (Korsching et al. 1992).

Clusters can be an important rural development strategy because they provide new opportunities for high-wage employment, as well as offer more long-term sustainability to communities. In the context of a global economy, rural clusters can increase productivity, as well as lead to a higher quality of life. Cluster development builds on local social relationships and offers opportunity for indigenous, rather than absentee, ownership. These attributes address many of the weaknesses of traditional development strategies in rural areas.

Regionalism

A growing number of policy makers and academics have argued for the need to promote regional approaches toward rural development (Drabenstott 2005). Regionalism addresses a key problem facing rural communities: political jurisdictions often do not match the geography of economic, social and environmental problems. For example, communities may be unable to manage environmental problems because the source of the problem is located in another jurisdiction. Similarly, many rural communities have become bedroom communities for larger urban areas. The evidence suggests that there may be more costs than benefits to this type of development for communities. Finally, many rural communities are extremely limited by resources in providing a wide variety of services to their residents. Thus, there is a need for greater coordination and/or cooperation among communities.

Regionalism assumes that urban and rural areas are intimately linked and policy makers need to develop policies that promote greater integration (Katz 2000). A minimal amount of coordination can occur with information exchange or cooperation on a few activities. On a more formal level, it can involve coordinated regional transportation systems, land use planning and even tax sharing.

Regionalism can take several other forms (Orfield 1997). In some cases, it may involve a separate government for the region and/or provisions for taxation at the regional level. Tax base sharing is an important element because it helps reduce some of the differences in service delivery and educational funding across a region. Other important policies might include affordable housing, transportation and land use planning. Providing more affordable housing options outside central cities helps reduce concentrated poverty and provides housing opportunities in suburban and rural areas. Regional transportation systems enable workers throughout the region to have access to good jobs. Land use decisions are usually made by local jurisdictions without consideration of externalities or impacts on neighboring municipalities. Regional planning can address some of these limitations by insuring that municipalities throughout a region have a coordinated plan for growth and development (Rusk 1995).

There are several potential benefits of promoting regionalism as a rural development strategy. First, regionalism can generate economies of scale because resources and efforts are not duplicated in several jurisdictions. These economies of scale are often realized in the provision of services, such as health care or social services. Second, it can capture spillover effects across jurisdictions, and help internalize costs. For example, developing regional land use plans can work against municipalities limiting undesirable land use and pushing them to neighboring municipalities. Third, regionalism has the potential for increasing expertise and empowerment. Through coordination and concentrating resources, rural communities can have more leverage to address social and economic problems.

There are multiple constraints to implementing regional economic development strategies in rural areas. Many states allocate resources to localities based on population and/or jobs, which establishes a competitive system among places. Regionalism may involve some planning and sharing of resources among multiple communities, which may necessitate the establishment of new institutions. These institutions usually require a legal status that does not exist in many states. For example, many states have constitutionally limited government bodies to counties, cities and villages, and towns. Finally, regional approaches to development in rural areas are often challenged by a strong sense of community and sense of local pride that makes it difficult to mobilize residents around multi-community issues. Regional approaches to rural development do not necessarily mean a loss of community autonomy. There is always, however, the potential for the loss of meaningful participation as decisions and policies are made at a higher level. This weakness can be compensated with structured decision making that begins at the grassroots level.

Overall, we have argued that regional approaches to rural development can improve the efficiency of organizations and institutions without the loss of accountability and participation. Similarly, regionalism provides rural areas with the ability to address social, economic and environmental issues at the appropriate level and increase the availability of resources as well. Regional approaches may be the most appropriate response to the limitations of many rural areas that are related to low population density. Regionalism improves the scale of operation to provide additional resources. Finally, there are good models of regionalism that maintain grassroots public participation and involvement in decisions.

CONCLUSIONS

Researchers and policy makers continue to debate the appropriate role of the state, markets and community in promoting rural development. Many rural development policies in the past have encouraged increased dependency on agriculture, forestry, mining and other extractive industries. This dependency has made rural communities more vulnerable to fluctuations in markets and technological change. Globalization of commodity markets has injected new risks to many rural regions. The singular focus on markets in rural development has proven to be disastrous for many communities. We have argued that rural development policy should balance market, government and community.

Although many rural localities have adopted community-based development strategies, they often lack the capacity and/or resources to be effective (Green et al. 1990). There is a need to build rural development programs and projects that build on community-based approaches, but are also market-oriented and utilize state resources to effectively improve the quality of life of rural residents. Contrary to many arguments about the effects of globalization, government policy still plays an important role in regulating markets and providing resources to rural communities. In addition, community-based development efforts need access to resources, information and support.

In addition to external resources and support, rural community-based development strategies need to be rooted in participatory processes that engage residents (Cernea 1985). Full participation requires that residents are able to effectively influence decisions, and are involved in the implementation and evaluation of rural development strategies. Participation in community-based development strategies is often constrained, however, by the local power structure that limits involvement by residents. In many cases, full participation is difficult to achieve due to the lack of community capacity. Building local capacity, then, is essential for rural communities to realize their potential in a global economy.

REFERENCES

Aldrich, Howard E. and Roger Waldinger (1990), 'Ethnicity and entrepreneurship', *Annual Review of Sociology*, 16, 111–35.

Aldrich, Howard, Roger Waldinger and R. Ward (1990), *Ethnic Entrepreneurs*, Newbury Park, CA: Sage Publications.

Bartik, Tim J. (1991), *Who Benefits from State and Local Economic Development Policies?*, Kalamazoo, MI: W.E. Upjohn Institute.

Boyd, Robert L. (1990), 'Black and Asian self-employment in large metropolitan areas: a comparative view', *Social Problems*, 37, 258–74.

Boyd, Robert L. (1991), 'A contextual analysis of black self-employment in large metropolitan areas, 1970–1980', *Social Forces*, 70, 409–29.

Bruno, A.V. and T.T. Tyebjee (1982), 'The environment for entrepreneurship', in C.A. Kent (ed.), *Encyclopedia of Entrepreneurship*, Lexington, MA: D.C. Heath Company, pp. 288–315.

Burt, Robert S. (1992), *Structural Holes: The Social Structure of Competition*, Cambridge, MA: Harvard University Press.

Cernea, Michael (ed.) (1985), *Putting People First: Sociological Variables in Rural Development*, New York: Oxford University Press.

Cernea, Michael and K. Schmidt-Soltau (2006), 'Poverty risks and national parks: policy issues in conservation and resettlement', *World Development*, 34, 1808–30.

Drabenstott, Mark (2005), 'A review of the federal policies in regional economic development', Federal Reserve Bank of Kansas City.

Galston, William and Karen Baehler (1995), *Rural Development in the United States: Connecting Theory, Practice and Possibilities*, Washington, DC: Island Press.

Green, Gary Paul (2001), 'Amenities and community economic development', *Journal of Regional Analysis and Policy*, 31, 61–76.

Green, Gary Paul and Anna Haines (2012), *Asset Building and Community Development*, Thousand Oaks, CA: Sage Publications.

Green, Gary P., Jan L. Flora, Cornelia B. Flora and Frederick E. Schmidt (1990), 'Local self-development strategies: national survey results', *Journal of the Community Development Society*, 21, 55–73.

Green, Gary P., David Marcouiller, Steven Deller, Daniel Erkkila and N.R. Sumathi (1996), 'Local dependency, land use attitudes and economic development: comparisons between seasonal and permanent residents', *Rural Sociology*, 61, 427–45.

Green, Gary Paul, Steven C. Deller and David W. Marcouiller (eds) (2005), *Amenities and Rural Development: Theory, Methods and Public Policy*, Cheltenham, UK and Northampton, MA, USA: Edward Elgar Publishing.

Green, Gary Paul, Greg Wise and Evan Armstrong (2007), 'Inventor and entrepreneur clubs: investment in an innovative approach to entrepreneurship', paper presented at the conference on Frameworks for Entrepreneurship Research in Food, Agriculture, Natural Resources and Rural Development: A National Conference on Entrepreneurship Research, October 18–19, Kansas City, MO. Available at: http://www.ssu.missouri.edu/agecon/mccel/materials/green-wise.pdf (accessed 8 January 2013).

Katz, Bruce (ed.) (2000), *Reflections on Regionalism*, Washington, DC: Brookings Institution Press.

Korsching, Peter F., Timothy O. Borich and Julie Stewart (1992), *Multicommunity Collaboration: An Evolving Rural Revitalization Strategy*, Ames, IA: North Central Regional Center for Rural Development.

Light, Ivan and Edna Bonacich (1988), *Immigrant Entrepreneurs*, Berkeley, CA: University of California Press.

20 *Handbook of rural development*

Lin, X., T.F. Buss and M. Popovich (1990), 'Entrepreneurship is alive and well in rural America', *Economic Development Quarterly*, 4, 254–9.
Logan, John and Harvey Molotch (1987), *Urban Fortunes: The Political Economy of Place*, Berkeley, CA: University of California Press.
Long, Norman (1987), *An Introduction to the Sociology of Rural Development*, Boulder, CO: Westview Press.
Marans, Robert W. and John D. Wellman (1978), *The Quality of Life of Nonmetropolitan Living: Evaluations, Behaviors and Expectations of Northern Michigan Residents*, Ann Arbor, MI: Institute for Social Research.
Marsden, Terry, Jonathan Murdoch, Philip Lowe, Richard Munton and Andrew Flynn (1993), *Constructing the Countryside*, Boulder, CO: Westview Press.
McKibben, Bill (2007), *Deep Economy: The Wealth of Communities and the Durable Future*, New York: Times Books.
McMichael, Philip (2004), *Development and Social Change: A Global Perspective*, Thousand Oaks, CA: Pine Forge Press.
McMichael, Philip (ed.) (2010), *Contesting Development: Critical Struggles for Social Change*, New York: Routledge Press.
Mokry, R. (1988), *Entrepreneurship and Public Policy*, New York: Quorum Books.
Newby, Howard (1980), 'Rural sociology: a trend report', *Current Sociology*, 28, 3–109.
Orfield, Myron (1997), *Metropolitics: A Regional Agenda for Community and Stability*, Washington, DC: Brookings Institution Press.
Peterson, Paul E. (1981), *City Limits*, Chicago, IL: University of Chicago Press.
Porter, Michael E. (2000), 'Location, competition and economic development: local clusters in a global economy', *Economic Development Quarterly*, 14, 15–24.
Putnam, Robert D. (2000), *Bowling Alone: The Collapse and Revival of American Community*, New York: Simon & Schuster.
Rogers, Everett M. (1995), *Diffusion of Innovations*, 4th edition, New York: Free Press.
Rusk, David (1995), *Cities Without Suburbs*, Washington, DC: Woodrow Wilson Center Press.
Sears, David W. and J. Norman Reid (eds) (1995), *Rural Development Strategies*, Chicago, IL: Nelson-Hall Publishers.
Sen, Amartya (1999), *Development as Freedom*, New York: Anchor Books.
Stiglitz, Joseph E., Jose Antonio Ocampo, Shari Spiegel, Ricardo Ffrench-Davis and Deepak Nayyar (2006), *Stability with Growth*, New York: Oxford University Press.
Thornton, P.H. (1999), 'The sociology of entrepreneurship', *Annual Review of Sociology*, 25, 19–46.
Tigges, Leann M. and Gary P. Green (1994), 'Small business success among men- and women-owned firms in rural areas', *Rural Sociology*, 59, 289–310.

2. Globalization
Alessandro Bonanno

INTRODUCTION

In recent decades, globalization has occupied center stage in both scientific and popular debates. This popularity engendered a wealth of contributions on the cultural, political, social and economic sides of globalization. Within this production, it is not uncommon to find strikingly divergent interpretations. At the cultural level, globalization has been viewed as a complex process that molds distant groups into networks, allows enhanced communication, and fosters understanding and communality of views and purposes. Ultimately, it brings people closer together, creating cooperation and synergy (Croucher 2004; Jagdish 2004). Simultaneously, it has been seen as a phenomenon that promotes the oppression of local groups and cultures, erases differences, represses identity and, as a result, instigates radical resistance. Fundamentalism, it has been argued, is one of the undesirable outcomes of globalization (Barber 1995; Giddens 2000; Hosseini 2009; Ritzer 2008).

Globalization has been interpreted as a process that increases interdependence, mutual exchange and respect, and fortifies society's cohesiveness (Friedman 2005). The free circulation of capital, labor and products has been heralded as one of the primary conditions for social growth (Woolf 2004). At the same time, globalization has been regarded as a process that enhances the centrifugal power of capitalism, dismembers communities and undermines the stability of society (Amoore 2005; Giddens 2000; Harvey 2006).

Politically, globalization has been portrayed as a force that deters unilateralism and promotes cooperation among people and nations. Although the United States remains the 'benign hegemon' in the world system of nations, the working of the global system is based on, and fosters, a greater participation of all people in the governing of the world. This enhanced global participation in decision making is seen as the characterizing force of current political arrangements (Friedman 2000). This view is contrasted by concerns about the reduced power of the nation-state and the limited ability of people to be represented in political debates and decision making. The crisis of political representation (the declining connection between the rulers and the ruled), and the growing inability of democratic political institutions to control the actions of global corporations have often been mentioned as the most distinctive outcomes of globalization (Boggs 2000; Wettstein 2009).

Economically, globalization has been described as the engine for growth and the elimination of socio-economic inequality. Global income inequality has decreased and income among nations is now distributed in a much more equitable manner. Additionally, the idea that one or few nations can dominate other nations (imperialism) is viewed as obsolete and the emergence of a global ruling class promotes just development (Becker and Sklar 1999; Firebaugh and Goesling 2004). Opponents of globalization have indicated that globalization is a class project that increases the exploitation of the lower classes and the global South (Harvey 2006; Robinson 2004). Others have contended that the growth of transnational corporations and the declining power of political and economic institutions (in other words, the nation-state, unions and social movements) resulted in the concentration of wealth in the hands of the top 1 percent of the world population and worsening socio-economic conditions of the rest of society (Milanovic 2011; Sassen 1998; Stiglitz 2003).

Although contrasting interpretations characterize the debate on globalization, there is convergence on the definition of this phenomenon. It refers to the acceleration of the time within which social relations take place, and the compression of their spatial scope. In other words, globalization means that the social world is 'smaller' and people 'move about it in a much faster way than before'. In his analysis of modernity, the noted British sociologist Anthony Giddens argues that the evolution of capitalist social relations has brought distant communities progressively closer together (Giddens 2000). Accordingly, at the outset of capitalism, social relations were largely contained within the 'local'. As capitalism expanded and gendered increased homogenization and standardization, distant actors and events progressively shaped local social relations. In essence, the current phenomenon of globalization is the culmination of this process of linking together actors and processes across the globe.

The remainder of this chapter is devoted to an analysis of globalization through the review of salient debates. The first section discusses early debates of the 1970s and 1980s. At that time, the term 'globalization' was not yet employed to refer to the transnationalization of social relations. The second section covers salient debates of the 1990s. In particular, it illustrates the debate on the 'Washington Consensus' and the emergence of transnational corporations. The final two sections deal with debates in the two decades of the new millennium. Also identified are salient scientific gaps and topics for future research.

THE ORIGIN OF THE DEBATE: THE CONCEPT OF GLOBALIZATION AND ITS EARLY FORMULATIONS

The origins and first use of the term 'globalization' are not very clear. There are unconfirmed claims that references to global socio-economic processes were made in the first portion of the twentieth century. It was only in 1951, however, that the Merriam-Webster dictionary of the English language officially acknowledged the word 'globalization'. In academic circles, the term gained some recognition in the early 1980s after Theodore Levitt published the article 'The globalization of markets' in the *Harvard Business Review* (Levitt 1983). In that article, Levitt contended that the world had entered a new era in which national differences in consumer preferences had become largely irrelevant. Changes at the technological and social levels allowed corporations to market their products worldwide in ways that were impossible before. The essence of Levitt's argument was that a set of new and qualitatively different factors enhanced the ability of companies to conduct business globally.

As far as the study of development is concerned, the 1980s were characterized by a three-camp debate. The once dominant Modernization School had lost most of its popularity. Its key argument of the independent and autonomous development of nations (Parsons 1971; Rostow 1960) was criticized for blaming poor countries for their conditions, justifying the unequal redistribution of resources and power, disregarding the relationship between development and underdevelopment and, ultimately, ignoring the historical conditions that shape development. In its ahistorical formulation of growth, modernization theory proposed a view in which each country would develop by adopting the culture and institutions of the United States. This process of cultural and economic modernization or Americanization (Parsons 1971) would be reached through stages that would be achieved according to each country's own ability to mobilize the necessary resources to grow (Rostow 1960).

Marxian structuralists raised particularly strong objections. This camp consisted of two major sub-groups. The first included the World System School led by Immanuel Wallerstein (1974, 1980, 2005) while the second referred to the Regulationist School (Aglietta 1979; Lipietz 1987, 1992). The World System School borrowed from the Longue Duree School (Annales School) and emphasized the long-term evolution of social relations.[1] For Wallerstein, development could be understood only by analyzing the emergence of capitalism in Europe and its evolution. This evolution, he contended, culminated in a 'world system' in which all nations were connected together in patterns of growth, but also underdevelopment. Rejecting the assumption that the growth of each nation evolves following indigenously based stages and strategies of development, World System theorists demonstrated that the development of advanced societies (core countries) was the result of processes of underdevelopment of countries in the periphery (underdeveloped countries) and semi-periphery (less developed countries). Under world capitalism, the socio-economic growth of core nations was the direct outcome of concomitant processes of underdevelopment of periphery and semi-periphery countries.

At this stage of the debate, the contribution of World System theory was relevant for at least two reasons. First, it proposed a view in which the global system was understood as a process that initiated with the growth of capitalism. Accordingly, World System theorists rejected the thesis that attributed the genesis of globalization to recent events and insisted on the long-term dimension of the phenomenon. Second, World System theory reaffirmed the centrality of the nation-state in contemporary capitalism. Although they stressed the historical nature of the nation-state, it is only one of the historical forms of the state. They also viewed the world system as a system among nations, an international system. In this respect, World System theorists remained skeptical of statements that associated globalization with the crisis of the nation-state.

World System theorists' skepticism about the novelty represented by globalization remained, and statements about this concept's inadequacy were re-proposed periodically. Wallerstein (2000), for instance, has frequently argued that globalization is not a new phenomenon. Christopher Chase-Dunn (1998) argued:

> Most discussions of globalization assume that, however defined, it is a fairly recent phenomenon … [I]f we take a long-term view of the structural constants, cyclical processes, and secular trends that have operated in the Europe-centered system for several centuries we can understand that there have been no recent major transformations in the developmental logic of the world-system. (Chase-Dunn 1998, p. ix)

Members of the Regulationist school maintained that each era of capitalism was defined by a 'regime of accumulation' and a 'mode of regulation'. The concept of regime of accumulation refers to the system of wage relations that defines a particular era of capitalism. Mode of regulation indicates the social norms that govern each regime of accumulation. In the 1980s, regulationists concentrated their efforts on the analysis of the end of Fordism and the emergence of a new and post-Fordism regime of accumulation. At the time, Post-Fordism was used widely to refer to conditions that later would be associated with globalization.

According to the regulationists, Fordism indicated the 'regulated capitalism' that characterized most of the twentieth century. Introduced by the

Italian philosopher Antonio Gramsci (1971) to define the advanced Taylorist capitalism of the 1930s, it was re-proposed by the regulationists to refer to the combination of Keynesian political economy and state intervention at the social level that characterized the development of advanced Western societies in the post-World War II decades. The crisis of Fordism, they contended, was the result of the so-called 'rigidities' of this regime of accumulation. Theorized from a number of different perspectives (see O'Connor 1974; Habermas 1975), the concept of rigidities referred primarily to the fiscal and ideological dimensions of Fordism. At the fiscal level, the cost of maintaining state intervention became too high. A combination of an increased demand for state-sponsored services and the world economic crisis of the early 1970s prevented many nation-states from continuing their support of corporate activities at previous levels. State attempts to increase tax and introduce more regulations motivated corporations to export profit and by-pass state requests. The result was a fiscal crisis of the nation-state. Simultaneously and at the ideological level, the inability of nation-states to address many of the existing social issues discredited the political elites and their ideologies. This legitimation crisis engendered widespread calls for changes in the administration of society and the economy. The regulationists viewed these changes as indications of the emergence of a new global regime that they called Post-Fordism.

Postmodernity was the third major camp that characterized the debate on development and globalization in the 1980s. Dwelling on poststructuralist contributions (Foucault 1969, 1975; Derrida 1978), postmodern theorists (Baudrillard 1983; Laclau and Mouffe 1985, 1987) argued that the issue of global development could not be adequately addressed employing 'grand narratives'. By 'grand narratives' they referred to holistic explanations that could be applied across time and space. In their critique, they maintained that the complexity of human existence could not be explained by modern theories and their assumption of universalism. Similarly, development could not be understood by using these modern theories. Denouncing the oppressive character of grand narratives, postmodernists maintained that the elimination of class inequality would not necessarily address other forms of oppression such as gender, race and ethnic dominations. Furthermore, liberation strategies that spoke for the disenfranchised often silenced the very voices they claimed to support. In contemporary society, theories of development and liberation were transformed into theories of oppression.

Their critique of left-leaning and socialist theories was often more strident than those coming from the far right. Their argument centered on the historical failure of socialist projects and the 'exclusion' and 'oppression' of many groups that these theories and practices engendered. The global society, they contended, requires the acknowledgement of the existence of a plurality of voices and patterns of action as repression emerges from all sides of the political spectrum.

THE DEBATE IN THE 1990S: TRANSNATIONAL CORPORATIONS, THE WASHINGTON CONSENSUS AND THE POWER OF THE NATION-STATE

In the 1990s the debate on globalization expanded significantly and globalization became one of the most discussed topics in the social sciences. The term 'Post-Fordism' was gradually abandoned as the processes and trends associated with it were now referred to as globalization. The debate dwelled on three aspects of globalization: the emergence of transnational corporations, the changed power of the nation-state and the Washington Consensus.

Since their creation in the nineteenth century, multinational corporations (MNCs) operated globally yet maintained strong ties with their home countries. Their home countries' governments provided the political and military support that corporations needed to penetrate and later control international markets. In return, MNCs repatriated profit to the benefit of national elites and the socio-economic stability of the home country. During most of the twentieth century, MNCs operated with the so-called mother–daughter industrial system (Dunning 1993). A mother company with headquarters in the home country opened daughter subsidiaries overseas. The subsidiaries were directly controlled by the home headquarters. In this scheme, MNC ownership, management and image remained associated with the company's home country.

This beneficial association between multinational corporations and major nation-states entered a crisis in the early 1970s (Dunning 1993; Harrison and Bluestone 1988; Harvey 1989). The period's world economic downturn and consequent austerity measures prevented nation-states from maintaining desired levels of corporate support while adding more taxation and regulations. Simultaneously, because of the negative economic consequences of the oil crisis, the loss of legitimacy of the modernization project and shifts to the political left of many governments, more host countries overtly antagonized MNCs with a presence on their territories. The corporate response consisted in the transnationalization of operations. Companies began to decouple their presence overseas with the interests of home countries, assumed national identities at their convenience, avoided undesirable locations, and began global searches for convenient production sites featuring favorable political contexts, business climates and neoliberal policies. Corporations actively worked to create production networks that transcended the classical mother–daughter system. Decentralization of production, the creation of production and distribution networks, and the global mobility of profit and investment defined the new transnational corporations.

Supporters of globalization celebrated the end of Fordism and its 'regulated capitalism' and the dominance of transnational corporations as the beginning of a new and more prosperous era. Based on the adoption of neoliberal measures, the globalization project centered on the idea of a free market as the ultimate regulator of capitalism and the system through which its unwanted consequences would be controlled. These ideas justified the dismantling of the interventionist nation-state. Framed as an effective manner in which to attract fleeing corporate investment, reignite stagnating economies and generate jobs and profit, nation-states began to adopt globally oriented macro-organizational strategies that shifted emphasis away from socially oriented goals (in other words, social stability, equitable socio-economic growth, welfare spending) to profit-enhancing objectives. Originally theorized as the inability of nation-states to control and regulate global flows, this new posture of the state was now seen as the outcome of internal transformations. Although corporate groups' demands for more profit- and free-market-oriented policies increased, it was stressed that the election of neoliberal tickets created a new political leadership that re-oriented state actions in a pro-market direction. Even the administrations of traditionally left leaning parties, such as the Democratic Party in the US, did not escape this trend.[2]

Francis Fukuyama stressed this positive view of globalization. In his now classical work *The End of History* (1992), he spoke about the advantages of a free-market-based system to counter the distortions and rigidities generated by the intervention of the Fordist state. Stressing a much less radical version of the virtues of the unregulated market (see the version of neoliberalism introduced in the 1960s by Milton Friedman (1982 [1962]), Fukuyama believed that the open market of the post-Berlin Wall era could address the unwanted consequences of the expansion of capitalism. Although aware of the problems arising from social and economic inequality, he contended that stressing state intervention in social matters opens the way for 'infinite abuse of the democratic principle'. In his view, post-war liberalism's efforts to reform, redistribute and regulate are prone to authoritarian abuses rivaling communism. Simultaneously, he maintained that competitive capitalism allows the most able, ambitious people to rise to the top and create wealth that benefits everyone (Fukuyama 1992). According to Fukuyama, economic inequality follows inevitably from people getting their just deserts; thus, populist reactions to increased inequality do not call for economic reform or redistribution, but for efforts to allow the market to function properly.

Fukuyama's optimism about the self-adjusting property of the free market was relatively short lived. While the ideal of the market as the ultimate regulatory entity remained, the complexity of global markets and the problems that transnational corporations encountered in operating in a liberalized global economy engendered corporate calls for more effective regulation. Capturing the corporate mood of the time, the executive Alex Rubner (1990) claimed that corporations have a weak position in the global economy that does not allow them to take full advantage of the benefits of the free market. He contended that globalization's much more accelerated, expanded and interdependent economic interactions, lacking centralized regulatory authority, require some form of business-friendly re-regulation to reduce the risks associated with corporations' global movements and transactions. Sharing these concerns, corporate leaderships and their allies proclaimed that the anti-regulatory zeal of free-market ideologues was contradictory to corporate goals and profitability and supported the creation and strengthening of new global regulatory organizations. They supported the creation of organizations that favored the mobility of capital, regulated trade and shifted decision making processes from the political to the technical and administrative sphere.

These institutions took a number of forms. There was the creation of global trade organizations such as the World Trade Organization (WTO), continental trade agreements such as North American Free Trade Agreement (NAFTA), the establishment of global political organizations such as the G8, and the redesigned presence of established organizations such as the International Monetary Fund (IMF) and the World Bank. All these institutions contributed to the re-regulation of capitalism worldwide.

The accelerated economic growth and rapid technological advancements that characterized the 1990s allowed observers to equate globalization with sustained development. This optimism was captured by the theory of the Washington Consensus, a set of practices and related ideology that legitimized globalization. Written in the late 1990s and published for the first time in 2000, Thomas Friedman's *The Lexus and the Olive Tree* (2000) is arguably the text that most aptly captures the essence of the Washington Consensus. Friedman viewed globalization as an historical period that supports an affluent, integrated, spontaneous, efficient, participatory, socially conscious, informational capitalism. Stressing the benefits associated with the overcoming of the Cold War era's East–West split that hindered development, Friedman contended that globalization generates global integration and dynamism that generate economic well-being and democracy and freedom for individuals and communities (2000, pp. 44–

72). He argued that globalization delivers economic prosperity through the creation of a 'New Economy' of weightless goods that overcomes the old capitalism's socio-political and spatio-temporal constraints and approximates the neoclassical ideal of perfect markets.

Friedman acknowledged that globalization increases economic inequality. But he saw the problem as an inevitable cost of providing just rewards to meritorious people and denying the slothful and incompetent undue encouragement. Arguing that globalization's 'winners take all society' benefits everyone, Friedman implied that substantially increased US economic inequality likely has legitimacy with all but the least able, displaced or warped workers. His revision of the functional theory of stratification held that the globalization system provides exceptional rewards for exceptionally skilled people, but that the benefits of their labors flow down to persons with average abilities (Friedman 2000, pp. 306–24). Friedman admitted that poor countries, on the margins or outside of the globalization system, suffer extreme inequalities and misery, but he said that only the neoliberal regime offers any hope for improvement (2000, pp. 355–57).

GLOBALIZATION IN THE NEW MILLENNIUM

The rosy picture presented by globalization advocates was shattered by 9/11 and the world events that characterized the first decade of the new millennium. The wars in Afghanistan and Iraq, the continued political tension in the Middle East and Iran, and the social and economic instability in countries of Africa, Latin America and Asia, made clear that the harmonious globalized system envisioned by Friedman was a wish more than a reality. About two months after 9/11, Ulrich Beck (2001) commented that the attacks were 'globalization's Chernobyl' and that the 1990s' expectations about the future of globalization were forever vanished.

In this context, the debate was characterized by opposing arguments on the viability of the globalization project as a system for socio-economic development. Critics of globalization argued that the collapse of the stock market after 9/11, the mounting number of corporate scandals – such as that of the energy giant Enron – and the dramatic increase in the world price of oil revealed a situation in which polarization and inequality characterized the distribution of income and wealth globally. While corporate profits soared, the economic conditions of large segments of the world population, in both developing and developed countries, dramatically deteriorated; throughout the roaring 1990s and beyond the economic gap between the rich and the poor increased. They stressed that in 1993 the richest 1 percent of the world population controlled as much wealth as the lowest 57 percent, while the richest 5 percent had an average income 114 times larger than the poorest 5 percent. From 1988 to 1993, the latter group grew poorer by losing 25 percent of its income. Simultaneously, the top 20 percent of the population saw its income increase by 12 percent. In 1980, the richest 10 percent of the countries had a median income that was 77 times greater than that of the poorest 10 percent. By 1999, this gap had increased to 122 times. From 1980 to 2001, the average personal income of developing regions as a percentage of that of the United States diminished significantly (Milanovic 2011). The average income in Latin America was 36 percent of that of the US in 1980, but only 26 percent in 2001. Similarly, the average income of African countries was 10 percent of that of the US in 1980, but only 6 percent in 2001. In the entire political South, the average per capita income as a portion of that of the US dropped from 16 percent in 1980 to 14 percent in 2001 (Milanovic 2011).

Critics of globalization further contended that income and wealth inequality grew also in the United States (Mishel et al. 2003). They argued that in 2000 economic inequality in the US was at the highest levels since the 1920s as the top 5 percent of all US households had a combined income that was six times larger than that of the lower 20 percent of households. This gap was four times larger than it was in 1970. Additionally, between 1979 and 2000 the gap between the rich and the poor increased. During this period the income of the top 20 percent of the households in the US grew by an astonishing 68 percent. The income of the lowest 20 percent of households and that of the middle fifth experienced much more contained increases: 9 and 15 percent respectively. Also, from 1979 to 2002 the after-tax income obtained by the highest fifth of the US population grew from 42 percent to 51 percent. Simultaneously, the after-tax income of the lowest 20 percent remained constant. Inequality was much more dramatic if measured in terms of overall wealth. In 2001, the top 1 percent of the US population controlled 33 percent of the wealth while the bottom 90 percent of the population was left with only 28 percent of the wealth. One of the most remarkable consequences of globalization was that the gap between the wealthy and the poor increased while the economy enjoyed an extended period of sustained growth.

Supporters of globalization responded to these criticisms by emphasizing that the world economic inequality has actually diminished during the last two decades. Arguably one of the most cited studies in this regard is the article published by Glenn Firebaugh and Brian Goesling in the September 2004 issue of the *American Journal of Sociology* (Firebaugh and Goesling 2004). Firebaugh and Goesling maintain that global income distribution is now more equal than it was in the early 1980s. This reduction, they continue, is primarily the result of average income growth in the most populous countries of Asia: China and India. Setting aside arguments that see growth in class inequality in these countries, they maintain that China and India are instances in which the expansion of globalization has significantly increased the overall socio-economic well-being. As in the cases of many other less developed countries, growth in these two emerging markets is directly related to the expansion of industrialization – and in particular manufacture – and the insertion of local firms in global networks. The growth occurring in less developed countries, they contend, is the direct result of processes that have been augmented by globalization. It is their policy recommendation, therefore, that globalization should be promoted and that actions that would delay its application would result in less, rather than more, development. Gavin Kitching (2001) also concludes that more globalization is actually beneficial for the world's poor and for developing regions. For Kitching, globalization's decentralization of production and hypermobility of capital create new opportunities for developing regions and workers. While jobs may have been lost in developed regions with the consequent protest by local unions and left-leaning political groups, new jobs are created in less developed regions. He contends that if one job created is equal to one job lost, the fact that jobs reappear in the less developed South is a positive sign in the struggle to reduce socio-economic inequality worldwide.

Regardless of its consequences, the importance of globalization for rural development remained a central aspect of this literature. Two primary implications emerged. First, it was argued that the development of rural regions was increasingly connected to the growth of production and consumption networks. Membership in these networks determined the ability and direction of rural communities' growth. For some, this signified that rural communities had to be prepared to compete globally and attract new investments and business initiatives. For others, it signaled a loss of political control and the subordination of the community to global interests that can be countered by avoiding connection with these corporate-led global networks. Second, development could not be analyzed and planned simply by thinking in local or national terms. Regardless of the power and importance of local institutions and the nation, rural development was now an issue that required a global approach.

THE DEBATE IN THE 2010s, GAPS IN THE LITERATURE AND IMPORTANT RESEARCH QUESTIONS

The theme of globalization continues to characterize the debate on socio-economic development in the second decade of the twenty-first century. I will employ five issues to summarize it, identify salient research questions as well as underscore analytical gaps. I will explore the themes of: (1) the power of transnational corporations and resistance to them; (2) the crisis of the state; (3) the phenomenon of financialization; (4) the position and use of labor under globalization; and (5) the possible legitimation crisis of neo-liberalism.

The growth of corporate power has not only characterized globalization since its outset, but has remained a persistent theme in the literature. In current debates, there is consensus that transnational corporations (TNCs) continue to be powerful actors in the economy and society. Disagreement exists in regard to the extent to which TNCs have the same level of power as a decade ago, and the consequences generated by the application of this power. According to one camp, TNCs will continue to be powerful actors and their ability to control nation-states, social groups and economic policies will continue (Busse 2004; Macleod and Lewis 2004). Within this camp, some argue that TNCs' power is actually beneficial to society (Becker and Sklar 1999; Henderson 2000; Kitching 2001). These authors contend that the emergence of global corporate power promotes business, profit and socio-economic well-being and a more equitable development among countries. Opposing this view, other authors contend that the power of TNCs reduces the level of democracy and prevents national and regional constituencies from participating in decision making processes (Boggs 2000). Furthermore, soaring corporate power has negative consequences for the economy and society as economic inequality increases, and the unchecked actions of corporations often have had destabilizing effects on the economy (Harvey 2010; Krugman 2007).

A second camp consists of authors who argue that the power of TNCs is not as absolute as some analysts would contend. Although TNCs remain powerful actors in the global context, their power is resisted at various levels. Resistance emerges from a number of actors including nation-states, local groups and social movements such as the environmental movement and organized labor. In the case of socio-economic development in agriculture and food a number of studies have underscored the role that consumers play in shaping TNCs' actions (Humphery 1998; Marsden 2003; Wright and Midderndorf 2007). It is argued that consumers' behavior is increasingly affected by social values such as the protection of the environment; health and nutritional concerns; the protection of producers and communities in less developed areas; fair processes of trade – rather than price. Accordingly, as consumers' social consciousness affects demand, it also affects the behavior of corporations and their power. It is further argued that the power of transnational corporations is also limited by internal organizational constraints and contradictions (Bonanno and Constance 2008).

Because they compete with other corporations and have relatively limited organizational strength given the scope of their actions, TNCs encounter difficulties in exercising power at the global level.

The issue of the power and growth of TNCs remains central in the second decade of the new millennium. The thesis that global corporations' actions engender benefits for the community continues to be debated and requires further analysis. In particular, future research should clarify the hypothesis that the growth of corporate actions would create more interdependence and, as a result, more cooperation and respect among all components of society.

The crisis of the nation-state has also been one of the phenomena traditionally associated with the expansion of globalization. Because of the implementation of neoliberal policies and the growth of transnational corporations, it has been argued that nation-states could not regulate the economy and society to the extent that they did in previous eras of capitalism. Framed as the ability of TNCs to by-pass state requirements, the crisis of the state has been identified as one of the most distinctive features of globalization (Constance and Heffernan 1991; Ohmae 1995). Some authors questioned these conclusions by arguing that they are based on unsubstantiated claims. An exemplar of this position is the work of Paul Hirst and Graham Thompson (1996). For these authors, true TNCs do not exist, so the purported socio-economic changes that resulted in the creation of TNCs are unsubstantiated. They maintain that most corporations are still national as they are still connected to their country of origin in significant ways, regardless of their international activities. Additionally, data do not indicate the existence of trends toward the emergence of truly global corporations. In effect the examination of foreign direct investment (FDI) reveals that it is generated by companies located in North America, Europe or Japan. Hirst and Thompson further maintain that, while the post-war system that regulated capitalism has exhausted its role, a new system of regulation has been set in place. This new mechanism allows the three superpowers (the US, the European Union and Japan) to govern the world and ensure adequate levels of socio-economic stability.

Two critics of this position are Mauro Guillen (2001) and William Robinson (2004). Although Guillen maintains that Hirst and Thompson contributed to the clarification of often taken-for-granted aspects of globalization, he contends that they failed to see the new cultural and economic phenomena associated with it. In particular they failed to acknowledge the greater interdependence generated by globalization and the mutual awareness that it engenders. Robinson (2004) argues that there are quantitative and qualitative differences between globalization and previous periods of capitalist development. Accordingly, it is misleading to argue that globalization is simply the continuation of trends established in the past. From a quantitative point of view, Robinson maintains that trade is much larger under globalization than in other historical periods, and that this is the case also for the scale of capital flows, and the level of information and communication technology. He also stresses the differences associated with the global presence of transnational corporations and a transnational labor force. Qualitatively, Robinson underscores that globalization:

> has entailed the fragmentation and decentralization of complex production chains and the worldwide dispersal and functional integration of the different segments of these chains … In this way globalization is unifying the world into a single mode of production and a single global system and bringing about the integration of different countries and regions into a new global economy. (2004, p. 15)

He concludes that because of these changes the nation-state has lost the central role that it played for most of the twentieth century.

The role of the nation-state and its ability to regulate social and economic matters remains a key topic of research in the study of socio-economic development. In particular, it is important to better understand the extent and characteristics of the assumed limits of state power.

Under neoliberal globalization financial capital has become the most dominant form of capital. The expansion of financial capital is generated by financialization. This phenomenon refers to processes that tend to reduce all value produced into financial instruments. A financial instrument is any tradable asset in financial markets. Following neoliberal deregulation, corporate agents operated to produce new financial instruments by combining existing and/or to-be-created financial assets and marketing these repackaged entities to investors. Financialization further indicates the increased importance of financial capital over real (manufacturing and agricultural) capital in determining the profit expected from investments as well as the increased subordination of investments to the demands of global financial markets.

The financialization of the economy has engendered at least five important consequences. First, profit has been transferred from the productive sector to the financial sector. This phenomenon has transformed the financial sector into the most profitable sector of the economy. Second, wages have been decoupled from productivity growth, resulting in a stagnation of labor remuneration and rising income inequality. Income has been shifted from labor to capital as a greater percentage of remuneration is allocated to profit. Third, as wages and salaries stagnated and/or decreased, the level of household debt has grown significantly. The growing gap between household debt and income points to the declining well-being of families and communities. Fourth, profit generation has been decoupled from the creation of jobs. Defined as the jobless recovery, the era of financialization has been characterized by steady high levels of unemployment while corporate profit remained high. Finally, financialization has increased the instability of the economy. At the outset, the creation of financial products tends to increase collateral value. This expanded value allows more borrowing that finances investment spending and fuels economic expansion. As collateral value decreases, borrowing and investment fall, triggering a downward spiral that results in a crisis. Attempts to address these recurrent crises have consisted in state-sponsored bailouts and/or austerity measures that strained nation-states' finances, created unemployment and undermined social stability.

Pertinent literature has discussed the characteristics and implications of financialization. The attention paid to these phenomena, however, has not been commensurate to their importance and impact. In effect, the centrality of the inter-capital conflict between financial and productive capital remains an area that requires further investigation. The extent to which financial companies' short-term strategies and thinking have become more relevant over the long-term strategies of productive capital should be accurately studied.

There is a similarity between the conditions that engendered the crisis of legitimation of Fordism and the current conditions under which of the ideology of neoliberalism supports globalization. Defining the financial crisis of 2008 as an epiphenomenon of the structural crisis of advanced capitalism, the French philosopher Gérard Raulet (2011) contends that the current situation is reminiscent of the legitimation crisis of Fordist capitalism illustrated by the renowned German social theorist Jürgen Habermas in his book the *Legitimation Crisis* (1975). As in the case of the 1970s, under the current global regime the state cannot meet the demands stemming from the economy and the expectations of the masses. The neoliberal withdrawing of the state has magnified the unwanted consequences of the functioning of the market and significantly diminished the ability of large segments of society to participate in decision making processes. Studies such as this call into question the consequences of the application of neoliberal ideology and its claims about enhanced freedom, democracy and socio-economic development. Employing a definition of legitimation that rests on the gap between the ability of global constituencies to democratically participate in decision making processes and the very processes with which decisions are made, Lupel (2005) argues that globalization has eroded the collective capacity to make 'legitimately binding decisions'. The current conditions, he concludes, open a crisis of legitimacy as established mechanisms of decision making are ineffective and new, and more democratic ones, are lacking. Underhill and Zhang (2008) further this argument by contending that current global arrangements undermine the legitimacy of the global system by shifting power overtly away from public entities and forums into the hands of private actors. Under globalization, the public good is increasingly defined and decided upon in private settings by private actors, and escapes collective scrutiny. Focusing on the governance of the financial sector, they conclude that the unchecked dominance of private interests in decision making strips the process of governance of the necessary legitimacy. Discussing the same substantive area, Helleiner (2010) contends that the neoliberal claims of the effectiveness and desirability of market mechanisms clash with calls for state intervention and regulation that followed recent crises (for example, economic crises, natural and man-made disasters, risky actions by large corporations and banks). These moves unveil a delegitimizing gap between ideology and practice under globalization.

In essence, the current dominant normative structure is inadequate to address social demand and stimulate mechanisms of development. Criticized are the claims that neoliberal globalization brings about enhanced freedom, democracy, socio-economic development and reliable instruments to achieve them. While the arguments in favor of the legitimation crisis are many, analyses on the reasons for the continuous dominance of neoliberalism are lacking. More specifically, this debate has not been able to pinpoint the elements that allow neoliberalism to remain the ideology of choice for many groups around the world. Studies of the future of socio-economic development should shed some light on this issue.

Between the late 1960s and the end of the 1990s, research on social change and development paid significant attention to the theme of labor. Topics such as the proletarianization of labor, workers' class position, the role of rural workers as reservoir of labor for the expansion of urban areas, and the marginalization and use of wage labor were frequently analyzed. In recent years, however, studies on social change and development have moved away from this traditional subject of investigation. Surprisingly, this trend evolved in a period in which labor relations were significantly altered and new and more serious forms of labor marginalization and control emerged. As the conditions of workers worsened under globalization, studies paid less attention to the theme of labor.

In a situation characterized by the enhanced mobility of commodities and capital, labor remains highly regulated. This is hardly a coincidence. In effect, stricter mechanisms of labor control not only diminished the ability

of labor to resist corporate actions but also allowed for the faster acceleration of capital accumulation (Harvey 2006). In the past, labor was effectively controlled through labor market and institutional mechanisms.
Historically, the assumption that high labor demand would generate higher
wages and labor strength was often supported by empirical evidence.
Simultaneously, the creation of labor surpluses – or labor reserve armies –
constituted one of the most effective tools to depress wages and contain
workers' claims. Under Fordism, however, labor was most effectively
controlled through state intervention and the so-called 'labor-management
accord' (Antonio and Bonanno 1996). This Fordist state-sponsored pact
allowed the pacification of labor relations and promoted a steady growth in
productivity, production and wages as well as a relative stability of employment.

Under globalization, the creation of transnational networks generated a
demand for labor. Contrary to the past, however, this demand did not
translate into labor strength. Corporations' ability to search the globe for
convenient factors of production (global sourcing) placed production facilities and activities in regions where labor was abundant and politically
docile. In effect, the search for docile labor has been one of the most
defining objectives of global sourcing. Global sourcing also limited the
power of stronger labor pools as these workers were placed in competition
with less expensive and less combative labor in different regions. As
demand weakened in labor-rich regions, workers were forced to migrate.
Because labor migration remained highly controlled, these migratory processes often took place through short-term immigration programs – workers
migrated for limited time periods and/or to execute specific tasks – or illegal
migration. In both cases, labor market mechanisms became secondary as
employment opportunities were regulated by legal-political mechanisms.
Under globalization, therefore, immigration laws and their enforcement
emerged as fundamental factors in the control of labor and predictors of
labor availability. The net result is that globalization often signifies lower
wages, unstable employment and the worsening of working conditions.

The high vulnerability of immigrant labor is further reinforced by ideological mechanisms that stigmatize migrants. In the United States, dominant discourses identify immigrants as undesirable individuals who break
the law, threaten community stability and national security, and take away
jobs from local workers. These discourses provide political fuel for the
proliferation of repressive anti-immigrant laws. Simultaneously, the
demand for immigrant labor continues to exist as companies are reluctant to
halt and/or reduce the use of this inexpensive, efficient and docile labor. The
continuous desire of business to employ immigrants contradicts the ideology and moves to limit immigration.

The issue of labor should be brought back to the forefront of research in socio-economic development. Among the many themes associated with labor, particular attention should be paid to the non-market mechanisms that regulate labor use and to the ideological discourses that characterize immigration policies and policy proposals.

CONCLUSIONS

The essence of this discussion on globalization is that it is one of the most important social phenomena of the twenty-first century. It is also an item that will continue to characterize the evolution of rural development and inform the manner in which rural communities will evolve. Accordingly, national and local leaders, rural community members, as well all the stakeholders should take this phenomenon into account as they consider future actions. As the literature presented above indicates, globalization's complexity mandates careful understanding of its characteristics and implications, not only to avoid its negative consequences but also to promote its positive outcomes.

NOTES

1. The Longue Duree group refers to that group of scholars that were originally associated with the journal *Annales d'histoirie économique et sociale*. First popularized in 1930s and 1940s by the work of Marc Bloch and Lucien Febvre, and later in the post-World War II decades by that of Fernand Braudel, their historiography centered on the importance of the evolution of long-term historical conditions (from this came the name Longue Duree, or Long Term) and the view that contemporary socio-economic phenomena find their roots and explanations in established historical trends. Wallerstein, along with other important representatives of the World System School, was associated with the Braudel Center at the State University of New York, Binghamton, USA.
2. The Clinton Administration's reform of the welfare system (Personal Responsibility and Work Opportunity Act, 1996) is an exemplar. The traditionally held idea of a welfare system to 'support the poor' was replaced by a rationale that stressed participation in the labor market. It implied that work would lift people out of poverty without taking into account that a significant portion of welfare recipients already worked and that earning minimum wages does not lift families out of poverty.

REFERENCES

Aglietta, Michel (1979), *A Theory of Capitalist Regulation*, London: New Left Books.
Amoore, Louise (ed.) (2005), *The Global Resistance Reader*, New York: Routledge.
Antonio, Robert J. and Alessandro Bonanno (1996), 'Post-Fordism in the United States: the poverty of market-centered democracy', *Current Perspectives in Social Theory*, 16, 3–32.

Barber, Benjiamin (1995), *Jihad vs. McWorld: Terrorism's Challenge to Democracy*, New York: Ballantine Books.

Baudrillard, Jean (1983), *Simulations*, New York: Semiotext(e).

Beck, Ulrich (2001), 'Globalisation's Chernobyl', *FT. Com (Financial Times)*. Available at http://www.news.ft.com (accessed November 6, 2001).

Becker, David and Richard Sklar (eds) (1999), *Postimperialism and World Politics*, Westport, CT: Praeger.

Boggs, Carl (2000), *The End of Politics: Corporate Power and the Decline of the Public Sphere*, New York: Guilford Press.

Bonanno, Alessandro and Douglas Constance (2008), *Stories of Globalization: Transnational Corporations, Resistance and the State*, University Park, PA: Penn State University Press.

Busse, Matthias (2004), 'Transnational corporations and repression of political rights and civil liberties: an empirical analysis', *Kyklos*, 57, 45–65.

Chase-Dunn, Christopher (1998), *Global Formation. Structure of the World-Economy*, Lanham, MD: Rowman & Littlefield.

Constance, Douglas H. and William D. Heffernan (1991), 'The global poultry agro-food complex', *International Journal of Sociology of Agriculture and Food*, 1, 126–42.

Croucher, Sheila (2004), *Globalization and Belonging: The Politics of Identity in a Changing World*, New York: Rowman & Littlefield.

Derrida, Jacques (1978), *Writings and Differences*, Chicago, IL: University of Chicago Press.

Dunning, John (1993), *The Globalization of Business*, New York: Routledge.

Firebaugh, Glenn and Brian Goesling (2004), 'Accounting for the recent decline in global income inequality', *American Journal of Sociology*, 110, 283–312.

Foucault, Michel (1969), *The Archaeology of Knowledge and the Discourse of Language*, New York: Harper Colophon.

Foucault, Michel (1975), *The Birth of the Clinic: An Archaeology of Medical Perception*, New York: Vintage Books.

Friedman, Milton (1982 [1962]), *Capitalism and Freedom*, Chicago, IL: University of Chicago Press.

Friedman, Thomas L. (2000), *The Lexus and the Olive Tree*, New York: Anchor Books.

Friedman, Thomas L. (2005), *The World is Flat*, New York: Picador.

Fukuyama, Francis (1992), *The End of History and The Last Man*, New York: Free Press.

Giddens, Anthony (2000), *Runaway World: How Globalization Is Reshaping Our Lives*, New York: Routledge.

Gramsci, Antonio (1971), *Selections from the Prison Notebooks*, transl. Quintin Hoare and Geoggrey Nowell Smith, New York: International Publishers.

Guillen, Mauro F. (2001), 'Is globalization civilizing, destructive or feeble? a critique of five key debates in the social science literature', *Annual Review of Sociology*, 27, 235–60.

Habermas, Jürgen (1975), *Legitimation Crisis*, Boston, MA: Beacon Press.

Harrison, Bennett and Barry Bluestone (1988), *The Great U-Turn: Corporate Restructuring and the Polarizing of America*, New York: Basic Books.

Harvey, David (1989), *The Condition of Postmodernity*, Oxford: Basil Blackwell.

Harvey, David (2006), *Spaces of Global Capitalism*, London: Verso.

Harvey, David (2010), *The Enigma of Capital*, New York: Oxford University Press.

Helleiner, Eric (2010), 'A Bretton Woods moment? The 2007–2008 crisis and the future of global finance', *International Affairs*, 86, 619–36.

Henderson, Hazel (2000), 'Transnational corporations and global citizenship', *American Behavioral Scientist*, 43, 1231–61.

Hirst, Paul and Grahame Thompson (1996), *Globalization in Question*, Cambridge: Polity Press.

Hosseini, Hamed (2009), 'Global complexities and the rise of the global justice movement', *Global Studies Journal*, 2, 15–36.

Humphery, Kim (1998), *Shelf Life: Supermarkets and the Changing Cultures of Consumption*, Cambridge: Cambridge University Press.

Jagdish, Bhagwati (2004), *In Defense of Globalization*, New York: Oxford University Press.

Kitching, Gavin (2001), *Seeking Social Justice through Globalization: Escaping a Nationalist Perspective*, University Park, PA: Pennsylvania State University Press.

Krugman, Paul (2007), *The Conscience of a Liberal*, New York: W.N. Norton.

Laclau, Ernesto and Chantal Mouffe (1985), *Hegemony and Socialist Strategy: Towards a Radical Democratic Politics*, London: Verso.

Laclau, Ernesto and Chantal Mouffe (1987), 'Post-Marxism without apologies', *New Left Review*, 166, 79–106.

Levitt, Theodore (1983), 'The globalization of markets', *Harvard Business Review*, 61, 92–102.

Lipietz, Alan (1987), *Mirages and Miracles*, London: Verso.

Lipietz, Alan (1992), *Towards a New Economic Order: Post-Fordism, Ecology, and Democracy*, New York: Oxford University Press.

Lupel, Adam (2005), 'Tasks of a global civil society: Held, Habermas and democratic legitimacy beyond the nation-state', *Globalizations*, 2, 117–33.

Macleod, Sorcha and Douglas Lewis (2004), 'Transnational corporations – power, influence and responsibility', *Global Social Policy*, 4, 77–98.

Marsden, Terry (2003), *The Condition of Rural Sustainability*, Assen, The Netherlands: Royal Van Gorcum.

Milanovic, Branko (2011), *The Haves and the Have-Nots: A Short and Idiosyncratic History of Global Inequality*, New York: Basic Books.

Mishel, Lawrence, Jared Bernstein and John Schmitt (2003), *The State of Working America 2002–03*, Washington, DC: Economic Policy Institute.

O'Connor, James (1974), *The Fiscal Crisis of the State*, New York: St Martin's Press.

Ohmae, Kenichi (1995), *The End of the Nation State: The Rise of Regional Economies*, New York: Free Press.

Parsons, Talcott (1971), *The System of Modern Societies*, Englewood Cliffs, NJ: Prentice-Hall.

Raulet, Gérard (2011), 'Legitimacy and globalization', *Philosophy and Social Criticism*, 37, 313–27.

Ritzer, George (2008), *The McDonaldization of Society*, Los Angeles, CA: Pine Forge Press.

Robinson, William I. (2004), *A Theory of Global Capitalism. Production, Class and State in a Transnational World*, Baltimore, MD, USA and London, UK: Johns Hopkins University Press.

Rostow, Walter W. (1960), *The Stages of Economic Growth: A Noncommunist Manifesto*, Cambridge: Cambridge University Press.

Rubner, Alex (1990), *The Might of the Multinationals: The Rise and Fall of the Corporate Legend*, New York: Praeger.

Sassen, Saskia (1998), *Globalization and its Discontents*, New York: New Press.

Stiglitz, Joseph (2003), *The Roaring Nineties*, New York: W.W. Norton & Company.

Underhill, Geoffrey and Xiaoke Zhang (2008), 'Setting the rules: private power, political underpinnings, and legitimacy in global monetary and financial governance', *International Affairs*, 84, 535–54.

Wallerstein, Immanuel (1974), *The Modern World-System: Capitalist Agriculture and the Origins of the European World Economy in the 16th Century*, New York: Academy Press.

Wallerstein, Immanuel (1980), *The Modern World System II: Mercantilism and the Consolidation of the European World-Economy, 1660–1750*, New York: Academy Press.

Wallerstein, Immanuel (2000), 'Globalization or the age of transition', *International Sociology*, 15, 251–67.

Wallerstein, Immanuel (2005), 'After development and globalization, what?', *Social Forces*, 83, 1263–78.
Wettstein, Florian (2009), *Multinational Corporations and Global Justice: Human Rights Obligations of a Quasi-Governmental Institution*, Stanford, CA: Stanford University Press.
Wright, Wynne and Gerad Midderndorf (eds) (2007), *The Fight Over Food*, University Park, PA: Penn State University Press.

3. Rural policy

Thomas G. Johnson

WHAT IS RURAL POLICY?

There are no clear definitions of rural policy that help us determine the issues that should either be included in, or excluded from, the domain of rural policy. Bryden (2007) distinguishes between narrow and broad rural policies. Narrow rural policies are those that have as their stated purpose the improvement in economic and social conditions of rural people and places. Broad rural policies include all policies that have significant impacts on rural people and places but which have goals not directly related to rural economic and social conditions. Using these definitions, broad rural policies would include agricultural, transportation, health, education, economic development, regional, environmental and other policies that have implications for rural populations. Obviously, many of these largely sectoral policies and programs have different impacts over space and thus have differential consequences for rural people and places.

Narrow rural policies are explicitly spatial rather than sectoral. Because they have spatial rather than sectoral dimensions, they are often more difficult to identify and categorize. Our government agencies are more often organized along sectoral lines (departments of agriculture, health, transportation, commerce, and so on), which means that narrow rural policies are distributed across many agencies. One useful way to think of narrow rural policies is to look for features of policies that are in some way conditional on a definition of 'rural'.[1] For example, health policies that make provisions for populations or service providers in less dense regions should be considered rural policies. Similarly, a policy that provides economic development support for traditionally rural businesses might be considered a rural policy even though eligibility may not be tied to a definition of rural. In this chapter I will primarily be concerned with narrow rural policy, but it is inevitable that the discussion will sometimes stray into issues that relate to broader policy domains.

Another definitional issue relates to the terms 'rural policy' and 'rural development policy'. These terms are frequently used synonymously but there is value in distinguishing between them. To some, rural development policy implies efforts to raise the economic performance in underdeveloped rural areas, whereas rural policy is broader, dealing with the provision of services, and improvements in non-economic standards as well as economic development. In this chapter I generally refer to the more general interpretation of rural policy.

Finally, the discussion here will focus mostly on the history, evolution and current state of rural policy in developed countries. To many people, the terms 'rural development' and 'rural development policy' are predominantly focused on developing countries. A search for articles on 'rural development policy' on Google Scholar, for instance, returns almost exclusively articles on the developing world. This chapter, however, focuses on the policies of relevance to Organisation for Economic Co-operation and Development (OECD) countries. As rapid development occurs in much of the world, the issues covered here will become more and more relevant to more countries of the world.

WHY RURAL POLICY?

Policy interventions are intended to bring about changes that benefit society. The goals and objectives of policy vary across the spectrum of societal issues – another reason that rural policy is difficult to define, and as we will see, difficult to develop. Justifications for rural policy interventions are typically of two types.

The first justification for rural policy interventions is to promote fairness or equity.[2] At one extreme, the definition of fairness is that all residents, no matter where they live, deserve equal access to services and economic opportunities. Some countries, in fact, have explicit policies referred to as 'equivalency' in which the goals of rural policy are to assure that rural and urban residents can expect to enjoy roughly equal access to services such as health care, education and so on (Bryden 2010). Complete equivalency, even among rural regions, is probably impossible because of the degree of remoteness and low population density of many rural regions, but for those countries that adopt equivalency as a goal it provides benchmarks against which policies and programs may be measured, and which can be used to guide policy realignment.

Other countries define fairness as the assurance that all residents have at least some minimum access to public services and economic opportunities. This definition of fairness leads to much more modest policy goals, but still justifies rural policy on the basis of fairness and again provides benchmarks against which achievements can be assessed.

Given their choice of residence, it is likely that rural and urban residents have different preferences for public services, natural, social and cultural amenities, and economic opportunities. For this reason, it is unlikely that total equality of service provision is necessarily the ideal or optimum outcome of policy. A 'fair' outcome of policy is probably not the same as an 'equivalent' outcome of policy. Furthermore, because of the diversity among rural places, it is likely that what is considered a fair outcome by the residents of one rural community or region is different from that which is considered a fair outcome by residents of other rural communities and regions.

The second justification for rural policy is increased economic efficiency. Policy interventions potentially increase efficiency in cases where markets, in the absence of this intervention, would fail to allocate resources optimally. Market failure occurs when any of several conditions occur including the production of public goods, the propagation of externalities, or the existence of information asymmetry or monopolistic power. These conditions occur throughout the economy but rural regions are particularly prone to some forms of market failure. Both theory and empirical analysis suggest that rural economies are particularly susceptible to monopolistic power because of their sparse population and distance to major markets (Kilkenny 2010). An even more obvious source of market failure, and thus a compelling justification for policy intervention is the wide range of public goods and externalities (both positive and negative) produced as a consequence of rural resource use. The OECD points out that '[e]xternalities related to rural land use are pervasive' (OECD 2003, p. 106). Many of the public goods and positive externalities generated in rural regions are collectively referred to as multifunctionalities of rural land use (Hediger and Lehmann 2007; Jordan et al. 2007) or rural development (McCarthy 2005; Refsgaard and Johnson 2010). In other cases these public goods and externalities are simply referred to as rural amenities or environmental and ecosystem services (Baylis et al. 2008).

In general, most policies will have both equity and efficiency goals and justifications. It is commonly believed that over most ranges of possible policy outcomes, equity and efficiency are substitutes, and that policies and programs designed to improve the distributional outcomes will necessarily reduce the Pareto efficiency of the outcomes (Pascual et al. 2010). Rural policy is particularly challenging in this respect due to the great deal of spatial diversity involved.

On the other hand, equity and efficiency are occasionally complementary goals. Policies designed to encourage and facilitate human capital investment for example tend to reduce income inequities while increasing overall economic efficiency and productivity (Benabou 1996; Wößmann and Schütz 2006; Woessmann 2008). Where complementarities between equity and efficiency goals exist, rural policies may be made less controversial and more cost-effective. I will explore this possibility more below.

A BRIEF HISTORY OF RURAL POLICY

Historically, rural policy has been equated with agricultural policy in most parts of the world. In the past, when farm families accounted for a large share of the rural population, and agriculture (farming, food and fiber processing and marketing) was the backbone of rural economies, this approach worked relatively well. Government programs designed to financially support agriculture and farmers assured a strong and relatively stable engine for rural economies. Non-agricultural rural firms provided inputs, services and markets for farms and agribusinesses. Farms and agribusinesses provided a strong tax base for local governments in rural areas. In this context, policies designed to increase agricultural productivity and profitability also promoted rural development goals.

However, due to the success of public and private investments in productivity-enhancing research, technology and infrastructure, agriculture, as well as other rural sectors such as mining, forestry, fishing and manufacturing, now employ far fewer workers than in the past, while producing more commodities than ever. The increased capital intensity of these traditionally rural sectors released labor, allowing them to take employment in the services, financial, transportation, trade and other sectors. Some of these new jobs were located in rural areas, but most were located in urban areas where economies of scale and agglomeration economies meant the productivity of both labor and capital was higher.

Today the traditional economic bases of rural areas – farming, agribusiness, forestry, fishing, mining and manufacturing – account for a small share of total employment, income and gross domestic product. The indirect economic activities generated by these basic sectors (the multiplier effects) are relatively small. And in many cases these indirect jobs are themselves located in urban areas. Thus, public policy focused on these traditional rural sectors has a small and declining impact on the prosperity and opportunities available to rural residents. In fact, many of these sectoral policies have net negative effects on rural economies. For example, Thompson (2007) speculates that US agricultural policy, which subsidizes farm income and stabilizes agricultural commodity prices, has several deleterious effects on rural communities including farm consolidation and concomitant population losses, higher land values thus reducing competitiveness of rural businesses, and reduced entrepreneurship among farmers and related businesses. Similarly, Bryden (2010) argues that the European Union's Common Agricultural Policy, despite having explicit rural development goals of increasing social cohesion,[3] has 'anti-cohesion' (p. 3) impacts. In fact, few rural and agricultural policy analysts today would argue, as many did in the past, that good farm policy was good rural policy.

THE NEW RURAL PARADIGM

About the turn of the twenty-first century, rural policy theory and practice entered a renaissance period of sorts in many developed countries. A key observer and communicator of changes and best practices in rural policy has been the Organisation for Economic Co-operation and Development. In 2002 the OECD held a global conference on rural policy in Sienna, Italy that has since been followed by annual conferences around the world to assess the progress of its member nations in modernizing their rural policies. The proceedings of this conference (OECD 2003) summarized several themes that were shaping rural regions and have guided the emerging rural policies in many countries since that time. First, agriculture is a significant sector in many rural regions, but it is declining in importance and no longer can be counted on to drive the economies of most rural regions. Second, sectoral policies can no longer solve the problems faced by rural regions. Sectoral policies are blunt instruments that fail to address the idiosyncratic issues of most rural regions. Instead, place-based policies are called for that recognize and exploit these same idiosyncrasies. Third, it is important to recognize that rural and urban places are parts of interrelated regions, but the rural components of these regions require policies that are sensitive to their particular strengths and constraints. Policies designed for urban areas will typically be inappropriate for the rural territory in the same region. Fourth, rural areas are not just problems that must be solved to avoid being drags on urban economies. The diversity and unique assets of rural areas are opportunities that, if captured, will increase the competitiveness and sustainability of the larger economies of which they are components.

Since 2003, these concepts have been further developed, formalized and tested. In 2006 the OECD unveiled its New Rural Paradigm (OECD 2006b). The New Rural Paradigm was both a conceptual framework and a summary of best practices. The New Rural Paradigm is summarized in Table 3.1.

The key shifts proposed by the New Rural Paradigm were a replacement of sector-based policies with place-based policies, and a shift in instruments from subsidies to investments. The paradigm called for a greater role for local and regional governments as well as non-governmental institutions, and for more horizontal and vertical coordination among governments.

Using the New Rural Paradigm as a standard, the OECD has, since 2006, assessed and documented the policies of several countries and regions of the world (OECD 2007a, 2007b, 2008a, 2008b, 2008c, 2009a, 2009b, 2009c, 2010, 2011). These reviews chronicle a broad array of innovative attempts to redirect the trends occurring in rural regions, the interaction of policies and politics, and of failures as well as successes. These reviews find that the underlying drivers of change in rural regions – technological change,

Table 3.1   The New Rural Paradigm

	Old approach	New approach
Objectives	Equalization, farm income, farm competitiveness	Competitiveness of rural areas, valorization of local assets, exploitation of unused resources
Key target sector	Agriculture	Various sectors of rural economies (ex. rural tourism, manufacturing, ICT industry, etc.)
Main tools	Subsidies	Investments
Key actors	National governments, farmers	All levels of government (supranational, regional and local), various local stakeholders (public, private, NGOs)

Source: OECD (2006a, p. 4).

changing demographics, changing economic bases of rural areas and declining political influence – are common to rural regions throughout the world. But they describe processes which differ according to political institutions, history, culture and contemporaneous events. They provide a rich menu of best practices, but at the same time demonstrate that policies cannot be simply borrowed from another country. Institutions are path dependent and critical determinants of policy success, and for this reason, rural policies must be fine-tuned to local conditions.

THE CURRENT CONTEXT FOR RURAL POLICY

Today, rural policy is made and executed in an environment of rapid technological change, globalization and urbanization. Each of these trends influences the needs for and success of alternative policy strategies.

Rural regions are not unfamiliar with technological change. Agriculture was arguably the earliest sector to be significantly transformed by technology. More recently, technological change in mining, forestry and other extractive sectors have continued to create wrenching change in the rural economy. Today, the services, the largest employer in rural economies, are also being transformed by technology. The growing role of information and communication technologies (ICTs) represents both opportunities and threats for rural residents and employers. These opportunities and threats create both efficiency and equity reasons for policy intervention, but require quite different strategies than in the past. Today's policy challenges include such issues as the rural broadband deficit, telemedicine and distance education, e-commerce and others.

Globalization, the growing integration of the world economy, is related to technology but leads to different stresses and challenges. It has been argued that globalization has accelerated the process of economic agglomeration, by increasing competition and expanding market size for many products (Scott and Storper 2003). Furthermore, globalization has led to a diversity of responses by regional economies. Some regions have found their niches and adapted to the new competitive realities. Other regions have found it difficult to adapt and have resorted instead to resisting change. Ironically, this growing diversity and specialization makes one-size-fits-all policy even less effective than in the past.

Urbanization is clearly related to technological change and globalization but it has implications of its own. Urbanization has created a political and social gulf between rural and urban areas, even as regional economic specialization has made rural and urban areas more interrelated. Urban voters and politicians are less likely to understand the needs of rural areas, and less likely to appreciate how vulnerable they have become because of their dependence on water, energy and food that is produced by an ever-declining portion of the population.

Together this policy context requires a different approach to rural policy but simultaneously makes rural policy making more difficult and less responsive to these changing needs. The follow sections explore the current state of rural policy in this context.

THE CURRENT STATE OF RURAL POLICY

The New Rural Paradigm challenges the approaches to rural policy that have prevailed for decades. It provides a rough outline for new policies but does not prescribe policies. The observations and conclusions contained in the description of this paradigm reflect ongoing policy experimentation in many countries. This section explores some of these policy approaches. Some have had modest success, others are still untested, and none are panaceas for issues faced by rural regions, especially in a world where issues are very dynamic. Interestingly, policy innovation often proceeds ahead of conceptual and empirical evidence for its efficacy (Johnson 2007). This challenges theorists and empiricists to keep up with practitioners, but it also provides them with ample and diverse evidence with which to study the issues.

Place-Based Policy

The first of these new policy experiments is placed-based policy. Barca defines place-based policy as:

> a long-term strategy aimed at tackling persistent underutilisation of potential and reducing persistent social exclusion in specific places through external interventions and multilevel governance. It promotes the supply of integrated goods and services tailored to contexts, and it triggers institutional changes. In a place-based policy, public interventions rely on local knowledge and are verifiable and submitted to scrutiny, while linkages among places are taken into account. (Barca 2009, p. vii)

The goal of place-based rural policy is to redress both inefficiencies and inequities by addressing impediments and opportunities in specific places, especially those that are lagging behind more dynamic places. The hope is that by tailoring programs to address a place's weaknesses and exploiting its strengths, higher returns to policy investments can be achieved. It is also hoped that policy will have its greatest impact in lagging regions, thus reducing regional disparity and leading to regional convergence. There is reason to believe that such a strategy not only lifts up the lagging regions but also boosts the national efficiency and rate of growth as well (Barca et al. 2012). Thus place-based policies may be one of those cases where complementarities between efficiency and equity can be found.

The theoretical rationale for place-based policy builds upon many of the concepts discussed above but adds spatial, cultural, social and institutional dimensions. The spatial dimension cites the importance of diversity in the process of economic change and development. Diverse natural resources and amenities, diverse labor forces, and unique spatial arrays of markets and infrastructure all suggest the need for policies that allow flexibility in program implementation.

Cultural and social dimensions of place-based policy introduce the role of preferences, collective societal goals and interpersonal relationships into the process of prioritizing economic development goals and strategies. Culture introduces numerous, often subtle, effects on behaviors that influence people's response to policy (Guiso et al. 2006). For example, communities and regions with a stronger cultural affinity to natural landscapes will find industrial development less attractive. Communities with a stronger association with land will be less likely to sell, rent or dramatically change land uses. Attitudes toward education, risk taking, entrepreneurship, women's roles, democratic processes and many others are both culturally based and economically relevant. Thus policy that allows for spatial variation in its approach to cultural differences is likely to be more effective.

The institutional dimension has more recently been recognized as a critical and formidable concern for rural and regional policy (Wood and Valler 2004). In short, institutions are unique to place, historically based, change very slowly and are critical to economic development. For these reasons, policies and programs are not easily transferred from one place to another, because without the necessary institutions in place the programs will have quite different consequences in a new place than they had in a previous location. Even more vexing is the likelihood that some institutions, in some places, make any kind of change difficult. Barca et al. (2012) argue that development at the local and regional level is often impeded by dysfunctional institutions. In some cases these are institutions that are intentionally designed to impede development to protect local elites, while in other cases institutions are simply outdated and inadequate.

For all of these reasons, effective policies must be place-based. This does not preclude national or state rural policies, but it suggest that these policies must be flexible enough to adapt to the natural, cultural, social, environmental and economic conditions of each place.

Rural Wealth Creation

The emphasis of rural development policy has traditionally been on increasing the rate of growth in productivity and income of rural residents. When rural policy was essentially equated to agricultural policy, this meant that higher farm incomes equaled rural development. Thus it was accepted that farm income supports, and programs designed to increase the price of agricultural commodities, were the most direct paths to rural development. Our most common indicator of economic performance (efficiency), gross domestic product (GDP), could be applied to rural sectors and rural regions to gauge the level of success of our rural policy. Measures of median and average family and per capita disposable income were used as indicators of welfare and the distribution of income as an indicator of equity.

More recently the concept of wealth has reappeared as a goal and as an indicator of progress toward economic development. The distribution of wealth has been suggested as an alternative to distribution of income as an indicator of equity. Why wealth? Surely people's welfare is more dependent on their ability to access and consume goods and services (broadly defined) than it is to their amassed wealth. While this is true it turns out that the sustainability of people's consumption of goods and services depends on societal wealth (broadly defined).

A sustainable level of consumption, as Nordhaus (2000) posits, is 'the maximum amount that a nation can consume while ensuring that members of all current and future generations can have expected lifetime consumption or utility that is at least as high as current consumption or utility' (p. 259). Nordhaus demonstrates that to assure this constant or growing level of consumption requires a growth in societal wealth. And this wealth is comprised of more than financial capital and fixed investments. It includes various non-market and intangible capitals that must all be maintained or enhanced to assure a sustained level of consumption into the future. Hoffer and Levy (2010) identify seven types of capital: intellectual, social, individual, natural, built, financial and political. These capitals may be individually owned and controlled (human capital, for example) or publicly owned and available (built infrastructure, natural capital and various types of intellectual capital).

Our most widely used measure of economic performance is gross domestic product. GDP is a gross flow measure that ignores changes in (investment in or depreciation of) assets. Wealth is a stock measure that is solely focused on the changing stock of assets. Like GDP, well-being is a flow, but one which depends critically on net wealth measured in a number of dimensions in addition to income. During the last two decades there have been significant advances made in expanding our indicators of economic performance to include various non-market and intangible capitals (especially the natural and environmental capitals) and their associated flows of goods and services to estimate broader indicators of wealth (Nordhaus 1996).

The policy implications of this focus on wealth are numerous, especially for rural people and places. First, a focus on wealth assures a longer-term perspective, and more sustainable results. Second, rural policy-based on a wealth perspective will become more focused on investment and less on income support, a key tenet of the new rural paradigm. Third, a greater policy focus on natural capital is particularly important for rural areas where a majority of a nation's natural capital exists and which represents a very large portion of rural wealth despite its non-market characteristics. The growing focus on rural wealth creation strategies is evidence that this type of rural policy will have significant visibility for some time.

WHY IS RURAL POLICY DEVELOPMENT SO HARD TO ACCOMPLISH?

The process of policy development for rural regions is generally difficult. A number of policy scholars have speculated on why this is the case. The most common conclusion is that rural policy is difficult to develop because rural people and places lack a well-defined constituency. Unlike sector-based stakeholders, many rural residents do not identify common interests with other rural residents as readily as they do with the sectoral cooperators and competitors. Farmers are more likely to recognize their interests in policies dealing with agricultural commodities, crop insurance and even environmental regulation. Rural manufacturers will pay close attention to immigration, tax, transportation and regulatory policies. But farmers, rural manufacturers, rural educators and rural residents in general may not recognize their common interest in policies to encourage the strengthening of rural innovation systems or improved rural broadband access.

Meanwhile, urban residents have less familiarity with rural problems as they become increasingly distanced from their agrarian origins. With each generation, the rapidly growing urban population has fewer familial and social connections to rural people. At the political level elected leaders increasingly lack rural constituents or personal experience with rural issues and are thus less likely to give rural issues priority.

Together the lack of a cohesive rural constituency and the declining connection to other constituencies makes rural policy making more difficult and less likely to be responsive to rural needs unless policy analysts work with policy advocates to increase understanding of the issues and appropriate responses.

CONCLUSIONS

As I have noted, the economic context for rural policy is in a state of rapid change and is likely to continue changing. In response, rural policy must not only change but must become more flexible and dynamic in order to accommodate the constantly changing context. At the same time the political and social contexts for rural policy do not make policy change easy.

Confounding these growing challenges to rural policy making is the growing criticality of rural vitality and growing dependency of urban populations on the health of rural economies. A common outcome of this policy-making dilemma is a tendency for policy makers to apply policies designed for urban areas, across the rural–urban spectrum, without regard for the unique needs and constraints of rural regions.

However, as we have seen there are promising new policy strategies and tools emerging, especially at the local level. These tools are not yet proven, and most will need to be adapted to local institutions and conditions to be successful. Policy theorists, analysts and educators will play an important role in testing, improving and implementing the new and future policy strategies for rural areas.

NOTES

1. This, of course, raises the issue of what is rural, something that will not be addressed in this chapter but which continues to be debated in the literature (Coburn et al. 2007; Isserman 2005, 2007; Waldorf 2007).
2. There is a large literature debating what is meant by fairness, equity, equality and equivalence. Here we use the terms 'fairness' and 'equity' as synonymous, but distinguish these concepts from 'equality' or 'equivalence'.
3. The Council of Europe defines social cohesion as 'a concept that includes values and principles which aim to ensure that all citizens, without discrimination and on an equal footing, have access to fundamental social and economic rights' (Council of Europe 2001, p. 5).

REFERENCES

Barca, Fabrizio (2009), 'An agenda for a reformed cohesion policy: a place-based approach to meeting European Union challenges and expectations', Independent Report prepared at the request of Danuta Hübner, Commissioner for Regional Policy, European Union Parliament. http://www.europarl.europa.eu/meetdocs/2009_2014/documents/regi/dv/barca_report_/barca_report_en.pdf.
Barca, F., P. McCann and A. Rodríguez-Pose (2012), 'The case for regional development intervention: place-based versus place-neutral approaches', *Journal of Regional Science*, 52, 134–52.
Baylis, K., S. Peplow, G. Rausser and L. Simon (2008), 'Agri-environmental policies in the EU and United States: a comparison', *Ecological Economics*, 65, 753–64.
Benabou, R. (1996), 'Equity and efficiency in human capital investment: the local connection', *Review of Economic Studies*, 63, 237–64.
Bryden, J.M. (2007), 'Changes in rural policy and governance: the broader context', in A. Copus (ed.), *Continuity or Transformation? Perspectives on Rural Development in the Nordic Countries*, conference report, Nordregio Report 2007.4, Stockholm, pp. 23–31.
Bryden, J.M. (2010), 'European rural policy: old wine in old bottles: is it corked?' Keynote address for the Nordic Rural Futures Conference, Sweden.
Coburn, Andrew F., A. Clinton MacKinney, Timothy D. McBride, Keith J. Mueller, Rebecca T. Slifkin and Mary K. Wakefield (2007), 'Choosing rural definitions: implications for health policy', Rural Policy Research Institute Health Panel Issue Brief #2, March. http://www.rupri.org/Forms/RuralDefinitionsBrief.pdf.
Council of Europe (2001), *Promoting the Policy Debate on Social Exclusion from a Comparative Perspective*, Trends in Social Cohesion, no. 1, Strasbourg: Council of Europe Publishing.
Guiso, L., P. Sapienza and L. Zingales (2006), 'Does culture affect economic outcomes?' No. w11999, Cambridge, MA: National Bureau of Economic Research. http://www.nber.org/papers/w11999.
Hediger, W. and B. Lehmann (2007), 'Multifunctional agriculture and the preservation of environmental benefits', *Schweizerische Zeitschrift für Volkswirtschaft und Statistik*, 143(4), 449–70.
Hoffer, D. and M. Levy (2010), 'Measuring community wealth', report for the Wealth Creation in Rural Communities Project of the Ford Foundation. http://www. yellowwood. org/wealthcreation. aspx.
Isserman, A.M. (2005), 'In the national interest: defining rural and urban correctly in research and public policy', *International Regional Science Review*, 28, 465–99.

Isserman, A.M. (2007), 'Getting state rural policy right: definitions, growth, and program eligibility', *Journal of Regional Analysis and Policy*, 37, 73–9.

Johnson, T.G. (2007), 'Place-based economic policy: innovation or fad?', *Agricultural and Resource Economics Review*, 36, 1.

Jordon, N., G. Boody, W. Broussard, J.D. Glover, D. Keeney, B.H. McCown, G. McIsaac, M. Muller, H. Murry, J. Neal, C. Pansing, R.E. Turner, K. Warner and D. Wyse (2007), 'Sustainable development of the agricultural bio-economy', *Science*, 316, 1570–71.

Kilkenny, Maureen (2010), 'Urban/regional economics and rural development', *Journal of Regional Science*, 50, 449–70.

McCarthy, James (2005), 'Rural geography: multifunctional rural geographies – reactionary or radical?', *Progress in Human Geography*, 29, 773–82.

Nordhaus, W.D. (1996), 'Budget deficits and national saving', *Challenge*, 39(2), 45–9.

Nordhaus, W.D. (2000), 'New directions in national economic accounting', *American Economic Review*, 90, 259–63.

Organisation for Economic Co-operation and Development (2003), *The Future of Rural Policy: From Sectoral to Place-Based Policies in Rural Areas*, Paris: OECD.

Organisation for Economic Co-operation and Development (2006a), 'Reinventing rural policy: policy brief'. http://www.oecd.org/regional/37556607.pdf.

Organisation for Economic Co-operation and Development (2006b), 'The New Rural Paradigm: policies and governance', Paris: OECD. http://www3.unisi.it/cipas/ref/OECD_2006_Rural_Paradigm.pdf.

Organisation for Economic Co-operation and Development (2007a), *Rural Policy Reviews: Mexico*, Paris: OECD.

Organisation for Economic Co-operation and Development (2007b), *Rural Policy Reviews: Germany*, Paris: OECD.

Organisation for Economic Co-operation and Development (2008a), *Rural Policy Reviews: Scotland*, Paris: OECD.

Organisation for Economic Co-operation and Development (2008b), *Rural Policy Reviews: The Netherlands*, Paris: OECD.

Organisation for Economic Co-operation and Development (2008c), *Rural Policy Reviews: Finland*, Paris: OECD.

Organisation for Economic Co-operation and Development (2009a), *Rural Policy Reviews: Spain*, Paris: OECD.

Organisation for Economic Co-operation and Development (2009b), *Rural Policy Reviews: Italy*, Paris: OECD.

Organisation for Economic Co-operation and Development (2009c), *Rural Policy Reviews: China*, Paris: OECD.

Organisation for Economic Co-operation and Development (2010), *Rural Policy Reviews: Quebec, Canada*, Paris: OECD.

Organisation for Economic Co-operation and Development (2011), *Rural Policy Reviews: England, United Kingdom*, Paris: OECD.

Pascual, U., R. Muradian, L.C. Rodríguez and A. Duraiappah (2010), 'Exploring the links between equity and efficiency in payments for environmental services: a conceptual approach', *Ecological Economics*, 69, 1237–44.

Refsgaard, K. and T.G. Johnson (2010), 'Modelling policies for multifunctional agriculture and rural development–a Norwegian case study', *Environmental Policy and Governance*, 20, 239–57.

Scott, A. and M. Storper (2003), 'Regions, globalization, development', *Regional Studies*, 37, 549–78.

Thompson, Robert L. (2007), 'Globalization and rural America', *Chicago Fed Letter*, Federal Reserve Bank of Chicago.

Waldorf, B. (2007), *What is Rural and What is Urban in Indiana*, West Lafayette, IN: Purdue Center for Regional Development. http://www.pcrd.purdue.edu/documents/publications/What_is_Rural_and_What_is_Urban_in_Indiana.pdf.

Woessmann, L. (2008), 'Efficiency and equity of European education and training policies', *International Tax and Public Finance*, 15, 199–230.

Wood, Andrew and David Valler (2004), *Governing Local and Regional Economies: Institutions, Politics and Economic Development*, Aldershot: Ashgate Publishing.

Wößmann, L. and G. Schütz (2006), 'Efficiency and equity in European education and training systems', Analytical Report for the European Commission prepared by the European expert network on economics of education (EENEE) to accompany the Communication and Staff Working Paper by the European Commission under the same title. http://ec.europa.eu/education/policies/2010/doc/eenee.pdf.

4. Grassroots rural development: models of development, capacity and leadership

Stephen P. Gasteyer and Cameron (Khalfani) Herman

INTRODUCTION

Grassroots development is a process of intentional social change that privileges local organizing, visioning and decision making. According to Gaventa and Lewis (1989), it is an alternative to trickle-down approaches to local development in poor communities. Trickle-down approaches have a long history in rural community development and have been associated by some scholars with legacies of colonialism, corruption and attempts by powerful, urban-based elites to extract resources from rural communities and places (Tacoli 1998). While most prominently discussed in the developing-country context, the concept is also applied to local organizing in the United States, Canada and Europe, specifically through the study of 'grassroots organizations' in marginalized communities (see, for example, Scott 2002).

This chapter focuses on grassroots approaches to development in rural communities in the United States and the global arena. The overview draws on relevant community development literature to contextualize the practice of grassroots development. Additionally, the chapter examines a few case studies to illustrate how grassroots development is implemented in different rural communities throughout the world. A brief discussion of grassroots development's capacity to improve the human condition closes the chapter.

THE CONTEXT OF GRASSROOTS DEVELOPMENT

Whether in developing or industrialized nations, the process of rural community development has often been driven by agencies and forces outside of rural communities themselves. For centuries, nation-states have encouraged development based on export-oriented extraction of natural resources from rural areas as a critical component of national wealth creation. Modernization of transportation and basic services such as electricity accompanied these efforts to varying degrees, depending in part on the need for legitimation from local or international political elites (McMichael 2012). While national governments have often pursued development agendas in and around rural communities, too often this has been done with little consideration of rural community concerns – sometimes with disastrous effects on rural livelihoods (Gaventa and Lewis 1989).

The process of top-down development has taken different forms in different contexts. Colonial governments imposed new means and forms of production on rural communities to increase export earnings (McMichael 2012). In South and East Asia and Southern Africa, for instance, colonial administrations effectively provided military cover for private investors from Europe, some of whom made their fortunes extracting minerals, spices, agricultural commodities and other products that became staples of European culture (see, for example, Peluso 1992; Ribot 2003).

Even in sovereign and powerful nations, central governments often imposed systems that privileged moneyed elites over the interests of local subsistence producers. Within the United States, for instance, federal and state governments facilitated corporate control of land and mineral rights for extraction of raw materials to encourage processes of industrial development. Government investments laid the infrastructure for capitalist development through damming rivers, laying railroad lines, building roads, putting in water, communications and electricity, and introducing new technologies for increasing agricultural and other rural extractive production (Flora and Flora 2013).

During the post-World War II era of decolonialization, capitalist countries with colonial histories developed land tenure policies that often encouraged expatriate corporate investment, sometimes at the expense of collective ownership structures that had long been in place (see, for example, Peluso 1992). While some have argued that capitalist development has been the culprit in these forms of development, it is worth remembering that the Soviet Union and post-colonial Marxist countries were even more top-down in collectivizing individual farms into enormous aggregated units, and reorganizing rural labor around established industries. This was often done over the objections of rural residents – with disappointing outcomes in some places and catastrophic impacts in others (McMichael 2012).

In all cases, rural development projects have too often been facilitated through top-down approaches, initiated and overseen by corporations, government agencies, non-governmental organizations (NGOs), global institutions such as the World Bank and United Nations, and private corporations (Carroll 1992). These approaches to rural development have all too often ensured that the profits from farming, natural resources extraction and other production activities have gone to outside investors, leaving community members (while possibly benefiting from jobs in the short term) to live with the social and environmental ramifications of development initiatives – be they energy extraction, forestry, agriculture or manufacturing (Flora and Flora 2013; Freudenburg and Krannich 2003; McMichael 2012).

Grassroots development emerged as a response to concern about these kinds of detrimental impacts of top-down development initiatives. It is important to note that grassroots development often involves fundamentally challenging the presumed rationale for development as an enterprise itself.

GRASSROOTS DEVELOPMENT AS A CHALLENGE TO MODERNIZATION

It would be a mistake, however, to consider all top-down development initiatives to be purely cynical attempts at natural resources extraction. The development initiative was through the 1970s, and in many ways still is, driven by a narrative of modernization. This narrative argued that modernization could improve quality of life through providing greater economic well-being, as well as improving basic aspects of life indicators such as health and education. As opposed to toiling just to make ends meet, people could live better. Modern infrastructure that connected rural places to urban and international markets was a key component of this process, but the quid pro quo was that traditional ways of life had to yield to more 'modern' forms of daily activity (Harvey 1990).

To achieve these modern innovations, new kinds of community leaders were needed who would see these initiatives as advantageous. Development initiatives to improve rural community 'leadership' and human capital were part of the development process throughout the first part of the twentieth century. The British and French colonial systems, for instance, had explicit programs to educate rural indigenous youth (Adas 1991; McClellan 1991).

Sanderson (1947) was part of a growing chorus calling for rural community leadership development in the United States – so that rural communities could gain the decision-making skills to address head on new challenges such as growing mobility and telecommunications. The notion, however, was generally that through improving human capital, rural people would be better equipped to adopt the technologies that had been developed to modernize their lives.

While the 'tree top development' (Stiles 1987, p. 14) could lead to modernization of infrastructure, improvements in wealth, greater diversity in thought and less physically demanding labor through technological changes such as the mechanization of agricultural processes, this type of development also exposed local people to fluctuations in regional and national economies affecting rural communities around the world (Flora and Flora, 2013).

As critical development scholar Arturo Escobar (1995) notes, the development enterprise itself has too often been driven to encourage undemocratic modernization and wealth creation, very often disempowering and further impoverishing people in rural communities, while providing wealth for corporate and political elites. In some cases, there is no desire on the part of developers to include community members in the planning or implementation processes (McMichael 2012).

The results have been seen in growing unemployment, income disparity and depopulation of rural communities in industrialized and developing countries alike. Grassroots development is increasingly espoused as a rural community development strategy to combat these trends.

WHAT IS GRASSROOTS DEVELOPMENT?

The term 'grassroots development' emerged as a reaction to the bureaucracy-centered development system that has typified the post-World War II modernization era. As Stiles (1987) notes, classical economic development has the purported goals of improved quality of life and happiness through better education, alleviation of poverty, clean water, food, housing, electricity and the other trappings of industrialized 'developed' society. Stiles notes that the typical pattern for classical development has involved interactions between government and agency bureaucracies:

> The usual approach to development has involved a donor bureaucracy (for example, USAID [United StatesAgency for International Development], World Bank, UNDP [United Nations Development Programme], EEC [European Economic Community]) dealing with a recipient government bureaucracy (for example, Ministry of Planning and National Development, the Treasury, etc.). Development project proposals are formulated based on priorities established nominally by the recipient government, but usually influenced by what the donor is willing to finance ... formulated by 'expert' consultants, usually paid for by the donor agency. (Stiles 1987: 11)

Usually, development initiatives like this are facilitated through a network of technical experts and consultants. These outside experts are employed to develop project proposals through short visits to the proposed project area to study the technical, economic and, hopefully, the social and environmental aspects of their project (Stiles 1987, p. 11).

This process is heavily bounded by bureaucratic rules and regulations. The project priorities are often based on priorities set in national or state capitals by government and/or donor agencies. Projects are large-budget, since large-budget projects are more easily administered. Local priorities tend not to fit agency objectives, and are thus often ignored. The rates of failure for projects within this development paradigm are far too high – and are sometimes disastrous for local people (Seyfang and Smith 2007; Stiles 1987).

It is notable that these promised improvements were very much part of the goals of rural development in the United States through the 1980s as well (Christenson and Robinson 1989). While there are now legal requirements for at least a minimal level of public participation associated with permitting processes, community development in rural America in the twenty-first century is still too often driven by non-local interests and values (Flora and Flora 2013).

In response to concerns about high failure rates of projects, scholars such as Chambers (2005), Toulmin and Chambers (1990) and Galjart (1981) increasingly called for greater public participation in the rural development process dating to the 1960s. They argued that the opportunities for input or participation from affected communities would not only be more just, but would also strengthen project implementation and impact. Some have indeed argued that 'participation' became a buzzword in development circles because it was viewed as a way to improve project outcomes (Cornwall and Brock 2005).

While the rhetoric of and language of participatory development has been increasingly widely adopted since the 1980s, the practice of participatory development has been variable. Many scholars (Allan et al. 2008; Matta et al. 2005; Pimbert and Pretty 1995; Smith and McDonough 2001 – to name just a few) have noted that participation varies significantly depending on the project, agency culture, and the national or regional context.

Building on Arnstein's (1969) work, the International Association for Public Participation (IAP2 2007) defines citizen participation in terms of a continuum. Too often, for government agencies, public participation is performed only through consultation with the public. Agencies will hire consultants either to survey public concerns or to facilitate meetings where the public is informed about the project and given a chance to voice concerns. On the other end of the continuum, meaningful engagement is where development decisions are the result of citizen initiative and action. Based on the development type, goals of development, the local community and the agency involved, initiatives fall closer or farther from meaningful engagement. Agencies have tended to implement 'participatory development' in manners that maintained agency control of the agenda and the process.

Pretty and Chambers (1994) and Pretty and Hines (1999) build on Arnstein's work in proposing a typology of participatory development. This is summarized in Table 4.1.

Table 4.1   Typology of public participation

Typology	Characteristics
Manipulative participation	Participation is simply pretence, with 'people's' representatives on official boards but who are not elected and have no power.
Passive participation	People participate by being told what has been decided or has already happened. It involves unilateral announcements by an administration or project management without listening to people's responses. The information shared belongs only to external professionals.
Participation by consultation	People participate by being consulted, and external people listen to views. These external professionals define both problems and solutions, and may modify these in light of the people's responses. Such a consultative process does not concede any share in decision-making, and professionals are under no obligation to take on board people's views.
Participation for material incentives	People participate by providing resources, for example labour, in return for food, cash or other material incentives. Much on-farm research falls into this category, as farmers provide their land but are not involved in the experimentation or the process of learning. It is very common to see this called participation. People have no stake in prolonging activities when the incentives run out.
Functional participation	People participate by forming groups to meet predetermined objectives related to the project, which can involve the development or promotion of externally initiated social organisation. Such involvement does not tend to be at early stages of project cycles or planning, but rather after major decisions have been made. These institutions tend to be dependent on external initiators and facilitators, but may become self-dependent.
Interactive participation	People participate in joint analysis, which leads to action plans and formation of new local institutions or the strengthening of existing ones. It tends to involve interdisciplinary methodologies that seek multiple perspectives and make use of systematic and structured learning processes. These groups take control over local decisions, and so people have a stake in maintaining structures or practices.
Self-mobilisation	People participate by taking initiatives independently of external institutions to change systems. They develop contacts with external institutions for the resources and technical advice they need, but retain control over how resources are used. Such self-initiated mobilisation and collective action may or may not challenge existing inequitable distribution of wealth and power.

Source: http://www.dse.vic.gov.au/effective-engagement/introduction-to-engagement/participatory-engagement.

Pretty and Chambers (1994), and many other scholars, have considered participatory development approaches that leaned toward interactive participation and self-mobilization most desirable, as they implied local determination of development priorities. They acknowledge, however, that these are often harder to implement given the time and bureaucratic constraints. What must be noted as well, however, is the extent to which these more engaged forms of participation – which begin to approach notions of grassroots development – may relate to political mobilization and empowerment.

The notion of grassroots development might be said to have its roots in the work of Paolo Freire (1970), the Brazilian education scholar whose literacy campaigns sowed the seeds of conscientization of oppressed rural populations. He argued that teaching could be done through discussion that privileges the lived experience of those at the community level, especially the poor, providing only the information that fills in the gaps and helps them to better understand the broader context in which local knowledge is nested. Freire's (1970) *Pedagogy of the Oppressed* fundamentally changed the perspective on rural development and education alike, calling for much greater interaction, privileging community tacit knowledge, arguing that the role of the expert should be to add to that tacit knowledge as needed by the community.

Grassroots development also often has an organizing component. Much of the grassroots development work is really organizing to demand development resources from the state (Gaventa 1995). Alinsky's power model of organizing has been a major part of the theory of development. Alinksy-style organizers view conflict between the local community and external antagonists as the beginning point for community development. Alinksy, an organizer himself, defined 'community power' as a community's successful participation in the decision-making processes of local and extra-community arenas (Reitzes and Reitzes 1980). Community power is cultivated through a community's successive victories in small conflicts with extra-community institutions. Each victory galvanizes additional local support for community groups and cultivates a collective belief in their ability to address community-wide issues. Organizers have completed their task when the community is capable of losing to external antagonists without losing its cohesiveness.

Grassroots development, in short, happens on the fully engaged end of the IAP2 participatory development continuum. There have been efforts to define this field by multiple agencies. Internationally, many smaller development foundations have embraced this notion. The Inter-American Foundation (IAF) in Washington, DC, for instance, works with local communities and operates on principles of grassroots development. This means that projects are much less oriented to development agendas set in Washington, DC and much more about empowering local, non-governmental organizations and community-based development organizations. As the IAF website states:

> The Inter-American Foundation, an independent U.S. government agency, was created by Congress in 1969 to channel development assistance directly to the organized poor in Latin America and the Caribbean. The IAF has carried out its mandate by responding with grant support for the most creative ideas for self-help received from grassroots groups and nongovernmental organizations. It also encourages partnerships among community organizations, business and local government directed at improving the quality of life for poor people and strengthening democratic practices. (IAF 2013)

The kinds of interventions discussed by IAF imply development activities that are different than large donor agencies like the US Agency for International Development or the international development banks. While there is an overarching goal of 'improving quality of life for poor people', the explicit method for achieving this is through working with and empowering 'grassroots groups and nongovernmental organizations'.

In a comparative analysis of rural development across 16 countries in Asia, countries with the best linkages between central government and rural government through institutional networks had the best performance in social and agricultural indicators (Uphoff 1993, p. 613). Again, the grassroots development initiatives are necessary to draw attention to the needs of communities overlooked by larger governing bodies. Whether the issue is a matter of social, political or economic need, it is often the case in the contemporary era that grassroots organizations must collaborate with external entities to address internal needs. In many cases, grassroots organization is only the beginning of institutionalizing change in communities. Rural communities that can employ their local resources and guide the use of extra-local resources while maintaining high levels of autonomy stand a considerable chance of achieving their developmental goals (Flora et al. 1992).

Development organizations have struggled to create methodologies for this kind of development. Over time, best practices have emerged, however. These involve starting the development process with the assumption that the goal is empowerment of local and community level actors – specifically the poor and marginalized in the development process (Buell 1987). If the goal is empowerment, rather than some more concrete development objective, this means engaging differently with local residents. Rather than approaching as experts with facts, development professionals are encouraged to facilitate processes that allow for local visions and knowledge to emerge. Facts can be deployed, but only to further processes that are led by the local people and not so much to devalue, but as part of broader community processes around indicators of change (O'Meara et al. 2007).

Key, however, to grassroots development is the explicit acknowledgement that sometimes mobilization for particular resources or changes to structural conditions is necessary as part of the development process. Thus, Posterman et al. (1990), for instance, devote much of their volume titled *Agrarian Reform and Grassroots Development* to effectively making the case that real empowerment of grassroots farmers and agricultural communities in ten different contexts is contingent on land tenure reform. At the same time, they argue that efforts to then impose development models on small farmers would undermine the very goals of such reform. For grassroots development to work, the structural conditions must be in place to facilitate local empowerment, but that alone is not sufficient.

There has been increasing attention to the need for capacity development of the grassroots movements so that they have the tools to become empowered. This has taken different forms. Martinez and Boglio (2008) discusses a need for 'grassroots support organizations' that work with communities and local non-governmental organizations to build the skills and networks to facilitate improvements to quality of life. This kind of notion is increasingly popular and has fostered not only a literature on intermediary NGOs (Carroll 1992) but also a leadership development movement that is targeted at grassroots organizations. Zachary (1998) documents how grassroots leadership training has been key to actual lasting empowerment, through greater conscientization of structural barriers but also better strategies for creating local visions for change. Groups such as the Leadership Learning Consortium (http://www.leadershiplearning.org/) have adopted a model of contextualized leadership development that is intended to create grassroots mobilization and development through skill development and relationship building. Indeed, a key to grassroots development is breaking the isolation that can come with marginalization in broader society (Zachary 1998).

For leadership development to successfully create grassroots capacity, it must be based on a more relational model of leadership development (Pigg 1999; Rost 1990). At the core of these initiatives is the recognition that rural community leadership must involve an expansion beyond the 'usual suspects'. This is not only because, as will be discussed below, current community leaders find themselves without the time to initiate necessary changes, but also because of the basic underlying principle that leadership in the twenty-first century must be about creating relationships rather than purely skill sets (Rost 1993). Problems in communities will be solved by collaborative networks rather than individuals (Chrislip and Larson 1994; Castells 2000; Haus and Heinelt 2005; Lyson and Tolbert 2003; O'Brien et al. 1998; O'Brien and Hassinger 1992). It is here that models of community development are worthy of consideration.

Scholars such as Green and Haines (2012), Matarrita-Cascante and Brennan (2012) and Christenson and Robinson (1989) argue that there are three basic ideal types of community development: imposed, directed and self-help development. Self-help development is similar to grassroots development in that it presumes that local actors drive the process. Imposed and direct forms of development reflect the relationship that external community entities have with communities in shaping development initiatives ranging from no relationship (imposed) or selective input (direct). Inter-community groups and institutions initiate grassroots development by collectively identifying issues and developing processes to create the community they want to live in (Flora and Flora 2013; Matarrita-Cascante and Brennan 2012; Green and Haines 2012). While this approach is not oblivious to outcomes, they are secondary goals in the self-help process. Institutionalizing the processes that engender a community's capacity to work together on current and future problems is the central goal of grassroots development (Flora and Flora 2013; Matarrita-Cascante and Brennan 2012). At the core of the grassroots approach is the belief that community development is about people working collectively to help themselves (Green and Haines 2012).

GRASSROOTS DEVELOPMENT IN RURAL CONTEXT

Rural grassroots development initiatives have taken on different forms in different contexts. In the context of developing countries, grassroots development is frequently part of broader initiatives to assert national autonomy and independence against global international elites such as international financial institutions and wealthy international finance organizations that support those organizations. These initiatives may have an explicit tie to movements to resist the hegemony of development initiatives that are seen to constrain economic sovereignty.

Grassroots development initiatives in Canada, the United Kingdom or the United States may be implemented with the same principles of inclusiveness and participatory democracy, but may not be as explicitly tied to international anti-global capitalist or imperialist movements. Indeed, it is notable that grassroots organizing in Appalachia has tended not to embrace the international mobilizing themes around concepts such as sustainability and anti-corporate global movements (Rice 2002). It is certainly the case that community context is critical to the form that grassroots development takes.

By the same token, the economic history, dominant ethnic origin and political history of the community in question is critical to the meaning and linkages of grassroots development in a particular context. In the United States, for instance, Chicano/Hispanic or American Indian communities may be more likely to see a link between their economic history and the relationship to larger global struggles for indigenous rights than the community in the Midwest. The following cases offer some insight into the processes and context of grassroots development in communities beyond the United States.

HOW IS GRASSROOTS DEVELOPMENT IMPLEMENTED IN RURAL COMMUNITIES?

Kerala

A long history of grassroots mobilization among agrarian laborers in the south Indian state of Kerala was a driving force behind significant land reform legislation in the 1970s (Herring 1990). Agrarian mobilization was facilitated by a long history of oppression against indigenous Muslims, known as the Mappilla. Their social oppression and economic exploitation manifested in a series of uprisings against Hindu landowners and the state, culminating in the Malabar Rebellion of 1921. This history of critical resistance against state policies provided a source of collective identity in the struggle to abolish landlordism in the mid-twentieth century.

Landlordism was 'a coherent and multidimensional social system of oppression and inequality' in which 'the hierarchy of land control and privilege roughly paralleled the hierarchy of social status' within the caste system (Herring 1990, p. 56). Rural slavery was common practice in Kerala. The dehumanization of the Untouchables, the lowest caste order in Indian society, was exacerbated under landlordism. Lower caste orders were relegated to the status of laborer, and excluded from land ownership as well as 'public discourse, participation and dignity' (Herring 1990, p. 56). Muslim and poor laborers tilled land primarily owned by the Hindu elite and paid them for the use of their labor. Landlordism allowed rentiers to collect rent and labor from workers as well as the profit stemming from cultivated crops. This system of land ownership maintained a highly polarized structure of economic inequality that informed the cultural and political contexts of Kerala.

The political context of Kerala society played an important role in the demise of landlordism. The presence of the Communist Party was a unique feature of Kerala's political life. According to Herring, the early Kerala

Congress fused issues of social reform with demands for democratic social justice and self-governance (Herring 1990, p. 57). The leftist Communist Party grew in power during the 1930s and 1940s, galvanizing support from socially and economically marginalized groups including the laborers. Indigenous dissent and disgust with the landlordism system was critical to mobilizing agrarian laborers in the political sphere. The leftist Communist Party presented oppressed groups with a viable alternative to an incumbent government that was unconcerned with the demands emanating from the grassroots. Local peasant associations and landless laborer unions provided platforms for community member participation in politics. Support from the widely literate and organized underclass propelled the leftist Communist Party to power in the free election of 1957.

Following a decade of subsequent land reform bills, the newly elected government passed legislation leading to the effective abolishment of landlordism on January 1, 1970. The legislation abolished the rentier class and outlawed land leasing, and limited the amount of land one person could legally own. While the aim was to make land available to landless tenants, the slow implementation of reform allowed landowners to redistribute property to family members, effectively retaining control of the land. Subsequent amendments to the land reform legislation established sub-district land boards to address land reform issues that arise in Kerala.

Herring's work on Kerala sheds some important insights on grassroots development in rural communities. Mobilization of the poor was central to the effectiveness of grassroots development projects. However, the mobilization of political parties in the electoral system played a crucial role in formalizing a new system of social and economic relations. Herring notes that widespread literacy among agrarian laborers, effective local organizations and extensive politicization were key factors contributing to the abolition of a long-standing system (Herring 1990, p. 61). What the Kerala case illustrates is how the self-help mobilization efforts of agrarian laborers shaped the institutionalization of a new social and economic system by influencing the state's political decision-making system. In the continuum, the work of agrarian laborers as a self-help form influences the structural framework of society which may be a function facilitated by agents of imposed development forms. The next case demonstrates how external organizations can be employed in the service of grassroots development initiatives.

The Miraflores Community

The Miraflores community in the Central American nation of Nicaragua presents a more recent perspective on rural development in the international context (Horton 2007). Horton's study demonstrates how new communities create collective capacity when a common or long-standing history in the area is not available as a resource to unify the community.

The Miraflores community, largely comprised of self-described poor, has been in contentious relations with the upper class over land claims and subsistence rights since the Sandinista National Liberation Front (FSLN) government lost power in the 1990 elections. Following the elections, the new government voted to parcel out lands individually, adhering to the World Bank's call for individual ownership of land as a key to furthering economic development. The Miraflores, initially divided on the decision to parcel lands, has focused on obtaining individual land titles to maintain some level of land control under less favorable political conditions.

The Miraflores community cultivated a shared sense of identity through their interactions with external entities over the course of two decades. First, the FSLN took power in 1979, encouraging the proliferation of grassroots organizations among the Miraflores including youth organizations, unions, farmer's organizations and neighborhood associations (Horton 2007, p. 83). Under the FSLN, the Miraflores had control of the land which they tilled collectively promoting equality, social solidarity and community while maintaining subsistence levels of production (Horton, 2007).

In the face of land ownership claims from upper class interests, the Miraflores utilized the skills cultivated through relationships with the growing number of locally based NGOs. Horton (2007) recounts an instance in 1994 where the Miraflores received a letter from the family of an original landowner claiming the community owed the bank a sizeable amount of money, and ordering them to leave the land (p. 88). Rather than succumbing to the demands of land claims, the Miraflores sent a message stating that they owed no money, and falsely claimed that they hired a lawyer to defend their land rights. Seeing that they were not going to easily give up their land, the former owner's family withdrew their legal action against the community and the Miraflores won this battle amidst a series of similar claims.

While the victory above may seem particularly simple, the Miraflores community's ability to fight and win against land claims is a product of several factors coming together to support their grassroots initiative. The Miraflores community is largely comprised of functional illiterates and a lack of formal education is a significant obstacle in navigating the increasingly complex terrain of legal claims of the land. Members of the Miraflores community credit the NGOs with providing 'substantial material and moral support, information and access to social networks' that have helped them maintain their fight for land control and household subsistence (Horton 2007, p. 83). The NGOs have continued working to empower the Miraflores community which the Sandanista government initiated during the 1980s. The Miraflores incorporated the resources provided by the NGOs and the support of the Sandinista government to protect the community's interests.

Intermediary Organizations

As discussed above, intermediary organizations often play an important role in development projects. Intermediary organizations are very involved in rural development projects in the international sphere. While top-down approaches are not necessary to enable poor communities to initiate bottom-up participation (Carroll 1992), NGOs can offer a number of resources to aid grassroots groups. It is imperative that communities implementing grassroots-level strategies for development strive to maintain control of their activity while incorporating resources from external organizations (Flora et al. 1992).

Although they do not represent an exhaustive representation of rural development experiences, the cases in Kerala and Nicaragua illustrate the growing necessity of resource networks beyond the grassroots level employed to address community-level issues. In an increasingly global and networked society, it is becoming less possible to rely solely on the resources located in one's own community to solve local problems and address local issues. The interconnectedness of the rural communities to the urban, state, regional, national and global spheres requires cooperation and collaboration to address local issues. The vision of grassroots development as an independently initiated, operated and sustained project is less applicable in the current era of globalization. As such, rural groups often work with extra-local entities as long as the partnership serves the interests of the community and the community maintains control over itself and its resources (Flora and Flora 2013). Intermediary organizations' ability to serve as the catalyst for grassroots development within a locality is not impossible, however it is very unlikely (Caroll 1992). In the context of a global economy, grassroots organizations can make a difference in their communities with the aid of external support.

Horizontal linkages are a form of extra-community networking not present in the case studies but worth noting here. Horizontal linkages are external partnerships between communities, typically communities who have experienced similar issues. Members from each community connect, share ideas and experiences about how they handle an issue, and that information can be used to inform local decision-making processes of self-help projects (Flora and Flora 2013). This form of support can lead to collaborative efforts that sustain rather than impede the collective agency of grassroots organizations, which is a potential hazard that accompanies the use of external partnerships in a networked society.

DOES GRASSROOTS DEVELOPMENT CONTRIBUTE TO IMPROVING THE HUMAN CONDITION?

Grassroots development's ability to improve the human condition in rural communities is indefinite. As discussed above, the success of self-development initiatives is not determined by the outcomes but by their ability to institutionalize processes for collectively addressing the current issue at hand and future issues that will arise in the community. The case studies discussed above illustrate that grassroots initiatives, with the support of external entities – from political parties to business groups to other rural communities – have the potential to improve the conditions facing people living in rural communities. Part of this process of improving the human condition is likely tied initially to the belief that groups have the capacity to impact the well-being of their community, subsequently demonstrated through collective action. In all cases discussed above, new problems arose following the communities' responses to challenges. Yet they were apparently better equipped to respond to new challenges, a fundamental measure of grassroots development's success.

Grassroots organizations provide a number of advantages in comparison to other forms of development: closeness to the people, knowledge of the local conditions often from the people themselves (indigenous knowledge) and responsiveness to local needs (Uphoff 1993, p. 619). However, the voluntary thrust of grassroots organizations and the long period of time it may take to see problem-solving tasks through to completion may render grassroots development efforts less than sustainable over time (Uphoff 1993). A potential solution to this problem is collaborative partnerships with external entities to address internal needs. Uphoff (1993) proposes 'assisted self-reliance' calls on external support from state and market institutions to buttress local efforts of grassroots organizations over extended periods.

REFERENCES

Adas, Michael (1991), 'Scientific standards and colonial education in British India and French Senegal', in Teresa A. Meade and Mark Walker (eds), *Science, Medicine, and Cultural Imperialism,* New York: St Martin's Press, pp. 5–26.
Allan, Catherine, Allan Curtis, George Stankey and Bruce Shindler (2008), 'Adaptive management and watersheds: a social science perspective', *Journal of the American Water Resources Association,* 44, 166–74.

Arnstein, S.R. (1969), 'A ladder of citizen participation', *Journal of the American Institute of Planners*, 35, 216–24.

Buell, Rebecca (1987), 'Grassroots development: a question of empowerment', *Cultural Survival Quarterly*, 11, 27–45.

Carroll, Thomas F. (1992), *Intermediary NGOs: the supporting link in grassroots development*, West Hartford, CT: Kumarian Press.

Castells, M. (2000), *The Rise of the Network Society*, Malden, MA: Blackwell Publishers.

Chambers, Robert (2005), *Ideas for Development*, London: Earthscan.

Chrislip, D. and C. Larson (1994), *Collaborative Leadership: How Citizens and Civic Leaders Can Make a Difference*, San Francisco, CA: Jossey-Bass Publishers.

Christenson, James A. and Jerry W. Robinson, Jr. (1989), *Community Development in Perspective*, Ames, IA: Iowa State University Press.

Cornwall, Andrea and Karen Brock (2005), 'What do buzzwords do for development policy? A critical look at participation, empowerment and poverty reduction', *Third World Quarterly*, 26, 1043–60.

Escobar, Arturo (1995), *Encountering Development: The Making and Unmaking of the Third World*, Princeton, NJ: Princeton University Press.

Flora, Cornelia Butler and Jan Flora (2013), *Rural Communities: Legacies and Change*, 4th edition, Boulder, CO: Westview Press.

Flora, Jan L., Gary P. Green, Edward A. Gale, Frederick E. Schmidt and Cornelia Butler Flora (1992), 'Self-development: a viable rural development option?', *Policy Studies Journal*, 20, 276–88.

Freire, Paolo (1970), *Pedagogy of the Oppressed*, New York: Herder & Herder.

Freudenburg, W. and R. Krannich (2003), 'Boomtowns', in K. Christensen and D. Levinson (eds), *Encyclopedia of Community: From the Village to the Virtual World*, Thousand Oaks, CA: Sage Publications, pp. 100–101.

Galjart, Benno (1981), 'Participatory development projects: some conclusions from research', *Sociologia Ruralis*, 21, 142–59.

Gaventa, John (1995), 'Citizen knowledge, citizen competence and democracy building', *Good Society*, 5, 28–35.

Gaventa, John and Helen Lewis (1989), 'Rural area development: participation by the people', *Forum for Applied Research and Public Policy*, 4, 58–62.

Green, Gary Paul and Anna Haines (2012), *Asset Building and Community Development*, Thousand Oaks, CA: Sage Publications.

Harvey, David (1990), *The Condition of Post-Modernity*, New York: Wiley-Blackwell.

Haus, M. and H. Heinelt (2005), 'How to achieve governability at the local level? Theoretical and conceptual considerations on a complementarity of urban leadership and community involvement', in M. Haus, H. Heinelt and M. Stewart (eds), *Urban Governance and Democracy: Leadership and Community Involvement*, Abingdon: Routledge, pp. 12–44.

Herring, R.J. (1990), 'Resurrecting the commons: collective action and ecology', *Items*, 44, 64–8.

Horton, Lynn (2007), *Grassroots Struggles for Sustainability in Central America*, Boulder, CO: University Press of Colorado.

Inter-American Foundation (IAF) (2013), 'At a glance', Arlington, VA: Inter-American Foundation. Available at http://www.iaf.gov/index.aspx?page=201 (accessed 1 May 2013).

International Association for Public Participation (IAP2) (2007), *IAP2 Core Values*. Available at http://www.iap2.org/.

Lyson, T. and C. Tolbert (2003), 'Civil society, civic communities and rural development', in D.L. Brown and L.E. Swanson (eds), *Challenges for Rural America in the Twenty-first Century*, State College, PA: Penn State Press, pp. 228–40.

Martínez, Rafael and A. Boglio (2008), 'Grassroots support organizations and transformative practices', *Journal of Community Practice*, 16, 339–58.

Matarrita-Cascante, D. and M.A. Brennan (2012), 'Conceptualizing community development in the 21st century', *Community Development*, 43, 293–305.

Matta, Jagganadha Rao, John Kerr and Kimberly Chung (2005), 'From forest regulation to participatory facilitation: forest employee perspectives on organizational change and transformation in India', *Journal of Environmental Planning and Management*, 48, 475–90.

McClellan III, A. James (1991), 'Science, medicine and French colonialism in old-regime Haiti', in Teresa A. Meade and Mark Walker (eds), *Science, Medicine, and Cultural Imperialism*, New York: St Martin's Press, pp. 27–52.

McMichael, Philip (2012), *Development and Social Change*, Thousand Oaks, CA: Pine Forge Press.

O'Brien, D.J. and E.S. Hassinger (1992), 'Community attachment among leaders in five rural communities', *Rural Sociology*, 57, 521–44.

O'Brien, D.J., A. Raedeke and E.W. Hassinger (1998), 'The social networks of leaders in more or less viable communities six years later: a research note', *Rural Sociology*, 63, 109–27.

O'Meara, Peter, Cathy Pendergast and Anske Robinson (2007), 'Grassroots community engagement: the key to success in a community building program', *Rural Society*, 17, 155–64.

Peluso, Nancy Lee (1992), *Rich Forests, Poor People: Resource Control and Resistance in Java*, Berkeley, CA: University of California Press.

Pigg, Kenneth (1999), 'Community leadership and community theory', *Community Development*, 30, 196–212.

Pimbert, M. and J.N. Pretty (1995), 'Parks, people and professionals', Discussion paper DP 57, United Nations Research Institute for Social Development, Geneva.

Posterman, Roy L., Mary N. Temple and Timothy M. Hanstad (1990), *Agrarian Reform and Grassroots Development*, London: Lynn Reiner Publishers.

Pretty, J.N. and R. Chambers (1994), 'Towards a learning paradigm: new professionalism and institutions for agriculture', in I. Scoones and J. Thompson (eds), *Beyond Farmer First: Rural People's Knowledge, Agricultural Research and Extension Practice*, London: Intermediate Technology Publications, pp. 182–202.

Pretty, Jules and R. Hine (1999), 'Participatory appraisal for community assessment', Centre for Environment and Society, University of Essex.

Reitzes, Donald C. and Dietrich C. Reitzes (1980), 'Saul D. Alinsky's contribution to community development', *Journal of the Community Development Society*, 11, 39–52.

Ribot, Jesse C. (2003), 'Democratic decentralisation of natural resources: institutional choice and discretionary power transfers in Sub-Saharan Africa', *Public Administration and Development*, 23, 53–65.

Rice, Christopher Scott (2002), 'Discourses of sustainability: grassroots organizations and sustainable community development in Central Appalachia', PhD dissertation, Lexington, KY: University of Kentucky.

Rost, Joseph C. (1990), *Leadership for the Twenty-First Century*, New York: Praeger.

Rost, J. (1993), *Leadership for the 21st Century*, Westport, CT: Praeger Publishers.

Sanderson, Dwight (1940), *Leadership for Rural Life*, New York: Association Press.

Seyfang, Gill and Adrian Smith (2007), 'Grassroots innovations for sustainable development: towards a new research and policy agenda', *Environmental Politics*, 16, 584–603.

Smith, P.D. and M.H. McDonough (2001), 'Beyond public participation: fairness in natural resource decision making', *Society and Natural Resources*, 14, 239–49.

Stiles, Daniel (1987), 'Classical versus grassroots development', *Cultural Survival Quarterly*, 11. http://www.culturalsurvival.org/publications/cultural-survival-quarterly/c-te-divoire/classical-versus-grassroots-development (retrieved March 17, 2013).

Tacoli, Cecelia (1998), 'Rural–urban interactions: a guide to the literature', *Environment and Urbanization*, 10, 147–66.

Toulmin, Camilla and Robert Chambers (1990), *Farmer-First: Achieving Sustainable Dryland Development in Africa*, London: International Institute for Environment and Development.

Uphoff, Norman (1993), 'Grassroots organizations and NGOs in rural development: opportunities with diminishing states and expanding markets', *World Development*, 21, 607–22.

Zachary, Eric Julian (1998), 'An exploration of grassroots leadership development: a case study of a training program's effort to integrate theory and method', PhD dissertation, City University of New York.

PART II

THEMES

5. Resource dependence and rural development
Richard C. Stedman

INTRODUCTION

It is conventional wisdom (indeed, it is nearly a truism) among rural development boosters that the extraction and processing of natural resources – timber resources, fisheries, energy and minerals – contributes to employment, prosperity and development for rural places. Logically, this occurs in several ways: most evident are the direct returns – royalties, employment – that occur during the period of extraction, processing and transport. Secondary benefits may endure beyond the period of extractive operations through the linkage to subsequent economic development forms (Freudenburg and Gramling 1998), whether processing and/or transport of the raw materials, or through linkages to additional forms of development (Bunker 1989).

These development strategies are often characterized as the natural advantage enjoyed by many rural locations over urban areas; associated employment has contributed mightily to the mythos of rural life. When I ask my freshmen or sophomore-level class to estimate what percentage of all jobs in the rural United States are in fisheries, forestry, mining, energy and agriculture (combined), the guesses usually start at 30 percent and range upward from that. The reality, of course, is that these students – bright as they are – are off by an order of magnitude: less than 5 percent of employment in the rural United States is in these natural resource sectors. Although the mythos does not really match the socio-demographic reality, it is one that is powerful and has real staying power, not just among these students, but in rural development circles: 'real' rural jobs are not those found in the service industries, or government, but involve the harvest and processing of the fruits of nature. The other element of this mythos, of course, is that these jobs are not only numerous, but they are 'better' jobs for rural places, higher paying, less susceptible to seasonal shifts, and bringing outside monies into circulation (Power 1996). Generally speaking, data also fail to support this contention, as witnessed by academic writings that stress the resource curse or the paradox of poverty in the midst of plenty.

Regardless of the empirical evidence, these are the forms of development that promoters suggest will make rural places better off.

Rural sociologists and other rural development scholars often recognize as false – or at minimum, oversimplified – these images of rural places as dominated by resource-based jobs. They point to the relative scarcity of such jobs, their empirical association with problematic community outcomes, and to the general decline in importance of this form of rural development. Such conventional academic thinking has emphasized rural places as continuing to shift away from 'productivist' landscapes toward landscapes of consumption (Halfacree and Boyle 1998). Rural change, so the conventional academic logic goes, will be characterized by continued out-migration from traditional resource-dependent regions that are low in amenities or other forms of advantage, and growth in amenity-based phenomena (in other words, tourism, second home development, the growth of the 'creative class') (Florida 2012) in regions that have the amenity resources to support such forms of development.

These conventions may be called into question in the context of recent energy development in the Great Plains, the Northeast and elsewhere, where new energy landscapes – related to wind, biofuels and (especially) natural gas – are rapidly emerging. This shift back toward resource dependence reinvigorates the evaluation of resource dependence as a rural development strategy. In this chapter, I suggest that it is important to open up this mythos, and, in so doing, engage this recent resurgence. Fundamentally, doing so requires more precision in our thinking. This chapter describes basic relationships between resource dependence and well-being but, more critically, opens up questions about: (1) what we mean by (how do we operationalize) our core concepts of development and well-being, resources, dependence; and (2) how the relationship is variable across different forms of development, for whom, and in what contexts. Finally, (3) the potential effects of large-scale changes – with a focus here on climate change – are engaged.

DEPENDENCE AND DEVELOPMENT: THE TRAJECTORY OF METAPHORS

The link between resource dependence and community development has been of interest to rural scholars for well over a half-century. It is instructive to track the evolution of the metaphors used to describe the relationship. Beginning with the image of community 'stability', Kaufman and Kaufman (1946) suggested that forest harvests could be conducted in such a way (rotated around a central community, with sufficient time to allow forest regeneration) that the industry and its associated worker base need not migrate across the landscape, but remain in a given community. This would allow them to raise families and become committed to a place, thus producing stable communities.

Critiques of the 'stability' metaphor resulted in it being supplanted by that of 'sustainability' (most notably by the Rio Declaration and the now-famous Brundtland Commission report of 1987) which suggested that sustainable development ensures that the needs of the present generation is met, without compromising the ability of future generations to meet their needs, and that natural capital is preserved to yield ecosystem services into the future (Rees 1997). This era of thinking produced numerous 'indicators of sustainability of resource dependent community' works (for example, Beckley et al.; Parkins et al. 2001).

More recently, the sustainability metaphor has been critiqued as overemphasizing the flow of goods and services based on natural resources as being too 'development' and accumulation oriented. In response, community resilience and adaptive capacity (Wall and Marzall 2006) have been invoked as better describing the ability of a community and its people to respond to unexpected social–ecological changes and still be able to retain basic structure and function (Walker and Salt 2006). Resilience, in contradistinction to sustainability, places greater emphasis on managing uncertainty and potential harm rather than the sustainable distribution of resources.

Resilience, so the logic goes, is promoted by diversity – in ecology and community development as well (Adger 2000; Walker and Salt 2006; but see Stedman et al. 2012 for a review and critique). As described in Freudenburg (1992) and elsewhere, economic diversification is widely promoted by community development as contributing to per capita income, employment, and other positive outcomes (Dissart 2003; Wilson and Leach 2002). This enthusiasm is based at least in part on the idea that diversity is commonly regarded as the conceptual opposite of dependence. Economic diversity reduces the impact of market and social fluctuations that pose problems for single-industry resource-dependent communities (Kennedy et al. 2001). Diversity also connotes increased resilience of coupled social–ecological systems by creating redundancies and response capacity: diverse systems better maintain options and reduce risk, especially in the context of high uncertainty (Folke et al. 2002). If it is difficult to anticipate the future trajectory of change, more diverse communities are generally thought to be in a better position to respond when uncertainty is high; but see Stedman et al. (2012) for a critique of these claims.

DEFINING DEVELOPMENT IN THE CONTEXT OF RESOURCE DEPENDENCE

Understanding the relationship between resource dependence and rural development requires more specific articulations of what we mean by our core constructs, especially given the range of indicators of well-being used to assess the relationship between dependence and development. Green and Zinda (Chapter 1 in this volume) note that defining development is exceedingly difficult and 'is one of the most controversial concepts in the social sciences'. Because their chapter engages this in some detail, this chapter re-emphasizes a few points especially germane to discussions of resource dependence. Most fundamentally, development is not synonymous with growth – in jobs, income, infrastructure – as assessments must factor in the costs of growth, as well as accounting for non-material factors (for example, quality of life, happiness, social capital, and so on) that may bear scant empirical relation to growth.

Another key element to consider is how any outcomes are distributed through a population: inequitable distribution of benefits (whether viewed cross-sectionally or longitudinally) undercuts development goals (Sen 1999). Short-term growth at the expense of long-term sustainability is not a desired outcome of development strategies, but is often found with certain forms of resource extraction, especially that related to rapid energy development (more on this below).

I will suggest in this chapter that historically, natural resource-based rural development has utilized – and suffered from – narrow and/or reified definitions of dependence and well-being. This has been especially true of development boosters, but researchers as well have suffered from what Freudenburg (1986, p. 463) termed 'the edifice complex', or an over-focus on readily measurable tangible economic indicators.

Part of the task of this chapter is to show the implications of broadening the definitions: of development and well-being, and of dependence itself. To begin, it is important to note that much of the indicator-based empirical literature does not really address 'development', but instead uses the language of 'community well-being indicators'. It is instructive to begin by reviewing a few key basic findings from the literature. This will be followed by a deeper engagement of how these findings vary by indicator of development/well-being, place, time and operational definition of dependence.

DESCRIPTIVE FINDINGS: RESOURCE DEPENDENCE AND COMMUNITY WELL-BEING

Most studies show negative relationships between resource dependence and community well-being. Places that have a greater proportion of employment in industries such as fishing, forestry, mining and energy (sometimes agriculture is thrown into the mix as well) have negative outcomes. However, this broad generalization masks a great degree of variation (especially by sector) that needs to be considered, especially given that many of these findings come from single-industry studies, briefly reviewed here. Mining and energy dependence often emerges rapidly and is consequently associated with rapid growth and the creation of boomtown conditions, reflecting earlier assertions that growth is not synonymous with development. Many of the early studies, especially those based in the American West in the 1970s (see Krannich 2012 for a summary) describe rapid growth in employment opportunities in energy extraction and construction, along with linked service industry expansion. This growth is associated with rapid in-migration and community change (Freudenburg 1984; Gilmore and Duff 1975; Krannich and Greider 1984). Energy boomtowns may have distinct 'stages' (see Jacquet 2009 for a cogent summary), suggesting that any conclusions drawn by 'snapshot' data analyses may be potentially misleading. Nord and Luloff (1993) noted that mining-dependent counties differ little from other counties on median family income, individual, poverty, unemployment or education, but that these summations may mask a great deal of variation. Partially in response to these claims, Freudenburg and Wilson (2002) conducted a meta-analysis of existing studies and found extensive variation. Recent studies and studies from outside the Western United States show that mining dependence is more likely to be associated with decreased human well-being indicators. Mining dependence appears to have more positive effects when the measure of well-being is income rather than poverty or unemployment. Probably most attention has been paid to the relationship between forest reliance and well-being. Outcomes of forest reliance on economic indicators of well-being are often seen as negative: for example, US studies, although somewhat dated, reveal that unemployment (for example, Howze et al. 1993) and poverty rates (for example, Bliss et al. 1992; Cook 1995) usually are higher in forest-dependent places, as are rates of social pathology such as divorce (for example, Drielsma 1984) or crime (for example, Force et al. 1993). These findings also are potentially variable, especially by particular subsector: Overdevest and Green (1995) reveal that some forest sectors, particularly pulp and paper, produce higher incomes (see Stedman et al. 2005 for similar findings in Canada). Fishing reliance, in contrast, is typically associated with negative outcomes, without the variation seen in forestry, mining and energy. Hamilton and Seyfrit (1994), for example, find that fishing dependence devalues education, and that policy discriminates against marginal operations that often characterize the industry.

The findings revealed above were part of a spate of attention in the mid-1990s paid to the relationship between resource dependence and rural poverty. The journal *Society and Natural Resources* devoted several special issues to the topic, and the Rural Sociological Society Task Force on Rural Poverty (Humphrey et al. 1993) offered a series of theory-based explanations for the negative findings described above, arguments that remain extraordinarily relevant 20 years later. Briefly, their explanations include those based on the following: (1) human capital theory, which suggests that underinvestment in human capital skills such as education often characterizes rural resource-dependent places, and is a 'rational' response to the availability of high-wage employment that does not require these skills; (2) power and natural resource bureaucracy suggests that governmental bureaucracy may become captured by large-scale corporate interests (see also Freudenburg and Gramling 1994b; West 1994); (3) industrial structure, or economic segmentation, where resource jobs become 'peripheral' in that they often are low wage, part time and provide few benefits (based especially on undifferentiated products in the context of market relations that comprise many sellers and few buyers); and (4) the social construction of nature, which suggests that certain groups or uses may become 'morally excluded', where popular sentiment about the nature of resources may marginalize and subsequently exclude extractive interests from the resource base. Freudenburg (1992) also articulates the effects of a 'cost–price squeeze' that can undercut employment or wages even when resources are still abundant, but are tied to resource price volatility and associated variability in employment. Machlis et al. (1990) note that underlying all resource dependence is the issue of land as a factor in production, resulting in decreased mobility of industry (one cannot mine or cut what is not there). Freudenburg and Gramling (1994a, 1998) note that the degree to which resource extraction and processing becomes linked to subsequent economic development and infrastructure is key to fostering well-being as long as the associated development is relatively independent of the parent resource industry. If it is not, shocks to the resource industry will reverberate through the linked industries, potentially exacerbating rather than counterbalancing shifts in well-being.

VARIABILITY BY OPERATIONAL DEFINITIONS AND CONTEXT

As revealed above, the relationship between resource dependence and well-being is highly variable according to the particular industry, context and definitions. Therefore, it is crucial that we are clear about definitions of key constructs, because – quite simply – the story of the relationship between resource dependence and development outcomes changes (potentially quite dramatically) depending on the particulars: what form of resources, what form of dependence, and what indicators are chosen to represent well-being. This section of the chapter reviews several comparative studies (based on my research) that have examined variation in findings based on the criteria described above.

Variation by Indicator Chosen

This chapter has already engaged in what we mean by development at a conceptual level. We have also seen, based on the single-industry studies, that there is considerable variation in the outcome of studies depending on whether income-based or other indicators are chosen to represent well-being. A comparative study of resource dependence and well-being across all rural census subdivisions in Canada revealed that general relationships varied strongly depending on the particular indicator chosen to represent community well-being (Stedman et al. 2004). Even within a region and for a particular example industry, the impact of resource dependence changes depending on whether the discussion focuses on income, employment, migration, crime, divorce, educational attainment or other elements (Stedman et al. 2004). Stedman et al. (2004) revealed, for example, consistent with the boomtown conception, that energy dependence had a widespread association with high income levels and high poverty, migration and unemployment levels; each of these is a legitimate indicator of well-being, but the conclusions about the effects of dependency and related community development activity will vary dramatically depending on the indicator chosen.

Variation by Resource Industry and Sector

As described above, most work has focused on individual natural resource sectors, rarely examining these in comparative context or their joint effects. With my colleagues at the Canadian Forest Service, I (Stedman et al. 2004; see Stedman et al. 2012 for a summary) engaged in a comparative analysis to examine variation in outcomes of resource dependence by resource industry (agriculture, energy, mining, forestry and fishing), as well as (following Overdevest and Green 1995) variation within the forest industry by sector: pulp, logging, forest services and timber (Stedman et al. 2005). This disaggregation revealed strong and consistent differences by industry or sector, leading us to the conclusion that just as there is no single 'best' indicator of well-being, there really is no such thing as a 'resource-dependent community', as the effects on well-being of the particular type of resource (for example, energy, forest, farm, mining) provide highly variable outcomes (Stedman et al. 2012).

A Deeper Look at Forestry

Using 2001 data, Stedman et al. (2005) examined the relationship between type of forest dependence (pulp and paper, logging, services and lumber) and well-being. Consistent with previous work examining core–periphery theories (for example, Overdevest and Green 1995), pulp is the only sector not associated with lower educational attainment or higher unemployment. Pulp employment also is positively related to median family income, whereas this relationship for all of the other forest sectors is significantly negative. As such, pulp dependence presents itself in contrast to the other forestry sectors, which are all similar: consistent with core–periphery theories, logging, services and lumber are associated with lower educational attainment, higher poverty and unemployment, and lower income.

Variation by Region

The studies cited above also revealed that the relationship between resource dependence and well-being varies strongly across regions: the natural resource endowments, policy responses and market characteristics of the location where the dependence occurs apparently have a great deal to do with the outcomes of dependence (Parkins et al. 2003; Stedman et al. 2004, 2005, 2011). Briefly, the Canada work revealed that stronger resource reliance (overall) is correlated with lower median family incomes in the Atlantic and Central regions, but higher income in the Prairie region and the North.[1] These differences are partly based on differences in the particular resource industries that characterize different regions: in Atlantic Canada, the negative relationship between resource dependence and income is primarily based on the fact that 'resource' dependence here is most likely to be fishing dependence (almost half of all resource-based employment), which is strongly related to low income. In the Central region, the slight negative effect of resource dependence is driven primarily by forest industry reliance. Over one-third (35 percent) of resource employment is in forestry, and the overall effect of forest reliance is negative here as well. In the Prairie region, the positive effect is driven primarily by high reliance on agriculture. The small positive effect of resource dependence on well-being in British Columbia is driven primarily by the forest industry. This is an effect both of higher levels of dependence (forestry accounts for nearly 60 percent of all resource employment in British Columbia), but also especially on the strong performance of the industry here relative to other regions. Finally, the strong positive relationship between resource reliance and income observed in the North is almost entirely attributable to the mining and energy industries.

Variation Over Time

The vast majority of studies focusing on the relationship between resource dependence and well-being use 'snapshot' secondary data, gathered during a particular census period. Accordingly, it is easy to forget that the relationship between dependence and development can vary strongly not simply by place and indicator, but over time as well. We (Stedman et al. 2011) examined the forest industry, and the relationship of its component sectors, in Canada in more detail between 1986 and 2001.[2] The work explored change in the distribution of sectors within the forest industry (consistent with the core–periphery discussion above); and in the relationship between economic dependence on each of these sectors and well-being. Also consistent with the regional comparisons described above, regional variation was also explored for each of these questions. Nationally, forest dependence declined between 1986 and 2001, but these changes ranged from a 35 percent decline in Atlantic Canada to a slight increase in the Prairie region. The composition of the forest industry changed somewhat as well. Logging dependence declined (as a proportion of the total forest industry) in more established regions of the east (Atlantic and Quebec), held steady in central Canada (Ontario and the Prairies) and increased in the west (British Columbia) and north (Canada's Territories) where the industry is still in the early phases of development. Forest service-based employment generally declined except in British Columbia and the North. Lumber dependence increased everywhere except in British Columbia and the North, and pulp dependence held relatively steady.

Is resource dependence associated with more negative outcomes over time, and does this vary by sector and region? We examined two indicators: unemployment and median family income. In brief, we obtained results consistent with core–periphery models: the most peripheral forest sectors (logging and forest services) generally (with some regional variation) were associated with higher unemployment and lower median family income in

2001 than in 1986. In contrast, the relationship between well-being and lumber and pulp dependence (the more core sectors) was much more consistent (did not worsen) over time and region.

Variation by Definitions of Dependence

In addition to examining variation by place, time and resource industry or sector, this chapter has already explored the implications of different ways that well-being and development are defined on any conclusions we might draw about the relationship between dependence and well-being. We need also to reflect critically on what exactly it is we mean by 'dependence' itself. Stedman et al. (2007) has noted that compared to discussions about the implications of different measures of community well-being, little work addresses the implications of how forest dependence is defined. Staying within the confines of employment-based methods, we analyzed the Canadian census subdivision (CSD) level described elsewhere in this chapter. We examined the relationship between employment and dependence defined four different ways: (1) percentage of employment; (2) percentage of employment income in resource industries; and through location quotient[3] calculations for (3) employment; and (4) employment income. We obtained different results based on which operational definition of dependence was used. For example, income (Base) approaches identified larger communities with a stronger presence of pulp as resource dependent, likely influencing the performance of these communities according to a number of indicators of well-being. As such, the conclusions researchers may draw about the effects of resource dependence on community outcomes are therefore method dependent. We also noted in that paper (see also Stedman et al. 2012) the need to move decisively beyond definitions of dependence that are restricted to employment in the extraction and processing of raw materials to include employment in resource-based tourism and psychological and/or community identity-based dependence. Empirical work in this domain is in its infancy, but this trajectory is crucial to more nuanced understandings of resource dependence and its relationship to rural development.

GLOBAL CLIMATE CHANGE, RESOURCE DEPENDENCE AND RURAL DEVELOPMENT

The '900 pound gorilla in the room' is the emergence of climate change dialogue and impacts on resource dependence and rural development. The dialogue is undoubtedly affecting, for example, enthusiasm for biofuel development and other alternative energy sources such as wind development projects that have a potentially transformative effect on rural landscapes (see Devine-Wright 2005; Jacquet and Stedman, forthcoming), and have heightened debates around heightened fossil fuel development in much of rural America. In particular, rural forest-dependent communities may have difficulty adapting to rapidly changing climate and the associated discourse. Davidson et al. (2003) provide an excellent analysis of the reasons for this, summarized here. There are multiple vulnerabilities of forest-dependent communities to climate change, tied to (for example) changing species assemblies, extreme weather events, insect infestations, and drought and fire events.

Given these multiple vulnerabilities, one might think that forest-dependent communities would be at the forefront of conversations about adaptation to climate change. However, a fundamental point raised by Davidson et al. (2003) is that such communities may be 'underconcerned' about climate change impacts on their livelihood.

First, resource-dependent communities often lack resilience in the classical sense of being able to respond proactively and effectively to disturbances, such as that represented by climate change. Community institutions may have little capacity to make decisions about their own future which is controlled by larger-scale market and governance, coupled with low human capital produced by (as discussed earlier) rational underinvestment. Further, often there is outside pressure to reduce harvests: political attention given to deforestation as a cause of climate change; sentiments that forest harvest should be reduced. Rural forest-dependent communities may be caught in the political struggle. Long time horizons in decision making (from planting to harvest often takes 50 years or more), may make it difficult to be proactive, especially given that climate change-related uncertainty increases market exposure and risk. The often relatively conservative nature of resource-dependent communities may result in concern about climate change being equated with environmentalism. Employers and decision makers may not be inclined to align with the very people who are often perceived as trying to put them out of business. Finally, the nature of the perceived risk matters as well: decision makers may not connect discrete events (for example, fire, drought, pest outbreaks) to climate change because many of these manifestations are phenomena that they are already familiar with. As such, they may not be linked to longer-term patterns, and the impacts of any given event may not be perceived as problematic, given historical uncertainty and stochasticity. There is much work in this area that remains to be done; especially given the emerging dialogue about climate, energy and rural community.

SUMMARY AND CONCLUSIONS

Natural resource dependence is traditional rural development strategy populated by multiple (even potentially oppositional) cherished assumptions: rural developers and resource boosters emphasize the traditional nature of resource-based employment in rural areas, and emphasize the benefits that such forms of development may bring. Rural sociologists and rural planners recognize the potential fallacies of these arguments. Community dependence on these forms of development often comes at a cost: poor outcomes and increased vulnerability are commonplace. As such, these scholars assert that rural places, at least in the more developed countries, have (as they should) largely moved past such forms of rural development. Recent booms in energy development, however, in North America and beyond, have reinvigorated the relevance of these discussions.

The materials covered in this chapter, therefore, are intended to provide both an overview of existing research in this area, and a call for those who would engage in such work, or apply it, to recognize and appreciate the forms of variability that characterize the area of inquiry. Simply put, the relationship between dependence and development varies dramatically: across space, over time, and according to definitions and operationalizations of core constructs. Thus, this chapter suggests that both historical optimism and pessimism about resource dependence and rural development need to be tempered, and boosters and skeptics alike (whether academics, policy makers or firms) should beware of overgeneralizations.

The majority of the results and reflections presented herein are from analyses of Canadian data. In some ways, this represents a historical accident (my employment with the Canadian Forest Service), but other factors are at play as well: the national support through the Canadian Council of Forest Ministers and the concomitant emphasis on both resource development and community well-being. Rural Canada was (and continues to be) more economically and culturally dependent on the harvest and processing of raw materials, thus providing not only support for such inquiries, but also higher levels of dependence providing better data analysis potential. Historically, Statistics Canada data have been superior to US Census data as well: the former are collected at five-year intervals (rather than ten years in the US). Further, Canada has had strong data availability at the 'census subdivision' level. These CSDs are finer spatial scales than the county-level data in the US. As such, they probably come closer to representing real 'communities' than do US counties, thus neatly sidestepping a nagging controversy we see in the US that is making statements about 'communities' while using county-level data.

I hope that researchers engage in work of this type in the United States. Recent changes to the Canadian Census (only requiring participation in a very abbreviated short-form version) will make further analyses of the type conducted herein very difficult to replicate. Further, the questions explored in our analyses will become more salient – and the stakes higher – as our rural communities increasingly are looked at as potential sites for multiple forms of energy development. As such, precise answers to precise questions will take on even more importance, especially in the context of the ever-expanding role of global level factors such as climate change debates.

NOTES

1. Although, as has been already pointed out, outcomes vary by indicator chosen to portray them, we chose median family income as a key indicator to compare across industry and region. Standard regional classifications in Canada describe Atlantic Canada as being comprised of the provinces of Newfoundland and Labrador, Prince Edward Island, Nova Scotia and New Brunswick; Central Canada contains the provinces of Quebec and Ontario; the Prairie region consists of the provinces of Alberta, Saskatchewan and Manitoba; and the North consists of Canada's territories: Northwest Territory, Yukon Territory and Nunavit. British Columbia tends to be considered as a standalone 'region' because of the uniqueness of its natural features.
2. Data post-2001 were not comparable due to changes in CSD boundaries and/or measurement of key indicators.
3. The location quotient (LQ) is the proportion of a given community's share of employment in a particular industry that is above a benchmark region's level. In our analysis the province is used as the benchmark for all of the communities within it. See Stedman et al. (2007) for details on the calculation of location quotient in this study.

REFERENCES

Adger, W.N. (2000), 'Social and ecological resilience: are they related?', *Progress in Human Geography*, 24, 347–64.
Beckley, T., J. Parkins and R.C. Stedman (2002), 'Indicators of forest-community sustainability: the evolution of research', *The Forestry Chronicle*, 78, 626–36.
Bliss, J.C., C. Bailey, G. Howze and L. Teeter (1992), 'Timber dependency in the American South', paper presented at the 8th World Congress for Rural Sociology, Penn State University, University Park, PA.
Bunker, S.G. (1989), 'Staples, links, and poles in the construction of regional development theories', *Sociological Forum*, 4, 589–610.
Cook, A.K. (1995), 'Increasing poverty in timber-dependent areas in Western Washington', *Society and Natural Resources*, 8, 97–109.
Devine-Wright, P. (2005), 'Beyond NIMBYism: towards an integrated framework for understanding public perceptions of wind energy', *Wind energy*, 8, 125–39.
Dissart, J.C. (2003), 'Regional economic diversity and regional economic stability: research results and agenda', *International Regional Science Review*, 26, 423–46.
Drielsma, J.H. (1984), 'The influence of forest-based industries on rural communities', Doctoral dissertation, Yale University.

Florida, R. (2012), *The Rise of the Creative Class – Revisited: Revised and Expanded*, New York: Basic Books.

Folke, C., S. Carpenter, T. Elmqvist, L. Gunderson, C.S. Holling and B. Walker (2002), 'Resilience and sustainable development: building adaptive capacity in a world of transformations', *AMBIO: A Journal of the Human Environment*, 31, 437–40.

Freudenburg, W.R. (1984), 'Boomtown's youth: the differential impacts of rapid community growth upon adolescents and adults', *American Sociological Review*, 49, 697–705.

Freudenburg, W.R. (1986), 'Social impact assessment', *Annual Review of Sociology*, 12, 451–78.

Freudenburg, W.R. (1992), 'Addictive economies: extractive industries and vulnerable localities in a changing world economy', *Rural Sociology*, 57, 305–32.

Freudenburg, W.R. and R. Gramling (1994a), 'Natural resources and rural poverty: a closer look', *Society and Natural Resources*, 7, 5–22.

Freudenburg, W.R. and R. Gramling (1994b), 'Bureaucratic slippage and failures of agency vigilance: the case of the environmental studies program', *Social Problems*, 214–39.

Freudenburg W.R. and R. Gramling (1998), 'Linked to what? Economic linkages in an extractive economy', *Society and Natural Resources*, 11, 569–86.

Freudenburg, W.R. and L.J. Wilson (2002), 'Mining the data: analyzing the economic implications of mining for nonmetropolitan regions', *Sociological Inquiry*, 72, 549–75.

Gilmore, J.S. and M.K. Duff (1975), *Boom Town Growth Management: A Case Study of Rock Springs-Green River, Wyoming*, Boulder, CO: Westview Press.

Halfacree, K. and P. Boyle (1998), *Migration, Rurality and the Post-Productivist Countryside*, New York: Wiley.

Hamilton, L.C. and C.L. Seyfrit (1994), 'Resources and hopes in Newfoundland', *Society and Natural Resources*, 7, 561–78.

Howze, G., C. Bailey, J. Bliss and L. Teeter (1993), 'Regional comparisons of timber dependency: the northwest and the southeast', paper presented at the Annual Meetings of the Rural Sociological Society, Orlando, FL.

Humphrey, C., G. Berardi, L. Fortmann, C. Geisler, C. Johnson, J. Kusel, R. Lee, S. Macinko, M. Schulman and P. West (1993), 'Theories in the study of natural resource dependent communities and persistent rural poverty in the United States', in Rural Sociological Society Task Force on Persistent Rural Poverty (eds), *Persistent Poverty in Rural America*, Rural Studies Series, Boulder, CO: Westview Press, pp. 136–72.

Jacquet, J. (2009), 'Energy boomtowns & natural gas: implications for Marcellus shale local governments & rural communities', Northeast Regional Center for Rural Development, Rural Development Paper 43.

Jacquet, J. and R.C. Stedman (forthcoming), 'The risk of social-psychological disruption as an impact of energy development and environmental change', *Journal of Environmental Planning and Management*.

Kaufman, H.F. and L.C. Kaufman (1946), *Toward the Stabilization and Enrichment of a Forest Community: The Montana Study*, Missoula, MT: University of Montana.

Kennedy, J.J., J.W. Thomas and P. Glueck (2001), 'Evolving forestry and rural development beliefs at midpoint and close of the 20th century', *Forest Policy and Economics*, 3, 81–95.

Krannich, R.S. (2012), 'Social change in natural resource-based rural communities: the evolution of sociological research and knowledge as influenced by William R. Freudenburg', *Journal of Environmental Studies and Sciences*, 2, 1–10.

Krannich, R.S. and T. Greider (1984), 'Contrasting results', *Rural Sociology*, 49, 541–52.

Machlis, G.E., J. Force and R.G. Balice (1990), 'Timber, minerals, and social change: an exploratory test of two resource-dependent communities', *Rural Sociology*, 55, 411–24.

Nord, M. and A.E. Luloff (1993), 'Socioeconomic heterogeneity of mining dependent counties', *Rural Sociology*, 58, 492–500.

Overdevest, Christine and Gary P. Green (1995), 'Forest dependency and community well-being: a segmented market approach', *Society and Natural Resources*, 8, 113–34.

Parkins, J., R.C. Stedman and J. Varghese (2001), 'Moving towards locally defined indicators of sustainability in forest-based communities: a mixed-method approach', *Social Indicators Research*, 56, 43–72.

Parkins J.R., R.C. Stedman and T.M. Beckley (2003), 'Forest sector dependence and community well-being: a structural equation model for New Brunswick and British Columbia', *Rural Sociology*, 68, 554–72.

Power, T.M. (1996), *Lost Landscapes and Failed Economies: The Search for a Value of Place*, Washington, DC: Island Press.

Rees, W.E. (1997), 'Urban ecosystems: the human dimension', *Urban Ecosystems*, 1, 63–75.

Stedman, R.C., J. Parkins and T.M. Beckley (2004), 'Resource dependence and community well-being in rural Canada', *Rural Sociology*, 69, 213–34.

Stedman, R.C., J. Parkins and T. Beckley (2005), 'Forest reliance and community well being in rural Canada: variation by forest sector and region', *Canadian Journal of Forest Research*, 35, 215–20.

Stedman, R.C., W. White, M. Patriquin and D. Watson (2007), 'Measuring community forest sector dependence: does method matter?', *Society and Natural Resources*, 20, 629–46.

Stedman, R.C., M. Patriquin and J. Parkins (2011), 'Forest dependence and community well-being in rural Canada: a longitudinal analysis', *Forestry*, 84, 375–84.

Stedman, R.C., M. Patriquin and J. Parkins (2012), 'Dependence, diversity, and the well-being of rural community: building on the Freudenburg legacy', *Journal of Environmental Studies and Sciences*, 2, 28–38.

Walker, B. and D. Salt (2006), *Resilience Thinking: Sustaining Ecosystems and People in a Changing World*, Washington, DC: Island Press.

Wall, E. and K. Marzall (2006), 'Adaptive capacity for climate change in Canadian rural communities', *Local Environment*, 11, 373–97.

West, P.C. (1994), 'Natural resources and the persistence of rural poverty in America: a Weberian perspective on the role of power, domination, and natural resource bureaucracy', *Society and Natural Resources*, 7, 415–27.

Wilson, A. and B. Leach (2002), 'Economic diversity, sustainability, and manufacturing communities', in Belinda Leach and Anthony Winson (eds), *Contingent Work, Disputed Lives: Labour and Community in the New Rural Economy*, Toronto, Ontario: University of Toronto Press, pp. 155–73.

6. Migration and rural development: resettlement, remittances and amenities
Shaun A. Golding and Katherine J. Curtis

MIGRATION AND RURAL DEVELOPMENT: A SYNOPSIS

Economic growth and population growth are interdependent. Vibrant economies can be veritable magnets that attract newcomers, but population growth, conversely, is critically important for fostering vibrant economies. A growing workforce increases economic productivity and distributes the expense of caring for a society's children, elderly and non-workers. Local population growth also appeals to outside investors looking to expand their profitability. On the contrary, population decline warrants careful fiscal planning at the national level, and locally it can demand more urgent measures.

Migration has long been a means for securing rural economic strength through population growth, but contemporary declines in birth and death rates have made it increasingly important. The world over, humans generally have fewer children and live longer than previous generations, a phenomenon known as the demographic transition (Caldwell and Caldwell 2006; Davis 1945). However, different places are at different stages in the demographic transition, and they remain widely disparate in their levels of economic and political stability. Under these geographically unequal circumstances, modern economies rely on flows of workers moving across national and regional borders, typically from poorer, unstable places to wealthier and politically stable places (Castles and Miller 2009). These migration patterns have proven crucial for development prospects in the world's rural communities.

Rural populations in most of the world experience some form of instability related to in- and out-migration. Their instability tends to follow the ups and downs of resource-dependent rural industries in the global economy, because people move to where they can find steady sources of income. As rural economies have shifted away from manufacturing and traditional forms of agriculture and resource extraction, the dominant rural population trend has been decline. The world is becoming more urban as rural residents migrate to cities in search of employment, and as cities increase the momentum of their growth with higher birth rates. This trend has advanced in developed nations for several generations, but is currently accelerating most rapidly in developing nations. However, migration to these places occurs under myriad different social and legal circumstances, and by shaping newcomers' civic and commercial experiences, those circumstances ultimately determine their contribution to local economic vitality.

Rural development and migration relate to each other differently across places. Rural communities located beyond the peripheries of cities generally experience development related to their natural resource base, and because natural resources are not distributed evenly and tend to fluctuate in value, rural population growth and prosperity also occur unevenly. Further, not all population growth has the same implications for development. In developing countries, migration to rural places often originates in other rural places, while in developed nations rural places are experiencing growth from cities as well. Rural–rural migrants tend to move in pursuit of work, while urban–rural movers relocate in pursuit of leisure with increasing frequency. International moves occur for both family repatriation and employment, and international movers tend to vary widely in their legal status and, thus, impact destination communities in contrasting ways.

In this chapter, we describe three patterns of migration-based rural development, distinguishable by sending and receiving communities' experience of economic restructuring and the circumstances surrounding migrants' motivations to move. The three patterns on which we focus are: (1) rural development in developed nations associated with resettlement; (2) rural development in developing nations associated with remittances made by out-migrants working abroad; and (3) rural development in both developed and developing nations associated with amenity migration.

To describe migration's impacts, we draw from literature that details changes to populations' composition and the associated economic implications. Specifically, we review scholarship that illuminates the role that in-migration plays in local economic development for remote, rural communities, where cities are not close enough to buoy their growth. Although we build our discussion around cases investigated in the United States and Mexico, we illustrate ways in which the North American experience is similar or different from other developed and developing countries in the world. In doing so, we highlight the increasingly interconnected global forces impacting rural development.

Migration research varies widely in its scope, and so our discussion necessarily encompasses different spatial scales and units of analysis. Global development literature discusses disparity across nations or levels of population density, as well as disparity between regions and communities. In the United States, for example, the community development literature emphasizes counties, towns or villages because they constitute the domains in which local governance and social continuity occur. Alternatively, remittance research from developing countries focuses on impacts that accrue at the family and household levels. Drawing from these diverse literatures, we discuss a variety of impacts.

Further, scholars study migration with different emphases on migrants and their origins. Though disproportionate attention is awarded to international moves, we know domestic moves have important development impacts as well. And though research often presents migration as individual journeys, it also views development as an outcome of those journeys' aggregation. Here, we discuss migration in the aggregate, focusing on the predominant migration streams arriving in rural places, and the large flows of migrants that make up those streams.

IN-MIGRATION MITIGATES RURAL POPULATION LOSS IN DEVELOPED COUNTRIES

In-migration is central to sustaining economic activity in developed counties' most economically peripheral rural communities. Where resource dependence has given way to population loss, and where still-viable rural industries need additional labor, newcomers are driving the economy. However, migration to these places occurs under myriad different social and legal circumstances, and by shaping newcomers' civic and commercial experiences, it is those circumstances that ultimately determine their contribution to local economic vitality.

Community Decline and Resident Recruitment

In developed countries, the majority of remote rural communities struggle to keep their residents. Long identified as the rural 'brain drain', the United States has observed this trend for decades. Since the 1940s, population in the US has shifted from living predominantly in rural counties to living primarily in metropolitan counties (Beale 1975), a shift that had been observed in other developed nations including those in Northern and Western Europe (Bairoch 1991 [1985]). Local schools, churches, sports teams, hospitals, post offices and small businesses cannot survive without a robust count of local households. Many communities have seen declines in primarily young and working-age households, leaving them populated disproportionately by elderly residents. In some of these rapidly aging communities, the key local institutions have already been shut or scaled down.

Rural population loss is a direct consequence of economic restructuring. Prime farmland, though productive and profitable, can support fewer families due to mechanization and consolidation. The same is true in many timber-dependent communities, where large firms vertically integrate the cultivation, harvesting, processing and sale of wood products. These industries demand fewer workers and with international competition, offer narrower profit margins than ever before. As a result, rural populations that depend on them have declined (Curtis White 2008). To illustrate, a few people can now manage a farm that once required several family members to maintain, but no longer can that farm actually sustain a family financially (Galston and Baehler 1995).

In tandem with the economic forces working against them, remote rural communities now confront a crisis of social constructions. Too small to attract employers, some shrinking rural communities concentrate their efforts on recruiting new residents (Wood 2008). However, in the parlance of advertising, remote rural communities have an image problem. The transformation of cities into cultural and entertainment centers has made small towns comparatively less appealing to many young people. The media portrayal of rural life as insular and unsophisticated reinforces rural places' status as social peripheries, making the retention of young people even more challenging (Carr and Kefalas 2009). Rural students who pursue a university degree may develop cosmopolitan tastes and meet spouses from other communities. Moreover, by earning an education they may inadvertently limit their ability to find suitable work in their home communities.

Declining rural communities have turned to different strategies to entice new residents to resettle in them. For example, those with particularly serious need on the American Great Plains have offered free land, and in some cases free homes to families who relocate. Communities in Kansas have instituted formal recruitment strategies, soliciting new residents with employment contacts and information about local schools and recreational opportunities (Wood 2008). These programs resemble the incentives used by the American government over a century ago to populate its western frontier. Reports suggest that some of these contemporary programs have been successful, at least by the objectives described by the communities themselves (Lu and Paull 2007).

Rural communities may also receive a modest boost from state and federal rural initiatives. Some support comes from the maintenance of federal infrastructure located in rural communities, such as military installments, national parks, forests and other public lands. More explicit subsidies come in the form of programs that maintain rural health infrastructure. To address the hospital closures accompanying rural America's population decline, the federal government now subsidizes rural health care facilities through its Medicaid program (Mueller 2001). The US government also joins some states in recruiting health care workers to remote communities, offering them educational loan repayment and visa waivers for international candidates. These efforts have helped keep over 1000 rural hospitals in operation, which not only maintains important health services, but also helps to keep local economies afloat and attract new families.

The North American experience of rural population decline is representative of urbanization trends experienced in developed nations around the world. Compared to North America, Australia and New Zealand, Europe has generally been able to maintain a greater proportion of its populations in rural areas (United Nations 2011). However, in Russia the countryside has experienced accelerated depopulation following market reforms of the post-soviet era (Ioffe et al. 2004). Rural depopulation is similarly extreme in Japan, where young people flock to the archipelago's enormous cities and leave behind some of the world's most rapidly aging communities (Traphagan and Knight 2003). Knight (2003) describes concerted development efforts made by Japanese municipalities to reverse the trend, which include infrastructural improvements to transportation networks, soliciting new employers, incentivizing marriage and child rearing, and hosting information sessions to promote resettlement.

Booms, Busts and Moves

Mineral and petroleum deposits are proving to be major engines of rural development as small communities ramp up their workforces and infrastructure. For example, in the currently booming petroleum and natural gas sector of the American Great Plains, Southwest and Appalachia, very high wages attract native-born job seekers, often siphoning workers from other rural industries (Adams and Menkhaus 1980). Echoing the oil boom of the 1970s, population growth in petroleum-rich communities has captured the attention of national media outlets which marvel at the dramatic reversal of fortunes that some previously declining rural communities are experiencing (Ellis 2012; Konigsberg 2011).

However, history has shown that rural communities developing around energy sectors are thought to experience unique growing pains (Wilkinson et al. 1982). Boom communities must expand services such as schools, waste management, and utilities fast enough to both accommodate growth and protect the environment and the public's long-term health and safety. The most notable drawback associated with extractive booms is community longevity. A community can prosper only so long as the demand for its resources remains high because history has shown that resource-dependent communities without diverse economies are unprepared for economic shocks. When resource extraction becomes less profitable or a resource nears its effective depletion, these communities tend to experience a slow decline as corporations downsize their workforces (Freudenburg 1992). While communities may eventually return to a normal level of social solidarity and cohesion after a boom (Smith et al. 2001), they may also return to pre-boom levels of disadvantage.

INTERNATIONAL LABOR MIGRATION IN CONTEXT: DEVELOPMENT AND IMMIGRATION POLICY

Dairying, meatpacking and agricultural processing exemplify a third economic scenario with a distinct implication for migration and development. The consolidation of these labor-intensive sectors has created concentrated demand for low-wage workers, often in places where local populations are either shrinking or transitioning away from engagement in manual labor (Harrison and Lloyd 2012; Kandel and Parrado 2005). Thus, many agriculture-focused rural communities rely on immigrant labor, recruited under circumstances that are highly variable.

A growing number of rural communities maintain stable populations because of labor migration. Outside laborers can be crucial for thriving rural industries to survive shrinking populations and changing job preferences among locals. For example, fish farming and processing, meatpacking, and mineral and petroleum extraction are predominantly rural industries that depend on large workforces. Increasingly, consolidation in the dairy industry has given rise to similar demand for workers to help manage growing herds (Harrison and Lloyd 2012). In communities that house these labor-intensive industries, employers hire outside workers with greater frequency, as local residents pursue less strenuous, more consistent and higher-paying jobs. These new worker inflows have differing impacts depending on their origins and household characteristics.

Offering lower wages than petroleum companies, the agricultural sector turns with greater frequency to foreign-born workers (Cuadros 2006; Harrison and Lloyd 2012; Kandel and Parrado 2005). In the United States, the Current Population Survey estimated approximately 40 million foreign-born immigrants resided in the United States in 2011, with nearly one-third of them originating in Mexico. The worldwide magnitude of international migration is staggering. In fact, Coleman (2006) contends that the growth of immigrant populations in the US and other large Western democracies is a sign that they are undergoing a third demographic transition, culminating when immigrant groups eventually attain majority status. As we discuss throughout this chapter, the impact that international migration has on development can depend on how national governments orient their policy toward migrants, and how communities and individuals react to social and cultural change in their daily lives.

Newcomers have the potential to infuse their adopted communities with social and economic vitality. A limited number of case studies indicate that immigrant workers make purchases locally and, in doing so, help to revitalize deteriorating commercial districts. Eventually, immigrants open small businesses to cater to their growing community. If they relocate with young children, they contribute to school enrollments, which keeps schools open, maintains civic vitality and thus supports middle-class jobs in local government and the private sector (Bickmeier 2001; Potter et al. 2004; Slesinger and Deller 2002).

However, foreign workers' capacity to engage in public life and strengthen rural economies can depend on the citizenship status granted them by state and national immigration policies. While most developed countries sanction legal immigration to strategically augment their labor forces, unsanctioned labor migration remains prevalent, particularly across the US–Mexico border. An estimated 11.9 million US workers and family members have entered the country illegally or have overstayed their work visa, subjecting them to scrutiny by law enforcement (Passel and Cohn 2008). These workers are generally referred to as 'illegal', or 'undocumented'.

In the United States, foreign workers' tenuous legal status presents several challenges for economic development. First, immigrant workers are most often men separated from their families, and thus, they remit a sizeable portion of their wages back to their home country. (We discuss this phenomenon as a development mechanism in greater detail below.) It follows that money returned to immigrant workers' home countries amounts to a lost economic opportunity for their host communities.

Second, undocumented workers have multiple incentives to limit their engagement in community and civic life. As immigration reform re-emerged as a contentious political issue in advance of the 2008 presidential election, deportations increased and some states enacted extremely harsh enforcement legislation. A 2012 study by the Pew Hispanic Center found that the share of Mexican immigrants caught by aggressive police raids at workplaces and homes grew from 3 percent in 2005 to 17 percent in 2010, marking a quadrupling of the rate. In response, undocumented workers harbor a justified mistrust of US institutions that require proof of identification, such as public safety, banks and hospitals (Paulson et al. 2006). With many families comprised of both 'legal' and 'illegal' members, entire groups are compelled to withdraw from civic life (Harrison and Lloyd

2012). And though many undocumented workers pay taxes on their earnings and send their children to school, they receive few legal protections in the workplace and experience high rates of turnover and relative transience (Grey 1997).

Third, workers confront cultural barriers in becoming socially integrated community members. With weakening institutional pressure for groups to assimilate culturally, the social fabric of rural immigration destinations is growing more vividly contrasting. To illustrate, churches offer services in two languages, and businesses reach out to their new clientele by selling different products and posting signs in foreign languages (Bickmeier 2001). For some in the majority, these multicultural displays fan the flames of xenophobia (Gouveia et al. 2005). And despite compelling evidence that foreign workers perform their jobs with minimal impacts on the native labor force, the notion that they are 'stealing' work from locals remains prevalent (Waldinger and Lichter 2003). For immigrants to enjoy complete participation in community life requires overcoming these social barriers.

Immigration and labor scholars describe developed countries' growing reliance on immigrant labor as evidence of 'dual' or 'segmented' labor markets, meaning that immigrant workers in developed nations help constitute a second-class workforce (Peck 1996; Piore 2001). Immigrants' limited legal protections are evidence of this distinction. The fewer rights workers have, the better suited they are for employers who need dispensable workforces under volatile economic conditions. Without leverage of any kind, most immigrant workers' wages are rarely increased, they experience limited upward mobility, and they move more frequently between different jobs and different communities (Gouveia et al. 2005). Theorists argue that host nations benefit from utilizing foreign laborers, both legal and illegal, because they bear no legal responsibility to provide for their health or education (Chavez 2001). But at the local scale, the segmentation of labor markets engineered by immigration policy limits benefits that could potentially accrue to communities.

Europe has instituted an alternative policy regime, permitting workers' passage to rural locations through legal border crossings. Under policies set forth by international collaboration, Europe's more developed countries benefit from relatively easy access to labor pools from less developed counties in the South and East (Hing 2010). Norway, for example, can staff the thriving fish farms dotting its vast and sparsely settled Atlantic coast with legal, documented workers from Poland and Romania, despite Norwegian independence from the European Union. Furthermore, workers can resettle their families and send their children to school without threat of deportation. These policies have generated a veritable renaissance for several of Norway's most remote rural communities (Berglund 2010). This is not to suggest that Europe avoids immigration conflict, as Norwegian agriculture relies primarily on seasonal migrant labor paid below national standards who confront cultural isolation and anti-immigrant sentiment (Rye and Andrzejewska 2010). However, in general, Europe's experience with intra-continental immigration is configured to promote more permanent economic development because it facilitates long-term and family-based settlement.

In summary, to realize the benefits of in-migration, small communities must accommodate not just population growth, but increasingly, new cultures and traditions. The rewards of accommodating these changes can be numerous, particularly when immigrant families move, as whole households invest in local housing, and fully participate in local activities. New residents sustain local businesses with their labor, and reverse the decline of schools, churches and civic life, leaving widely felt ripples across the community. However, newcomers' legal status is what articulates their rights as workers, residents and citizens, and ultimately determines the extent to which they contribute to local economies.

THE SENDING END: OUT-MIGRATION AND REMITTANCES IN DEVELOPING COUNTRIES

When workers leave their home country to work in more developed economies, they generate development in their home communities by sending their earnings back to family members. India ($64 billion), followed by China ($62 billion), Mexico ($24 billion), and the Philippines ($23 billion) account for the top four recipients of remittances from workers abroad (Ratha and Silwal 2012). A growing body of research has explored the effects of these remittances, offering several points to consider when assessing the impacts of out-migration on development. In-depth research frequently focuses on the Mexican experience because it has persisted throughout widely varying immigration policies over several decades. Accordingly, we emphasize here the experience of rural Mexico in discussing how immigration policy in migration-receiving countries influences development in migration-sending countries.

Global Development and the Depopulating Countryside

Understanding remittances in North America requires some background on changes seen in Mexico's economy and emigration patterns over the last 50 years. Historically, the US government promoted seasonal migration from Mexico to the United States under the Bracero program. The Bracero program opened the American border for Mexican laborers recruited by US agricultural producers, beginning in World War II and lasting into the 1960s (Castles and Miller 2009). In the 1970s, international development regimes contributed to major changes in migration patterns. Trade liberalization and foreign investments in large-scale agricultural production rendered small-scale and subsistence farming in Mexico gravely unprofitable (Fernandez-Kelly and Massey 2007). At the same time, Mexico was proceeding through its demographic transition, and so its labor markets flooded with workers. As a result, migration to the United States grew more prevalent and more permanent, despite less permissive immigration policy.

Migration between Mexico and the US reached a crescendo with the enactment of the North American Free Trade Agreement (NAFTA) in 1994 (Fernandez-Kelly and Massey 2007). NAFTA has been criticized for further eroding Mexico's ability to sustain equitable economic growth within its borders, instead favoring outside investment geared toward low-wage laborers (Delgado-Wise and Márquez Covarrubias 2007). Since NAFTA, Mexico's cities and border regions have swelled with low-paid industrial workforces, and now approximately 10 percent of native-born Mexicans live abroad (Passel et al. 2012). Both domestic and international out-migrants remit portions of their wages to their home communities, offering a lifeline to the families they leave behind (Boucher et al. 2005).

As development architecture, similar to NAFTA, is deployed throughout the world, trans-border labor migration created several national economic co-dependencies. Developed nations have come to rely on low-wage foreign workers, while in developing countries, labor migration has evolved as a cultural norm and a critical source of income. An annual World Bank report indicates that remittances between developed and developing countries had reached nearly $372 billion in 2011, an increase of 12.1 percent over 2010 (Ratha and Silwal 2012). In many cases, remittances rival the foreign direct investments made to these countries (IADB 2004), and in certain countries remittances account for nearly a third of national gross domestic product (GDP) (Ratha and Silwal 2012). In addition to Mexico, the US receives labor from throughout Central America and the Caribbean and from as far as China and Southeast Asia. Globally, labor migration connects the booming petroleum economies of the Persian Gulf to South Asia and the Pacific Islands, and the social democracies of Northern and Western Europe to Eastern Europe and the Middle East and North Africa. Australia and New Zealand are major destinations for workers from throughout Asia (Castles and Miller 2009). A large proportion of the world's migrant labor force travels from one developing country to another, and on the African continent, internal migration far outpaces migration to Europe, particularly among sub-Saharan nations (Castles and Miller 2009).

To illustrate the extent to which remittance have become institutionalized as a development strategy, the Philippines' national dependence on remittances grew from formal programs meant to address unemployment. A 2005 working paper reported that nearly 8 million Filipinos worked overseas, comprising a quarter of the national workforce (Burgess and Haksar 2005).

Remittances and Local Development

Questions about the extent to which remittances between developed and developing nations are beneficial for local economic development form a contentious debate among scholars in the field of demography and beyond. Most experts agree that remittances comprise an important income supplement for families in places with few immediate job opportunities. However, other major points to consider include the long-term efficacy and sustainability of remittances, community-wide benefits of remittances, and the overall variability in how different communities and locations fare.

A primary critique of remittance-based development asserts that absent laborers are in effect absent consumers. With young, healthy and productive community members working abroad, local infrastructure and the capacity of local institutions suffers. Departed workers living abroad cannot contribute to local spending, or in the longer term, contribute to population growth. From a demographic standpoint, fertility in sending communities suffers when workers in their most productive years depart to find jobs abroad, especially when women work abroad (Lindstrom and Saucedo 2002). From the family health and human development perspective, the hardship associated with absentee parents is not conducive to fostering a stable environment for raising children (Wright 2006) although recent research has found that father–child separation due to migration is distinct from that precipitated by divorce (Nobles 2011).

Some scholars draw attention to the volume and variety of benefits made possible by remittances, arguing that they play a vital part in sustaining otherwise destitute localities. Massey et al. (1998) estimate that every dollar remitted from the US to Mexico contributes an additional $2.90 to Mexico's gross national product. Another study estimates that the $2 billion remitted from the US to Mexico has the effect of $5.9 billion in wages in Mexico. Keely and Tran (1989) observed that remittances helped make sending communities more economically stable than other communities. Jones (2008) found that over successive years of labor migration, remittances offered rural Mexican communities greater income growth than urban areas, where a smaller proportion of the populace participates in international labor migration.

With favorable exchange rates, a modest quantity of US dollars can make a sizeable impact on Mexican families, and in turn, communities. Research indicates that many families receiving remittances use the funds to improve their long-term social standing. Detailed analyses show that workers' families use their remitted wages to pay for their children's education, make investments in land, small business enterprises and agricultural inputs, and to modernize their homes (Adams and Page 2005). However, a counter-argument has been lodged by studies that have observed that remittances can foster dependency, weakening young people's motivation to engage in schooling or local agricultural labor, ultimately weakening the potential for local economic development (Chami et al. 2003).

Increasingly, studies point to these emerging disparities in arguing that remittances reinforce inequality within and between households and communities in developing countries. For example, higher-status workers have more earnings to remit, and are often able to bring more family members with them. Further, workers from the poorest backgrounds remit a portion of their earnings on a regular basis, incurring wire fees each time, while those from more stable socio-economic positions return with their earnings to avoid fees (Durand et al. 1996). These relatively privileged workers tend to have more stable employment in the US, own homes in Mexico, and be more educated. Taylor et al. (2005) finds that these disparities may dissipate over time as more family members work in the US for longer durations, but because migration is an important way for families to match the material status of their neighbors, relative hardships emerge for families who cannot send workers to the US. What is more, remittances are rarely taxed and therefore offer few communal benefits to directly mitigate the growing disparities between families.

Similar inequality is emerging across rural Mexican communities. Research has observed that remittances generate economic development most successfully in places that already enjoy robust economies. Mexican communities were less likely to receive remittances if they had few development prospects than if they were vibrant entrepreneurial environments (Durand et al. 1996). In sum, the remittance of US earnings to Mexico strengthens the position of families and communities engaged in labor migration. But with an already stratified labor force and a stratified landscape, labor migration reinforces existing privilege, and therefore remittances have different implications for families and for communities in Mexico.

Remittances and Changing Politics of Migration

One major problem in assessing remittances as a development mechanism is the difficulty of accounting for the external economic and political factors that influence migration patterns. Just as immigration policies impact the potential for immigrant workers to contribute to local economies in the US, they ultimately shape the distribution of benefits that come from remittances. Evidence from the United States and Mexico indicates that the legal restrictions on migration and labor dilute the benefits of remittances. For example, immigrants pay a portion of remittances to smugglers, or 'coyotes', who demand fees to lead them across the border. Durand et al. (1996) found that workers who paid the most to coyotes for their entry to the US remitted more of their US earnings to Mexico, in order to pay off their debt.

Several studies suggest that strict immigration policies stifle remittance's long-term provision of development needs, because they often extended workers' stay in their host nation. Cyclical movements across borders such as those once sanctioned by the Bracero program allowed workers to maintain strong ties to their homes. However, as the US has experienced more recently, border enforcement and immigration policies are helping to make migration more permanent because border crossings are treacherous and expensive, and thus less cyclical. In North America, increases in border security between the US and Mexico are associated with a decrease in remittances overall (Glytsos 2002; Massey et al. 2003).

The most recent American financial crisis, along with new regimes in border security and deportation, are responsible for an unparalleled decline in Mexican–US migration, which reflects an obvious reduction in remitted wages. In a 2012 study by the Pew Hispanic Center, illegal immigration between Mexico and the United States was shown to have slowed considerably in both directions (Passel et al. 2012). The study found a precipitous decline in total entries to the US from Mexico, resulting in a slightly larger flow from the US to Mexico than vice versa. Further, more repatriated Mexican migrants than ever claim to be finished with their attempts to work in the US. This finding underscores remittance-based development strategies' vulnerability to external political and economic factors. The high costs of assistance in crossing borders, the difficulty of finding work in the US, and the growing threat of deportation have decreased the volume of Mexican workers in the US, erasing what had been a growing piece of local economic activity in Mexico.

Europe's experience with international migration offers a counter-example to the effects observed in other regions of the world. Multilateral cooperation under various economic and social agreements has relaxed

Europe's border controls for workers and their families in a highly structured fashion (Hing 2010). Less developed countries entering the economic agreements must wait as many as three years before their citizens can engage in work in other member countries, which ultimately mitigates the differential in wages that entices workers away from their homes. Most importantly, however, with relatively free movement across borders, partners and families can accompany laborers, reducing dependence on remittances. Ultimately, harnessing remittances' potential to create sustained economic development in rural places will require more formal multilateral policy interventions than what exists outside Europe (Farrant et al. 2006).

AMENITY DESTINATIONS, GENTRIFICATION AND INEQUALITY

Both developed and developing nations are home to communities that attract affluent newcomers, garnering investment in local development with relative ease. These places appeal to tourists and permanent and seasonal residents with 'natural amenities', and on average, they are more prosperous and more resistant to population decline than other rural places. Prime examples in the United States include Aspen, Colorado, the Texas hill country, and Stowe, Vermont. Amenity destinations cluster similarly in alpine valleys and along subtropical coastlines in Europe, and increasingly they are scattered throughout coastal and tropical developing nations including Costa Rica, the Dominican Republic and Thailand. Rural amenity destinations experience increased demand for seasonal and year-round homes, giving way to service economies built around newcomers' spending, and eventually spurring the arrival of service workers. Our review of amenity literature draws heavily from the deep well focusing on economic changes in North American destinations.

Amenities and Economic Growth

Amidst the decline of traditional rural industries, in-migration has delivered amenity communities an alternative source of prosperity. In contrast to rural development characterized by jobs that attract newcomers, newcomers in amenity communities play a major role in creating jobs (Vias 1999). Newcomers' connectivity to outside communities and consumer markets helps to generate additional income, advancing growth in sectors related to new home construction, the repair or conversion of existing homes, and home sales (Beyers and Nelson 2000). With many newcomers in their retirement years, economic development observed in amenity communities

derives largely from consumption patterns as opposed to labor force participation. Accordingly, growth seen in amenity communities occurs in the
construction and sale of residential real estate as well as in service-based
and retail sectors that cater to both urban tourists and newcomers.

With wealth from their careers in cities, and urban preferences as
homeowners and consumers, urban newcomers can dramatically improve
rural economies. Rural sociologists and regional economists have noted the
correlation between in-migration and development by showing that American retirement and recreation destinations have exhibited striking economic
expansion. For example, Deller (1995) observed through economic simulations that migrant retirees impact retail, health and construction sectors in a
non-metropolitan Maine community. Warnick (1996) reported from the
Berkshires in Massachusetts that the presence of seasonal homes meant
both lower tax rates and more spending per capita for high-amenity communities there. Similarly, Goe and Green (2005) find that high-amenity
localities, particularly those where multiple types of amenities overlap,
experienced significant improvements in well-being between 1980 and
2000.

With focus on the relative prosperity seen in rural destinations, development practitioners have encouraged communities to capitalize upon their
natural amenities. Amenity-based development initiatives typically involve
orienting policies toward visitors and newcomers (Chipeniuk 2004; Keith et
al. 1996). They include ecotourism and agritourism, the development of
special themed tourist routes, local museums, seasonal festivals, and other
agglomerations of niche businesses such as Amish crafts, cheese makers
and vineyards. These approaches to development have been heralded as
opportunities to preserve natural resources and accentuate cultural heritage
while sustaining local livelihoods (Galston and Baehler 1995; Reeder and
Brown 2005).

Critical Perspectives of Amenity Migration and Development

While their prosperous migrants make them generally more resilient to
economic shocks, amenity destinations face their own development challenges. Evidence of amenity migration's economic benefits often over-
shadows the complex demographic changes that accompany population
growth. With amenity-based economic strategies rising to prominence
among rural development practitioners, a body of more critical scholarship
has presented evidence that economic growth comes with consequences
and several caveats (Gosnell and Abrams 2009). We do not intend through
our discussion of these caveats to discredit amenity-based development, but

rather to illuminate considerations that are important for evaluating the costs and benefits of amenity migration to local development.

First, focusing solely on destinations' growth diverts attention from the reality that different types of migrants arrive and depart at different rates, and in doing so, have different impacts. Non-working newcomers impact communities differently than those who join the local workforce, just as permanent residents are different from seasonal residents, and older residents are different from younger residents. Glasgow and Reeder (1990) noted, for example, that retirement-age migrants' external sources of income mitigated their impact on local economies. Retirees, who dominate the growth in amenity destinations, are also likely to relocate again as their health declines.

As demand for property pushes the costs of living upward, research also suggests that young people leave amenity counties in proportions exceeding those at which they leave other rural counties (Winkler et al. 2011). Despite their appeal, destination counties in the US are in fact less able to retain younger in-migrants than either mining-dependent counties or other rural counties. This hinders development because it is young people who raise families, maintain local jobs and contribute to more long-term stability. Winkler (2010) also finds that young people's interests in community life may be placed directly at odds with those of the aging population, who shape local policy through their voting and spending behavior. Additionally, in contrast to year-round residents, seasonal residents, who are typically wealthier, contribute less to local economies because they make their purchases elsewhere as they come and go between different homes (Deller et al. 1997).

A second consideration is that there is a need to better ascertain the impacts of amenity migration as they progress over time. Studies have found that in-migration comes with long-term costs that may outweigh the short-term benefits. Deller et al. (1997) found that the tax revenue from seasonal housing failed to produce fiscal benefits that offset the additional costs of municipal services. Mullins and Rosentraub (1992) come to similar conclusions, finding that communities with large retired populations devote more spending to public services. Additionally, research tends to ignore destination communities' historical experience with in-migration as a key indicator of future in-migration. Golding (2012) observes that patterns of urban–rural migration have been tightly concentrated over time and that the majority of American destination counties in the 1990s had been destinations in previous decades. This finding may suggest that amenity development is not replicable or practical in communities that were not popular destinations already. Recognizing that most research examines a very short temporal window, Serow (2003) suggests in his literature review that development initiatives need better information about in-migration's long-term impacts.

Third, researchers generally pay inadequate attention to the distribution of amenity migration's benefits across different households, income groups and occupations, which is particularly problematic given the close association between in-migration and out-migration. Destinations' apparent advantages may be effectively negated by exorbitant housing prices that trigger the loss of low-income residents (Hammer and Winkler 2006; Hettinger 2004; Winkler 2010). To accommodate the service demands of wealthy newcomers, local employers rely on economically vulnerable and often foreign-born newcomers who accept low wages and unfavorable terms, a phenomenon which Nelson and Nelson (2011) term 'linked migration'. Their national analysis of linked migration documents the prevalence of inequality consistently found in case studies, such as Park and Pellow's (2011) study of Aspen, Colorado. Emphasizing outcomes, scholars rarely consider how in- and out-migration throughout the process of amenity development determine who receives the benefits and who shoulders the burdens of local economic changes. Put simply, we should assess the benefits of amenity development with caution because demographic data reveals that the population of beneficiaries is highly mobile, which diminishes their stake in the process over time.

In sum, while the aggregate social and economic improvements seen in amenity communities are notable, evidence suggests that the relationship between migration and amenity development is more complex than simple cause and effect. When viewed in concert with findings of inequality, these complexities illustrate the need to evaluate the relationship between migration and economic development with caution and reflection. This is especially important in developing countries, where the extremes of inequality between locals and newcomers are more widely split, where communities' financial interests in land can be limited, and where labor standards are more variable. And finally, as the massive 'baby boom' birth cohort reaches retirement age, their dominance in the population of developed countries may place unparalleled pressure on real estate in the world's rural amenity communities.

It is also important to note that amenity development is not perfectly uniform across national contexts. In Norway, for example, amenity migration may offer weaker opportunities for local development than in the US (Van Auken 2010). Urban Norwegians enjoy widespread access to rural cabins that tend to be located within a reasonable drive from their relatively clean and safe home cities. With a high quality of urban life, cabin owners see little need to permanently relocate to their cabins (Müller 2007). In

addition, Norwegian cabins are governed by zoning that mandates separation from year-round homes (Overvåg 2009). This separation limits the use
of most cabins as year-round residences, weakening the upward pressure on
home prices that repels low-income residents, but curtailing second homeowners' participation in local commerce. Thus, amenity migration is a less
viable development strategy for Norway because few households relocate
permanently to the countryside. Most importantly, perhaps, Norway's need
for amenity-based development is mitigated by policies that have propped
up its other rural industries, including the immigration policies that channel
Eastern European laborers to rural jobs.

CONCLUSIONS

Certainly, migration catalyzes and sustains economic development in contemporary rural communities. Some communities require labor to sustain
long-established industries, while others risk total dissolution if they cannot
attract new residents to participate in social and economic life. Seemingly
privileged communities enjoy natural resource endowments that appeal to
wealthy and urban newcomers, but typically rely on new workers to meet
newcomers' consumer demands. Migration's effectiveness as an economic
development engine in these scenarios is variable and complex. When
newcomers are recruited to sustain booming extractive economies, development can be extensive but short-lived and environmentally devastating.
When newcomers are hired in agriculture or service industries, development can worsen inequality. And given that migrants to rural places are
increasingly foreign-born, equitable rural development is now a matter of
international migration.

Migration's local economic benefits are sensitive to national immigration
policy because they set the boundaries for workers' participation in social
and commercial life. Policies that allow permanent moves by families can
promote more substantive and meaningful economic development. However, many nations that depend on foreign workers restrict their rights to
residency, reducing their local economic footprint, creating demand for
professional smugglers, and perpetuating segmented labor markets that
offer low wages with few opportunities to advance.

The corollary of these restrictive conditions in receiving nations is the
potential for remittance-based development in sending nations, because
limited passage across borders compels workers to support the families they
leave behind. While remittances provide a critical source of financial
support to otherwise impoverished places, they carve out a disparate social

landscape at the neighborhood, community and global scales. The remittance phenomenon highlights one of several ways that immigration policies engender unequal development.

Increasingly, international amenity destinations offer a more concise portrait of the extreme disparities that immigration policies promote. In developing countries, amenity migration is made possible by unhindered passage for wealthy foreigners, while in developed countries amenity destinations are serviced by workers whose legal status makes them both affordable and dispensable. In both scenarios, inequality persists locally because it exists globally.

More generally, immigration policies promote different levels of pay, security and rights for migrant workers by accepting different types of workers under different quotas and through different visa programs. They funnel specialists in the fields of science and medicine away from developing countries, while compelling the poorest workers to sacrifice rights for wages, and to pay more for their passage between countries and to send their wages home. Put simply, communities who benefit from this system do so because other communities are losing. The progress made within Europe towards integrating immigration and development policy illustrates that more broadly distributed benefits are possible by explicitly acknowledging these interconnections.

REFERENCES

Adams, R.H. and J. Page (2005), 'Do international migration and remittances reduce poverty in developing countries?', *World Development*, 33, 1645–69.

Adams, R.M. and D. Menkhaus (1980), 'The effect of mining on agricultural hired labor in the northern Great Plains', *American Journal of Agricultural Economics*, 62, 748.

Bairoch, P. (1991 [1985]), *Cities and Economic Development: From the Dawn of History to the Present*, trans. Christopher Braider, Chicago, IL, USA and Paris, France: University of Chicago Press.

Beale, C.L. (1975), *The Revival of Population Growth in Nonmetropolitan America*, Washington, DC: Economic Research Service.

Berglund, N. (2010), 'Immigrants "save" outlying areas', *Views and News from Norway*. http://www.newsinenglish.no/2012/03/19/immigrants-save-outlying-areas/ (retrieved March 10, 2012).

Beyers, W.B. and P.B. Nelson (2000), 'Contemporary development forces in the nonmetropolitan West: new insights from rapidly growing communities', *Journal of Rural Studies*, 16, 459–74.

Bickmeier, Gary (2001), *The Impact of Immigration on Small- to Mid-Sized Iowa Communities*, Ames, IA: Iowa State University Extension.

Boucher, S.R., O. Stark and J.E. Taylor (2005), 'A gain with a drain? Evidence from rural Mexico on the new economics of the brain drain', Davis, CA. http://escholarship.org/uc/item/9p13n1nv (retrieved March 10, 2012).

Burgess, R. and V. Haksar (2005), 'Migration and foreign remittances in the Philippines', International Monetary Fund working paper. www.imf.org/external/pubs/ft/wp/2005/wp05111.pdf.

Caldwell, J.C. and B.K. Caldwell (2006), *Demographic Transition Theory*, Dordrecht: Springer.

Carr, P. and M.J. Kefalas (2009), *Hollowing Out the Middle*, Boston, MA: Beacon Press.

Castles, S. and M.J. Miller (2009), *The Age of Migration, Fourth Edition: International Population Movements in the Modern World*, New York: Guilford Press.

Chami, R., C. Fullenkamp and S. Jajah (2003), *Are Immigrant Remittance Flows a Source of Capital for Development?*, New York: International Monetary Fund.

Chavez, L.R. (2001), *Covering Immigration: Popular Images and the Politics of the Nation*, Berkeley, CA: University of California Press.

Chipeniuk, R. (2004). 'Planning for amenity migration in Canada: current capacities of interior British Columbian mountain communities', *Mountain Research and Development*, 24, 327–35.

Coleman, D. (2006), 'Immigration and ethnic change in low-fertility countries: a third demographic transition', *Population and Development Review*, 32, 401–46.

Cuadros, P. (2006), *A Home on the Field: How One Championship Team Inspires Hope for the Revival of Small Town America*, New York: Harper.

Curtis White, K.J. (2008), 'Population change and farm dependence: temporal and spatial variation in the US Great Plains, 1900–2000', *Demography*, 45, 363–86.

Davis, K. (1945), 'The world demographic transition', *Annals of the American Academy of Political and Social Science*, 237, 1–11.

Delgado-Wise, R. and H. Márquez Covarrubias (2007), 'The reshaping of Mexican labor exports under NAFTA: paradoxes and challenges, *International Migration Review*, 41, 656–79.

Deller, S.C. (1995), Economic impact of retirement migration, *Economic Development Quarterly*, 9, 25–38.

Deller, S.C., D.W. Marcouiller and G.P. Green (1997), 'Recreational housing and local government finance', *Annals of Tourism Research*, 24, 687–705.

Durand, J., W. Kandel, E.A. Parrado and D.S. Massey (1996), 'International migration and development in Mexican Communities', *Demography*, 33, 249–64.

Ellis, B. (2012), 'Oil boom strikes Kansas', *CNN Money*. http://money.cnn.com/2012/05/23/pf/america-boomtown-kansas/index.htm (retrieved July 30, 2012).

Farrant, M., A. MacDonald and D. Sriskandarajah (2006), *Migration and Development: Opportunities and Challenges for Policy Makers*, Geneva: International Organization for Migration.

Fernandez-Kelly, P. and D.S. Massey (2007), 'Borders for whom? the role of NAFTA in Mexico–US migration', *ANNALS of the American Academy of Political and Social Science*, 610, 98–118.

Freudenburg, W.R. (1992), 'Addictive economies: extractive industries and vulnerable localities in a changing world economy', *Rural Sociology*, 57, 305–32.

Galston, W.A. and K.J. Baehler (1995), *Rural Development in the United States: Connecting Theory, Practice, and Possibilities*, Washington, DC: Island Press.

Glasgow, N. and R.J. Reeder (1990), 'Economic and fiscal implications of nonmetropolitan retirement migration', *Journal of Applied Gerontology*, 9, 433–51.

Glytsos, N.P. (2002), 'The role of migrant remittances in development: evidence from Mediterranean countries', *International Migration*, 40, 5–26.

Goe, W.R. and G.P. Green (2005), 'Amenities and change in the well-being of nonmetropolitan localities', in Gary Paul Green, Steven C. Deller and David W. Marcouiller (eds), *Amenities and Rural Development: Theory, Methods and Public Policy*, Cheltenham, UK and Northhampton, MA, USA: Edward Elgar Publishing, pp. 95–112.

Golding, S.A. (2012), 'Rural gentrification in the United States 1970–2000: a demographic analysis of its footprint, impacts, and implications', PhD dissertation, Madison, WI: University of Wisconsin at Madison.

Gosnell, H. and J. Abrams (2009), 'Amenity migration: diverse conceptualizations of drivers, socioeconomic dimensions, and emerging challenges', *GeoJournal*, 76, 303–11.

Gouveia, L., M.A. Carranza and J. Cogua (2005), 'The Great Plains migration: Mexicanos and Latinos in Nebraska', in Victor Zuniga and Hernandez-Leon Ruben (eds), *New Destinations: Mexican Immigration in the United States*, New York: Russell Sage, pp. 23–49.

Grey, M. (1997), 'Secondary labor in the meatpacking industry: demographic change and student mobility in rural Iowa schools', *Journal of Research in Rural Education*, 13, 153–64.

Hammer, R.B. and R.L. Winkler (2006), 'Housing affordability and population change in the Upper Midwestern North Woods', in W.A. Kandel and D.L. Brown (eds), *Population Change and Rural Society*. Dordrecht: Springer, pp. 293–309.

Harrison, J.L. and S.E. Lloyd (2012), 'Illegality at work: deportability and the productive new era of immigration enforcement', *Antipode*, 44, 365–85.

Hettinger, W.S. (2004), *Living and Working in Paradise: Why Housing Is Too Expensive and What Communities Can Do About It*, Windham, CT: Thames River Publishing.

Hing, B.O. (2010), *Ethical Borders: NAFTA, Globalization, and Mexican Migration*, Philadelphia, PA: Temple University Press.

Inter-American Development Bank (IADB) (2004), *Sending Money Home: Remittances to Latin America and the Caribbean*, Washington, DC: Inter-American Development Bank.

Ioffe, G., T. Nefedova and I. Zaslavsky (2004), 'From spatial continuity to fragmentation: the case of Russian farming', *Annals of the Association of American Geographers*, 94, 913–43.

Jones, R.C. (2008), 'Remittances and inequality: a question of migration stage and geographic scale', *Economic Geography*, 74, 8–25.

Kandel, W. and E.A. Parrado (2005), 'Restructuring of the US meat processing industry and new Hispanic migrant destinations', *Population and Development Review*, 31, 447–71.

Keely, C.B. and B.N. Tran (1989), 'Remittances from labor migration: evaluations, performance and implications', *International Migration Review*, 23, 500–525.

Keith, J., C. Fawson, and T. Chang (1996), 'Recreation as an economic development strategy: some evidence from Utah', *Journal of Leisure Research*, 28, 96–107.

Knight, J. (2003), 'Repopulating the village?', in J.W. Traphagan and J. Knight (eds), *Demographic Change and the Family in Japan's Aging Society*, Albany, NY: SUNY Press, 107–24.

Konigsberg, E. (2011), 'Kuwait on the prairie', *New Yorker*, New York. http://www.newyorker.com/reporting/2011/04/25/110425fa_fact_konigsberg (retrieved July 30, 2012).

Lindstrom, D. P. and S.G. Saucedo (2002), 'The short- and long-term effects of US migration experience on Mexican women's fertility', *Social Forces*, 80, 1341–68.

Lu, M. and D.A. Paull (2007), 'Assessing the free land programs for reversing rural depopulation', *Great Plains Research: A Journal of Natural and Social Sciences*. http://digitalcommons.unl.edu/greatplainsresearch/875 (retrieved July 30, 2012).

Massey, D.S., J. Arango, G. Hugo, A. Kouaouci, A. Pellegrino and J.E. Taylor (1998), *Worlds in Motion: Understanding International Migration at the End of the Millenium*, New York: Oxford University Press.

Massey, D.S., J. Durand and J. Malone (2003), *Beyond Smoke and Mirrors: Mexican Immigration in an Era of Economic Integration*, New York: Russell Sage.

Mueller, K.J. (2001), 'Rural health policy: past as a prelude to the future', in S. Loue and B.E. Quill (eds), *Handbook of Rural Health*, New York: Kluwer/Plenum, pp. 1–23.

Müller, D.K. (2007), 'Second homes in the Nordic countries: between common heritage and exclusive commodity', *Scandinavian Journal of Hospitality and Tourism*, 7, 193–201.

Mullins, Dan R. and Mark Rosentraub (1992), 'Migrating dollars? The impact of elders on local resource bases and public expenditures', *Urban Affairs Quarterly*, 30, 337–54.

Nelson, Lise and Peter B. Nelson (2011), 'The global rural: linked migration in the rural USA', *Progress in Human Geography*, 35, 441–59.

Nobles, J. (2011), 'Parenting from abroad: migration, nonresident father involvement, and children's education in Mexico', *Journal of Marriage and Family*, 73, 729–46.

Overvåg, K. (2009), 'Second homes in eastern Norway', Doctoral thesis, Norwegian University of Science and Technology, Trondheim, Norway.

Park, L.S. and D.N. Pellow (2011), *The Slums of Aspen: Immigrants vs. the Environment in America's Eden*, New York: New York University Press.

Passel, J.S. and D. Cohn (2008), *Trends in Unauthorized Immigration: Undocumented Inflow Now Trails Legal Inflow*, Washington, DC: Pew Hispanic Center.

Passel, J.S., D. Cohn and A. Gonzalez-Barrera (2012), *Net Migration from Mexico Falls to Zero – and Perhaps Less*, Washington, DC: Pew Hispanic Center.

Paulson, A., A. Singer, R. Newberger and J. Smith (2006), *Financial Access for Immigrants: Lessons from Diverse Perspectives*, Washington, DC: Brookings Institution.

Peck, J. (1996). *Work-Place: The Social Regulation of Labor Markets*, New York: Guilford Press.

Piore, M.J. (2001), 'The dual labor market: theory and implications', in D.B. Grusky (ed.), *Social Stratification: Class Race and Gender in Sociological Perspective*, Boulder, CO: Westview Press, pp. 435–9.

Potter, J., R. Cantarero, S. Larrick and B. Ramirez-Salazar, B. (2004), 'A case study of the impact of population influx on a small community in Nebraska', *Great Plains Research: A Journal of Natural and Social Sciences*, 14, 219–30.

Ratha, D. and A. Silwal (2012), *Remittance Flows in 2011 – An Update*, Washington, DC: World Bank.

Reeder, R.J. and D.M. Brown (2005), 'Recreation, tourism, and rural well-being', USDA Economic Research Service, Economic Research Report Number 7, Washington, DC: US Department of Agriculture.

Rye, J.F. and J. Andrzejewska (2010), 'The structural disempowerment of Eastern European migrant farm workers in Norwegian agriculture', *Journal of Rural Studies*, 26, 41–51.

Serow, W.J. (2003), 'Economic consequences of retiree concentrations: a review of North American studies', *Gerontologist*, 43, 897–903.

Slesinger, D.P. and S.C. Deller (2002), 'Economic impact of migrant workers on Wisconsin's economy', Working Paper, Madison, WI: University of Wisconsin Center for Demography and Ecology, Madison.

Smith, M.D., R.S. Krannich, and L.M. Hunter (2001), 'Growth, decline, stability, and disruption: a longitudinal analysis of social well-being in four western rural communities', *Rural Sociology*, 66, 425–50.

Taylor, J. Edward and Jorge Mora and Richard H. Adams, Jr. (2005), 'Remittances, inequality and poverty: evidence from rural Mexico', paper presented at the annual meeting of the American Economics Association, Providence, RI.

Traphagan, J.W. and J. Knight (2003), *Demographic Change and the Family in Japan's Aging Society*, Albany, NY: SUNY Press.

United Nations (2011), 'World urbanization prospects'. http://esa.un.org/unpd/wup/Documentation/highlights.htm (retrieved July 30, 2012).

Van Auken, P. (2010), 'Seeing, not participating: viewscape fetishism in American and Norwegian rural amenity areas', *Human Ecology*, 38, 521–37.

Vias, A.C. (1999), 'Jobs follow people in the rural Rocky Mountain West', *Rural Development Perspectives*, 14, 14–23.

Waldinger, R. and M.I. Lichter (2003), *How the Other Half Works: Immigration and the Social Organization of Labor*, Berkeley, CA: University of California Press.

Warnick, R.B. (1996), 'Seasonal homes in Berkshire County, Massachusetts: an exploratory study', *Proceedings of the 1996 Northeastern Recreation Research Symposium*, Radnor, PA: US Department of Agriculture, Forest Service, Northeastern Forest Experiment Station.

Wilkinson, K., R. Reynolds, J. Thompson and L. Ostresh (1982), 'Local social disruption and western energy development', *Pacific Sociological Review*, 25, 275–96.

Winkler, R.L. (2010), 'Rural destinations, uneven development and social exclusion', unpublished PhD dissertation, Madison, WI: University of Wisconsin at Madison.

Winkler, R., C. Cheng, and S. Golding (2011), 'Boom or bust? how migration impacts population composition in different types of natural resource dependent communities in the rural US', in L.J. Kulcsar and K.J. Curtis (eds), *International Handbook of Rural Demography*, New York: Springer, pp. 349–67.

Wood, R.E. (2008), *Survival of Rural America: Small Victories and Bitter Harvests*, Lawrence, KS: University Press of Kansas.

Wright, C. (2006), 'Missing in action – mass male migration and Mexican communities', *Georgetown Journal of International Affairs*, 7, 167–72.

7. Agriculture and rural development
Linda Lobao and Jeff Sharp

INTRODUCTION

The traditional economic base in rural areas globally is agriculture. Not surprisingly, in the minds of both the public and policy makers, the farm sector tends to be viewed as the lead generator of rural development across nations. Policy directed to agriculture has historically been synonymous with rural development policy in the United States (Browne et al. 1992), as well as most other nations (Barrett et al. 2010). In the US case, this sectoral approach to rural development persists even though less than 5 percent of rural Americans live on farms (Lobao and Meyer 2004, p. 14). Researchers have long leveled the criticism that agricultural policy remains the de facto US rural development policy, with the result that rural elites (in other words, farm owners) are the major beneficiaries as opposed to the vast majority of rural people (Browne et al. 1992; Irwin et al. 2010; Lobao and Meyer 2004).

In this chapter, we examine the manner by which agriculture has been studied as a sector generating rural development. By 'agriculture', we refer to and focus on the farm sector of the food and fiber industry. By 'rural development' we refer to a package of indicators of populations' well-being, focusing particularly on socio-economic conditions. By the latter we include standard indicators of economic development as measured by economic performance such as aggregate income and employment; and a broader range of indicators on the distribution of material well-being, such as poverty rates and income inequality. In addition to socio-economic conditions, rural development is also conceptualized via at least two other components: populations' social attributes (health, education, civic society) and the quality of the natural environment (United Nations 2007, p. 145). However, socio-economic conditions are at the core of any conceptualization of rural development. Most research on farming centers on these conditions as outcome indicators and they are key antecedent variables with regard to other outcome indicators.

We examine two research traditions that scrutinize the relationship between agriculture and rural development. The largest and most long-standing focuses on national patterns of agricultural structure, that is, the number and size of farms and organizational structure, and the impacts on an array of socio-economic and other well-being indicators. In the US case, this tradition centers on conventional production agriculture, that is, specialized commodity-based farming such as in cash grains, cotton and animal agriculture produced for national and global markets. Numerous studies address the degree to which conventional agriculture affects rural development. The literature dates from the first half of the twentieth century and systematic reviews are found in Lobao (1990) and Lobao and Stofferhan (2008). The second tradition entails a more recent literature on locally and regionally oriented farms or 'alternative agriculture', a term that distinguishes it from conventional commodity-based farming. This tradition documents the distinct qualities of alternative agricultural enterprises, the social actors participating in them, and their networks of consumption and production. Far less is known empirically about whether and how the alternative agriculture sector impacts development. While in principle analysts have assumed positive impacts on development (Lyson 2004), research is fragmented and largely anecdotal. Over time the promise of alternative agriculture for community development has been increasingly debated (Allen 2010).

FARMING AND RURAL DEVELOPMENT GLOBALLY

Rural areas, their populations and farming systems are diverse globally. Nevertheless, some generalizations about shifts in agricultural structure are relevant for understanding how researchers have conceptualized the relationship between farming and rural development. Two general questions have been posed about farming and rural development: (1) To what extent does farming relative to other economic sectors (and/or net of other conditions) influence development? (2) To what extent do different types of farming (in particular, large-scale industrialized versus smaller-scale farms) have positive or negative impacts on rural development or well-being?

Historically, the number of farms and size of farm populations decline as nations transition to industrial and post-industrial economies. Most nations have experienced the long-term out-migration from rural to urban areas classically noted by Kuznets (1955). This out-migration is fostered by both the pull of growth in urban manufacturing and the push of production agriculture whereby farms become larger, more capital intensive, and oriented toward commercial national or global markets (Barrett et al. 2010).

Globally, farm structure has tended to follow general patterns found in developed nations and exemplified by the United States: larger, fewer, capital-intensive farms increasingly account for the bulk of a nation's agricultural sales and the resident farm labor force shrinks dramatically (Barrett et al. 2010). This is not in any way to say that family farming (defined as family ownership or control over key production factors of land, labor and capital) disappears and is edged out by corporations as the agricultural transition proceeds (Lobao and Meyer 2001). In the United States, 95.1 percent of farms are family-run unincorporated businesses (McDonald 2012). The proportion of non-family-held incorporated farms has grown little over the past several decades (Lobao and Meyer 2001) and stands at 0.4 percent (McDonald 2012). However, globally, farming as an employment sector and generator of family livelihoods and community well-being tends to decline as development progresses. This was seen dramatically in the US where the farm population declined from 34 percent of the population in 1910 to less than 2 percent by the century's end, and particularly after World War II. From 1940 to 1980, the farm population declined tenfold (Lobao and Meyer 2001, p. 108). For US farms today over 90 percent of family income comes from non-farm sources.

With regard to question one, above, the degree of influence that farming itself has on development depends on the manner by which the aforementioned structural changes have occurred in any nation. For developed nations, non-farm manufacturing and service employment will exert a stronger impact on national as well as rural development relative to farming. For developing nations even as recently as the late 1990s, from 75 percent to 35 percent of their populations were employed in agriculture, the least developed nations having the largest share (United Nations 2007, p. 27). For less developed nations the majority (56.8 percent) still lived in rural areas in 2005 (United Nations 2007, p. 11). Farming and rural development is now given most empirical attention in these nations (Barrett et al. 2010).

Question one is connected to the second question: as the agricultural transition proceeds across nations, and the number of farms, farm population and farming itself declines as a livelihood strategy, how does the structure left in its wake affect rural development? Two contrasting views, one grounded in neoclassical economics and the other from sociology and related critical political economy research, can be seen (Lobao and Meyer 2001). The first denotes long-term benefits to rural development and society overall; the second disputes this assumption.

With regard to the first, neoclassical economics view, a nation's aggregate well-being is expected to improve overall and rural and urban areas are expected to converge in development. Deller (2003) builds from Kuznets (1955) to explain the neoclassical view which assumes the mobility of labor and capital is flexible and unproblematic. In the course of development, rural labor is siphoned off to higher-paid manufacturing sectors in urban areas, diminishing its supply in rural areas. Production agriculture also takes hold and farms become larger and industrialized. Over time, the demand for farm labor and wages in the farm sector increase (particularly since farm labor supply has decreased relatively). Rising earnings and employment in the farm sector result in improved rural development overall and a decrease in rural–urban inequality within nations. From this view, then, large-scale farms enhance rural and national development.

By contrast, sociologists and other social scientists dispute the neo-classical economics view. Much of this work builds from Marxian political economy. Numerous studies over decades summarize the political economy view of how the transformation of farming affects rural development (Buttel 2001; Buttel and Newby 1980; Friedland et al. 1991; Lobao 1990; Lobao and Meyer 2001). The nature of capitalism produces farming systems that are inherently uneven in their effects, conferring different costs and benefits across regions, communities and social classes. Market competition, the technological treadmill or need for farmers to continually adopt new capital-intensive technology to compete, and state programs and policies promote the growth of larger and fewer farms. Larger and fewer farms reduce the aggregate farm population and alter the farm and rural community class structure. In contrast to neoclassical assumptions that regional equilibrium will be established and rural areas eventually catch up to urban areas over time, the political economy view sees no such necessary relationship. By contrast, cumulative, uneven development is more likely. Some rural communities suffer long-term out-migration and persistent poverty, never fully recovering. Also, in contrast to neoclassical assumptions about labor mobility, the political economy view sees labor as 'sticky'. Farmers and other labor are not atomistic decision-makers but are embedded in family and community contexts. Household livelihood strategies, off-farm employment, kinship relationships and daily patterns of social life connect people to communities. People may remain rooted in place even though farming is no longer a viable livelihood strategy.

Compounding regional development processes within nations are changes in the global agricultural system. A large literature addresses the development of multinational corporations in agriculture, their control over the world's food supply, and the manner by which they touch down through commodity chains to affect rural communities. McMichael (2012) provides a recent update of this literature. Building from the political economy framework, he explains how the power of capitalist elites, multinational corporations and governments' acquiescence are leading to the development of a neoliberal food regime that unfolds across nations, jeopardizing public well-being.

Overall, from the political economy view, nations are embedded in a global food system whose path of development tends to result in larger and fewer farms, in some sense following the production agricultural systems that have emerged in developed nations. Nations vary in the degree to which this path is manifest. Counter-trends, such those discussed below with alternative agriculture, have also emerged. From the political economy perspective, conventional production agriculture benefits national and global elites along with affluent segments of farm populations. But it tends to be detrimental to rural communities, the public at large and the environment.

In the following section, we summarize the long-standing research that has empirically examined how the structure of production agriculture has influenced rural development and well-being across the United States. We then turn to more recent literature on alternatives to production agriculture and the promise they hold for rural development.

PRODUCTION AGRICULTURE AND RURAL COMMUNITY DEVELOPMENT

Extensive research exists on farm structure and its impacts on community development. This research is usually concerned with three interrelated trends that have occurred as production agriculture has evolved: the decline of the farm population; the relative growth of large, more hired-labor-dependent, 'industrialized' farms; and the relative decline of conventional family farming. We summarize the findings of this literature, building from previous reviews from the case of the United States (Buttel 2001; Lobao 1990; Lobao and Meyer 2001; Lobao and Stofferhan 2008). The first trend, a demographic shift, the decline in farm population, was of foremost concern in the pre-1970s period when US farm decline was most rapid. Fear that widespread rural decline would occur as families left farming generally did not materialize as the nation prospered in the post-World War II era and communities became more industrialized and integrated into the urban economy. Still, some communities in the south and Appalachia appear not to have overcome the past legacies of farm population decline (Wimberley and Morris 1996; Duncan 1999). Other communities in farm-dependent regions of the Midwest and Great Plains declined during the last 1980s farm crisis (Lasely et al. 1995). In the contemporary period, however, farming itself has waned as a causal force in population decline even in the most farm-dependent regions (Salamon 2003).

Most attention to the farm sector centers on structural shifts, the growth of large-scale, hired-labor-dependent industrialized farms and the decline of conventional family farming. Research addressing these structural shifts references either or both; they are treated as opposite sides of the same social problem – the growth of inequality in the farm sector. US farming has long been described as a dualistic system, composed of a few large farms with ever-expanding market shares of agricultural products, and many small farms. Moderate-sized farms are increasingly squeezed out of this system (Buttel 2001).

Past research thus mainly frames the production agriculture and community impacts in terms of large-scale, industrialized farms versus family farming (in other words, essentially treating together small and moderate-scale farms). This framing originates from the pioneering research of Walter Goldschmidt (1978). In the 1940s, he conducted a comparative case study of two California towns: Arvin, a community dominated by large farms, and Dinuba, a family farming community. Goldschmidt found poorer conditions in Arvin: a smaller middle class, lower family incomes, poorer public services and less civic participation. Goldschmidt argued that the scale of farming affected farm and local stratification patterns and community well-being overall. Controversy ensued after Goldschmidt published a US Department of Agriculture (USDA) report. Large farmers became angry over the findings and staged burnings of Goldschmidt's report along with Steinbeck's *Grapes of Wrath*. This contributed to the neglect of social science research on industrialized farms for over 30 years. With the development of the sociology of agriculture as a research field in the 1970s, numerous scholars turned to testing the 'Goldschmidt hypothesis' about the detrimental community effects of industrialized farms.

By and large, as past research has framed the rural development–production agriculture debate as large, industrialized farms versus family farms (moderate and small farms), we frame our overview through that lens as well. Numerous studies spanning the 1930s onward have addressed the differential impacts of large versus small farms. We denote conceptual issues including research gaps raised by these studies, then turn to a summary of findings. An elaboration of these points is provided in Lobao (1990), Lobao and Meyer (2001) and Lobao and Stofferhan (2008).

Conceptual Issues and Research Gaps across Studies

Over the decades, the large literature on the impacts of farming on rural development has become increasingly systematized into an overarching series of research protocols. There are customary conceptualizations of farm structure, research designs, units of analyses and outcome measures. While this gives some uniformity to the literature, it also results in some gaps.

Conceptualizing and measuring farm structure
To study the impacts of farming, analysts most commonly use measures of scale, with scale usually measured by sales and less frequently acreage (which varies more by commodity). The actual dollar amount of sales will

vary over time and data source. USDA, for example, sees farms grossing less than $250 000 per year as small farms, unable to support families through farming alone; they make up 88 percent of all US farms and account for about 16 percent of US agricultural sales (Hoppe and Banker 2010, p. v). Sales are usually assumed to coincide with other measures of farm organization and are used as a proxy measure of these organizational features. But as a measure, scale is limited because: (1) the degree to which sales and organizational features (see below) coincide remains an open empirical question; (2) family-owned and operated farms are increasingly large scale owing to technology; (3) scale alone cannot capture organizational factors that social scientists hypothesize might adversely affect communities. These organizational features include: absentee ownership; use of hired labor; vertical integration of corporations into farming such as through contract farming arrangements; and legal status as a family farm versus non-family-held corporations. These organizational measures are also used in studies but scale tends to be the common denominator variable across studies.

A current research gap is the manner in which scale indicators along with organizational attributes of farming coincide, and how they might provide insight into national and regional patterns of farm structure. Past research devoted attention to this question in attempting to understand complexity in patterns of production agriculture structure (Wimberley 1987). But over the years, this question has waned and scale seems to be a continued proxy. In keeping with the large-versus-small farm debate, sales have also been assumed to simply be related in linear fashion to community well-being.

Although researchers generally frame the rural development debate as large versus small or 'family' farming, some past research has grappled with the variations within the family farming sector and their impacts on community development. Researchers traditionally conceptualized family farming as moderate-sized farms where operators owned or controlled land, labor and capital; employed little hired labor; and family livelihood came largely from farming. From the political economy literature, small, part-time operations have been conceptualized as 'semi-proletarianized' operations and in a manner different from conventional moderate-sized 'family farming', which is conceptualized as classic petit bourgeois businesses. Lobao (1990) provides a discussion of these differences and demonstrates that community dependence on moderate-sized versus part-time operations indeed had different outcomes for community well-being during her historical period of study, 1970–1980. The former were related to higher median family income, lower poverty and lower income inequality across US counties, and the latter were related to poorer conditions along the same indicators. It should be noted that Lobao (1990) was examining the tail of the agricultural transition, when small, marginal farms were in rapid decline largely owing to competitive disadvantages from the technological tread-mill, the escalating need for costly, capital-intensive technologies. Whether differences between moderate-sized and smaller farms in rural development impacts remain today is unclear. With the development of alternative agriculture whereby small farms increasingly produce commodities for niche markets, this relationship is likely to have shifted.

In sum, there is a pressing need to revisit long-standing conceptual and methodological questions. How should we conceptualize and measure the structure of contemporary production agriculture? More broadly, what types of farming patterns characterize regions and communities? How have these patterns changed over time, and with what impact? Attention needs to be given to multiple indicator measures of farm structure, understanding variations within small- and moderate-scale farming, and documenting the degree to which farming across US regions and communities is shifting from traditional production agriculture to newer alternative agriculture.

Conceptualizing rural development outcomes and mechanisms by which farming affects them

In a meta-analysis of past research, Lobao and Stofferhan (2008) classify outcomes typically studied into three types. Socio-economic well-being is most frequently studied; typical indicators are standard measures of economic performance such as employment growth, income levels and growth, and broader distributional conditions (poverty rates and income inequality). Community social fabric refers to social organizational features that reflect community stability and quality of social life. Indicators include population change, social disruption indicators (for example, crime rates, births-to-teenagers, social-psychological stress, community conflict and interference with enjoyment of property), educational attainments and schooling quality, health status and civic participation (for example, voluntary organizations and voting). Environmental indicators include quality of water, soil and air, and health-related conditions. Most focus is on socio-economic well-being, partly because measures are widely available and because these indicators are also linked to other social fabric and environment outcomes.

The mechanisms or paths by which farming affects the aforementioned outcomes are another research gap. For the most part these mechanisms, if discussed at all, are schematic and vague. Few studies explore or even denote the many direct and indirect paths by which farming affects communities, but rather assume these paths exist and will be manifest in turn with positive or negative outcomes. While potential for long-term versus shorter-term impacts may be noted, the time periods at which these should be manifest are rarely discussed. This gap varies by study design with case studies better able to trace these mechanisms. But overall the issue is complex. Lobao and Stofferhan (2008) provide some example of the complexity that needs to be considered. Farming directly influences community well-being: through the quantity and quality (for example, earnings) of jobs produced; by the extent to which farms purchase inputs and sell outputs locally; by affecting the quality of local environmental conditions; and by affecting local decision making about economic development and other public-policy areas. Numerous indirect effects should also occur. First-order, indirect effects on local economic performance and well-being occur because the quantity and quality of jobs plus purchases affect total community employment, earnings and income (for example, economic multiplier effects), the local poverty rate and income inequality. First-order, indirect effects on the local social fabric occur because the jobs created by local farms affect community population size and class composition. Second-order, indirect effects on local social fabric work through the first-order effects above. Population size and social class composition are related to indicators of community social disruption (for example, crime, family instability, the high school dropout rate), local demand for schooling and other public services, and the property tax base and fiscal conditions of local government.

Common research designs: strengths and limitations
To study the impacts of farming and rural development, analysts typically focus on the community as a unit of analysis. In general, two study designs – case studies and quantitative studies across many communities – are used most frequently, and each has different strengths and limitations.

Case study designs provide in-depth analysis of the impacts of farming. Usually, a comparative case study design is implemented whereby a community (or communities) characterized by industrialized farming is contrasted with one characterized by smaller farms. Typical 'community' units of analyses are counties – important in rural areas because they function most like labor markets – or subcounty areas such as cities and towns with their hinterlands. Communities are usually matched on background attributes such as non-farm economy and farm dependence. An example is Goldschmidt's (1978) classic study; for others see Lobao and Stofferhan (2008).

The strengths and limitations of case studies are well known. Detailed analysis of farm structure and different sets of impacts over time are strengths, but generalizability and ability to control for extraneous causal factors open up case studies for potential criticism. Even Goldschmidt's study, which has endured over time and predicted fairly accurately future outcomes in Arvin, has been subjected to extensive methodological critique

(Lobao 1990, p. 65–6). But the problem looming largest is that existing case studies are highly uneven in their quality and scope of assessing impacts of farming.

Quantitative multivariate studies across communities entail statistical analysis to document relationships found in many communities across the US. Secondary data such as from the Census of Agriculture, Census of Population and other sources are usually used. Counties are the most common unit of analysis. To assess the consequences of industrialized farming, analysts usually compare its effects relative to other farming using scale (for example, proportion of sales in farms of different sizes) or organizational measures (for example, the proportion of owner-operated farms). Multivariate statistical techniques, such as regression analyses, are used so that the effects of farm structure are assessed net of other community conditions. Numerous examples exist and include Crowley and Roscigno (2004), Lobao (1990) and Lyson et al. (2001). Strengths of these studies include their ability to produce results for empirical relationships that are generalizable across many communities and/or the nation, and a variety of outcome indicators, though most focus on socio-economic conditions. Quantitative studies usually depend on secondary data which constrains measures and time periods of study.

Existing quantitative studies have also a number of gaps. Nearly all are based on data prior to the 2000 period and need serious updating in terms of conceptualizing farm structure and in assessing whether outcomes vary from the past. Updating is also needed, with two key conceptual problems that regional researchers now recognize affect analyses using population aggregates, spatial dependence and endogeneity. With regard to spatial dependence, socio-economic outcomes in any single community are likely to be linked to socio-economic and other conditions in nearby communities. Hence, in multivariate regression models, there are theoretical reasons to account for spatial dependence in the residual and dependent variable, as well as spillovers in control variables. Endogeneity refers to the classic problem of determining causality: farm structure and well-being are likely to be jointly determined – that is, farming may affect growth and poverty, and vice versa. Strategies that have now become prominent in the regional science literature to deal with spatial dependence and endogeneity (see Irwin et al. 2010) need to be integrated into future research.

Other designs are also used to study the impacts of farming. Sociologists have used surveys of farm households and/or community residents to assess whether living near or working on a large versus a family farm has varying effects on socio-economic well-being and community social fabric measures. An example is Lasely et al. (1995). Economists use two other designs:

input–output analysis and hedonic price modeling. The former was classically established to study the large–small farm debate with the work of Heady and Sonka (1974). It provides detail about economic performance such as projected estimates for the total number of jobs and income produced in a region based on its farming system. But noted limitations are that models involve assumptions about relationships from past years and different places that may be less applicable to the community at hand. Hedonic price models are often used to study the impacts of large-scale confined animal feeding operations (CAFOs) on local real-estate markets; in general, home values fall the closer they are located to CAFOs.

Farming and Rural Development: General Findings

Systematic summaries of research findings from the literature on farming on communities dating from the 1930s onward are provided in Lobao (1990) with a more recent update in Lobao and Stofferhan (2008). The latter study notes four generations of research that have investigated the effects of farming starting prior to Goldschmidt's study, moving to quantitative studies beginning in the 1970s, revisionary work that continues, and recent studies giving particular attention to CAFOs. Out of the total 56 studies analyzed by Lobao and Stofferhan (2008), the authors report largely detrimental impacts with regard to large-scale, industrial farms in 82 percent (32) of the studies, some detrimental impacts in 14, and no evidence of detrimental impacts in 10. Such relative consistency in findings continues to lead to the working hypothesis that industrialized farming jeopardizes communities. For the studies where social scientists reported predominantly detrimental impacts, these occurred across study designs and time periods. Detrimental impacts are found across different measures of socio-economic, social fabric and environmental well-being, for both farm scale and organizational indicators, and throughout regions of the country. Negative outcomes for local social fabric indicators were more likely to be reported by case studies that focus more on these types of indicators and also in studies of CAFO communities. Residents located closer to CAFOs often see their ability to enjoy their property deteriorate; younger and mid-sized producers face restricted access to markets; and community conflict tends to increase as residents become divided by the costs and benefits of these operations.

Nevertheless, research also provides evidence of mixed or trade-off effects. These occur particularly with studies finding that large farms increase total community income but reduce farm employment overall and increase income inequality.

There also is some evidence that recent studies tend to find less negative impact of large-scale farming. Lobao and Stofferhan (2008) note that this could, in part, be due to government policy pertaining to both the farm and non-farm rural economy, including regulation of corporate farming and income transfer programs for the disadvantaged. It could also be due to more robust methodology, particularly in the case of quantitative studies. As more robust methods of controlling for external community conditions are employed, farming's effects might be more likely to dissipate.

Production Agriculture and Rural Development Policy

Researchers have long questioned the degree to which agricultural policy can be a mechanism for improving rural development. For developing nations, this work often denotes the positive role that appropriate agricultural policy can play in improving economic performance and alleviating rural poverty (Barrett et al. 2010). By contrast, in the United States, social scientists stress the limits and problems with farm programs, particularly those earmarked for conventional commodities such as cash grains and cotton (Browne et al. 1992; Irwin et al. 2010; Lobao and Meyer 2001; Winders 2009). While 61 percent of farmers receive no government payments, for those that do, the largest farmers reap greater benefits, even though payments are capped for the largest farms (Hoppe and Banker 2010). Researchers charge farm programs with contributing to rising land values and reducing the risks of farming, which over time promotes the growth of larger and fewer farms (Brown et al. 1992), a trend demonstrated in much of the literature above that appears to harm rural well-being. Farm programs tend to subsidize rural elites, farmers and other property owners, as opposed to the mass of rural people (Brown et al. 1992). Farm households overall have higher median incomes than US non-farm households, and farm-dependent counties fare well nationally in terms of economic development indicators (Irwin et al. 2010, pp. 531–2). Though clamor for change is voiced every time a new farm bill is introduced, Democrats and Republicans have both balked historically at cutting back on government aid to farmers (Lobao and Meyer 2001).

Researchers note that non-farm programs tailored to local populations are far more effective than farm programs if the goal is to stimulate rural development. By the twenty-first century about 1 percent of the US population lived on farms, only 6 percent of rural employment was in farming and only 20 percent of non-metropolitan counties are classified as farming dependent by USDA (Irwin et al. 2010, pp. 523–4). Policies that could be tailored to specific rural populations include investments in local human capital via education, job training, skills upgrading, and entrepreneurship and community-wide infrastructure. Federal income transfer and other programs are also important for improving the lives of less affluent people across the board irrespective of place (Irwin et al. 2010).

In sum, researchers conclude that programs directed to production agriculture have limited or even counterproductive effects on rural development (Browne et al. 1992; Irwin et al. 2010). Given the long-standing concern that production agriculture and farm policies are limited at best in improving well-being, does alternative agriculture hold more promise? We turn to that issue.

ALTERNATIVE AGRICULTURE AND RURAL DEVELOPMENT

As the industrialization of farming has progressed, resulting in an expansive agricultural landscape populated by fewer farmers, larger fields, and large-scale production facilities and equipment, a counter trend has gained steam that seeks to support small and medium-scale farms to assure their continued viability. We refer to this counter trend as the development of an alternative agricultural system, to contrast it with production agriculture described above. Most research on alternative agriculture focuses on its emergence, characteristics and enterprise sustainability. In this sense, the causal relationship mainly explored is the manner by which rural development context affects farm survival, essentially the reverse relationship explored in the classic Goldschmidt literature that centers on how farming affects rural development. Deller (2012) notes that little rigorous research exists on whether an alternative agriculture system composed of smaller farms aimed at local and regional markets affects local development as measured by socio-economic and other well-being indicators.

Our discussion below addresses three issues: the reasons why alternative agriculture is increasingly viewed as a strategy for improving public well-being; the contexts where alternative agriculture is most likely to thrive, specifically in communities at the urban–rural interface; and the importance of developing mid-scale value chains to support moderate-sized and small farmers producing commodities of all types.

The Promise of Alternative Agriculture in Promoting Local Well-being

Public support for local farming and artisanal food has been stimulated by a variety of popular books (Kingsolver 2008; Pollan 2009) and magazines (such as the *Edible* series published in many US cities), although small- and medium-scale farm development has long been touted as an important public need for decades (for the lay audience, see Hightower 1972, and Berry 1977; for scholars see Buttel et al. 1990). Proponents of local food system development speak to its potential to better meet the economic needs of small- and medium-scale agricultural producers while improving consumer access to food of the quality they desire (Allen 2004; Hinrichs and Lyson 2008). Alternative and more sustainable production systems (National Research Council 2010) and a focus on regional production serving local markets are touted as alternative developments distinct from the industrial commodity system (Allen 2004; Feenstra 1997; Gale 1997).

There are a number of policy and economic arguments in support of local and urban agricultural development. Some of the earliest claims arose from a concern about the demise of family farming and rural communities in the face of agricultural industrialization (Feenstra 1997; Gale 1997). As discussed below, the rural–urban interface is a context where local and urban-oriented food system development has garnered considerable attention in hopes of improving farm profitability and reducing the loss of farmland to non-farm development (Lockeretz 1987; Lyson et al. 1999). The goals of preserving urban-edge agriculture and/or medium-scale farms persist today (Jussaume and Kondoh 2008; Lyson et al. 2008). Achieving regional food security or improving healthy food access through alternative agricultural development are also touted (Allen 2004; Hamm 2008). And with the recent economic downturn, alternative food system development has also garnered new attention from community development professionals and business entrepreneurs seeking ways to generate new economic activity via the production, processing, distribution and retailing of local foods.

Although historically many efforts to support medium-scale farm prosperity originated at the federal level from the US Department of Agriculture, there is an increasing focus on strategies and development activities that originate at the local level. Of course, rural development professionals over the years have attended to the potential for endogenous or community self-development (Flora et al. 1991; van der Ploeg and Long 1994), but in many rural communities, agriculture has been an important but overlooked or taken-for-granted sector of the local economy. Lyson (2007, p. 29) argues that 'it is time to put agriculture and food on the political agendas of local communities', further observing that 'local agriculture and food businesses need the same access to economic development resources – such as grants, tax incentives, and loans – as nonfarm-related business' (p. 30). There are a number of reasons why agriculture may be overlooked as a developable asset. One is the persistence of an agricultural exceptionalism that suggested agriculture was different from the rest of the economy and best governed by its own institutional structures that are not necessarily central to the community. In our own research, the fact that economic development organizations and chambers of commerce, in both rural and urban areas, often refer us to the Farm Bureau and County Extension when we seek information about agricultural-related economic development activity is indicative of how agriculture has maintained its distinctiveness.

But that exceptionalism appears to be changing. For instance, in response to public interest in issues of health, food access and quality, the formation of local food policy councils is increasingly being called for in policy circles. Food policy councils are governmental or quasi-governmental entities that can serve a variety of functions, including: developing policy recommendations for governments to promote access to healthy food, local food production and local land-use planning; facilitating discussion and communication about critical food system issues among public and private sector actors; and overseeing projects that improve local food systems (Clancy et al. 2008). Sharp et al. (2011) found that food policy councils and local committees to promote agricultural economic development were associated with positive assessments of farm viability and the future of local agriculture. The logic underlying such local councils and their effectiveness is drawn from classic community development theory, which anticipates collective action processes that engage a diversity of local stakeholders as an important step in creating the conditions for successful development (Christensen 1989; Flora and Flora 1993; Wilkinson 1972).

At the programmatic level, there is proliferation of all kinds of development activity initiated by various combinations of farmers, consumers and local government agencies that seek to realize a variety of particular interest goals, ranging from improved farm profitability (for farmers), improved food security (to meet health and social justice needs) and improved food quality (for discriminating consumers). Lyson (2004, p. 84–5) characterizes many of these activities as 'civic' agriculture, arguing that 'communities that nurture local systems of agricultural production and food distribution as one part of a broader plan of economic development may gain greater control over their economic destinies, enhance the level of social capital among their residents, and contribute to rising levels of civic welfare and socio-economic well-being'. The development of community supported agriculture (CSA) arrangements that link farmers with consumers in a mutually rewarding fashion where risk is shared among the community, farmers' markets, produce auctions, farm-to-school and farm-to-restaurant activities, and development of community gardens are all examples of civic agricultural development. These activities tie local farmers more closely to the community and create new outlets for farmers to sell their production at a premium and ultimately achieve higher profitability. Barriers to these activities can exist (such as where to locate a farmers' market or community garden or health and quality assurance needs), and this is where the development of food policy councils and guidance of community development and planners is useful.

The local food system movement and consumer trends create new opportunities for small and medium-scale farmers, particularly those located in proximity to large urban markets. We turn our attention to how the rural development context supports farming as an economic activity in such areas.

Agriculture in the Context of the Rural–Urban Interface

The linkage between rural development and agriculture likely evokes images of rural small towns surrounded by large farms engaged in specialized production of one or two commodities. But a substantial amount of US agricultural production occurs in less remote rural places (Jackson-Smith and Sharp 2008; Thomas and Howell 2003), or what is termed the rural–urban interface (RUI). A comprehensive report on urban-oriented agriculture found that just under half of total US agricultural crop sales, 79 percent of fruit production and 68 percent of vegetable production originated in metropolitan counties in 1997 (Butler and Maronek 2002); in 2007, production in RUI counties with relatively vibrant agricultural sectors accounted for 41 percent of total US agricultural sales (Jackson-Smith and Sharp 2008).

While the presence of substantial agricultural production at the RUI may not be fully appreciated by social scientists and policy makers, the location of particularly higher-value and perishable types of agricultural production in these zones was long recognized by geographers. Perhaps the most widely known model of agriculture at the RUI was developed by the nineteenth-century geographer Von Thünen, who described how the type of farming would vary by its proximity to the urban edge according to the ease or difficulty of transporting the particular commodity to nearby urban markets (Nelson 1999; Sinclair 1967). Fragile and perishable commodities, such as fruits and berries, or other difficult-to-transport commodities, would locate nearest the urban edge; while easily transported goods, such as livestock, would locate at further distances from urban centers.

Due to substantial transportation and technological improvements during the twentieth century, Sinclair (1967) proposed a revised model that was less attentive to the influence of transportation and perishability, but rather recognized competition for land by both urban and rural interests as a key factor in increasing land rents and prices, and resulting in a need for more intensive production (such as vegetables and fruits that generate higher returns per acre) being located at the urban edge. Meanwhile, less intense and more land-extensive commodities, such as feed grains and pastures, would be more common in areas without significant urban competition. One implication of this theoretical view is an expectation of a farm sector that dynamically responds as urbanization pressures build up and as the zone of urban-influenced land expands. Hart (1991) likens this spatial expansion of the urban-influenced zone to a 'perimetropolitan bow wave' wherein the influence of urban growth precedes the visible arrival of new houses and population.

The RUI context creates unique development needs that warrant attention by rural development specialists. For example, our own work has focused on the adaptive response of farmers to increased land rents and challenges of farming amidst many non-farm neighbors (Inwood and Sharp 2012; Sharp and Smith 2003). One of the development needs identified is the importance of building social capital or networks of communication and familiarity among farmers and their non-farm neighbors. Individual farmers who build these relationships experience less conflict with neighbors over farming practices; they also create generalized benefit to local agriculture overall as non-farmers acquainted with farmers express greater support for farm development in the community (Sharp and Smith 2003). The practical implication of these findings is to denote the importance of purposive efforts to bring farmers and non-farmers together to generate social capital. Such action can be undertaken by individual farmers, but community-level efforts that bring diverse local interests together are also warranted.

A second development need concerns the intergenerational transmission of farming as an occupation. At the RUI, farmers face increased competition for land, which raises land costs and makes expansion of operations more difficult. This becomes particularly problematic as incorporating the next-generation farmer into a family farm operation often requires a period of farm growth to accommodate the needs of two generations (an older and younger farmer) during the succession process. We identify several strategies that RUI farmers adopt, including activities that intensify farm production on existing land, and developing complementary farm businesses, such as a retail or agritainment activity (Inwood and Sharp 2012). The implication for development policy and practice is the need for assistance in helping farmers improve their productivity and/or for the creation of new economic opportunities in the community that allow farmers to sell their product (perhaps at a premium) or add value to their product.

Value Chain Development among Small and Moderate Producers

A different approach to agricultural development that focuses less on developing markets for direct sales to consumers and less on building community capacity is the creation of mid-scale food value chains (Stevenson et al. 2011). Conceptually, this work is sensitive to the problem that many medium-scale farms within the current structure of agriculture are too big to direct-market their entire production directly to consumers but also too small to be economically competitive in industrial commodity chains. The value chain strategy seeks to link medium-scale farms and other food enterprises together in strategic alliances capable of delivering larger volumes of high-quality food to regional and multistate markets. A key element of this approach is to capitalize on the volume and quality that medium-scale farms can deliver in partnership with complementary firms. An important value associated with this sort of development is an equitable distribution of the profits among the value chain partners.

In theory, the mid-scale value chain may make strategic sense in terms of providing an outlet for medium-scale farm production and a better return to production as profits are more equitably spread across the value chain. In practice, many challenges exist, including the basic logistics of how to coordinate and manage value chains, how to effectively market or differentiate products from others in the marketplace, and how to finance their formation (Stevenson et al. 2011). Bloom and Hinrichs (2011) also note the difficulties for firms accustomed to competing with each other now learning to work together in a value chain. These challenges will vary by regional context. In Ohio, we found a surprisingly large number of mid-scale distributors who were well positioned and motivated to explore strategic alliances with medium-scale producers capable of providing sufficient volume of high-quality product (Clark et al. 2011).

In Summary: Alternative Agriculture and Rural Well-being

Research on alternative agriculture tends to center on the development context that supports it, rather than its direct impacts on rural development or well-being. When well-being is analyzed, focus is mainly on individuals participating as consumers and producers, and measured by survey data. Subjective well-being indicators, particularly social–psychological measures and behavioral indicators of networks and community participation, are often used. Generalizing upward from the existing research to infer something about improvements in rural development is problematic. Causality is also not clear: communities supporting alternative agriculture are likely to support a large package of other benefits that together are tauto-logical such as high social capital, low inequality and better-quality non-farm businesses. For example, New England as a region ranks high in alternative agriculture and virtually all socio-economic indicators (Deller 2012).

A few studies have sought a more generalizable view of the effects of alternative agriculture on communities. Lyson et al. (2001) examines the proportion of small-scale farms (a measure of 'civic agriculture') and finds they are related to better socio-economic well-being. The study is a variant of the Goldschmidt tradition and it does not pick up indicators of alternative agricultural production per se. Nevertheless it does suggest that smaller-scale production may have become more beneficial to communities over time, following expectations from the civic-agriculture thesis.

Deller (2012) has produced one of the most robust and nationally generalizable studies. He creates a local food index composed of Census of Agriculture measures of farms (sales less than $25 000; production in vegetables, fruits and specialty meats; and sales volume of direct sales to consumers). The use of this index strategy is similar to traditional indexes that sociologists have created to examine production agriculture (Wimber-ley 1987). Using county-level data over 2000–2007, he finds higher levels of the local food index are associated with greater population growth, but lower rates of per capita income growth and no significant effect on employment growth. Deller (2012) concludes that currently, promotion of local foods is not a viable rural economic development strategy for most places. For a more localized farm system to contribute to rural development, he notes that farm profitability must be the first concern.

In addition to Deller's (2012) empirical study, others have leveled general critiques about the potential of alternative agriculture. A growing line of research is concerned with social justice in the local food sector. Research-ers extend some of the earlier political economy arguments forward. In a capitalist society, stratification or inequality in the costs and benefits of any form of economic production, including alternative agriculture, will exist across regions, communities and social groups (Allen 2010).

CONCLUSION

By and large, past research stresses the limits of agriculture in generating rural development globally as nations move toward industrial and post-industrial economies. In the US case, extensive research has addressed the production agricultural system that has emerged, and the costs and benefits for communities of moving toward larger and fewer farms. Far less research has examined directly the potential of an alternative farming system for rural development and much speculation remains. In providing an overview of the two research traditions on farming and rural development, we have delineated strengths, limitations and continuing gaps in both.

To move both literatures forward, greater dialogue between those working within each tradition is needed. Research dealing with production agriculture and national patterns has tended to fall by the wayside (at least in sociology) as attention has turned to alternative agriculture. The former body of work is in serious need of updating. Attention to alternative forms of agriculture and how they coincide and relate to traditional patterns of commodity production is needed.

For the study of local food systems and alternative agriculture more generally, the research is not as mature. The quality of existing research could be improved by drawing from the production agriculture literature that has long detailed conceptual, measurement and research design issues that need to be considered in studying farm impacts. Further, decades of findings from the production agriculture literature should be a caution to those studying alternative agricultural enterprises. Under capitalism, and especially in the present neoliberal era, the degree to which small producers can contribute to rural development and social justice in the food sector remains questionable.

In both traditions, and especially in alternative agriculture literature, continuing gaps remain. These include the need to improve conceptualization and measurement of farm structure and consideration of an array of community well-being outcomes. The paths by which farming affects communities are not well studied. Attention to assessing the direct and indirect paths of influence and to longer-term as well as shorter-term impacts is needed. Recognition that the impacts of farming vary by social groups within the community should be a working assumption. Research designs have different strengths and limitations, indicating that multi-method approaches are particularly useful. Finally, questions about causality will continue to be a barrier. Unless more serious efforts are made, it will be difficult to tout the benefits of one form of production over another.

In terms of policy, dialogue is also important. In the production agriculture literature, most focus has been at the federal level and on national policy. In the alternative agriculture literature, as commodities are not covered by traditional farm programs, more attention has been given to subnational governments' (state and local) policies and programs, including local zoning and planning, and to non-governmental and locally indigenous self-development efforts. Yet to study the effects of farming on rural development, attention to the role of federal, subnational and non-governmental efforts are needed.

Lastly, the world is changing quickly. Unanticipated global financial shocks, climate change, drought and other extreme weather events, continuing dependence on fossil fuels along with neoliberal globalization affect both farming and rural well-being. Whether or not an alternative food system might more strongly emerge under such conditions, and the promises it might hold for rural development, still remain to be seen.

REFERENCES

Allen, Patricia (2004), *Together at the Table: Sustainability and Sustenance in the American Agrifood System*, University Park, PA: Pennsylvania State University Press.

Allen, Patricia (2010), 'Realizing justice in local food systems', *Cambridge Journal of Regions, Economy, and Society*, 3, 295–308.

Barrett, Christopher B., Michael R. Carter and C. Peter Timmer (2010), 'A century-long perspective on agricultural development', *American Journal of Agricultural Economics*, 92, 522–33.

Berry, Wendell (1977), *The Unsettling of America: Culture and Agriculture*, San Francisco, CA: Sierra Club Books.

Bloom, J. Dara and C. Clare Hinrichs (2011), 'Moving local food through conventional food system infrastructure: value chains framework, comparisons and insights', *Renewable Agriculture and Food Systems*, 26, 13–23.

Browne, William P., Jerry R. Skees, Louis E. Swanson, Paul B. Thompson and Laurian J. Unnevehr (1992), *Sacred Cows and Hot Potatoes: Agrarian Myths in Agricultural Policy*, Boulder, CO: Westview Press.

Butler, Lorna M. and Dale M. Maronek (2002), *Urban and Agricultural Communities: Opportunities for Common Ground*, CAST Task Force Report No. 138, Ames, IA: Council on Agricultural Science and Technology.

Buttel, Frederick (2001), 'Some reflections on late twentieth century agrarian political economy', *Sociologia Ruralis*, 41, 165–81.

Buttel, Frederick H. and Howard Newby (eds) (1980), *The Rural Sociology of Advanced Societies*, Montclair, NJ: Allanheld Osmun.

Buttel, Frederick H., Olaf F. Larson and Gilbert W. Gillespie Jr (1990), *The Sociology of Agriculture*, Westport, CT: Greenwood Press.

Christensen, James A. (1989), 'Themes of community development', in James A. Christensen and Jerry W. Robinson Jr (eds), *Community Development in Perspective*, Ames, IA: Iowa State University Press, pp. 26–47.

Clancy, Kate, Janet Hammer and Debra Lippoldt (2008), 'Food policy councils: past, present and future', in C. Clare Hinrichs and Thomas A. Lyson (eds), *Remaking the North American Food System*, Lincoln, NE: University of Nebraska Press, pp. 121–43.

Clark, Jill K., Shoshanah Inwood and Jeff S. Sharp (2011), 'Scaling-up connections between regional Ohio specialty crop producers and local markets: distribution as the missing link', Columbus, OH: Department of Agricultural, Environmental and Development Economics. http://cffpi.osu.edu/docs/Scaling_Up.pdf.

Crowley, Martha L. and Vincent J. Roscigno (2004), 'Farm concentration, political economic process and stratification: the case of the North Central US', *Journal of Political and Military Sociology*, 31, 133–55.

Deller, Steve (2012), 'Local foods and rural economic growth', paper presented at the American Applied Economics Association, Seattle, WA.

Duncan, Cynthia M. (1999), *Worlds Apart: Why Poverty Persists in Rural America*, New Haven, CT: Yale University Press.

Feenstra, Gail (1997), 'Local food systems and sustainable communities', *American Journal of Alternative Agriculture*, 12, 28–36.

Flora, Cornelia B. and Jan L. Flora (1993), 'Entrepreneurial social infrastructure: a necessary ingredient', *Annals of the Academy of Social and Political Sciences*, 529, 48–58.

Flora, Jan L., James J. Chriss, Eddie Gale, Gary P. Green, Frederick E. Schmidt and Cornelia Flora (1991), *From the Grassroots: Profiles of 103 Rural Self-Development Projects*, Agriculture and Rural Economy Division, Economic Research Service, Staff Report No. 9123, Washington, DC: US Department of Agriculture.

Friedland, William H., Amy E. Barton and Robert J. Thomas (1991), *Manufacturing Green Gold*, Cambridge: Cambridge University Press.

Gale, Fred (1997), 'Direct farm marketing as a rural development tool', *Rural Development Perspectives*, 1, 19–25.

Goldschmidt, Walter (1978), *As You Sow: Three Studies in the Social Consequences of Agribusiness*, Montclair, NJ: Allanheld, Osmun & Company.

Hamm, Michael W. (2008), 'Localization in a global context: invigorating local communities in Michigan through the food system', in C. Clare Hinrichs and Thomas A. Lyson (eds), *Remaking the North American Food System*, Lincoln, NE: University of Nebraska Press, pp. 216–34.

Hart, John F. (1991), 'The perimetropolitan bow wave', *Geographical Review*, 81, 35–52.

Heady, Earl O. and Steven T. Sonka (1974), 'Farm size, rural community income, and consumer welfare', *American Journal of Agricultural Economics*, 56, 534–42.

Hightower, Jim (1972), *Hard Tomatoes, Hard Times*, Washington, DC: Agribusiness Accountability Project.

Hinrichs, C. Clare and Thomas A. Lyson (eds) (2008), *Remaking the North American Food System: Strategies for Sustainability*, Lincoln, NE: University of Nebraska Press.

Hoppe, Robert and David Banker (2010), *Structure and Finances of US Farms: Family Farm Report, 2010 Edition*, Economic Research Service Bulletin No. EIB-66, Washington, DC: US Department of Agriculture.

Inwood, Shoshanah M. and Jeff S. Sharp (2012), 'Farm persistence and adaptation at the rural–urban interface: succession and farm adjustment', *Journal of Rural Studies*, 28, 107–17.

Irwin, Elena, Andrew M. Isserman, Maureen Kilkenny and Mark D. Partridge (2010), 'A century of research on rural development and agricultural issues', *American Journal of Agricultural Economics*, 92, 522–33.

Jackson-Smith, Douglas and Jeff Sharp (2008), 'Farming in the urban shadow: supporting agriculture at the rural–urban interface', *Rural Realities*, 2, 1–12.

Jussaume, Raymond A. Jr. and Kazumi Kondoh (2008), 'Possibilities for revitalizing local agriculture: evidence from four counties in Washington State', in Wynne Wright and Gerard Middendorf (eds), *The Fight over Food: Producers, Consumers, and Activists Challenge the Global Food System*, University Park, PA: Pennsylvania State University Press, pp. 225–46.

Kingsolver, Barbara (2008), *Animal, Vegetable, Miracle: A Year of Food Life*, New York: Harper Perennial.

Kuznets, Simon (1955), 'Economic growth and income inequality', *American Economic Review*, 45, 1–28.

Lasley, Paul, F., Larry Leistritz, Linda Lobao and Katherine Meyer (1995), *Beyond the Amber Waves of Grain: An Examination of Economic and Social Restructuring in the Heartland*, Boulder, CO: Westview Press.

Lobao, Linda (1990), *Locality and Inequality: Farm Structure, Industry Structure, and Socioeconomic Conditions*, Albany, NY: State University of New York Press.

Lobao, Linda and Katherine Meyer (2001), 'The great agricultural transition: crisis, change and social consequences of twentieth century US farming', *Annual Review of Sociology*, 27, 103–24.

Lobao, Linda and Katherine Meyer (2004), 'Farm power without the farmers', *Contexts*, 3, 12–21.

Lobao, Linda and Curtis W. Stofferhan (2008), 'The community effects of industrialized farming: social science research and challenges to corporate farming laws', *Agriculture and Human Values*, 25, 219–40.

Lockeretz, William (ed.) (1987), *Sustaining Agriculture Near Cities*, Ankeny, IA: Soil and Water Conservation Society.

Lyson, Thomas A. (2004), *Civic Agriculture: Reconnecting Farm, Food, and Community*, Medford MA: Tufts University Press.

Lyson, Thomas A. (2007), 'Civic agriculture and the North American food system', in C. Clare Hinrichs and Thomas A. Lyson (eds), *Remaking the North American Food System: Strategies for Sustainability*, Lincoln, NE: University of Nebraska Press, pp. 19–32.

Lyson, Thomas. A., Charles C. Geisler and C. Schlough (1999), 'Preserving community agriculture in a global economy', in Richard K. Olson and Thomas A. Lyson (eds), *Under the Blade: The Conversion of Agricultural Landscapes*, Boulder, CO: Westview Press, pp. 181–216.

Lyson, Thomas. A., R.J. Torres and Rick Welsh (2001), 'Scale of agricultural production, civic engagement, and community welfare', *Social Forces*, 80, 311–27.

Lyson, Thomas A., G.W. Stevenson and Rick Welsh (2008), *Food and the Mid-Level Farm: Renewing an Agriculture of the Middle*, Cambridge, MA: MIT Press.

McDonald, James (2012), 'US Department of Agriculture, 2010 Agricultural Resource Management Survey', all versions, Washington, DC: US Department of Agriculture, Economic Research Service. Personal communication, August.

McMichael, Philip (2012), *Development and Social Change: A Global Perspective*, 5th edition, Los Angeles, CA: Sage Publications.

National Research Council (2010), *Toward Sustainable Agricultural Systems in the 21st Century*, Washington, DC: National Academies Press.

Nelson, Arthur C. (1999), 'Comparing states with and without growth management analysis based on indicators with policy implications', *Land Use Policy*, 16, 121–7.

Pollan, Michael (2009), *In Defense of Food: An Eater's Manifesto*, New York: Penguin Books.

Salamon, Sonya (2003), *Newcomers to Old Towns: Suburbanization of the Heartland*, Chicago, IL: University of Chicago Press.

Sharp, Jeff S. and Molly Bean Smith (2003), 'Social capital and farming at the rural–urban interface: the importance of nonfarmer and farmer relations', *Agricultural Systems*, 76, 913-27.

Sharp, Jeff S., Doug Jackson-Smith and Leah Smith (2011), 'Agricultural economic development at the rural-urban interface: community organization, policy and agricultural change', *Journal of Agriculture, Food Systems, and Community Development*, 1, 189–204.

Sinclair, Robert (1967), 'Von Thunen and urban sprawl', *Annals of the Association of American Geographers*, 57, 72–87.

Stevenson, G.W., Kate Clancy, Robert King, Larry Lev, Marcia Ostrom and Stewart Smith (2011), 'Midscale food value chains: an introduction', *Journal of Agriculture, Food Systems, and Community Development*, 1, 27–34.

Thomas, John K. and Frank M. Howell (2003), 'Metropolitan proximity and US agricultural productivity, 1978–1997', *Rural Sociology*, 68, 366–86.

United Nations (2007), *Rural Households' Livelihood and Well-Being: Statistics on Rural Development and Agriculture Household Income*, New York, USA and Geneva, Switzerland: United Nations.

Van der Ploeg, Jan Douwe and Ann Long (1994), *Born from Within: Practice and Perspectives of Endogenous Rural Development*, Assen, The Netherlands: Van Goreum.

Wilkinson, Ken (1972), 'A field-theory perspective for community development research', *Rural Sociology*, 37, 43–52.

Wimberley, Ronald C. (1987), 'Dimensions of US agristructure: 1969–1982', *Rural Sociology*, 52, 445–61.

Wimberley, Ronald C. and Libby V. Morris (1996), *The Reference Book on Regional Well Being: US Regions, the Black Belt, Appalachia*, Mississippi State, MS: Southern Rural Development Center.

Winders, Bill (2009), *The Politics of Food Supply*, New Haven, CT: Yale University Press.

8. Entrepreneurship
Stephan J. Goetz

INTRODUCTION

The study of entrepreneurship in the context of rural development has expanded markedly in recent years, with a growing number of contributions appearing mostly in economic development and regional science journals. This development is important because the promotion of entrepreneurship is nearly always a complement, if not an alternative, to traditional economic development strategies such as industrial recruitment. In fact, much of the economic development profession still places excessive emphasis on seeking economic salvation from outside the community rather than from internal sources.

This chapter starts with a general definition of entrepreneurship and how it can be measured empirically, including the measurement challenges that arise especially in rural areas. This discussion is followed by a review of perceptions of entrepreneurship, and how entrepreneurial activity usually changes during the course of economic development as economies shift from natural resource to manufacturing and services-based activities. The chapter then examines whether entrepreneurship matters in terms of having positive spillovers on other local economic variables, and whether there are in fact concrete strategies that policy makers can deploy for expanding entrepreneurial activity. The final section provides a conclusion and discusses remaining research questions.

DEFINING AND MEASURING ENTREPRENEURSHIP

There are many definitions of entrepreneurship, but most include the notion of risk taking and of innovation involving either new goods or processes and ways of doing things. One example of innovation is provided by the saying attributed to Ralph Waldo Emerson: 'Build a better mousetrap, and the world will beat a path to your door.' This statement implies improvement of an existing product rather than an entirely new good. Usually entrepreneurs are viewed as individuals who develop new products, such as the first computers developed by Hewlett and Packard in their garage, or new processes, such as Henry Ford's assembly line that allowed automobiles to be built at relatively low cost for mass consumption. Ford did not invent the automobile itself, a feat generally attributed to Karl Benz in Germany, but he revolutionized how it was assembled. Howard Schultz of Starbucks is also widely viewed as entrepreneurial, although his contribution was 'merely' that of taking an idea that worked in Italy – the corner coffee shop – and bringing it to the US. His chain has been highly successful, expanding deep into Europe, but so far has not cracked the Italian market, which remains home to some of the highest standards worldwide for coffee consumption.

Other legendary entrepreneurs include individuals such as Sam Walton, Mary Kay and Mitt Romney, all of whom put existing products or services together in new ways and became extremely wealthy in the process. For example, Walton carefully studied and learned from existing retailers (Lichtenstein and Lyons 2010, p. 22) and then figured out a way to improve the efficiency of distributing ordinary consumer products by exploiting economies of scale, but he did not invent new goods or improve upon existing physical products in a profound way. Critics of Wal-Mart often overlook that today's behemoth started out as a single store. Walton also exemplifies that innovation and entrepreneurship are not limited to urban areas but can, indeed, also successfully emerge in rural areas and elsewhere. In fact, farmers in rural areas are in many ways the archetypal entrepreneur: they are risk takers who settled the land both in the US and in Europe, investing capital to combine scarce resources of soil, seed and water, waiting for crops to mature, and then storing, delivering and marketing them to consumers.

Many farmers are indeed jacks of all trades, and not only work for themselves, but also routinely make their own decisions with respect to what to produce and how, and where to market and sell it (Goetz and Debertin 2001). Likewise, loggers and coal-miners who extract natural resources from remote areas can be viewed as quintessential entrepreneurs, in the same manner as the Staples big-box store format developed by Bain Capital investors for urban areas, which essentially outcompeted existing mom-and-pop stationery stores by selling a greater variety of products at lower cost to consumers.[1] The most highly acclaimed entrepreneurs are those who transform an industry or create an entirely new industry. Here Steve Jobs and Bill Gates should be mentioned, because of their key role in making possible and expanding personal computing to the masses.

Although entrepreneurship can thrive in rural areas just as well as in urban areas, as already noted, it is also the case that rural areas tend to lack the scale and density that are often needed for firms to mature effectively and expand (see Plummer and Pe'er 2010 for a discussion of the role of space and geography in explaining entrepreneurship). This includes access both to inputs as well as to consumer markets, which is important not only to save on transport costs but also for the ability to more closely track changing consumer preferences. For example, Loveridge (2007) describes the cases of Nokia in Finland and Gerber products in the US, both of which started in rural areas but moved to urban centers as they grew. In a so-called innovation-based economy a critical mass and density of highly skilled workers are necessary to foster entrepreneurship, especially as new insights are increasingly based on contributions from different fields (Johansson 2006; Ogle 2007). And, if human capital levels are low in rural areas, because the returns to such capital are lower there than in urban areas (Goetz and Rupasingha 2004; Tokila and Tervo 2011), then the ability of the local population to absorb new, innovative ideas and apply them successfully to achieve economic development may be limited (Rodriguez-Pose and Crescenzi 2008, p. 60).

Although a precise definition of entrepreneurship remains elusive, most observers would agree that 'they know it when they see it'. Accurately measuring the concept, on the other hand, remains a challenge especially at the subnational level (in other words, for rural areas) because of data limitations. The Organisation for Economic Co-operation and Development (Ahmad and Hoffman 2008) describes a number of indicators of entrepreneurship, ranging from the rate of employer firm (net) births to gazelle start-ups per labor force and employment shares in firms younger than five years, and to value-added or productivity contributions by young firms (also see Goetz et al. 2010 for more detail). One important recent innovation in this area has been the analytical distinction between entrepreneurs who are pushed into self-employment because of necessity (for example, a lay-off elsewhere), and those who are pulled into it because they have a novel idea (these are known as opportunity-based entrepreneurs or self-employed).

Internationally, the perhaps best-known data source in this area is the Global Entrepreneurship Monitor (GEM). This source provides industry-level and other detail, and in the US component it includes a zip code for individual-level respondents. These data permit stratification by rural and urban areas with a 2005–2010 sample average of 8.2 individuals per US county (Figueroa-Armijos et al. 2012, p. 8). In what is perhaps the first study to use the data in this way, the authors construct a data set in which 5.4 percent of the observations represent opportunity-based entrepreneurs and 1.2 percent are necessity-based. Although this is an interesting and novel use of the GEM individual-level data, and analyses could be extended to focus on subpopulations of entrepreneurs such as low-income, female or retirees, the results of any study using the survey data need to be viewed with caution given the small sample sizes.

The Kauffman Foundation's entrepreneurial index, which is based on the annual current population survey and measures new firms started by individuals within the last month, is available at the state level and with industry detail, but the sample surveyed is too small to provide meaningful rural data. The decennial US Census as well as the Economic Census administered in years ending in '02 and '07 provide some detail on self-employment activity (for example, industry, education and age of the self-employed), but with obvious time lags. For these reasons, researchers seeking both county-level coverage and the most current data available have relied on non-farm self-employment numbers as a proxy for entrepreneurship, although this is changing now, as the Figueroa-Armijos et al. (2012) study shows.

The self-employment data, which are used in much of the literature reviewed here, are not without problems. The numbers are constructed from Form 1040 Schedule C income tax filings and reported by the Bureau of Economic Analysis (BEA). Individual states do not provide or even track these kinds of numbers, so that the self-employed generally are ignored in state economic development policy making. The reported numbers are inflated because they can double-count individuals working for themselves in two or more industries or jobs, but they also miss all of the underreported economic activity, which is estimated to exceed $350 billion nationally in the US. It is important to stress that both Current Population Survey (CPS) and US decennial Census data show flat or even declining self-employment rates, whereas the BEA data show increases, as is evident below. This discrepancy is largely explained by the fact that the Census question is an either/or response while the BEA data accommodate multiple job holding, which is more consistent with the new reality of US labor markets. A number of peer-reviewed papers have been published in leading economics and regional science journals in recent years using the BEA data to shed light on the phenomenon of entrepreneurship in rural areas especially.

Figure 8.1 shows, using BEA data, that the share of the total rural workforce that is made up of self-employed workers increased from under 14 percent in 1969 to over 22 percent in 2010. Perhaps most noteworthy is the structural break that occurs in this series around the recession of 2000, which was followed by a 'jobless' recovery. After this year the share of self-employed increased at a markedly higher rate than previously, with the rise interrupted only temporarily in 2008 at the peak of the housing crisis. Clearly, the self-employed are becoming an increasingly important component of the rural labor force, and economic developers cannot afford to ignore this fundamental development. If the trends continue, there will be one self-employed worker for every two wage-and-salary employees in rural areas within a decade.

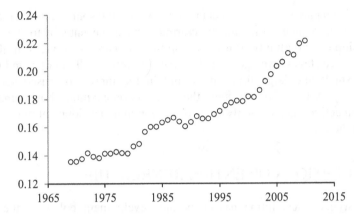

Source: From Bureau of Economic Analysis data available at http://www.bea.gov/regional/ (accessed June 29, 2012).

Figure 8.1 *Self-employed as a percentage of labor force, rural US, 1969–2010*

One other advantage of the BEA data is that they allow the returns to self-employment to be calculated consistently over time and at the county level. This is therefore a rich county-level data source, dating back as far as 1969, and it is unique in that it allows separate analyses to be conducted for rural and urban areas. As noted earlier, a key distinction in the literature is that of entrepreneurship of necessity versus opportunity, where the former is argued to capture laid-off workers who are forced into self-employment because of a lack of wage-and-salary employment, while the latter refers to a deliberate choice made to work for oneself because the individual has identified a remunerative opportunity. One proxy for distinguishing between these two types may be found in the returns to self-employment: those pursuing an opportunity have higher earnings, while those who are forced into working for themselves have lower earnings (along these lines, Low et al. 2005 refer to the quantity and quality of self-employment).

These examples can be used to illustrate conceptually the role of entre-preneurship in the course of economic development, as a nation shifts from being primarily natural resource- or factor-based to efficiency-based and, eventually, innovation-based. Acs et al. (2008) suggest that as income rises in a nation, the dominant economic sector shifts from natural resources to manufacturing and then services, and the sources of growth are based, respectively, on resource abundance; so-called copy-cat gap-filling; and new products, processes and services. It is during this economic develop-ment transition that the primary organizational form of a nation's businesses shifts from pure self-employment related to natural resources; to wage-and-salary employment within manufacturing firms; and eventually to entrepreneurship of opportunity or necessity in the provision of services. In these same three stages, average firm size changes from small to large, and then both small and large firms are found in the innovation-based service economy. With this background, the next section examines how entrepreneurial activity is commonly viewed by economic development practitioners in the US.

PERCEPTIONS OF ENTREPRENEURSHIP

One stylized description has economic development policy in the US evolving in the form of three 'waves' of development (Deller and Goetz 2009, p. 29). In essence, the first wave can be described as one in which communities exclusively look beyond their borders for economic salvation, which usually occurs in the form of industrial recruitment or grants from the federal government. The second wave is more inward-looking, focusing on entrepreneurs as well as retention and expansion of existing businesses (BRE). In the third wave emphasis is placed on increasing competitiveness through public–private partnerships. It is important to consider these three waves because while BRE programs are used in some communities, many still focus on industrial recruitment to the neglect of nurturing local entrepreneurs or businesses. Yet, as we will see, the latter represent an enormous opportunity.

There is perhaps excessive optimism about the potential for entrepreneurship to lift rural economies onto higher growth trajectories (see Shane 2008, who is perhaps the most vocal critic). At the same time, there is a great deal of ignorance about the potential importance of entrepreneurs. The lack of focus on entrepreneurs and the self-employed in the US relative to Europe is remarkable because the US prides itself as being made up of ruggedly independent and opportunity-seeking individuals; the US is still seen by many Europeans as the 'land of unlimited opportunity', and yet more research has been conducted in Europe rather than the US on entrepreneurship at the regional level. One reason for the lack of attention paid to entrepreneurs may be the perception that self-employment is merely a stop-gap measure of desperation and that the immediately visible economic impact of entrepreneurs is often difficult to decipher, or it is taken for granted, as in the case of Bill Gates (Glaeser et al. 2010). In comparison, successful recruitment of a large manufacturer or processor can lead to high-profile ribbon cutting ceremonies that attract the attention of news media.

Yet the number of likely future successes in attracting this kind of development from outside the county is increasingly small as capital and the means of production move with growing ease around the world to the site offering the lowest-cost labor with minimal skills required. At the same time, recruiting or spawning high-profile success stories such as a Sam Walton, Bill Gates or Mary Kay would seem to be even more out of the reach of the average county economic development agency. This also raises the question: if entrepreneurship is essentially an individual's endeavor, is there even a role for the public sector in helping to spawn such activity?

Promoters of entrepreneurship or self-employment who see it as a solution to lagging local economic development also tend to ignore that not everyone has the personal make-up or fortitude to survive as an entrepreneur. Just as the high-skill and high-education economy and related job opportunities are not available to all individuals, so too are not all individuals able to adapt to the rigors of working for themselves or possess the innate grit needed to succeed. Yet, if at least some individuals have the ability and drive to work for themselves, they may if successful become employers and even hire other laid-off workers. This raises the question of whether or not self-employment has any measurable local impact, an issue covered in the next section.

THE LOCAL IMPACT OF ENTREPRENEURSHIP

The perception that self-employment is an activity of last resort for at least some workers may not be inaccurate. In fact, Figure 8.2 shows that the returns to rural self-employment relative to wage-and-salary employment have declined almost without interruption since the commodities boom of the 1970s. The relative decline was especially sharp between 1978 and 1982: from above parity to less than three-quarters. After a period of relative stability during the 1980s and 1990s, when the self-employed earned about 75 percent the income of employed workers, the relative decline resumed post-2000, which coincides with the rapid rise in the share of self-employment shown in Figure 8.1. In 2010 these relative returns rebounded from their all-time low of 0.493 in 2009, but it remains to be seen how this evolves in the future. The data strongly suggest that while technology has made it possible for even small-scale operators to carry out tasks that previously were possible only in fully staffed, complex organizations (for example, with an information technology unit to maintain websites and secretarial staff to keep appointments), changes in the productivity of self-employed workers have not kept pace with those of wage-and-salary workers. At a minimum, this suggests that policy makers could consider whether public policy has a role to play in enhancing these relative returns.

In other words, is there an underlying public goods aspect to this new form of organizing labor that is worth public sector intervention? A gradually expanding collection of papers seeks to address this question; Wennekers and Thurik (1999) provide an early literature survey.

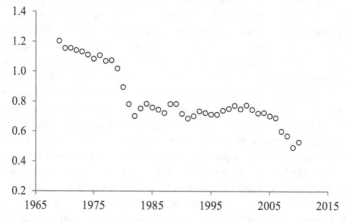

Source: From Bureau of Economic Analysis data available at http://www.bea.gov/regional/ (accessed June 29, 2012).

Figure 8.2   Returns to self-employment relative to employment, rural US, 1969–2010 (earnings per worker)

Goetz and Shrestha (2009) is one of the few US-based studies to examine why the 2000–2005 growth rates in the returns to self-employment varied across counties, and they find no statistically significant effect of metro or non-metro status. Using 2001 data from Finland, Tokila and Tervo (2011) are able to probe more deeply into this question, and they report that the returns to education (measured in years) for entrepreneurs are actually higher in rural areas than the returns to education for wage-and-salary workers, while they find no such differences in urban areas. These authors use Census and employment statistics files provided by Statistics Finland, in which employment is categorized according to how individuals are insured nationally and how they report their income; even for these entre-preneurs, income is considered to be derived from self-employment, and the measure is not without problems (Tokila and Tervo 2011, p. 695). It is noteworthy that density appears not to affect the returns to education, and these authors furthermore conclude that rural workers tend to be pushed into self-employment rather than being pulled.

In another study from Europe, Bosma and Schutjens (2011) use individual-level GEM data over 2001–2006 to analyze differences in attitudes towards entrepreneurship and related activities. Understanding how these vary across regions and demographic characteristics is important for designing and assessing any successful policy interventions. Although these authors do not have cleanly separated data for rural and urban areas, they are able to develop non-metro proxy regions using the NUTS (Nomenclature of Territorial Units for Statistics) data. For example, they decompose Bavaria into the Munich metro area and a non-metro residual, and in this manner arrive at a total of 147 regions. One of their interesting results is that the fear of failure related to a business start tends to be higher in less densely settled areas. They also confirm a pattern of success breeding more success, in that regions with more entrepreneurial activity also spawn more start-ups, which they attribute to a positive demonstration (or network) effect. They caution that regions differ in terms of entrepreneurial vigor, and that one-size-fits-all-regions programs and approaches are likely to fail.

Whether or not the public sector ought to support the self-employed or entrepreneurs depends on: (1) whether policy options are available in the first place; and (2) whether the self-employed produce any local economic benefits other than the money they themselves earn. While the low returns shown in Figure 8.2 at first glance suggest that there may be no benefits to supporting self-employment through public policy, the truth is the opposite. This issue is addressed next.

A key challenge that arises in identifying the impact of self-employment on the local economy is sorting out whether self-employment 'causes' local economic growth or whether local growth provides the conditions that allow more individuals to become self-employed (Fritsch 2008; Goetz et al. 2012; Wennekers and Thurik 1999). In this situation a regression of local economic growth on changes in local self-employment rates and other explanatory variables would produce biased parameter estimates and lead to potentially incorrect interpretations. A related consideration is that if the self-employed successfully compete with existing businesses this would imply they are more productive and efficient, and thus need fewer workers (see also Fritsch and Mueller 2008). In this case income should rise but total employment may actually shrink.

One of the first studies in the US to account for the potential endogeneity issues is Shrestha et al. (2007). These authors carefully specify regression models for three different time periods covering recessions and economic expansions as well as different lags for key variables, in addition to considering state fixed effects as well as spatial spillovers across county borders. They regress changes in non-farm wage-and-salary job growth in one five-year period on lagged wage employment growth, wage earnings growth and self-employment growth. The latter is measured as the change in self-employment over five years relative to base period total employment; this is known as the 'labor market' approach because it simulates the process of the self-employed emerging out of the total workforce (as opposed to the beginning period stock of existing businesses, known as the ecological approach). Although they do not provide separate regressions for rural areas, Shrestha et al. (2007) control for the metropolitan status of counties and also interact this status with the self-employment growth rate to test whether the latter has a different effect in metro than in rural counties. The conclusion of this study is that (p. 164) 'lagged proprietorship formations lead to increased job growth [in the ensuing period], controlling for other factors and regardless of the time period considered'. Perhaps not surprisingly, these authors find a stronger effect during economic expansions than during contractions. Furthermore, the effect of self-employment growth is found to be stronger in metropolitan compared to rural counties.

Extending this work by focusing on Appalachia as a lagging and mostly remote rural region, Stephens and Partridge (2011) carefully assess how self-employment rates and small business shares influence county-level per capita income growth over the period 1990–2006. They use the 420 counties officially designated as part of the Appalachian Regional Commission in addition to 134 counties that border this region as controls, and as instruments they consider 1969 proprietor shares and 1960 population density. They conclude that self-employment measured both at the 1990 level and the lagged 1980–1990 change in share raise both per capita income and job growth in the region, which is confirmed independently by Rupasingha and Goetz (2012). However, in contrast to the latter study Stephens and Partridge (2011) do not find a statistically significant impact on poverty rate reduction, in this lagging remote region.

In their study covering the decades of the 1970s through 1990s, Rupasingha and Goetz (2012) examine the effect of initial period self-employment rates (as a share of total employment) on changes in per capita income and poverty rates and overall employment growth. The panel nature of the data allows these authors to employ a state-of-the-art Spatial Durbin Model that has a number of advantages in that it further attenuates endogeneity concerns and also allows spatial spillovers to be captured explicitly. The authors conclude that self-employment has robust effects in non-metro areas not only in terms of raising per capita income and lowering poverty rates, but also leading to greater wage-and-salary growth. From this literature there is thus an impressive and growing body of evidence suggesting that self-employment or entrepreneurship at all scales contributes to local economic growth.

Although the bulk of the evidence is based on self-employment data that, as already noted, are not without problems, studies using other types of data lend further support to the claim that entrepreneurial firms have wider economic impacts. In particular, using a unique database, Fleming and Goetz (2011) find that locally owned small (defined as 10–99 employees) firms had a statistically significant positive effect on per capita income growth rates across the rural–urban continuum during the period 2000–2007. More specifically, a community that doubled the number of small, locally owned firms from about five to ten firms per 1000 population is predicted to increase average household income county-wide by $5280 annually. Although not all of these small, locally owned firms are necessarily entrepreneurial, this does lend further support to the claims made here. In contrast, large firms that are not owned locally (such as big box chains) are associated with a statistically significant smaller increase in per capita growth over time.

Similarly, in an exhaustive study of 12 years of NETS (National Establishment Time Series) data on nearly 15 million business establishments, Neumark et al. (2011) find that smaller firms are associated with stronger job growth. As a final piece of evidence, although it is not available separately for rural areas because of the data used, Goetz et al. (2011) find that the Kauffman Index of Entrepreneurial Activity is also statistically associated with faster employment growth at the state level over the period 2000–2007. For an overview of this evidence, interested readers are referred to Goetz et al. (2012).

OPTIONS FOR EXPANDING ENTREPRENEURSHIP

Given the relatively strong evidence suggesting that entrepreneurship and self-employment have tangible economic benefits in the local economies where they are based, the question arises whether concrete policy levers exist for expanding such activity especially in rural areas. Examples do exist of strategies that increase self-employment, and successful rural entrepreneurs were already identified earlier. There is no evidence, however, to suggest that Wal-Mart and Gerber Foods came into existence because of a government or other program fostering entrepreneurship targeted at them. Although Lichtenstein and Lyons (2010, p. 7) writes that the 'economic environment ushered in by Reagan ... relieved employers, especially the retailers and fast-food restaurants, of hundreds of billions of dollars in annual labor costs', this non-targeted policy would have benefited any would-be entrepreneur at the time in the same manner.

At the same time it is also clear that, increasingly, entrepreneurial innovation requires economic density and diversity that by definition are absent in rural areas. For example, Johansson (2006) describes the Medici Effect as consisting of the innovation that was made possible by the many individuals from very diverse backgrounds who were brought together from around the world to Florence, Italy. Richard Ogle (2007) provides compelling evidence that breakthrough innovations increasingly occur at the frontiers of disciplines, in so-called 'idea spaces'. In some universities, fundamental advances in science are now occurring not necessarily within interdisciplinary institutes, but at the intersections of these institutes.

Although a number of studies have been conducted on the determinants of entrepreneurship, considerably less work has been conducted on the causes relative to the consequences or effects of entrepreneurship (which were examined earlier). These studies are briefly reviewed in this section, and then applied strategies that have been used to stimulate entrepreneurship are presented. In terms of policy, five categories of variables can be considered (Acs et al. 2008): education (both general and specific); amenities, including an absence of crime; physical infrastructure, including transportation; legal and institutional factors; and both general and specific or targeted taxes.

An early exploratory study of the determinants of self-employment in different counties or regions of the US is Low et al. (2005). They define levels of entrepreneurship using self-employment as a share of total employment; self-employment income per proprietor; and average proprietor income divided by average non-employer earnings. In part these measures capture the quantity versus quality of entrepreneurship or self-employment. For example, the second variable is a productivity measure.

The explanatory variables that account for differences in the quality and quantity of entrepreneurship, according to Low et al.'s (2005) results, can have effects that are opposite in direction. For example, access to broadband and interstate highways is associated with a lower quantity but higher quality (earnings) of entrepreneurs or the self-employed. This would suggest that there are more self-employed proportionally in those areas where individuals are pushed into working for themselves because of a lack of alternative forms of employment. Likewise, having more foreign-born residents is associated with more quality but lower quantity of self-employment, whereas places with more scenic amenities have both higher quality and quantity of self-employment.

Goetz and Rupasingha (2009) provide the first systemic assessment at the level of all US counties of how demographic, regional and policy variables affect changes in self-employment densities over time. Their study is based on a utility-maximizing model in which individuals can choose between wage-and-salary and self-employment. Although they do not estimate separate regressions for rural areas, they do find a small but statistically significant higher rate of self-employment formation in rural counties, all else being equal. Although the average increase between 1990 and 2000 in the self-employment rate across all counties was 1.90 percentage points, in rural counties it increased by 1.95 points.

Although some of the other exogenous variables included in the study and found to be statistically significant in influencing self-employment rate changes over time are more difficult to change through policy (for example the ethnic mix and age of the population), state-level policies including greater economic freedom from government intervention and higher levels of taxation have positive effects. The latter result may seem paradoxical but it has been explained by reference to the fact that higher taxes are associated with a lower expectation of future tax increases, which is viewed as positive by businesses.

In a paper that focuses specifically on the determinants of rural self-employment across the 2003 rural–urban continuum codes (RUCC03), Goetz and Rupasingha (2011) estimate statistical equations that build on their earlier study (Goetz and Rupasingha 2009) as well as Acs and Armington (2006). The paper was commissioned by the Federal Reserve Bank and designed to explore rural options for federal intervention in the jobless recovery as fiscal and monetary policy options for stimulating economic growth become increasingly limited. By using the RUCC03 the authors are able to study determinants of self-employment change over the period 2000–2009 as affected by proximity to metro areas (yes or no), on the one hand; and population mass or density (large, medium and small), on the other. This period is critical in that it captures the last national business cycle, including the 2008 'Great' Recession.

Among the salient results for rural areas in particular, the following stand out. In rural counties that are adjacent to metro areas, population expansion in the previous period has a positive impact on self-employment rate changes regardless of county size or density. This suggests that there are positive effects simply resulting from population growth spillovers associated with ongoing suburbanization. Human capital (measured by educational attainment of the population) affects self-employment growth in the larger and medium-sized non-adjacent non-metro counties. One interpretation is that businesses in these communities are unable to hire educated workers from nearby metro areas and instead have to rely on their local human capital base.

The number of bank branches per capita, as a proxy for access to capital needed to launch and grow a business, matters in a positive direction only in the smallest county-types, which likely otherwise lack the required infrastructure of financial institutions. By examining the effect of age structure on self-employment growth, Goetz and Rupasingha (2011) also suggest that youth entrepreneurship programs may be most urgently needed in larger counties that are metro-adjacent. The reason for this is that here self-employment rates only increase for higher shares of older residents, which indicates an opportunity to help individuals start their own businesses earlier in life through educational programs, for example.

Figueroa-Armijos et al. (2012) use the US GEM data described earlier to make three innovations: a separate analysis of the individual-level data for rural counties; for necessity-based versus opportunity-based entrepreneurs; and for the periods before (2005–2007) and after (2008–2010) the recession. Although the results may suffer from endogeneity bias (for example, part-time employment status is included as a regressor), they are plausible in that they suggest individuals were more likely to enter into necessity-based entrepreneurship after the 2008 recession, or if they lived alone, and those with a college degree are more likely to engage in opportunity-based entrepreneurship.

Turning to the practice of stimulating entrepreneurship, one well-known practical program that is designed to increase the supply of entrepreneurs in a community is the Entrepreneurial League System (or pipeline) developed by Lichtenstein and Lyons (2001, 2010). The basic idea is that, just as the American baseball league has a farming system for players ranging from Rookies to AAA and the Major League, so too is it appropriate for nascent entrepreneurs to move up through a pipeline or skill ladder, where novice entrepreneurs move up through higher stages representing increasing sophistication and scale of entrepreneurial activity that ends up with profitable businesses in the major leagues for those who are successful. The skills sets involved include technical, managerial, entrepreneurial and personal maturity skills. These authors also describe six specific life-cycle stages of entrepreneurial firms, starting with pre-venture and existence, and moving through early growth to expansion, maturity and eventual decline (p. 70). Using the two variables of life-cycle stage of the business and skill levels of the entrepreneurs in a community, Lichtenstein and Lyons 2001 present a matrix that can be used to identify weak spots within the overall pipeline in any given community. As a next step, they then describe how economic developers can strategically recruit entrepreneurs from elsewhere to fill in the gaps (p. 116), as an economic development strategy. This specific tool can be used in communities to stimulate local economic development, based on 'performance enhancement, incubation and selective attraction' (p. 117). A complementary data-based approach for accomplishing this is presented below.

Loveridge and Nizalov (2007) are the first authors to test the entrepreneurial pipeline idea in the 83 Michigan counties, using firms of different sizes as measures of entrepreneurial pipeline stages. They examine the effect of the size distribution of businesses (starting with 1–4, 5–9, and so on, to over 1000 employees) on per capita income growth rates over time while controlling for other factors such as educational attainment, industry composition and population density. They conclude that there is a 'strong' connection between business size distribution and economic growth, and that this confirms the pipeline idea proposed by Lichtenstein and Lyons (2010). A general finding is that Michigan at present has a suboptimal mix of firms at different stages of entrepreneurial development (as measured by size) and that a shift to more smaller firms would lead to faster economic growth across most counties. In part they attribute this to the legacy effect of large-scale manufacturing in Michigan. One policy implication of this work is that instead of pursuing industrial recruitment efforts directed at large manufacturers, state policy makers should instead concentrate on helping to spawn new small businesses, for example through incubation programs.

Deller (2009, 2012) developed an innovative data-driven process that complements the Lichtenstein and Lyons entrepreneurial league system. In the so-called 'Wisconsin approach' IMPLAN (Impact Analysis for Planning, software developed by MIG, Inc.) is used to identify gaps and disconnects within communities, which in turn provide opportunities for import substitution. A gap exists whenever goods and services in a given sector are both imported and produced locally. The idea is that opportunities may exist for the local demand to be met from local sources, but for some reason local entrepreneurs are not yet taking advantage of the opportunity. A disconnect arises when all of the inputs used locally in a particular sector are imported. Although there may be good reasons for such an outcome, this at least raises the prospect that more of the good could be supplied locally. This sophisticated approach uses a county's input–output matrix to identify sectors that are candidates for import substitution, whereby imports are replaced with local products or services. In both cases, the potential for local entrepreneurial expansion may exist, and the advantage of the approach is that it is both data-based and sector-specific. Thus, the Wisconsin approach provides a tool that complements the Lichtenstein–Lyons strategic approach to developing entrepreneurship by identifying specific sectors or industries for investment.

The Wisconsin approach identifies specific sectors that may provide business opportunities for entrepreneurs. In addition, the US Land Grant university faculty has developed numerous programs to support local entrepreneurs. For example, Loveridge et al. (2012) at Michigan State University describe entrepreneurial cultures and how they vary across regions, and review alternative programs and policies that are used to assist entrepreneurs and improve their economic success. Marshall (2012) presents the results of two surveys that were administered to examine how

Purdue University could help improve the viability of small food-related businesses in Indiana. An important part of the educational objective here is also to help nascent entrepreneurs assess when their business ideas may not be profitable, or viable.

CONCLUSION AND REMAINING QUESTIONS

This chapter has demonstrated the substantial wealth of interest in the topic of rural entrepreneurship. Although there is mounting evidence about the economic impact of such activity, many questions remain for both research-ers and policy makers. This concluding section is organized around three unsettled issues: generalizations about the impact of entrepreneurship in particular; the roles of population density as well as spatial economic spillovers, with a particular focus on implications for rural areas; and technological changes that may enable increased future dispersion of economic activity, and entrepreneurship, into rural areas.

Despite the mounting evidence about the economic impact of self-employed workers, with one of the most recent studies (Rupasingha and Goetz 2012) showing unequivocal benefits for rural areas in terms of income and job growth as well as poverty reduction, questions continue about the relative roles of small and large businesses, the benefits they provide to their workers, and the degree to which they are innovative (for example, Edmiston 2007). Part of the issue here is whether small businesses are necessarily entrepreneurial and whether the economic impact measure used should be job growth or income (in other words, productivity) growth. Other issues include the geography covered as well as the time period over which impacts are evaluated. Studies using different data sets come to different conclusions, thereby contributing to the confusion.

Aside from these measurement issues, questions remain about the costs and benefits of any public sector intervention in support of entrepreneurs or the self-employed. Acs et al. (2008, p. 23) conclude, at least for urban areas, that limiting progressive state and local taxes and simplifying start-up-related approval processes are relatively straightforward beneficial actions, as are policies such as traffic congestion pricing which would reduce travel times. Although congestion is less of an issue in rural areas, travel distances and times remain large. At the same time, local programs to mentor and encourage entrepreneurs, and enhancements of road and internet (wireless) infrastructure, man-made amenities and local schools, have strong potential that needs to be rigorously evaluated.

Another important set of questions exists about the geography of innov-ation, especially related to entrepreneurship in rural areas and 'the trans-mission of economically productive innovation' (Rodriguez-Pose and

Crescenzi 2008, p. 63). These authors conclude that such transmission decays within a 200 km (125 mile) radius in Europe, but other studies have reported much shorter distances over which agglomeration economies are bounded both in the US and Europe (for example, Plummer and Pe'er 2010, p. 547). This is an area in which considerable potential for fruitful new research exists.

Looking into the future, one emerging area of technological change could lead to dramatic new opportunities for both entrepreneurship and innovation even in remote and more isolated rural areas. This relates to three-dimensional digital printing technologies known as additive manufacturing. The critical novelty here is that products and spare parts can be printed anywhere in the world without the necessity of having a reliable supply chain in place to ensure cost-effective and timely assembly of goods.[2] In turn this has the potential to up-end some of the critical agglomeration economies that are currently driving the growth of large cities. As Glaeser and Kerr (2009) point out in seeking to explain where manufacturing activity is located, new firms appear to be attracted especially to locations with numerous existing firms that can potentially supply them with inputs. Conceivably, the new form of additive manufacturing could make possible a similar ecology of firms in rural areas, thereby attenuating the strong link that currently exists between density and innovation.

NOTES

1. http://en.wikipedia.org/wiki/Bain_Capital (accessed June 29, 2012).
2. See the April 21, 2012, Special Report in *The Economist* on 'Manufacturing and innovation' at http://www.economist.com/node/21552901; the sub-title is 'A Third Industrial Revolution', following mechanization of textile mills and then the assembly lines allowing mass manufacturing. The report points to special opportunities for rural areas in a number of instances.

REFERENCES

Acs, Z.J. and C. Armington (2006), *Entrepreneurship, Geography, and American Economic Growth*, Cambridge: Cambridge University Press.
Acs, Z.J., E.L. Glaeser, R.E. Litan, L. Fleming, S.J. Goetz, W.R. Kerr, S. Klepper, R. Steven, S. Stuart, O. Sorenson and W.C. Strange (2008), 'Entrepreneurship and urban success: toward a policy consensus'. http://ssrn.com/abstract=1092493 or http://dx.doi.org/10.2139/ssrn.1092493.
Ahmad, Nadim and Anders Hoffman (2008), 'A framework for addressing and measuring entrepreneurship', Organisation for Economic Co-operation and Development. http://egateg.usaidallnet.gov/sites/default/files/A%20Framework%20for%20Addressing%20and%20Measuring%20Entrepreneurship.pdf.

Bosma, N. and V. Schutjens (2011), 'Understanding regional variation in entrepreneurial activity and entrepreneurial attitude in Europe', *Annals of Regional Science*, 47, 711–42.

Deller, Steven C. (2009), 'Import substitution and the analysis of gaps and disconnects', in S.J. Goetz, S.C. Deller and T.R. Harris (eds), *Targeting Regional Economic Development*, Abingdon: Routledge, pp. 365–88.

Deller, Steven C. (2012), 'Targeting industrial gaps and disconnects for community economic development', *Choices*, 3rd Quarter. http://www.choicesmagazine.org/choices-magazine/theme-articles/public-sector-options-for-creating-jobs/targeting-industrial-gaps-and-disconnects-for-community-economic-development.

Deller, S.C. and S.J. Goetz (2009), 'Historical description of economic development policy', in Goetz, S.J., S.C. Deller and T.R. Harris (eds), *Targeting Regional Economic Development*, Abingdon: Routledge, pp. 17–34.

Edmiston, K. (2007), 'The role of small and large business in economic development', *Economic Review*, Second Quarter, 73–97. http://www.kc.frb.org/PUBLICAT/ECONREV/PDF/2q07edmi.pdf (accessed July 7, 2012).

Figueroa-Armijos, M., B. Dabson and T.G. Johnson (2012), 'Rural entrepreneurship in a time of recession', *Entrepreneurship Research Journal*, 2. http://www.bepress.com/erj/vol2/iss1/3 (accessed July 7, 2012). DOI: 10.2202/2157-5665.1044.

Fritsch, M. (2008), 'How does new business formation affect regional development?', *Small Business Economics*, 30, 1–14.

Fritsch, M. and P. Mueller (2008), 'The effect of new business formation on regional development over time: the case of Germany', *Small Business Economics*, 30, 15–29.

Glaeser, E.L. and W.R. Kerr (2009), 'Local industrial conditions and entrepreneurship: how much of the spatial distribution can we explain?', *Journal of Economics and Management*, 18, 623–63.

Glaeser, E.L., S.S. Rosenthal and W.C. Strange (2010), 'Urban economics and entrepreneurship', *Journal of Urban Economics*, 60, 1–14.

Goetz, S.J. and D.L. Debertin (2001), 'Why farmers quit: a county-level analysis', *American Journal of Agricultural Economics* 83, 1010–23.

Goetz, S.J. and A. Rupasingha (2009), 'Determinants and implications of growth in non-farm proprietorship densities: 1990–2000', *Small Business Economics*, 32, 425–38.

Goetz, S.J. and A. Rupasingha (2011), 'The determinants of rural self-employment: insights from county-level data', prepared for the Federal Reserve Bank Conference on Small Business and Entrepreneurship During an Economic Recovery, Board of Governors of the Federal Reserve System, Washington, DC, November 9–10.

Goetz, S.J. and S.S. Shrestha (2009), 'Explaining self-employment success and failure: Wal-Mart vs. Starbucks or Schumpeter vs. Putnam', *Social Science Quarterly*, 91, 22–38.

Goetz, S.J., M. Partridge, S.C. Deller and D. Fleming (2010), 'Evaluating US rural entrepreneurship policy', *Journal of Regional Analysis and Policy*, 40, 20–33.

Goetz, S.J., M.D. Partridge, D.S. Rickman and S. Majumdar (2011), 'Sharing the gains of local economic growth: Race to the top vs. race to the bottom economic development', *Environment and Planning C: Government and Policy*, 29, 428–56.

Goetz, S.J., D.A. Fleming and A. Rupasingha (2012), 'The economic impacts of self-employment', *Journal of Agricultural and Applied Economics*, 44, 315–21.

Johansson, F. (2006), *The Medici Effect*, Boston, MA: Harvard Business School Press.

Lichtenstein, G. and T.S. Lyons (2001), 'The entrepreneurial development system: transforming business talent and community economies', *Economic Development Quarterly*, 15, 3–20.

Lichtenstein, G. and T.S. Lyons (2010), *Investing in Entrepreneurs: A Strategic Approach for Strengthening Your Regional and Community Economy*, Santa Barbara, CA: Praeger.

Loveridge, S. (2007), 'Getting started in community-based entrepreneurship', in N. Walzer (ed.), *Entrepreneurship and Local Economic Development*, Lanham, MD and Plymouth, UK: Lexington Books, pp. 255–73.

Loveridge, S. and D. Nizalov (2007), 'Operationalizing the entrepreneurial pipeline theory: an empirical assessment of the optimal size distribution of local firms', *Economic Development Quarterly*, 21, 244–62.

Loveridge, S., S. Miller and T. Komarek (2012), 'Residents support entrepreneurship, but policy lags', *Choices*, 3rd Quarter. http://www.choicesmagazine.org/choices-magazine/theme-articles/public-sector-options-for-creating-jobs/residents-support-entrepreneurship-but-policy-lags.

Low, S., J. Henderson and S. Weiler (2005), 'Gauging a region's entrepreneurial potential', *Economic Review*, 3rd Quarter, 61–89. http://www.kc.frb.org/publicat/econrev/pdf/3q05low.pdf (accessed July 7, 2012).

Marshall, M. (2012), 'Outreach and education boost entrepreneurs in Indiana', *Choices*, 3rd Quarter. http://www.choicesmagazine.org/choices-magazine/theme-articles/public-sector-options-for-creating-jobs/outreach-and-education-boost-entrepreneurs-in-indiana.

Neumark, D., B. Wall and J. Zhang (2011), 'Do small businesses create more jobs? New evidence for the United States from the National Establishment Time Series', *Review of Economics and Statistics*, 93, 16–29.

Ogle, R. (2007), *Smart World: Breakthrough Creativity and the New Science of Ideas*, Boston, MA: Harvard Business School Press.

Plummer, L.A. and A. Pe'er (2010), 'The geography of entrepreneurship', in Z.J. Acs and D.B. Audretsch (eds), *Handbook of Entrepreneurship Research*, 2nd edition, New York: Springer Science and Business Media, pp. 519–56.

Rodriguez-Pose, A. and R. Crescenzi (2008), 'Research and development, spillovers and innovation systems, and the genesis of regional growth in Europe', *Regional Studies*, 42, 51–67.

Rupasingha, A. and S.J. Goetz (2012), 'Self-employment and local economic performance: evidence from US counties', *Papers in Regional Science*. DOI 10.1111/j.1435-5957.2011.00396.x

Shane, S.A. (2008), *The Illusions of Entrepreneurship*, New Haven, CT: Yale University Press.

Shrestha, S.S., S.J. Goetz and A. Rupasingha (2007), 'Proprietorship formations and US job growth', *Review of Regional Studies*, 27, 146–68.

Stephens, H.M. and M.D. Partridge (2011), 'Do entrepreneurs enhance economic growth in lagging regions?', *Growth and Change*, 42, 431–65.

Tokila, A. and H. Tervo (2011), 'Regional differences in returns to education for entrepreneurs versus wage earners', *Annals of Regional Science*, 47, 689–710.

Wennekers, S. and R. Thurik (1999), 'Linking entrepreneurship and economic growth', *Small Business Economics*, 13, 27–55.

9. The rural development attributes of tourism

David Marcouiller

INTRODUCTION

Within developed economies, rural regions across the globe are progressing through a dramatic and sustained post-industrial transition. Household economic sustenance gained through family-run farms, small-scale timbering, mining and rustic tourism are yielding to large-scale corporate agriculture and forestry, footloose and globally competitive primary processing firms (manufacturing), the rise of the service sector, regional knowledge economies, leisure estates and mass tourism at unprecedented scales. The implications of this transition for rural development involve dramatic changes in regional economic structure; household income inequality driven by an increased presence of more affluent amenity migrants and retirees in concert with an increase in low-wage, seasonal work; and wholesale socio-demographic change. Although maintaining generational roots provides incentives for long-term rural residents to age in-place, there remains limited economic opportunity, persistent poverty and a continual drain of young people to urban areas.

This said, contemporary rural structure is complex and difficult to characterize with simple generalizations. Although standardized definitions of rural North America and the European Union allow initial distinctions to be made that reflect remoteness, population size and distance to metropolitan area (Brezzi et al. 2011; USDA 2004), others focus more on economic structure and dominant economic activity (Duncan 2007; Hamilton et al. 2008; Johnson and Beale 2002; Lapping et al. 1989). These latter definitions begin to sort out important rural characteristics that reflect underlying issues of rural welfare, economic structure, community development and amenity base. Doing so distinguishes relevant conceptual elements important to understanding regional change and the role of tourism within rural areas.

As an introduction, it is important to note that tourism definitions vary depending on the disciplinary bent of the writer. The one truly common element associated with definitions of tourism is leisure travel: activities of people partaken in away from their homes for purposes that involve pleasure. While later in this chapter I will more fully discuss definitional issues, there are some excellent references that begin to delineate the topic of defining tourism. The history of touristic travel and a theoretical overview of tourism theory are outlined by Edensor (2009). Spatially distinct definitional references exist for urban tourism (Hall 2009) and rural tourism (Cawley 2009) and reflect specific resources upon which tourism is based. The geographic perspective of tourism is defined by Williams and Shaw (2001). Regional economic specification of tourism and complexities associated with our ability to track tourism incidence over time is summarized by Smith and Massieu (2005). And finally, the regional transition described in my initial paragraph on post-industrialization and tourism is well described by Pike (2009). From a public policy and integrative tourism planning perspective, the latest edition of C. Michael Hall's text *Tourism Planning: Policies, Processes, and Relationships* is indispensable (Hall 2008). From a development perspective, one key defining attribute of tourism is lacking: a more complete definition of the tourism product and its relationship to rural condition. This key definitional limitation is addressed later in this chapter and, indeed, provides a central thematic of this contribution.

Tourism represents an increasingly important component of rural development. Depending on the rural region, tourism can serve as an economic engine; stimulating private sector entrepreneurial activity within retail and service sector business categories (Crompton 2001; Monchuk 2007; Reeder and Brown 2005; Smith and Massieu 2005). This said, tourism is not without its set of development detractors (Bernhardt et al. 2003; Goos and Manning 2007; Lacher and Oh 2012; Rothman 1998) who argue that tourism creates increased rural income inequality by providing a plethora of low-wage, low-skill, dead-end jobs while generating substantial profits for business owners, many of whom are not from the local rural regions in which they operate for-profit business (Aramberri 2001; McNaughton 2006). From a social class perspective, others argue that local planning and public decision making for tourism has been usurped by stakeholders representing merchants, chambers of commerce and local landed elites (Byrd et al. 2009; Currie et al. 2009; Sautter and Leisen 1999; Weaver and Lawton 2001). From an environmental justice perspective, still others argue that the environmental resources upon which rural tourism is based are differentially benefiting affluent absentee amenity migrants (short and long term), increasingly inaccessible to local residents and indigenous populations, reliant on publicly owned common-property resources rife with recreational use conflict, and supported by large-scale public subsidies (Marcouiller and Hoogasian forthcoming; Rudzitis et al. 2011; Vail and Hultkrantz 2000; Vail and Heldt 2004).

These issues raise important implications for the development of rural regions. Rural tourism and the generic attributes associated with amenity-led development of rural regions can be transformative (Hammer 2008). Transformation occurs within several thematic arenas: notably economic, socio-demographic and environmental. Although public policy makers tend to accept conventional wisdom that precludes in-depth assessment, most often leading to a planning approach known as regional tourism boosterism (Hall 2008), academics have made progress in uncovering the complexities associated with this with respect to rural development. Three specific elements allow insight into this topic and are central to this discussion: (1) the role that natural amenities play in producing the tourism product; (2) rural tourism and linkages between the partially industrialized set of regional business sectors and household income generation; and (3) important socio-demographic transitions of rural regions. These elements provide a focus for this chapter.

Several questions can help frame the set of issues around which this chapter is written. First, upon what theoretical basis do we begin to build understanding about the tourism product and the role of natural amenities in rural development? Second, how might we develop a more theory-driven characterization of the tourism product in its effect on rural condition? And, finally, how can we use this understanding to move forward with progressive, proactive and integrative tourism planning that serves to improve the welfare of people who reside in rural regions? These are the questions to which I attend, written with an eye on the current literature, pointing to gaps in our understanding and important topics for further research, and relevant public policy strategies and alternatives.

This chapter is organized into four subsequent sections. First, I present an overview of theory relevant to understanding tourism and rural development within a more complex, partially industrialized and experience-scape perspective. Next, I spend time developing and defining the concept of a rural tourism product. Following this discussion, I outline the linkages between the tourism product and effects of tourism on rural development. Finally, I conclude with a section that calls for a more integrative tourism planning approach that places improvement in the welfare of rural people and the development of rural communities at its core.

RELEVANT THEORY

There are a variety of theoretical constructs typically outlined to explain touristic phenomena. These span the disciplines of geography, sociology, anthropology, psychology and economics. As the focus of this chapter is on the rural development attributes of tourism, it is noteworthy to identify those theories that relate to the rural condition, regional change and basic elements associated with how tourism is produced. To be sure, my discussion here should not be construed as a comprehensive overview of tourism theories, rather describing only those that relate to the role of tourism in rural development and regional change. Thus, I begin with a description of spatial and temporal theories associated with tourism, then progress to a discussion of tourism as an industry, the tourism product, and conclude this section with a discussion of amenity theory.

Much of the conceptual development of spatial and temporal theory with respect to tourism originates from the work of economic geographers. One such theory, coined the 'tourism destination life cycle', helps explain change in place-based destinations as a result of increased regional incidence of tourism and leisure travel. A well-used description of the tourism destination life cycle was presented by Butler (1989) in the late 1980s. Later expanded into relevant issues addressed by tourism planning (Baum 1998; Getz 1992; Lundtorp and Wanhill 2001) and regional analytics (Cole 2007, 2009, 2012), this theory describes staged changes in community structure as influenced by increases in leisure travelers over time, as outlined in Figure 9.1.

Initial destination elements involve low levels of leisure travel to an area with demands reflective of exploratory interests. These often focus on local resources that are less developed or unique natural features provided by public ownerships. As visitation grows, responses take place within small business interests as demands for retail and service sector offerings shift from a local to a non-local customer base. This development phase is marked by rapid growth in both visitation and community response to increased congestion. Eventually, growth slows and destination tourism planning is faced with critical issues of capacity, consolidation and stagnation. Depending on the effectiveness of this forward thinking, the destination can then move to future phases of either rejuvenation or decline. Classic examples of this are fairly easy to spot, particularly around true destinations. Empirical examples are found throughout the tourism literature (Cooper and Jackson 1989; Kozak and Drew 2012; O'Hare and Barrett 1997; Rodriguez et al. 2008).

Spatially, destinations grow based on locational notoriety as perceived by non-locals. Indeed, crafting this locational notoriety has long been the primary responsibility of marketers, promoters and local tourism boosters. Early- and late- (mature) stage destination demands tend to increase gradually toward a customer base comprised by non-locals who are resident at greater distances from the destination as shown in Figure 9.2.[1] This definitional identification of 'local' and 'non-local' is central to understanding rural tourism and is identified in Figure 9.2 by where the number of tourists

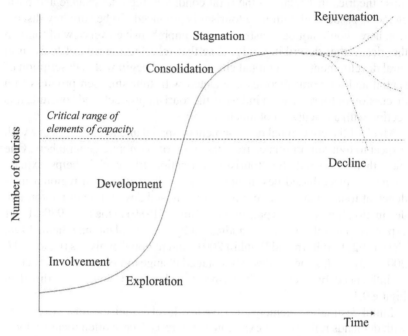

Source: Adapted from Butler (1989).

Figure 9.1   The tourism destination life cycle

is tracked. Note from this figure that early-stage tourism destinations attract tourists from nearby surrounding regions proximate to the destination. As a destination grows, it becomes increasingly attractive to broader geographic markets and the proportion of tourist origins expands away from the destination. At maturation, a true tourism destination will typically attract a primary customer base that is resident far distant from the destination itself as shown by the solid dark line in Figure 9.2 labeled 'Mature-stage tourism destination'.

An important complexity with tourism reflects the tourism product itself. An aging academic in the US Lake States is often quoted as saying 'people don't travel to the Northwoods for great hotel beds or food; they come for the lakes, trees and fresh air with a few fish and deer thrown in to boot!' Simply stated, there is an important disconnection between businesses that benefit from regional natural amenities and the provision of those same natural amenities. Thus, we are brought to an important juncture in our conceptual basis of tourism: exactly what is the tourism product?

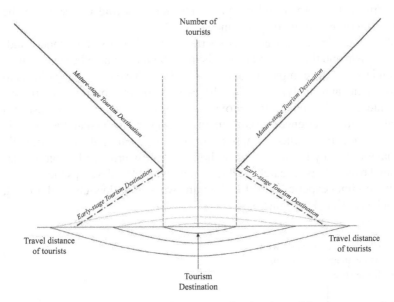

Figure 9.2   Spatial elements of a tourism destination with respect to origin of tourists

This element of how tourism is produced is neither simple nor supported by an abundance of relevant theory. The lack of a conceptual basis limits our ability to speak confidently about the role of tourism in rural development. With respect to conceptual basis, it is useful to understand the academic debate regarding tourism as an 'industry' and the tourism product. Colloquially known as the 'Smith–Leiper debate', this back-and-forth in the tourism literature follows the arguments of Stephen L.J. Smith and the late Neal Leiper. While Smith and others characterize supply-side retail and service sector involvement in catering to travelers (Smith 1988, 1992, 1994) and their resulting supply-chain issues (Rusko et al. 2009; Smith and Massieu 2005; Smith and Xiao 2008; Zhang et al. 2009), others have focused on tourism as a complex, partially industrialized phenomenon (Leiper 1979, 1990, 2008a, 2008b) that relies on latent demand–supply relationships and experience-based tourism products (Andersson 2007; Mossberg 2007; Ellis and Rossman 2008; O'Dell and Billing, 2005; Rossman and Ellis 2008; Rossman and Schlatter, 2008; Sylvester 2008). This 'Leiper-side' partially industrialized and experience-based approach to understanding the tourism product ultimately deals with the supply of visitor experience and resulting regional economic production-related elements. Although the latter arguments are ripe for development of theoretical constructs, the former reflects pure empiricism devoid of theory in the understanding of touristic phenomena.

A partially industrialized and experience-based approach to understanding tourism and the tourism product is important, if for no other reason than to underscore the complexity of the topic. There have been many efforts to understand and analyze what is the essence of the tourism experience. Ritchie and Hudson (2009) provide an excellent overview of research dealing with experience as a concept in defining and understanding touristic phenomena. Experience as applied to the empirical analysis of touristic behavior is a key to understanding how tourism is produced. From fundamental psychology research, Csikszentmihalyi (1990) develops the concept of the optimal experience within the framework of a 'flow-channel' model, which is outlined in Figure 9.3.

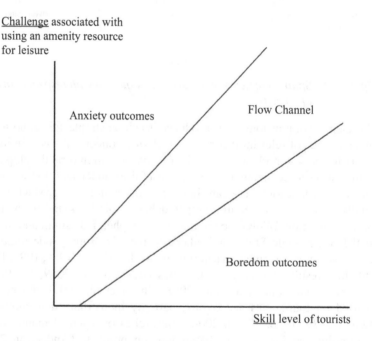

Source: Adapted from Csikszentmihalyi (1990).

Figure 9.3   The flow-channel concept adapted for the tourism product

The relevant tourism product question exists as follows. Why would tourists (non-local visitors) be willing to pay higher amounts for standard goods and services (mostly retail and service sector offerings) in one place (a destination) relative to another? To address this, it is necessary to more fully capture the experience within a production context. The key experiential elements that require planning involve challenge and user skill. Note from Figure 9.3 that the y-axis labeled 'Challenge associated with using an amenity resource for leisure' and the x-axis labeled 'Skill level of tourists' provide a multidimensional trade-off framework that can be related to by tourism mediators (planners, entrepreneurs, governmental units, amenity resource managers, multifunctional landscape beneficiaries). In tourism mediation, natural amenity resources themselves are a necessary but insufficient condition for optimality. Just as important are interpretation (education), recreational site development (physical access) and adaptive site planning (managing use interaction) that address participant skill in usefulness of the underlying resources as employed for leisure. Optimality and higher returns can be expected to accrue to tourism mediators and tourism destinations that are competent in translating local complexities based upon the skill set of the tourist demand base (Dissart and Marcouiller 2012).

The concept of a regional 'experience-scape' has been developed by several writers (Mossberg 2007; Pine and Gilmore 1999; Rossman and Schlatter 2008). O'Dell and Billing (2005) describe experiences as occurring regionally as a combination of individual site attributes. Further, the term 'experience-scape' is often defined as a result of market-based production activities, and planned for regionally by place marketers, city planners and local entrepreneurs such that consumer experiences are staged within stylized landscapes. Indeed, experience-scapes are increasingly understood as a central attribute of the touristic phenomenon and are consistently shown to be important in destination development (Melián-González and García-Falcón 2003; Murphy et al. 2000). So, how does an experience-scape concept add to our understanding of the rural development attributes of tourism? It stresses the fact that tourism experiences take place somewhere in space but involve the interplay between amenities, recreational sites, interpretation, adaptive site planning and the minds of the tourists themselves. There are ample opportunities to more fully operationalize and empirically test for experience and experience-scapes within the theory of tourism. This is particularly important for informing more proactive and progressive tourism planning and public policy (Bornhorst et al. 2010).

The rural tourism phenomenon often surrounds experiential leisure demands that have outdoor recreation at their core. Rural tourism relies on natural resource bases that often have alternative commodity-based uses. Joint production, or the intertwined production relationships of multi-output processes, require and depend on alternative use interaction. Use interaction was first posited by Clawson and Knetsch (1966) in their classic tome on the *Economics of Outdoor Recreation*. Casey van Kooten (1993) provides an excellent description of expanding the concept to incorporate multiple-use, joint-production trade-off concepts. These have been formalized within microeconomics as multi-product additivity (Bailey and Friedlaender 1982).

Environmental economists have developed a corresponding quantitative representation of this notion of compatibility in what is known as 'additivity'. Using diversity as a basis, Weitzman (1992) recognized how a multivariate system relates to individual functions. In this work, alternative forms of additivity were defined. In what is termed supra-additivity, complementarity in utility is defined as increasing returns to utility by combining uses. Subadditivity, on the other hand, occurs when alternative uses are substitutes and exist with decreasing returns to utility in their combination. Recent applications of the basic additivity notions to outdoor recreation and tourism planning are found within the recreational use conflict literature (Carothers et al. 2001; Church et al. 2007; Donnelly et al. 2000; Hall and Shelby 2000; Johnson and Dawson 2004; Marcouiller et al. 2008; Needham and Rollins 2005), and progress is being made. This said, incorporation of economic additivity concepts within theoretical development focused on the tourism product presents a wide opportunity set indeed.

Amenities, both naturally occurring and human-developed, serve as critical causal elements behind both motivations for rural leisure travel and this post-industrial transition in the rural condition of North America (Castle et al. 2011; Gartner 2005; Irwin et al. 2010; Olfert and Partridge 2010; Power 2005; Reeder and Brown 2005), Australia (Argent et al. 2005, 2007) and Europe (Waltert et al. 2011; Williams and Shaw 2009). In particular, the role of natural amenities in concert with developed recreational sites as they influence both the incidence of leisure travel and rural development is complex and generally unrecognized within public policy and tourism planning.

As for the role of amenities within rural development economics, we likewise suffer from a general dearth of policy-relevant theory to explain the tourism product. One dated theoretical basis that is often used to explain rural macroeconomic–amenity relationships extends the wage curve to trade off amenities for wage and salary income, job opportunities and higher land rents within household utility functions; amenities are capitalized into wage and salary incomes, rents and employment (Roback 1982, 1988). Regions with higher levels of amenities should expect equilibration with lower wage and salary income effects. This particular theory remains growth-focused and lacks an understanding of the multiple interactions between tourism and the rest of the economy, wholly missing relationships involving shifts in regional income distribution (Marcouiller 1998; Marcouiller and Clendenning 2005; Power 1996, 2005). Furthermore, economic-amenity theory remains disassociated from important land-based resource dependency and land developability elements.

Although providing mixed and inconsistent results (Deller 2009; Partridge and Rickman 1997), the existing empirical work related to this theory continues to suffer from a lack of standardized control metrics, questionable geographic scales (county level, versus finer-grained minor civil division, block-level or parcel-level specifications) and significant spatial dependency. Certainly, more work is needed to develop theory-based economic-amenity concepts defended by sound and robust empiricism that incorporates amenities and development metrics reflective of rapid transitions experienced by exurban and rural regions.

ON DEFINING RURAL TOURISM AND THE RURAL TOURISM PRODUCT

Leisure travel to rural regions has grown dramatically since the rise of mass tourism, which began the 1950s (Edensor 2009). Increased disposable incomes, leisure time, transportation technology and the development of rural infrastructure have contributed to this rise in retail and service sector activity considered to be tourism-sensitive (Eugenio-Martin et al. 2008; Hall 2008). Demand for rural natural amenities has also increased, most often reflective of development stage, underlying natural resources and nature-based attractions. Rural development impacts of leisure travel extend beyond traditionally defined tourism-sensitive retail and service sectors. Indeed, if we include amenity-driven residential development and its associated linkages to rural land, real-estate, construction and remodeling, and financial services, the rural development attributes of leisure travel become quite broad (Crompton 2001; Gosnell and Travis 2005; Gude et al. 2006; Löffler and Steinike 2006).

Practical regional development concepts associated with tourism are neither direct nor supported by an abundance of relevant theory. This 'Leiper-side' partially industrialized and experience-based approach to understanding the tourism product ultimately deals with the supply of visitor experience and resulting regional economic production-related elements. An adaptation to an early version of this partially industrialized and experience-scape approach, originally published by Lena Mossberg (2007), is found in Figure 9.4.

Note from this presentation that the rural tourism product is fundamentally a co-produced output marked by a decidedly joint private and public process. Experience-based tourism product outcomes, much like the flow channel and additivity concepts described previously, depend on a variety

Leisure travel sensitive business sectors:	Service Sectors			Retail Sectors			Finance, Insurance, & Real Estate (and sectors catering specifically to amenity migrants)	Leisure travel sensitive business sectors
	Hotels, Motels, B&Bs, Camping	Eating & drinking	Amuse-ments	Leisure Retail (sports, gifts, & equipment)	General merch-andise (groceries, furnishings, & durable goods)	Transport (planes, trains, & automobiles)		

Site-specific recreational services:		Indirect (joint) producers:
Local festivals and events		Agricultural producers
Marketing and site promotion		Forest and wildlife managers
Guides and recreational instruction		Watershed managers
Local tour management	**The Rural Tourism Product**	Park and trail managers
Interpretation & communication		Governance (tangible & intangible)
Arts and crafts display		Marketing and regional boosterism
Rural parks and trails		Stakeholders
Rural cultural and historic sites		Infrastructure providers

Site-specific recreational services:	Multi-functional Rural Landscape			Indirect (joint) producers
	Other rural experiencers (tourists in same rural area)	Natural and built amenities **Symbiotic interactions**	Rural heritage, culture, and history	
The experience-scape:				*The experience-scape:*

Source: Adapted from Marcouiller and Hoogasian (2013) and Mossberg (2007).

Figure 9.4   Co-production of tourism that explicitly incorporates experience-based public and jointly produced inputs with traditionally defined tourism sectors and site-specific recreational services

of public and private interactions. Across the top of this figure are listed the private for-profit firms who sell goods and services to tourists and non-tourists alike. Leisure-based non-local travelers (tourists) are combined with local consumers (non-tourists) to contribute to the receipt base of these firms, most of which are involved in the personal service and retail sectors of the regional economy. The tourism component of this demand (non-locals) are drawn to the area because of bucolic rural landscapes that are multifunctional; land which jointly produces agriculture, forestry and mineral commodities and their forward-linked processing outputs (food, wood products and processed minerals). Public outdoor recreation providers and private non-tourism actors play prominent and indispensable roles in producing a sustainable tourism product.

Acting as joint producers, providers of the experience-scape itself and the service supplier of site-specific recreational assets, non-tourism inputs ultimately provide unpriced amenity-based subsidies to those private firms involved in retail and service sector businesses. This amenity subsidy comes in the form of non-local leisure travel demand stimulation to these for-profit firms involved in transportation, overnight accommodations, eating and drinking, amusements and local retailers. Further, if we extend tourism definitions to include recreational homeowners and other amenity migrants such as retirees (indeed, these involve leisure travel), a significant amount of additional non-local contribution to receipts falls within finance, insurance, real estate and other related sectors (for example, construction and remodeling, arts and crafts, and recreational toys such as boats and their docking equipment). Indeed, empirical evidence increasingly suggests that amenities serve as primary motivators behind in-migration to rural regions (Chi and Marcouiller 2011; Cho and Newman 2005; Frentz et al. 2004; Isserman 2001; Isserman et al. 2009; Poudyal et al. 2008; Thompson et al. 2006; Waltert and Schläpfer, 2010; Ward and Brown 2009).

Restating the obvious, tourists rarely travel to rural regions because these regions possess great hotels or restaurants. Instead, they are motivated to travel to rural regions because these regions possess unique natural resource assets. Lakes, coastlines, mountains, forests and bucolic rural landscapes are driving inputs to the production of the rural tourism product. A large portion of the overall demand for rural travel and the rural tourism product is motivated by natural amenities accessed by recreational sites, often publicly owned and managed. Effectiveness of growing the rural tourism product depends on how well tourism mediators develop the underlying experience of leisure travelers. The tourism product is a co-produced and joint public and private set of goods and services; ultimately serving the experience-base of non-local leisure travelers.

RURAL DEVELOPMENT IMPLICATIONS OF THE TOURISM PRODUCT

The rural development implications associated with providing the tourism product have been alluded to by many (Butler et al. 1998; Cawley 2009; Gartner 2005; Reeder and Brown 2005; Ribeiro and Marques 2002). For purposes of clarification, an outline of relevant linkages is summarized in Figure 9.5. Note from this figure that the rural tourism product is represented by co-production, supplied by an array of private and public entities that extend beyond leisure travel-sensitive for-profit firms to include joint producers (park managers, agricultural and forestry producers and local units of government), site-specific recreational services (interpretation and education) and the experience-scape where amenities interact with other tourists. This complex array of tourism providers interacts directly and indirectly with those who demand the tourism product. Non-local travelers (tourists) can be short- or long-duration visitors. Local rural residents can also be leisure travel demanders; but not within the locale in which they reside. Within the host locale, the leisure travel of local residents can be thought of as an important offsetting set of leakages; rarely accounted for in impact assessment.

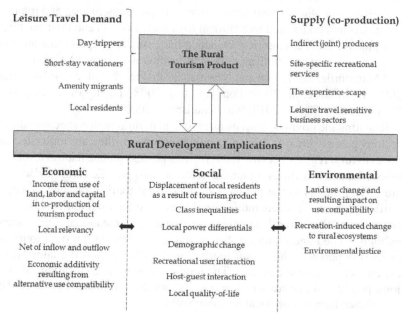

Figure 9.5   Rural development implications of the rural tourism product

The local rural tourism product impacts local residents as a quality-of-life factor, again rarely accounted for due to its nebulous set of non-market values. The presence of non-local visitors can often cause displacement and congestion which, in turn, can detrimentally affect the value of the tourism product (Harrill 2004). The differential benefits and costs can simultaneously result in the rural tourism product being viewed as a zero-sum net option. Non-local travel to rural communities further raises important distributional elements that have the potential for disconnects between local electorates and non-local benefactors of public subsidies. Local benefactors of these public subsidies include footloose entrepreneurs and local business leaders, which have led some to argue local growth machine inequities (Beaver and Cohen 2004; Crowe 2006; Green et al. 1996; Krannich and Humphrey 1983). Certainly, more research is needed with respect to distributional elements associated with benefits and costs of providing public outdoor recreation facilities (Lacher and Oh 2012).

Distributional elements aside, tourism has been shown to provide an important source of income to rural communities; particularly important as traditional forms of income growth decline within less diverse economic structures. This said, there are substantive issues of local relevancy and net effect associated with the inflow of money spent by non-local leisure travelers. Given the predominance of multinational hotel chains and restaurants, much of this inflow leaks straight back out of the rural region to serve non-local investors. Further, there is a pressing need to account for the net effect of the tourism product locally, not the gross effect which is the norm. This net effect requires regional specification and an accounting for local leisure travel to destinations outside of the region. The larger we define the region, the closer we get to a zero-sum outcome (discounting for the time being that space travel is now possible ...). Were we to look at the net effect of producing the tourism product, which regions would end up as gainers, and which would end up as losers? In total, is producing the tourism product a zero-sum game; simply a rearrangement of existing disposable incomes? Does tourism create wealth or simply rearrange urban and rural incomes, leading to an exacerbation of inter-regional income inequality?

From an environmental perspective, tourism creates pressures on land uses shifting from productive use capacity to speculative and amenity-driven values. Certainly, our experience with lake-front development leads us to believe that a significant premium on high-amenity sites serves to dislocate lower- and middle-income local residents, shifting their options for affordable housing to lower-amenity sites within the same rural region. Also, it is important to note that amenity-driven developments are not environmentally benign. Recreation congestion has the potential to detrimentally affect sensitive terrestrial and aquatic ecosystems: introducing invasive species, creating situations for degradation of bio-system function, water quality decline and a variety of pollutants. Further, leisure travel (which serves as a defining element of the tourism product itself) requires massive energy consumption and significant carbon footprints; particularly true today as the majority of travel is done by private vehicles or airplanes.

Finally, note from Figure 9.5 that the rural tourism product and its rural development implications have arrows that point both ways. The tourism product has important social, economic and environmental implications for rural communities. But also, the extent and quality of these implications feed back to the rural tourism product as important determinants of governance approach, effectiveness of tourism mediation, willingness to provide continued public subsidy and, ultimately, the quality of the visitor experience.

SUMMARY AND CONCLUSIONS

In this chapter, I have focused on rural development implications of tourism. This chapter provides a summary of extant knowledge from the current literature, points to gaps in our understanding and posits important roles for mediation, public policy, local governance and stakeholder collaboration. In doing so, I have addressed theoretical issues related to spatial and temporal incidence of tourism, use interaction, joint production, economic additivity and amenity production. I outlined an experience-scape approach to defining the tourism product. This approach accounts for co-production and joint public–private processes within multifunctional rural experience-scapes. This then led to an overview that related the tourism product with important implications for rural development; within issue sets surrounding economic, social and environmental themes.

A key aspect of producing the rural tourism product reflects the need to account for visitor experience: leisure outcomes that take place somewhere in rural spaces but involving the interplay between traditionally defined tourism businesses, jointly owned amenities, publicly managed recreational sites, interpretation, adaptive site planning and the minds of the tourists themselves. In tourism mediation, the traditionally defined tourism 'industry' (retail and personal service firms) exists as a necessary but insufficient condition for optimality. Likewise, natural amenity resources themselves are necessary, but insufficient means upon which an optimal tourism product is produced. Just as important are interpretation (education), public recreational site development (physical access) and adaptive site planning (managing use interaction) that address participant skill in usefulness of the underlying natural resource base as employed for leisure. Optimality and higher returns can be expected to accrue to rural regions endowed with tourism mediators and tourism destinations that are: (1) rich in natural amenities; (2) willing to invest in multifunctional rural landscapes; (3) able to utilize collaborative planning processes that allow for interplay between and among tourism interests, joint producers and public agencies; and (4) competent in translating local complexities based upon the skill set of the tourist demand base. There are ample opportunities to more fully operationalize and empirically test for experience and experience-scapes within the theory of tourism.

Acting as joint producers, providers of the experience-scape (local private landowners) and the service suppliers of site-specific recreational assets are a critical input into the tourism product. Unless compensated, these joint producers and service suppliers offer tourism inputs that exist as unpriced amenity-based subsidies to those private for-profit firms involved in retail and service sector business activity traditionally defined as the tourism 'industry'. In a like fashion, the public invests significant amounts of scarce public funds intent on the maintenance of and improvement to high-quality rural environments and publicly managed natural resources. In essence, these also serve as a subsidy to the same for-profit privately owned firms engaged in tourism.

Creative and proactive public policies with respect to rural tourism can help alleviate disconnects among private returns, costs associated with producing amenities, and public subsidies. Producing joint outputs of amenity resources in a fashion that is complementary to touristic experiences is not costless. Public policies that recognize these complexities can act to generate revenue streams from tourists to offset the costs of producing these key inputs in an equitable manner. Room taxes, user fees, recreational license fees and other incidence-shifting mechanisms can be useful only if returned to general-purpose revenue streams of local, regional and state-level institutions of governance. In turn, these governance structures can then apply these targeted funds to offset the cost of managing resources in a fashion complementary to touristic uses. Certainly, producing a sustainable and high-quality rural tourism product must extend beyond simple marketing and advertising.

In conclusion, rural tourism represents a complex co-produced experience-based product resulting from multifunctional rural landscapes and the activities of public and private actors. It represents an increasingly important component of rural welfare. A more integrative tourism planning approach (Hall 2008; Marcouiller 1997) needs to extend beyond regional tourism boosterism to include the complex interactions between public and private stakeholder groups. The intent of a more proactive approach can serve to place improvement in the welfare of rural people and the development of rural communities at its core.

NOTE

1. It is important to point out that definitions of tourism need to be clear with respect to regional origin of the customer base. One common definition used by many US state tourism agencies applies 50 miles as the necessary distance one must travel before being considered a 'tourist' (the customer base of tourism-sensitive businesses).

REFERENCES

Andersson, T. (2007), 'The tourist in the experience economy', *Scandinavian Journal of Hospitality and Tourism*, 7, 46–58.
Aramberri, J. (2001), 'The host should get lost: paradigms in tourism theory', *Annals of Tourism Research*, 28, 738–61.

174 Handbook of rural development

Argent, N., P. Smails and T. Griffin (2005), 'Tracing the density impulse in rural settlement systems: a quantitative analysis of the factors underlying rural population density across south-eastern Australia, 1981–2001', *Population and Environment*, 27, 151–90.

Argent, N., P. Smails and T. Griffin (2007), 'The amenity complex: towards a framework for analysing and predicting the emergency of a multifunctional countryside in Australia', *Geographical Research*, 45, 217–232.

Bailey, E. and A. Friedlaender (1982), 'Market structure and multiproduct industries', *Journal of Economic Literature*, 20, 1024–48.

Baum, T. (1998), 'Taking the exit route: extending the tourism area life cycle model', *Current Issues in Tourism*, 1, 167–75.

Beaver, W. and E. Cohen (2004), 'Power in a rural county', *Sociological Spectrum*, 24, 629–50.

Bernhardt, A., L. Dresser and E. Hatton (2003), 'The coffee pot wars: unions and firm restructuring in the hotel industry', in E. Appelbaum, A. Bernhardt and R.J. Murnane (eds), *Low-Wage America: How Employers are Reshaping Opportunity in the Workplace*, New York: Russell Sage Foundation, pp. 33–76.

Bornhorst, T., J.R.B. Ritchie and L. Sheehan (2010), 'Determinants of tourism success for DMOs and destinations: an empirical examination of stakeholders' perspectives', *Tourism Management*, 31, 572–89.

Brezzi, M., L. Dijkstra and V. Ruiz (2011), 'OECD extended regional typology: the economic performance of remote rural regions', OECD Regional Development Working Papers, 2011/06, OECD Publishing.

Butler, Richard C., C. Michael Hall and John Jenkins (eds) (1998), *Tourism and Recreation in Rural Areas*, New York: John Wiley.

Butler, R.W. (1989), 'The concept of a tourist area cycle of evolution: implications for management of resources', *Canadian Geographer*, 26, 5–12.

Byrd, E.T., H.E. Bosley and M.G. Dronberger (2009), 'Comparisons of stakeholder perceptions of tourism impacts in rural eastern North Carolina', *Tourism Manaagement*, 30, 693–703.

Carothers, P., J. Vaske and M. Donnelly (2001), 'Social values versus interpersonal conflict among hikers and mountain bikers', *Leisure Sciences*, 23, 47–61.

Castle, E.N., J. Wu and B.A. Weber (2011), 'Place orientation and rural–urban interdependence', *Applied Economic Perspectives and Policy*. doi:10.1093/aepp/ppr009.

Cawley, M. (2009), 'Rural tourism', in R. Kitchin and N. Thrift (eds), *International Encyclopedia of Human Geography*, Amsterdam: Elsevier Publishing, pp. 313–17.

Chi, Guangqing and D.W. Marcouiller (2011), 'Isolating the effect of natural amenities on population change at the local level', *Regional Studies*, 5, 491–505.

Cho, Seung-hoon and David H. Newman (2005), 'Spatial analysis of rural land development', *Forest Policy and Economics*, 7, 732–44.

Church, Andrew, Paul Gilchrist and Neil Ravenscroft (2007), 'Negotiating recreational access under asymmetrical power relations: the case of inland waterways in England', *Society and Natural Resources*, 20, 213–27.

Clawson, M. and J.L. Knetsch (1966), *Economics of Outdoor Recreation*, Baltimore, MD: Johns Hopkins Press.

Cole, S. (2007), 'Beyond the resort life-cycle: the micro-dynamics of destination tourism', *Journal of Regional Analysis and Policy*, 37, 266–78.

Cole, S. (2009), 'A logistic tourism model: resort cycles, globalization, and chaos', *Annals of Tourism Research*, 36, 689–714.

Cole, S. (2012), 'Synergy and congestion in the tourism destination life cycle', *Tourism Management*, 33, 1128–40.

Cooper, C. and S. Jackson (1989), 'Destination life-cycle: the Isle of Man case-study', *Annals of Tourism Research*, 16, 377–98.

Crompton, J.L. (2001), 'Parks and economic development', Planning Advisory Service Report Number 502, Chicago, IL: American Planning Association.

Crowe, J.A. (2006), 'Community economic development strategies in rural Washington: toward a synthesis of natural and social capital', *Rural Sociology*, 71, 573–96.

Csikszentmihalyi, M. (1990), *Flow: The Psychology of Optimal Experience*, New York: Harper & Row.

Currie, Russell R., Sheilagh Seaton and Franz Wesley (2009), 'Determining stakeholders for feasibility analysis', *Annals of Tourism Research*, 36, 41–63.

Deller, S. (2009), 'Wages, rent, unemployment and amenities', *Journal of Regional Analysis and Policy*, 39, 141–54.

Dissart, J.C. and D.W. Marcouiller (2012), 'Rural tourism production and the experience-scape', *Tourism Analysis*, 17, 691–704.

Donnelly, M., J. Vaske, D. Whittaker and B. Shelby (2000), 'Toward an understanding of norm prevalence: a comparative analysis of 20 years of research', *Environmental Management*, 25, 403–14.

Duncan, C.M. (2007), 'Rural America in transition: a comparison of conditions and perspectives in amenity rich, resource dependent and chronically poor communities', presented to the National Rural Assembly, June.

Edensor, T. (2009), 'Tourism', in R. Kitchin and N. Thrift (eds), *International Encyclopedia of Human Geography*, Amsterdam: Elsevier Publishing, pp. 301–12.

Ellis, G.D. and J.R. Rossman (2008), 'Creating value for participants through experience staging: parks, recreation, and tourism in the experience industry', *Journal of Park and Recreation Administration*, 26, 1–20.

Eugenio-Martin, J., N. Marin-Morales and M. Thea Sinclair (2008), 'The role of economic development in tourism demand', *Tourism Economics*, 14, 673–90.

Frentz, I.C., F.L. Farmer, J.M. Guldin and K.G. Smith (2004), 'Public lands and population growth', *Society and Natural Resources*, 17, 57–68.

Gartner, W.C. (2005), 'A perspective on rural tourism development', *Journal of Regional Analysis and Policy*, 35, 33–42.

Getz, D. (1992), 'Tourism planning and destination life-cycle', *Annals of Tourism Research*, 19, 752–70.

Goos, M. and A. Manning (2007). 'Lousy and lovely jobs: the rising polarization of work in Britain', *Review of Economics and Statistics*, 89, 118–33.

Gosnell, H. and W.R. Travis (2005), 'Ranchland ownership dynamics in the Rocky Mountain West', *Rangeland Ecology and Management*, 58, 191–8.

Green, G.P., D.W. Marcouiller, S.C. Deller, D.K. Erkkila and N.R. Sumathi (1996), 'Local dependency, land use attitudes, and economic development: comparisons between seasonal and permanent residents', *Rural Sociology*, 61, 427–45.

Gude, P.H., A.J. Hansen, R. Rasker and B. Maxwell (2006), 'Rates and drivers of rural residential development in Greater Yellowstone', *Landscape and Urban Planning*, 77, 131–51.

Hall, C. Michael (2008), *Tourism Planning: Policies, Processes, and Relationships*, 2nd edition, New York: Pearson Prentice.

Hall, T. (2009), 'Urban tourism', in R. Kitchin and N. Thrift (eds), *International Encyclopedia of Human Geography*, Amsterdam: Elsevier Publishing, pp. 318–23.

Hall, T. and B. Shelby (2000), 'Temporal and spatial displacement: evidence from a high-use reservoir and alternate sites', *Journal of Leisure Research*, 32, 435–56.

Hamilton, Lawrence C., Leslie R. Hamilton, Cynthia M. Duncan and Chris R. Colocousis (2008), 'Place matters: Cenges and opportunities in four rural Americas', *Reports on Rural America* 1, 4, Durham, NH: Carsey Institute.

Hammer, R. (2008), 'Recreation and rural development in Norway: nature versus culture', *Scandinavian Journal of Hospitality and Tourism*, 8, 176–86.

Harrill, R. (2004), 'Resident's attitudes toward tourism development: a literature review with implications for tourism planning', *Journal of Planning Literature*, 18, 251–66.

Irwin, E.G., A.M. Isserman, M. Kilkenny and M.D. Partridge (2010), 'A century of research on rural development and regional issues', *American Journal of Agricultural Economics*, 92, 522–53.

Isserman A. (2001), 'The competitive advantages of rural America in the next century', *International Regional Science Review*, 24, 35–58.

Isserman, A.M., E. Feser, D.E. Warren (2009), 'Why some rural places prosper and others do not', *International Regional Science Review*, 32, 300–342.

Johnson, A. and C. Dawson (2004), 'An exploratory study of the complexities of coping behavior in the Adirondack Wilderness', *Leisure Sciences*, 26, 281–93.

Johnson, K.M. and C.L. Beale (2002), 'Nonmetro recreation counties: their identification and rapid growth', *Rural America*, 17, 12–19.

Kozak, M. and M. Drew (2012), 'Tourism life cycle and sustainability analysis: profit-focused strategies for mature destinations', *Tourism Management*, 33, 188–94.

Krannich, R.S. and C.R. Humphrey (1983), 'Local mobilization and community growth: toward an assessment of the "Growth Machine" hypothesis', *Rural Sociology*, 48, 60–81.

Lacher, R.G. and Chi-Ok Oh (2012), 'Is tourism a low-income industry? Evidence from three coastal regions', *Journal of Travel Research*, 51, 464–72.

Lapping, Mark B., Thomas L. Daniels and John W. Keller (1989), *Rural Planning and Development in the United States*, New York: Guilford Press.

Leiper, N. (1979), 'The framework of tourism: towards a definition of tourism, tourist, and the tourism industry', *Annals of Tourism Research*, 6, 390–407.

Leiper, N. (1990), 'Partial industrialization of tourism systems (Rejoinder and Commentary)', *Annals of Tourism Research*, 17, 600–605.

Leiper, N. (2008a), 'Why "the tourism industry" is misleading as a generic expression: the case for the plural variation, "tourism industries"', *Tourism Management*, 29, 237–51.

Leiper, N. (2008b), 'Partial industrialization in tourism: a new model', *Current Issues in Tourism*, 11, 205–35.

Löffler, R. and E. Steinike (2006), 'Counterurbanization and its socioeconomic effects in high mountain areas of the Sierra Nevada (California/Nevada)', *Mountain Research and Development*, 26, 64–71.

Lundtorp, S. and S. Wanhill (2001), 'The resort lifecycle theory: generating processes and estimation', *Annals of Tourism Research*, 28, 947–64.

Marcouiller, D.W. (1997), 'Toward integrative tourism planning in rural America', *Journal of Planning Literature*, 11, 337–57.

Marcouiller, David (1998), 'Environmental resources as latent primary factors of production in tourism', *Tourism Economics*, 4, 131–45.

Marcouiller, D.W. and G.C. Clendenning (2005), 'The supply of natural amenities: Moving from empirical anecdotes to a theoretical basis', in G.P. Green, S.C. Deller and D.W. Marcouiller (eds), *Amenities and Rural Development: Theory, Methods, and Public Policy*, Cheltenham, UK and Northampton, MA, USA: Edward Elgar Publishing, pp. 6–32.

Marcouiller, D.W. and A. Hoogasian (forthcoming), 'The role of public outdoor recreation providers in supporting rural development', in S. Payson (ed.), *Public Economics: The Government's Role in American Economics*, New York: ABC-Clio Publishing.

Marcouiller, D.W., I. Scott and J. Prey (2008), 'Outdoor recreation planning: a comprehensive approach to understanding use interaction', *CAB Reviews: Perspectives in Agriculture, Veterinary Science, Nutrition and Natural Resources*, 3(90), 1–12.

McNaughton, D. (2006), 'The "host" as uninvited "guest": hospitality, violence, and tourism', *Annals of Tourism Research*, 33, 645–65.

Melián-González, A. and J.M. García-Falcón (2003), 'Competitive potential of tourism in destinations', *Annals of Tourism Research*, 30, 720–40.

Monchuk, D. (2007), 'People rush in, empty their pockets, and scuttle out: economic impacts of gambling on the waterways', *Journal of Regional Analysis and Policy*, 37, 223–32.

Mossberg, L. (2007), 'A marketing approach to the tourist experience', *Scandinavian Journal of Hospitality and Tourism*, 7, 59–74.

Murphy, P., M.P. Pritchard and B. Smith (2000), 'The destination product and its impact on traveler perceptions', *Tourism Management*, 21, 43–52.

Needham, M. and R.B. Rollins (2005), 'Interest group standards for recreation and tourism impacts at ski areas in the summer', *Tourism Management*, 26, 1–13.

O'Dell, T. and P. Billing (2005), *Experiencescapes: Tourism, Culture and Economy*, Copenhagen: Copenhagen Business School Press.

O'Hare, G. and H. Barrett (1997), 'The destination life cycle: international tourism in Peru', *Scottish Geographical Magazine*, 113, 66–73.

Olfert, M. Rose and M.D. Partridge (2010), 'Best practices in twenty-first century rural development and policy', *Growth and Change*, 41, 147–64.

Partridge, M.D. and D.S. Rickman (1997), 'Has the wage curve nullified the Harris–Todaro model? Further US evidence', *Economic Letters*, 54, 277–82.

Pike, A. (2009), 'De-Industrialization', in R. Kitchin and N. Thrift (eds), *International Encyclopedia of Human Geography*, Northhampton MA: Elsevier Publishing, pp. 51–9.

Pine, B.J. and J.H. Gilmore (1999), *The Experience Economy: Work is Theatre and Every Business a Stage*, Boston, MA: Harvard Business School Press.

Poudyal, N.C., D.G. Hodges and H.K. Cordell (2008), 'The role of natural resource amenities in attracting retirees: implications for economic growth policy', *Ecological Economics*, 68, 240–48.

Power, Thomas (1996), *Lost Landscapes and Failed Economies*, Washington, DC: Island Press.

Power, T.M. (2005), 'The supply and demand for natural amenities: an overview of theory and concepts', in G.P. Green, D. Marcouiller and S. Deller (eds), *Amenities and Rural Development: Theory, Methods, and Public Policy*, Cheltenham, UK and Northampton, MA, USA: Edward Elgar Publishing, pp. 63–77.

Reeder, R.J. and D.M. Brown (2005), 'Recreation, tourism, and rural well-being', Economic Research Service, Economic Research Report #7, Washington, DC: US Department of Agriculture, Economic Research Service.

Ribeiro, M. and C. Marques (2002), 'Rural tourism and the development of less favoured areas – between rhetoric and practice', *International Journal of Tourism Research*, 4, 211–20.

Ritchie, J.R.B. and S. Hudson (2009), 'Understanding and meeting the challenges of consumer/tourist experience research', *International Journal of Tourism Research*, 11, 111–26.

Roback, J. (1982), 'Wages, rents and quality of life', *Journal of Political Economy*, 90, 1257–77.

Roback, J. (1988), 'Wages, rents and amenities: differences among workers and regions', *Economic Inquiry*, 26, 23–41.

Rodriguez, J.R.O., E. Parra-Lopez and V. Yanes-Estevez (2008), 'The sustainability of island destinations: tourism area life cycle and teleological perspectives', *Tourism Management*, 29, 53–65.

Rossman, J.R. and G.D. Ellis (2008), 'A rejoinder to Charles Sylvester', *Journal of Park and Recreation Administration*, 26, 42–6.

Rossman, J.R. and B.E. Schlatter (2008), *Recreation Programming: Designing Leisure Experiences*, 5th edition, Champaign, IL: Sagamore Publishing.

Rothman, Hal K. (1998), *Devil's Bargains: Tourism in the Twentieth-Century American West*, Lawrence, KS: University Press of Kansas.

Rudzitis, G., D.W. Marcouiller and P. Lorah (2011), 'The rural rich and their housing: spatially addressing the "haves"', in D.W. Marcouiller, M.L. Lapping and O. Furuseth (eds), *Rural Housing, Exurbanization, and Amenity-Driven Development: Contrasting the 'Haves' and the 'Have Nots'*, Aldershot: Ashgate Publishing, pp. 129–56.

Rusko, R.T., M. Kylanen and R. Saari (2009), 'Supply chain in tourism destinations: the case of Levi Resort in Finnish Lapland', *International Journal of Tourism Research*, 11, 71–87.

Sautter, E.T. and B. Leisen (1999), 'Managing stakeholders: a tourism planning model', *Annals of Tourism Research*, 26, 312–28.

Smith, S.L.J. (1988), 'Defining tourism: a supply-side view', *Annals of Tourism Research*, 15, 179–90.

Smith, S.L.J. (1992), 'Return to the supply side (Rejoinder and Commentary)', *Annals of Tourism Research*, 19, 226–9.

Smith, S.L.J. (1994), 'The tourism product', *Annals of Tourism Research*, 21, 582–95.

Smith, S.L.J. and A. Massieu (2005), 'Tourism statistics', in K. Kempf-Leanard (ed.), *Encyclopedia of Social Measurement*, Amsterdam: Elsevier Publishing, pp. 863–8.

Smith, S.L.J. and Honggen Xiao (2008), 'Culinary tourism supply chains: a preliminary examination', *Journal of Travel Research*, 46, 289–99.

Sylvester, C. (2008), 'The ethics of experience in recreation and leisure services', *Journal of Park and Recreation Administration*, 26, 21–41.

Thompson, E., G. Hammond and S. Weiler (2006), *Amenities, Local Conditions, and Fiscal Determinants of Factor Growth in Rural America*, Kansas City, MO: Federal Reserve Bank.

US Department of Agriculture (USDA) (2004), *Measuring Rurality: Rural–Urban Continuum Codes*, Washington, DC: Economic Research Service, US Department of Agriculture.

Vail, D. and T. Heldt (2004), 'Governing snowmobiles in multiple-use landscapes: Swedish and Maine (USA) cases', *Ecological Economics*, 48, 469–83.

Vail, D. and L. Hultkrantz (2000), 'Property rights and sustainable nature tourism: adaptation and mal-adaptation in Dalarna (Sweden) and Maine (USA)', *Ecological Economics*, 35, 223–42.

van Kooten, G.C. (1993), *Land Resource Economics and Sustainable Development: Economic Policies and the Common Good*, Vancouver: University of British Columbia Press.

Waltert, F. and F. Schläpfer (2010), 'Landscape amenities and local development: a review of migration, regional economic and hedonic pricing studies', *Ecological Economics*, 70, 141–52.

Waltert, F., T. Schulz and F. Schläpfer (2011), 'The role of landscape amenities in regional development: evidence from Swiss municipality data', *Land Use Policy*, 28, 748–61.

Ward, N. and D.L. Brown (2009), 'Placing the rural in regional development', *Regional Studies*, 43, 1237–44.

Weaver, D.B. and L.J. Lawton (2001), 'Resident perceptions in the urban–rural fringe', *Annals of Tourism Research*, 28, 439–58.

Weitzman, M.L. (1992), 'On diversity', *Quarterly Journal of Economics*, 107, 363–405.

Williams, A.M. and G. Shaw (2001), 'Geography of tourism', in N.J. Smelser and P.B. Baltes (eds), *International Encyclopedia of the Social and Behavioral Sciences*, Amsterdam: Elsevier Publishing, pp. 15800–803.

Williams, A.M. and G. Shaw (2009), 'Future play: tourism recreation and land use', *Land Use Policy*, 26S, S326–S335.

Zhang, Xinyan, Haiyan Song and G.Q. Huang (2009), 'Tourism supply chain management: a new research agenda', *Tourism Management*, 30, 345–58.

10. Gender and rural development

Carolyn Sachs

Restructuring of employment opportunities in the rural US involves the precipitous decline in manufacturing employment and natural resource-related jobs in forestry and fisheries, the demise of agricultural employment, and an increase in service-related jobs. These shifts alter the gender composition of the rural workforce and call for new approaches to rural development.

This chapter focuses primarily on the US, but also provides analysis of efforts related to gender and rural development in developing countries. The chapter begins by examining how restructuring of employment in the rural US and globally has impacted women and men. Second, the chapter explores how the push for entrepreneurship and small business development as a strategy for coping with the loss of traditional jobs in rural areas impacts women and men. Third, the chapter examines how women are affected by global changes in agriculture, both in large-scale commodity production and in smaller-scale enterprises. Fourth, the chapter addresses how changes in employment, the global economy and government cutbacks in services impacts women's household and reproductive work. Finally, I assess how rural policies and gender mainstreaming offer the potential to address issues of gender equity and improving the lives of rural women.

SHIFTING WORK PATTERNS

One striking change in the US is in the work patterns of men and women in rural areas. The decline in jobs for rural men in manufacturing, natural resources and agriculture pushed women into the workforce for the purpose of increasing income in their households (Falk and Lobao 2003). At the same time, the shift from manufacturing to service sector employment has also pulled rural women into the workforce (Smith and Tickamyer 2011). Increases in service sector employment have opened opportunities for rural women in the workforce in both professional and non-professional jobs. Some of the professional jobs such as teaching and nursing provide decent incomes for rural women, but many of the jobs women perform in the service sector in retail trade, restaurants and house cleaning provide low levels of remuneration, few benefits, and limited job security.

Rural women are not the only ones to be disadvantaged by structural shifts in employment. In fact, as Jensen and Jensen (2011) show in their detailed analyses of data from the Current Population Survey, rural men have been more disadvantaged from structural shifts in the economy than either urban men or rural women. Rural men's situations in the labor market have worsened over time, in contrast to rural women whose employment situations have improved markedly. Higher-wage, unionized jobs with benefits for men have declined in rural areas with severe impacts on rural men, women and children. These shifts in men's and women's work patterns result in changes in household relationships as well. Sherman's (2011) ethnographic study of a sawmill closure in a small logging and mill town in rural California reveals the multiple ways that gender roles shift in response to men's job loss. Some men respond by adhering to rigid masculine identities and struggle to maintain traditional gender roles. This struggle often has devastating consequences including substance abuse and domestic violence. However, Sherman also found a surprising amount of resilience and adoption of flexible masculine roles that emphasized more active fathering roles.

The rise in women's paid employment from the 1970s to 2000 was strikingly similar in both rural and urban areas. Rural women's employment rose from 57 percent in 1970 to a high of 74 percent in 2001 with a slight decline to 71 percent in 2007 (Smith and Tickamyer 2011, p. 62). During the same period of time rural men's employment has declined from 92 percent in 1970 to 80 percent in 2007 (Smith and Tickamyer 2011, p. 63). The gender shifts in employment patterns impact household incomes, family dynamics and household composition. Although more rural women are employed, they often work in low-wage jobs. For rural workers these low-wage jobs are most prevalent in food preparation; health care support; building and grounds cleaning and maintenance; and farming, fishing and forestry (Anderson and Weng 2011). At the national level in both urban and rural areas, women are most likely to work in management, professional and related occupations (40.6 percent); 32.0 percent worked in sales and office occupations; 21.3 percent in service occupations; 5.2 percent in production, transportation and material moving occupations; and 0.9 percent in natural resources, construction and maintenance occupations (US Department of Labor 2010). Gendered segregation of occupations results in different impacts of changes in the labor force for men and women.

One exception to the declining employment opportunities for men in rural areas is in oil and gas expansion employment. Natural gas development in certain regions of the country has led to increasing employment opportunities for rural men in areas with large natural gas reserves such as Pennsylvania, North Dakota, Texas and Oklahoma. The majority of workers in the natural gas industry are men. As of November 2012, 196 300 people were employed in the US in the oil and gas extraction industry (US Department of Labor 2012). Limited data exist on the gender breakdown of workers in the oil and gas extraction industry.

The trend towards the feminization of employment in the US is mirrored in many regions of the world as a key component of neoliberal global-ization. The feminization of employment involves both the increasing proportion of women in the workforce and the deterioration of labor conditions for both men and women (Peterson 2005). Women's formal employment has increased worldwide, while male employment is declin-ing; this does not necessarily translate into the empowerment of women, but rather deteriorating working conditions for men. 'In short, as more jobs become casual, irregular, flexible and precarious, more women – and feminised men – are doing them' (Peterson 2005, p. 509).

Between 2007 and 2009, approximately 642 000 manufacturing jobs were lost in non-metropolitan US counties, a 19.3 percent decrease (USDA 2010). Now wholesale and retail trade employ more people in rural areas than manufacturing. Rural communities are often hard hit by plant closures and losses in manufacturing jobs due to economic restructuring or move-ment of plants to other locations or countries. In single-industry rural towns, plant closures can impact the entire community (Lichter and Graefe 2011). Due to the gender segregation of jobs, plant closures in rural areas can differentially impact men and women.

Even though rural women's employment has increased, they often work in unfavorable circumstances with low pay, unpredictable hours and insta-bility. Women's employment in the rural US fits into the broader context of globalization and neoliberalism. As Patricia Fernandez-Kelly suggests in comparing women workers in factories in the US with women factory workers in other parts of the world, most women's search for jobs is driven by their concern to maintain living standards for themselves and their families, rather than to achieve emancipation. As she states, 'despite their comparative prosperity – US women bear a striking resemblance to their counterparts in China, Nicaragua, and Mexico. Despite such common-alities, national background and race continue to fragment gender and class consciousness' (Fernandez-Kelly 2007, p. 520). Fraser (2009) argues that second wave feminism's focus on increasing women's paid employment provided a key ingredient for neoliberalism. What began as a critique of the family wage now justifies flexible capitalism with women in both the professional classes and working class viewing work for salaries and wages with more than earning an income but also with ethical meaning and the path towards personal empowerment. Whether trying to break the glass ceiling, working as temporary flexible workers in agriculture or food processing, or obtaining loans for microcredit, women's empowerment has been tied to capital accumulation.

Rural development efforts have seldom turned their eye towards gender issues or actively sought jobs for women. Nevertheless, the service jobs that have replaced manufacturing, agriculture and natural resource employment in rural areas are often held by women. These include higher-wage professional jobs such as teachers and health care professionals as well as lower-wage jobs such as waitresses, retail clerks and health care attendants. Some of these jobs provide women with a level of economic independence, but others keep them economically reliant on husbands, boyfriends, friends, relatives, other family members or the state. As local areas consider various options for attracting particular industries, and states design economic development initiatives, they must consider opportunities for both men and women given the persistence of gender segregation of jobs (McLaughlin and Coleman-Jensen 2011).

ENTREPRENEURSHIP AND SMALL-BUSINESS DEVELOPMENT

Entrepreneurship and small-business development have been touted as the key to resolving national and local employment problems as well as providing innovation and the possibility for long-term economic recovery. Typical small-scale businesses in rural areas have been undermined by the consolidation in rural industries such as agriculture, logging and coal mining, which does not bode well for the creation of jobs in these sectors. Similarly, rural retail small businesses such as grocery stores, pharmacies and hardware stores have been systematically pushed out of business by large boxstore companies such as Walmart, Lowes and Home Depot.

The extent to which small-business development and entrepreneurship can revitalize rural areas and provide good paying jobs for women or men remains questionable, but many rural women in both the US and other countries are turning to small-scale entrepreneurship opportunities to gain income.

Women are increasingly starting new businesses and many of these are small businesses. In 2002, women owned 28 percent of the business firms in the US, and the number of women-owned businesses increased by 20 percent from 1997 to 2002 (US Small Business Administration 2006). Since 2002, the number of women-owned businesses has leveled off, but as of 2007, women owned 7.8 million businesses and accounted for 28.7 percent of all businesses nationwide. The Small Business Administration reports that 88 percent of women-owned businesses are small businesses.

Women have started enterprises at a faster rate than men, but women-owned businesses are smaller than men's businesses and on average their revenues are only 27 percent of men-owned businesses.

Despite the growth in numbers of women-owned businesses, entrepreneurship continues to be viewed as the province of men. The characteristics of successful entrepreneurs are often coded as male qualities, although this is rarely explicitly articulated. The dominant discourse of entrepreneurship focuses on 'heroic masculinism' (Lewis 2006), with entrepreneurs defined as risk takers, leaders and rational planners (Bruni et al. 2004). Some scholars argue that women business owners challenge the definition of successful entrepreneurship and suggest that women's businesses create new possibilities for alternative models of enterprise and entrepreneurship (Fenwick 2003). Women's preference for small and stable entrepreneurial models provides them with opportunities for a better work–family balance (Lee-Gosselin and Grise 1990).

For women in rural areas with limited access to good jobs in formal employment, starting a small business may seem a good option. Women in rural areas often face long commutes, have limited options for child care or elder care, and may lean towards small business for non-economic as well as economic reasons (Tigges and Green 1994). By contrast, men business owners are less likely than women to be constrained by the geographic location of their business because they tend to have fewer family responsibilities (Mulholland 1996; Nelson and Smith 1999). Tigges and Green (1994) found that women's businesses had lower sales and fewer workers than men-owned businesses. Women's businesses were highly concentrated in personal services which offer limited remuneration. Other studies replicate their findings that women-owned businesses are in the least profitable industries and sectors. Bird's study of businesses in Iowa found less of a gender gap in business success in rural than urban areas. She suggests that policies that support women-owned businesses focus too narrowly on individual loans to women and training programs without addressing broader structural factors that limit the success of women-owned businesses (Bird and Sapp 2004).

One of the initial pushes for women's entrepreneurship came from the success of microcredit programs for women in South Asia. Outside of the US, especially in developing countries where limited formal employment opportunities exist for women, entrepreneurship and small businesses offer numerous possibilities for women. In Asia, microcredit programs such as the Grameen Bank and Self-Employed Workers Association (SEWA) have targeted women for small loans to support their business efforts. These programs rely on women's groups and result in excellent loan repayment rates. Many efforts in developing countries have replicated these micro-credit programs and have learned numerous lessons along the way. Two of the strengths of microcredit efforts are that they target poor women and they use group-based strategies (Kabeer 2005). Non-governmental organizations (NGOs) offering microcredit often target poor women and they have the possibility of addressing social inequality and improving the income of the poor. Second, the group-based strategies give poor women the opportunity to belong to groups and offer some possibilities for collective social action and change. There have been numerous critiques of microcredit programs, and as Kabeer (2005) suggests, they are not silver bullets in efforts to alleviate poverty and to empower women. First, the amount of money available to individual women and women's groups is often quite small and not sufficient to begin to pull poor women out of poverty. Second, women are not necessarily empowered through their participation in these credit groups. Third, the money is often spent on smaller-scale income-generating activities that are traditionally performed by women and offer little opportunity for them to move into less traditional sectors that offer opportunity to gain substantial income. And finally, finances alone are not sufficient to pull individuals out of poverty in the midst of structural factors that reinforce poverty. More recent microcredit programs have responded to critiques and now often include financial education, training, health care services and other strategies for improving women's possibilities of economic success and empowerment.

A strategy that goes beyond microcredit to improve working conditions for poor women in developing countries is the fair trade movement. Northern consumers' concerns with fair working conditions in developing countries have fostered many efforts to promote fair trade. Conflicting findings have emerged on the extent that these fair trade initiatives help women workers. Le Mare's (2012) study of women Fair Trade handicraft producers in Bangladesh finds that women's involvement in Fair Trade producers' groups has improved their status in the home, increased their involvement in decision making and provided economic empowerment. She acknowledges several issues that need to be addressed to reach the goals of empowering women, including: the low rates of return for handicraft work, increased workloads for women and the problem of increasing women's involvement in the public sphere. Other studies of fair trade show that codes for working standards are not gender neutral. As Smith and Dolan (2006) and Bain (2010) point out, fair trade codes designed to improve working conditions address the needs of formal workers, whereas women are very likely to be informal workers and not covered by these policies. Smith and Dolan (2006) suggest that fair trade policies could also be more sensitive to the needs of women workers by extending their codes to non-wage benefits such as maternity benefits, child care and transportation that enable women to better manage their work and family responsibilities.

For many rural women in different regions of the globe, small businesses and enterprises provide options for combining child care or elder care with income-generating opportunities that are not readily available in formal employment. Although small-scale entrepreneurship provides many potential opportunities for women, there are also significant barriers. Women-owned businesses confront more barriers and receive fewer services and support than men-owned businesses (Bardasi et al. 2007; Ellis et al. 2006; World Bank 2007a, 2007b).

SHIFTING GENDER RELATIONS IN AGRICULTURE

Shifts in the global restructuring in agriculture have differential gender impacts. Much of the scholarship on rural women in the US has focused on women in agriculture, especially women farmers. Recently scholars have noted the increase in women farmers, especially on sustainable and organic farms (Hall and Mogyorody 2007; Trauger et al. 2009), but with limited analysis of the impact of global agricultural restructuring on gender issues in farming in the US. Global and regional trade agreements that cut subsidies and supports for traditional commodities often result in shifts in gender relations on farms in different regions of the world. Global and national policies that favor large-scale corporate agriculture have led to the decline in the number of medium-sized farms and the heavy reliance of small and medium-sized farms on off-farm employment in the US and Europe. In some instances, men leave farms or seek employment off the farm, opening up space for women to move into farming; or in some places the gender balance shifts to such an extent that scholars have noted the feminization of agriculture. In Europe, policies that support multifunctional agriculture such as tourism have shifted gender relations on farms, undermined patriarchal power, and created more equitable and empowering opportunities for women (Brandth and Haugen 2010). Limited attention has been directed at how these global shifts impact gender relations or women on farms in the US.

Shifts in the global agrifood system created by various trade agreements, loan repayment policies and corporate agriculture have impacted women in agriculture in multiple ways (Sachs and Alston 2010). In efforts to increase exports and respond to the terms of structural adjustment, many countries in the global south have increased production and processing of non-traditional crops such as vegetables, fruits and flowers which rely heavily on women's labor. Women are valued laborers because they can be paid less and hired to work in more flexible and less stable work arrangements. The global and the local are highly linked in terms of women's employment opportunities, 'the comparative advantage of agrifood industries in global markets rests on the comparative disadvantage of rural women in national labor markets' (Preibisch and Grez 2010, p. 291). While women are often the preferred workers in corporate agricultural production in developing countries, single migrant men workers who are most often from Mexico are often preferred hired agricultural laborers in the US and Canada (Preibish and Grez 2010). The complex intersections of gender, race and ethnicity in corporate agriculture in the US have only just begun to be addressed.

Agriculture in the US is tied to global markets with the increasing industrialization and globalization of agriculture continually shifting and redefining agriculture and farming in the United States. Large-scale commodity production is at the center of agriculture in the US. The barriers to entry are steep and most women do not have the land or capital to invest in these large-scale operations. Women are less likely than men to be farmers on these large-scale commodity farms. Women are significantly less likely than men to be principal operators or primary operators on farms that produce major commodities such as corn, soybeans, cotton and cattle. The majority of women farmers do not produce these major commodities on large-scale operations but rather tend to be involved in smaller, diversified operations. Of course, women live on large commodity farms and are married to farmers, but many of these women do not consider themselves farmers. Many women on commodity farms help in the business of farming, but also work off the farm.

Nevertheless, the number of women farmers is increasing and as of 2007, women constitute 30 percent of farm operators in the US, a 17 percent increase from 2002 to 2007 (USDA 2007). Part of this increase is due to new counting procedures at the US Department of Agriculture (USDA) which uncovered that more women are farming than officially tallied in the past. Before 2007, only one operator was counted per farm and usually the male operator was counted. Tallying more than one operator per farm substantially increased the number of women who were officially counted as farmers. But in addition to farming with spouses and family members, more women are entering farming as the principal operator of their farms. USDA defines the principal farm operator as the person in charge of day-to-day decisions on the farm. The number of women principal farm operators increased from 237 819 in 2002 to 306 209 in 2007 for a 29 percent increase in women farmers in just five years (USDA 2007).

Women principal operators of farms have different types of operations than men farmers. Men's farms are far more likely to produce grains and cattle than women-operated farms. Male-operated farms are also more likely to produce tobacco, cotton, dairy and hogs than women-operated farms. Women's farms are often quite diverse in terms of crops and livestock and they are most likely to produce hay and animals categorized as 'other' by the agricultural census. They are also more likely than male farmers to have vegetables, fruits and nuts, horticulture, poultry, and sheep and goats (USDA 2007).

Clearly, women have different types of farming than their male peers but they also farm with fewer resources. Women's farms tend to be smaller with lower sales than male-operated farms. On average women's farms are less than half the size of men's farms: 210 acres compared to 452 acres (USDA 2007). The discrepancy in sales is even greater with the average sales on women-operated farms about one-fourth of men's: $36 440 compared to $150 671. Women farmers remain under-represented in large-scale commodity production, but are quite prominent in sustainable and local food production. At the smaller end of the farm scale continuum, many farmers are producing for local, sustainable and organic markets.

Although more women are farming, they often lack access to key resources for the success of their farm, including land, credit, capital and knowledge. These barriers are faced by women farmers in the US, other developed countries and developing countries. Land, which is obviously a key for agricultural production, is seldom owned by women. As noted above, more women are farming in the US but they are farming smaller amounts of land. In many developing countries, the pattern of limited land ownership for women is even more problematic. In addition to farming less land, women typically farm on poor-quality soils in segmented plots often located at a distance from markets. Women's tenure arrangements are often insecure and dependent on their husbands or other male family members. They often have use-rights to land, but no long-term security. Lack of secure land ownership translates directly into limited access to credit. Farmers often need credit to purchase seeds and animals due to the seasonal nature of production. Women often lack access to credit due to lack of land as collateral, although small-scale credit schemes have helped women farmers in certain locations. Women farmers in both the US and developing countries often lack capital necessary for scaling up their operations. While small-scale credit schemes provide minimal resources for women farmers, they seldom provide sufficient resources to purchase tractors, trucks to take their products to market, or funds to construct barns or cold storage facilities. Access to knowledge is another limiting factor for women farmers. Fewer women than men farmers receive formal training in agricultural production. Many efforts have been undertaken to reach women farmers in agricultural extension programs and farmers' field schools, but problems of access for women remain. In addition to limited training in production, many women farmers lack access to market and financial information.

One area of farming where women are standing out is in sustainable agriculture, which includes organic production, producing for local markets, running community supported agriculture operations and linking with urban consumers. Women are often leaders in the local food movement which links farmers with urban consumers and offers alternatives to conventional agriculture. Local food systems offer possibilities for both farmers and consumers through building greater trust between farmers and consumers (Hinrichs 2000; Jarosz and Qazi 2000), shorter food supply chains, and reduced social, economic and geographical distance between farmers and consumers. Women farmers play key roles and often find a niche in the increasing number of farmers' markets, direct sales of farm products to consumers and restaurants, and community supported agriculture. Nevertheless some contestation exists over exactly what constitutes local food and whether local food is necessarily produced in a more sustainable fashion that provides benefits to communities (Hinrichs and Allen 2008; Hinrichs 2000). At the international level, women comprise a major component of the burgeoning food sovereignty movement that emphasizes food as a right, values producers and farmer workers, and emphasizes local control over food. Raj Patel argues that we should use a feminist analysis to 'blow open an important set of priorities around food sovereignty' (2010, p. 193). He suggests using food sovereignty to address deep power inequalities based on sexism, racism, patriarchy, and class power. Questions remain about the possibilities that local food systems can reach their goal of achieving environmental and social justice aims while working in the broader context of the agroindustrial food system.

LOOKING AT VALUE CHAINS AS RURAL DEVELOPMENT

Increasing integration of global markets impacts small-scale and subsistence farmers as well as larger-scale corporate farms. These global markets bring about new distribution and consumption patterns. Multinational and national supermarkets often control these new value chains in developing countries. Women's integration into these agricultural value chains can be both opportunities and threats to women's employment (FAO 2010). Building on value chain analysis, recent development efforts have emphasized using agricultural value chain analysis to improve the performance of small producers in value chains. In many of these efforts, small-scale producers learn to analyze value chains including production, processing, inputs, distribution and consumers. Value-chain development hopes to demystify the food chain for farmers to help them more successfully compete in the food system. Barrientos (2009) has called for gender analysis of global value chains. She has studied horticulture value chains and noted the importance of understanding the gender dimension of value chains, especially the reliance on women's low wages in horticultural production. In some instances, new markets in specialty types of production such as organic or fair trade open up new opportunities for small-scale women farmers. High-value crops often require labor-intensive production techniques that many women can accommodate. For example, Las Hermanas, a women's coffee producers' cooperative in Nicaragua, supplies Peets Coffee in the US. The women's cooperative split from the main cooperative after managers found that the women's coffee was of superior quality. Las Hermanas coffee has been recognized by Peets' for high quality and is consistently recognized in coffee quality competitions (Chan 2010). In other instances, traditional crops are replaced by imported foods either directly or indirectly.

BEYOND THE MARKET: WHAT ABOUT REPRODUCTION?

Although neoliberal globalization clearly alters the employment landscape in rural areas, the impact of these shifts extends beyond formal employment. Economic restructuring is tied to family stability and structure. Loss of full-time jobs with higher wages for men disrupts traditional family formation and undermines the longer-term stability of families (McLaughlin and Coleman-Jensen 2011). As Peterson notes, these shifts 'reduce the emotional, cultural and material resources necessary for the wellbeing of most women and families' (Peterson 2005, p. 27). Women in most regions of the globe, and especially those who lack resources, are spending increasing amounts of time on reproductive labor including feeding their families, providing health care, taking care of children and the elderly, and providing emotional support. The legacy of structural adjustment programs that have reduced government services have left the provision of many of these services to the unpaid work of women. Although there is some evidence that rural men are taking up reproductive work, few studies have compared shifting gender divisions of labor in households between rural and urban areas. Also, the decline in government services also means declining employment for women in rural areas, especially in so-called 'good' jobs such as social work and teaching.

In many rural communities, reliance on government programs and services has historically been low due to limited availability of services, and lack of adequate transportation. With the neoliberal push for the decline of government services and social supports, rural programs are often the first to go. For example, fewer programs exist to support rural women who are victims of sexual assaults. In addition, women are often reluctant to report sexual assaults due to lack of anonymity, physical isolation and distrust of public agencies. People with HIV/AIDS in rural areas are also less likely to seek and obtain adequate treatment due to lack of appropriate health care providers, stigma attached to the disease, and transportation issues.

Clearly, global shifts in employment opportunities have altered gender relations in households. In some cases, traditional gender roles have been reinscribed, resulting in problematic family and household dynamics. In other cases, the detraditionalization of gender roles in rural areas offers possibilities for new and more equitable relations between rural men and women (Brandth and Haugen 2010). These gender dynamics play out differently for women and men in different regions, races and classes.

RURAL POLICIES RELATED TO GENDER IN THE US

Rural policies have centered on agricultural policy, food supply and natural resource management (Brown and Swanson 2004) with little consideration of issues of gender and family. At the conclusion of their edited collection on economic restructuring and rural families, Tickamyer and Smith (2011) point to dilemmas in rural policy. The needs of rural areas are pressing and stark and many of the glaring issues significantly impact women's lives. Rural areas need to expand jobs, improve working conditions, housing, health care, transportation, child care and infrastructure, but questions remain as to who will implement these activities and who will pay for them. As Tickamyer and Smith (2011 note), many of these needs will not be met by the market, but lack of support for government programs and services leaves these rural areas in a desperate state requiring actions at the federal, state and local level. They suggest three broad areas for rural policy: (1) meeting employment needs; (2) service and amenity needs; and (3) infrastructure development. To improve employment, stable jobs that pay decent wages with benefits and more predictable hours are needed. New and creative strategies for creating jobs need to be considered that do not merely provide tax subsidies to businesses that provide few good jobs. The new opportunities that exist in the energy industry for good jobs will favor men's employment, which could also help rural women who are married or live in households with men. The expansion of alternative agriculture and local foods will offer opportunities to women as well. But for women to directly benefit from employment in these areas, training, credit and targeted employment programs must be instituted to enable women to compete for jobs and earn decent incomes. In the area of improving service and amenities, Tickamyer and Smith (2011) suggest innovative funding and delivery methods for schools, health care, day care, transportation, recreation, social services and affordable housing. Increased funding for these services will serve multiple needs for rural women including provision of jobs, ameliorating work–family conflicts and lightening household responsibilities. Education, health care and social services often provide decent paying professional jobs for rural women. Availability of day care and transportation could improve women's ability to have the time and means to seek employment outside the home. In terms of infrastructure development Tickamyer and Smith suggest improvement of broadband and rural transportation systems. Efforts in some cities in Europe such as Vienna, which have implemented gender mainstreaming in city planning efforts, could provide guidance as rural places consider infrastructure issues. In rural development efforts beyond the US, gender mainstreaming has been at the center of efforts to improve women's lives.

GENDER MAINSTREAMING AT THE HEART OF POLICIES FOR RURAL GENDER ISSUES

Although gender issues are rarely considered in rural policies in the US, gender mainstreaming sets the tone for rural development policies relating to women in most other regions of the world. Gender mainstreaming has served as the guiding strategy for issues of gender equity and attaining women's rights since the Fourth United Nations (UN) Conference on Women in Beijing in 1995. International organizations including the UN, the World Bank, national governments and non-governmental organizations have adopted gender mainstreaming as a primary strategy for addressing women's issues. Gender mainstreaming developed as a response to the slow success of efforts to improve women's rights and livelihoods through targeting development efforts specifically to women. The UN defines gender mainstreaming as:

> the process of assessing the implications for women and men of any planned action, including legislation, policies or programs, in all areas and at all levels. It is a strategy for making women's as well as men's concerns and experiences an integral dimension of the design, implementation, monitoring and evaluation of policies and programs in all political, economic and societal spheres so that women and men benefit equally and inequality is not perpetuated. The ultimate goal is to achieve gender equality. (United Nations 1997, p. 1)

In many countries, rural development relating to gender has centered on gender mainstreaming policies. Gender mainstreaming was pushed by women's advocates in Beijing as a critique of the liberal, Western-led approach to women in development (WID) which seemed to only work at the margins of the development effort rather than push for major transformations in development. In rural areas, these WID projects often took the form of small-scale animal production, handicraft production, sewing school uniforms and other traditionally female tasks. While some of these projects did succeed in providing increased incomes for rural women, they failed to challenge the predominant paradigm of agricultural development which favored large-scale commodity production.

The jury is still out on whether gender mainstreaming has the potential to succeed. Some feminist scholars have advocated continuing with the policy (Moser and Moser 2005). But gender mainstreaming as the project for improving women's lives has been soundly critiqued by others. Mukhopadhyay's study on gender mainstreaming concludes that feminist efforts are 'being normalized in the development business as ahistorical, apolitical, de-contextualized and technical project that leave power relations intact' (Mukhopadhyay 2004, p. 95). She recognizes that gender mainstreaming has different results in different sectors, but provides excellent examples of why gender mainstreaming may be less effective in agriculture than in other sectors. She provides an example from Yemen of a project to help women farmers. The project was designed to build the capacity of agricultural extension to work with women farmers. In Yemen, women farmers contribute substantially to household food production but are rarely considered to be farmers by extension personnel. The project was originally housed under the Rural Women's Directorate in the Department of Agriculture. But as gender mainstreaming became the accepted strategy for dealing with rural women, the project was cut with the rationale that gender had been mainstreamed and therefore there was no need to spend resources on women. She also provides insight into the relatively limited success of gender mainstreaming in agriculture as compared to education in Ethiopia. Achieving gender equity was a major goal of the Ethiopian Ministry of Education, so the process of gender mainstreaming was taken quite seriously. By contrast, the goal of the Ministry of Agriculture was to create a profitable agricultural sector, with no support from the Ministry for Gender Equity. Therefore, efforts to mainstream gender produced guidelines that 'remained a cosmetic document with little or no power of enforceability' (Mukhopadhyay 2009, p. 100).

Others note that gender mainstreaming has resulted in conceptual confusion and the outlay of enormous resources that could have been better spent. Sandler and Rao (2012) agree with Cornwall (2008) that 'we need to rid ourselves of – in Andrea Cornwall's words – the rather triumphalist discourse of gender mainstreaming that presents gender transformation as a do-able, "technical" problem that can be overcome with sufficient determination and commitment'. This optimism coincides with neoliberal assumptions that the state, institutions and citizens can be easily engaged to promote gender equality. Sweetman (2012) sums up the overall failure and critique of gender mainstreaming after the UN Conference on Women in Beijing in 1995. She notes that almost 20 years after Beijing, women are still waiting for a transformation of global and national policies that would reflect the priorities of women in the global South. Development organizations are still primarily led by white elite males, and women's priorities are not well represented in decision making. Finally, feminist economic perspectives and insights are completely missing from the global economy as 'the world continues to follow a development model predicated on unlimited economic growth, despite the unsustainability of this from both an environmental and a human perspective' (Sweetman 2012, p. 389).

A final strategy that has often been overlooked with the focus on gender mainstreaming is the promotion of rural women's networks. In the US, rural women's agricultural networks such as the Pennsylvania Women's Agricultural Network, the Women, Food and Agricultural Network and Vermont Women's Agricultural Network provide education, empowerment and policy initiatives related to women in agriculture and rural America. In Africa and India, women agricultural producer organizations have worked to increase their access to markets and promote women entrepreneurs (FAO 2011). Developing women's networks and partnerships in specific locations, states, regions, and across the globe can provide much-needed resources for empowering women, increasing women's safety (Moser 2012) and improving their livelihoods.

REFERENCES

Anderson, Cynthia D. and Chih-Yuan Weng (2011), 'Regional variation of women in low-wage work across rural communities', in Kristen E. Smith and Ann R. Tickamyer (eds), *Economic Restructuring and Family Well-Being in Rural America*, University Park, PA: Penn State University Press, pp. 215–30.

Bain, C. (2010), 'Structuring the flexible and feminized labor market: GLOBALGAP standards for agricultural labor in Chile', *Signs: Journal of Women in Culture and Society*, 35, 343–70.

Bardasi, Elena, C. Mark Blackden and Juan Carlos Guzman (2007), 'Gender, Entrepreneurship, and Competitiveness in Africa', in Klaus Schwab (ed.), *Africa Competitiveness Report 2007*, Washington, DC: World Economic Forum, World Bank, and African Development Bank. www.weforum.org/en/initiatives/gcp/Africa%20Competitiveness%20Report/2007/index.htm.

Barrientos, Stephanie (2009), 'Gender, flexibility and global value chains', *IDS Bulletin*, 32, 83–93.

Bird, Sharon and Steve Sapp (2004), 'Understanding the gender gap in small business success', *Gender and Society*, 18, 5–28.

Brandth, Berit and Marit Haugen (2010), 'Doing farm tourism: the intertwining practices of gender and work', *Signs: Journal of Women in Culture and Society*, 35, 425–46.

Brown, David and Lou Swanson (2004), *Challenges for Rural America in the Twenty-First Century*, University Park, PA: Penn State Press.

Bruni, Attila, Silvia Gherardi and Barbara Poggio (2004), 'Doing gender, doing entrepreneurship: an ethnographic account of intertwined practices', *Gender, Work and Organization*, 11, 406–29.

Chan, Man-Kwun (2010), *Improving Opportunities for Women in Smallholder-based Supply Chains*, Bill and Melinda Gates Foundation. http://www.gatesfoundation.org/learning/Documents/gender-value-chain-guide.pdf.

Cornwall, Andrea (2008), 'Myths to live by? solidarity and female autonomy reconsidered', in A. Cornwall, E. Harrison and A. Whitehead (eds), *Gender Myths and Feminist Fables*, Oxford: Wiley-Blackwell, pp. 145–63.

Ellis, Amanda, Claire Manuel and C. Mark Blackden (2006), *Gender and Economic Growth in Uganda: Unleashing the Power of Women*, Washington, DC: World Bank.

Falk, W.W. and L.M. Lobao (2003), 'Who benefits from economic restructuring? Lessons from the past, challenges for the future', in David Brown and Louis Swanson (eds), *Challenges for Rural American in the 21st Century*, University Park, PA: Penn State Press, pp. 152–65.

Fenwick, T. (2003), 'Innovation: examining workplace learning in new enterprises', *Journal of Workplace Learning*, 15, 123–32.

Fernandez-Kelly, Patricia (2007), *NAFTA and Beyond*, Thousand Oaks, CA: Sage Publications.

Food and Agriculture Organization (FAO) (2010), *Agriculture Value Chain Development: Threat or Opportunity for Women's Employment*, Rome: FAO.

Food and Agriculture Organization (FAO) (2011), *The Role of Women Producer Organizations in Agricultural Value Chains: Practical Lessons from Africa and India*, Rome: FAO.

Fraser, Nancy (2009), 'Feminism, Capitalism and the cunning of history', *New Left Review*, 56, (March–April), 97–117.

Hall, A. and V. Mogyorody (2007), 'Organic farming, gender, and the labor process', *Rural Sociology*, 72, 289–316.

Hinrichs, C. Clare (2000), 'Embeddedness and local food systems: notes on two types of direct agricultural markets', *Journal of Rural Studies*, 16, 295–303.

Hinrichs, C. Clare and Patricia Allen (2008), 'Selective patronage and social justice: local food consumer campaigns in historical context', *Journal of Agricultural and Environmental Ethics*, 21, 329–52.

Jarosz, Lucy and Joan Qazi (2000), 'The geography of Washington's world apple', *Journal of Rural Studies*, 16, 1–11.

Jensen, Leif and Eric Jensen (2011), 'Employment hardship among rural men', in Kristin Smith and Ann R. Tickamyer (eds), *Economic Restructuring and Family Well-Being in Rural America*, University Park, PA: Pennsylvania State Press, pp. 40–59.

Kabeer, Naila (2005), 'Is microfinance a "magic bullet" for women's empowerment? Analysis of findings from South Asia', *Economic and Political Weekly*, October, 14–48.

Le Mare, Ann (2012), 'Show the world to women and they can do it: southern fair trade enterprises as agents of empowerment', *Gender and Development*, 20, 910–15.

Lee-Gosselin, H. and J. Grise (1990), 'Are women owner-managers challenging our definitions of entreprenership? An in-depth survey', *Journal of Business Ethics*, 9, 423–33.

Lewis, P. (2006), 'The quest for invisibility: female entrepreneurs and the masculine norm of enterprise', *Gender, Work, and Organization*, 15, 453–69.

Lichter, Daniel and Deborah Graefe (2011), 'Rural economic restructuring: implications for children, youth, and families', in Kristin Smith and Ann R. Tickamyer (eds), *Economic Restructuring and Family Well-Being in Rural America*, University Park, PA: Pennsylvania State Press, pp. 25–39.

McLaughlin, Diane and Alisha Coleman-Jensen (2011), 'Economic restructuring and family structure change, 1980–2000: a focus on female-headed families with children', in Kristin Smith and Ann R. Tickamyer (eds), *Economic Restructuring and Family Well-Being in Rural America*, University Park, PA: Pennsylvania State Press, pp. 105–23.

Moser, Caroline (2012), 'Mainstreaming women's safety in cities into gender-based policy and programmes', *Gender and Development*, 20, 435–52.

Moser, Caroline and A. Moser (2005), 'Gender mainstreaming since Beijing: a review of success and limitations in international institutions', *Gender and Development*, 13, 11–22.

Mukhopadhyay, Maitrayee (2009), 'Mainstreaming gender or streaming gender away: feminists marooned in the development business', *IDS Bulletin*, 35, 95–103.

Mulholland, Kate (1996), 'Gender power and property relations within entrepreneurial wealthy families', *Gender, Work and Organization*, 3, 78–102.

Nelson, Margaret and Joan Smith (1999), *Working Hard and Making Do: Surviving in Small Town America*, Berkeley, CA: University of California Press.

Patel, Raj (2010), 'What does food sovereignty look like?', in Hannah Wittman, Annette Desmarais and Nettie Wiebe (eds), *Food Sovereignty: Reconnecting Food, Nature and Community*, Halifax: Fernwood Publishing, pp. 186-96.

Peterson, V. Spike (2005), 'How the meaning of gender matters in the new political economy', *New Political Economy*, 10, 499–521.

Preibisch, Kerry and Evelyn Grez (2010), 'The other side of el Otro Lado: Mexican migrant women and labor flexibility in Canadian agriculture', *Signs: Journal of Women in Culture and Society*, 35, 289–316.

Sachs, C. and M. Alston (2010), 'Global shifts, sedimentations and imaginaries', *SIGNS: Journal of Women in Culture and Society*, 35, 277–88.

Sandler, Joanne and Aruna Rao (2012), 'The elephant in the room and the dragons at the gate: strategising for gender equality in the 21st century', *Gender and Development*, 20, 547–62.

Sherman, Rachel (2011), 'Men without sawmills: job loss and gender identity', in Kristin E. Smith and Ann Tickamyer (eds), *Economic Restructuring and Family Well-Being in Rural America*, University Park, PA: Penn State University Press, pp. 40–104.

Smith, K. and A. Tickamyer (eds) (2011), *Economic Restructuring and Family Well-Being in Rural America*, University Park, PA: Penn State University Press.

Smith, Sally and Catherine Dolan (2006), 'Ethical trade: what does it mean for women workers in African horticulture?', in Stehapnie Barrientos and Catherine Dolan (eds), *Ethical Sourcing in the Global Food System*, London: Earthscan, pp. 79–96.

Sweetman, Caroline (2012), 'Introduction', *Gender and Development*, 20, 389–403.

Tickamyer, Ann and Kristin Smith (2011), 'Conclusion', in Kristin Smith and Ann R. Tickamyer (eds), *Economic Restructuring and Family Well-Being in Rural America*, University Park, PA: Pennsylvania State Press, pp. 336–46.

Tigges, Leann and Gary Green (1994), 'Does small business ownership offer opportunties for women in rural areas?', *Rural Sociology*, 59, 289–310.

Trauger, A., C. Sachs, M. Barbercheck, K. Brasier and N.E. Kiernan (2009), 'Our market is our community: women farmers and civic agriculture in Pennsylvania, USA', *Agriculture, Food and Human Values*, 26, 43–55.

United Nations (1997), 'Report of the Economic and Social Council for 1997', A/52/3, September 18.

United States Department of Agriculture (USDA) (2007), *Women Farmers. Census of Agriculture*. http://www.agcensus.usda.gov/Publications/2007/Online_Highlights/Fact_Sheets/Demographics/women.pdf.

United States Department of Agriculture (USDA) (2010), 'Rural America at a glance'. http://www.ers.usda.gov/media/138737/eib68_1_.pdf.

United States Department of Labor (2010), 'Women in the labor force 2010', Women's Bureau, United States Department of Labor. http://www.dol.gov/wb/factsheets/Qf-laborforce-10.htm#.UNChVa_Nnb0.

United States Department of Labor (2012), 'Bureau of Labor Statistics'. http://www.bls.gov/iag/tgs/iag211.htm#workforce.

US Small Business Administration (2006), 'Women in business: a demographic review of women's business ownership'. http://archive.sba.gov/advo/research/rs280tot.pdf.

World Bank (2007a), 'Cultivating knowledge and skills to grow African agriculture: a synthesis of an institutional, regional, and international review', Washington, DC: World Bank. http://siteresources.worldbank.org/INTARD/Resources/AET_Final_web.pdf.

World Bank (2007b), *Gender and Economic Growth in Kenya: Unleashing the Power of Women*, Washington, DC: World Bank.

11. The successes and challenges of microfinance

Ian Carrillo

Microfinance was founded as a tool to break the cycle of poverty in which many residents of developing countries are trapped. Muhammad Yunus, one of the early microfinance leaders, believes that the poor are systematically marginalized from formal channels of finance and face numerous discriminatory barriers to capital accumulation, which frequently prevents them from retaining 'the genuine results of their labor' (Yunus 2003, p. 114–15). His interpretation of how poverty is created and maintained led him to found Grameen Bank in 1976 in Bangladesh. Buoyed by high repayment rates and reductions in poverty, the unequivocal success of Grameen Bank inspired the replication of Grameen-style microfinance institutions (MFIs) throughout the developing world in subsequent years. Today there are thousands of MFIs operating in nearly every developing country.

Initially many MFIs followed Grameen's lending methodology, but as the industry evolved so did the operating practices. Rather than solely distributing microcredit for income-generating entrepreneurial activities, MFIs began providing services related to savings, insurance, remittances and consumer credit. Lending methodology also changed, as MFIs started giving loans to individuals in addition to solidarity groups, to men rather than solely women, and to the moderately poor instead of only the impoverished. The most controversial shift involved the commercialization of microfinance activities, as some MFIs began operating on a for-profit model. Proponents of commercialization argued that this was the only method that could ensure both financial sustainability and more rapid growth; while detractors stated that such profit-seeking off of the labor of the impoverished would undermine the original goal of microfinance, which was to reduce poverty.

In this chapter I elaborate in more detail on the controversy surrounding commercialization, as well as describing what the goals of microfinance are and how microfinance works in practice. First, I address why microfinance was developed as an anti-poverty tool, how its unconventional lending techniques function and how the microfinance industry has been able to grow over the last 35 years. Second, using empirical data from academic studies, I explore how MFIs repeatedly confront trade-offs related to financial sustainability, efficiency and outreach. Third, I discuss how incomplete land markets in rural areas pose a challenge to asset collateralization and the development of microfinance. Finally, I look at the historical performance of microfinance and critically analyze long-term outcomes of poverty reduction and employment creation.

WHAT IS MICROFINANCE?

Credit performs an important function for many microentrepreneurs and poor households. In many homes, credit can help smooth consumption, including the acquisition of food, clothes and household goods. It can finance important cultural and religious events, such as weddings, funerals and birthdays. Credit is also necessary for planned and emergency costs related to education and health. For microentrepreneurs – owners of firms that have three or fewer employees – credit is useful for equipment repairs, inventory purchasing, licensing and registration costs, and business expansion. Overall, access to credit is an indispensable component to the daily functions of many poor households and businesses throughout the developing world. Microfinance has been broadly defined as 'banking and/or financial services targeted to low-and-moderate income businesses or households, including the provision of credit'. In addition, microcredit is 'part of the field of microfinance', which also includes services involving savings, insurance and remittances (ProMujer 2008).

Yet, access to formal credit markets has historically remained elusive for many poor communities throughout the globe, in spite of the frequent need for credit in daily life. The combination of underdeveloped financial and banking sectors in poor countries, along with the discriminatory belief held by banking officials that the poor are financially unreliable and not worthy of investment, has left poor populations isolated from formal economic institutions. Under such circumstances, the poor have frequently turned to informal outlets, such as moneylenders, to secure credit. These informal loans have traditionally been characterized by annual percentage rates that 'routinely rise into the hundreds', unstable collection practices and default consequences that may be harmful for poor borrowers whose precarious livelihoods leave them vulnerable to harmful economic shocks (Consultative Group to Assist the Poor 2012).

In rural areas of poor countries, formal credit institutions have long been underdeveloped. So, while the urban poor may have wider access to informal credit, due to population density, the rural poor, especially in areas that are geographically isolated and sparsely populated, have fewer options from which to choose. In order to expand access to formal credit in rural areas, many governments have implemented rural credit programs. These state programs, however, have had limited success. Repayment rates were frequently low due to the fact that borrowers viewed loans as government assistance rather than financial exchanges. Local patronage networks shaped lending patterns, which has resulted in the targeted recipients and the poorest community members not receiving loans, while the loans ended up in the hands of politically connected and wealthier clients. And, importantly, ever-changing political climates led to budget reprioritizations and rural credit programs either being suspended or having their funds reduced (Robinson 2001, pp. 52–3).

Early practitioners of microfinance recognized these systemic problems and viewed microfinance as a way to provide formal and reliable access to credit for poor communities in developing countries. In Bangladesh in the 1970s, Grameen Bank founder Muhammad Yunus identified anti-poor discrimination and disinterest from government and banking officials as the primary reason for not providing formal credit outlets in rural communities. The informal moneylender, as the most accessible option remaining, compounded the problem through high interest rates. These issues were exacerbated by other factors that served as barriers to entry into formal credit markets, such as geographic isolation, the absence of formal collateral and the lack of official state identification. One of the primary goals of microfinance is to overcome such structural obstacles.

MICROFINANCE OPERATIONS AND LENDING METHODOLOGY

The institution that is informally credited with founding the microfinance industry is Grameen Bank. It began in 1976 in Bangladesh as a university research project headed by Muhammad Yunus, who was an economics professor at the University of Chittagong. In the study, Yunus and his students lent small amounts of money, normally less than $30, to poor residents in nearby villages. Going against traditional philosophy, Yunus lent directly to poor residents without requiring any additional training. The study was a major success and Yunus expanded the program to more villages, eventually founding an institution called Grameen Bank (Grameen Bank 1998). Using a non-profit approach that primarily focused on social returns, Grameen Bank experienced considerable growth over a 30-year period. Grameen Bank's borrowers, of which there are 2.6 million, own 93 percent of the bank, which classifies the bank as a co-operative (Yunus 2003, p. 235). By 2007, Grameen had distributed more than $6 billion in loans and had a repayment rate of 98.6 percent (Yunus 2007, p. 51). With slight modifications to its methodology over time, Grameen Bank concentrated on social returns and empowerment through entrepreneurialism in order to grow operations and alleviate poverty simultaneously. Between 1973 and 2005, extreme poverty in Bangladesh decreased from 74 percent to 40 percent (Yunus 2007, p. 105). The Grameen model has been replicated throughout the world.

One of the most intriguing aspects of microfinance has been the way in which the industry grew by using unconventional lending methods, especially solidarity group lending. In this method, a collection of borrowers, between 15 and 30 individuals, rely on one another to insure payments and to create a collective incentive to apply the loans towards income-generating activities. A default by one member carries a negative consequence for all members. The concept of solidarity group lending arose from a simple barrier facing many potential borrowers: lack of collateral. In the absence of a property title or other types of formal collateral, MFIs felt that poor borrowers could use social capital in order to insure against the loan. It was believed that a group of individuals could monitor one another to make sure that loan repayments were made punctually and that they could also track the utilization of the loan itself in order to see if there would likely be a bad outcome. As Morduch writes: 'Group-lending contracts effectively make a borrower's neighbors co-signers to loans, mitigating problems created by informational asymmetries between lender and borrower. Neighbors now have incentives to monitor each other and to exclude risky borrowers from participation, promoting repayments even in the absence of collateral requirements' (Morduch 1999, p. 1570).

In addition to the innovative solidarity group lending technique, some early MFIs concentrated on targeting female clientele, rather than men. Early practitioners recognized that gender discrimination played a role in maintaining the cycle of poverty and women were more likely than men to invest in the household and human capital (Kennedy and Peters 1992). ProMujer, a Latin American MFI that lends only to women, states:

> We believe that the best way to fight poverty in Latin America is to empower women by giving them access to the resources and training they need to increase their income, maintain their own health and the health of their families, and achieve greater equity in their homes, workplaces and communities. (ProMujer 2012 p. 12)

Some major MFIs currently maintain very high rates of female borrowers. In 2011, female borrowers constituted 96 percent of the 2.6 million clients at Grameen Bank (Grameen Bank 2011). And at Mexico's Compartamos Banco, the biggest MFI in the Western Hemisphere, 98 percent of the more than 1 million borrowers are female (ACCION International 2012).

More recently, lending methodology and microfinance products have evolved. Although solidarity lending is still widely practiced, many MFIs now engage in individual lending, which was seen as a suitable alternative due to it being more flexible, less labor intensive and less time-consuming. Many MFIs now offer a more diverse set of products as well. Rather than just providing credit for business activities, clients can now access services related to savings, insurance, remittance transfers and consumer credit. These changes have largely been a consequence of the growth and expansion of the microfinance industry, which the next section addresses.

THE EXPANSION OF MICROFINANCE

Over the last three decades, the microfinance industry has grown from a number of pilot projects in South Asia and Latin America to a major industry with operations in nearly every country of the globe. In recent years the microfinance movement has passed through a series of watershed moments. In 2000, the United Nations identified microfinance as an integral component to the success of the Millennium Development Goals, which aimed to halve extreme poverty across the globe by 2015, among several other important objectives. The United Nations declared 2005 to be the International Year of Microcredit. In 2006 Muhammad Yunus was awarded the Nobel Peace Prize for his decades of work on microfinance and the role that it played in contributing to reducing extreme poverty in Bangladesh. The international recognition attached to the awards from the United Nations and the Nobel committee enhanced the public visibility of microfinance and brought widespread legitimacy to the strategy.

Figure 11.1 is based on information that MFIs self-report to the Mix Market, an organization that compiles data related to the financial composition and performance of MFIs across the globe. As Figure 11.1 illustrates, Latin America has seen the strongest levels of growth, possibly due to microfinance practitioners' long-term presence in the region and the deep level of institutional support, in the form of administrative and financial assistance, from multilateral development banks, non-governmental organizations (NGOs) and private donors. Notably, the financial crisis in 2008 marked either a downturn or stagnation for MFI

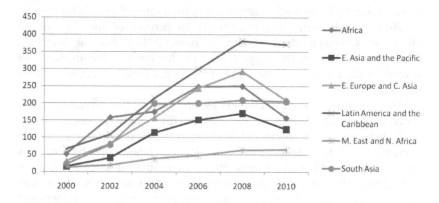

Source: based on data drawn from the Mix Market.www.mixmarket.org (accessed 14 June 2012).

Figure 11.1   Microfinance institutions by region, 2000–2010

growth in all regions, which was due to financial market contraction and/or an unwillingness of private donors and governments to invest in micro-finance activities.

Table 11.1 demonstrates the overall financial scope of microfinance activities in 2011. In terms of active borrowers, South Asia has the highest volume, largely due to active microfinance markets in countries with large, dense populations, such as Bangladesh and India. The number of depositors that a region has depends on how a nation's financial regulatory sector allows an MFI to receive client deposits, if any at all. The relevance of the average loan balance depends on the income level of the client base in question. Generally speaking, an MFI is considered to have deep outreach if its average loan balance consistently penetrates the poorest income deciles of the population. For many analysts, the average loan balance has been used as a proxy for poverty level. There is a general assumption that if an MFI's average loan balance increases, then the MFI is moving into a wealthier client base, a phenomenon called mission drift.

Concern over mission drift increased as microfinance activities shifted towards a commercialized model that emphasized profit maximization and efficiency-seeking. As it became clear that clients were frequently able to repay loans, more MFIs began to contemplate how they could impact a higher volume of people through increased outreach, which is characterized as an MFI's effectiveness in reaching its target market and distributing its product. Additionally, MFIs began looking for ways to achieve financial

Table 11.1   Performance characteristics of microfinance institutions, 2011

Region	Total MFIs	Gross loan portfolio	# of active borrowers	Avg. loan balance per borrower	Deposits	Assets	# of depositors
Africa	67	$5 billion	2.1 million	$426.1	$4.3 billion	$6.5 billion	4.3 million
East Asia and the Pacific	125	$9.6 billion	12.4 million	$391.5	$5.8 billion	$6.5 billion	5.1 million
East Europe and Central Asia	65	$3.6 billion	1.6 million	$1587.6	$2.0 billion	$4.2 billion	2.3 million
Latin America and the Caribbean	234	$26.9 billion	17.5 million	$1000.50	$17.8 billion	$33.2 billion	14.9 million
Middle East and North Africa	9	$236.6 million	290,306	$655.1	–	$274.9 million	–
South Asia	33	$2.2 billion	13.7 million	$168.8	$396.4 million	$1.6 billion	9.3 million

Source: based on data drawn from the Mix Market.www.mixmarket.org (accessed 14 June 2012).

sustainability that did not rely on state subsidies or private donors. Many policy makers and industry practitioners felt that pursuing a commercialized model of microfinance, which involves profit maximization and engaging private financial markets, would allow MFIs to expand outreach and generate enough capital to be financially sustainable. Critics of commercialization argue that profit maximization will come at the expense of poverty reduction, the original purpose of microfinance.

Proponents of commercialization see the shift in methodology as an inevitable and necessary change in microfinance operations. In order to provide credit access to the highest number of people, an MFI's outreach and ability to expand into new markets must be high, which requires large amounts of capital. Microfinance institutions that are dependent on government subsidies or private donations do not have such freedom to expand and respond to market needs. In order to acquire such capital, commercialized MFIs need to attract investors and generate profits. High financial returns appeal to investors who receive profits and are more likely to reinvest in a particular MFI, thus allowing the institution to grow and impact more poor individuals. This increased access to credit would potentially decrease the level of poverty in the particular market in which the MFI operates. Moreover, increased competition among MFIs would put downward pressure on interest rates. Industry leaders and policy makers, affiliated with multilateral development banks and private development agencies, have provided intellectual justification for the commercialization strategy through numerous publications.[1]

In 2007 the turn towards commercialization was famously marked by the US$458 million initial public offering (IPO) of Mexico's Compartamos Banco. The unequivocal financial success of Compartamos Banco ushered in many new entrants to Mexico's microfinance industry. Proponents of the IPO strongly defended it in the face of criticism. According to Accion International, a US Agency for International Development (USAID)-funded NGO that initially capitalized Compartamos Banco and profited from the IPO, the lucrative IPO was a 'market stimulus' (Accion International 2007). Álvaro Rodríguez Arregui, the chairman of Accion International, has called Compartamos's IPO a 'big win' in shoring up capital for the microfinance industry (*The Economist* 2008). Another Accion representative stated: 'The financial markets have shown the true value created by high performance, double bottom line-oriented microfinance institutions. We hope that this is the first of many [IPOs]' (Lewis 2008, p. 56). In a statement, Maria Otero, Accion's then chief executive offcer (CEO), hoped that 'many other MFIs will be able to replicate [Compartamos's] success, demonstrating that access to financial services for the poor has truly become integrated into international financial systems' (Lewis 2008, pp. 58). Mauricio Hubard, CEO of Compartamos competitor En Confianza, echoed Otero's sentiment:

> Yunus opened the eyes of the world to microfinance. Compartamos opened the eyes of the private sector and the financial markets. Thanks to the success of their IPO, we were successful in raising the initial capital we needed from private sector investors in less than a month. The success of Compartamos, even if people want to make it controversial has changed the financial sector and opened new opportunities for companies with a social commitment. (Carlos and Labarthe 2008, pp. 8–9)

Commercialization critics have frequently stated that an emphasis on profit maximization and efficiency-seeking contradicts the fundamental purpose of microfinance: poverty reduction. Many analysts have pointed to Compartamos's high interest rates, upwards of a 70 percent annual percentage rate, as evidence that they are profiting from the labor of the impoverished (*The Economist* 2008). Furthermore, once it was revealed that another for-profit MFI, Mexico's Banco Azteca, had engaged in extensive property seizures following loan delinquency, there was renewed and intensified scrutiny of profit-seeking MFIs and debate regarding whether for-profit microloans help or hurt poor clients (Epstein and Smith 2007). Muhammad Yunus strongly weighed in to the debate: 'When you discuss microcredit, don't bring Compartamos into it … Microcredit was created to fight the money lender, not to become the money lender' (*Business Week* 2007).

The commercialization debate[2] reached a climax in the fall of 2010 when a scandal ensnared India's SKS, which had been supported by the equity firm Sequoia Capital and in 2009 held a successful IPO. The following year more than 80 clients committed suicide, allegedly due to anxiety related to overindebtedness caused by predatory lending and aggressive collection practices from SKS loan officers. The microfinance industry in India subsequently fell into a deep crisis following the tragic episodes (Dutt 2010).

In addition to the difficulties associated with balancing profit-seeking with fair interest rates and collection practices, commercialized MFIs must also attempt to deal with serving rural clients along with urban clients. The market for commercialized MFIs has developed more rapidly in urban areas due to the fact that both higher population density and income levels of urban residents offer lower transaction costs and higher profits than what would be possible in rural markets. For MFIs that prioritize profit maximization and financial sustainability, the structural and environmental advantages of an urban area offer more appealing incentives for investment than a rural area. Rural residents may also be excluded from the commercialized MFI market for two reasons. First, many commercialized MFIs do not enter into contracts with individuals that exceed a specified distance from the MFI's branch office. For instance, a person is ineligible for a loan if he/she lives more than 30 minutes outside of a city's border, then that person will be ineligible for a loan. Second, rural residents are less likely to possess the necessary collateral, such as a property title, that a commercialized MFI requires for a loan. The issue of rural land titling and credit markets is explained in greater detail later in the chapter.

Although the experiences with commercialized microfinance in Mexico and India may be outliers in comparison with the majority of the world's MFIs, it is clear that as the microfinance industry evolves many MFIs must confront trade-offs related to efficiency and outreach. At times these trade-offs may correspond with the traditional concept of mission drift and rising average loan balances. However, as the next section discusses, many not-for-profit and for-profit MFIs persistently face challenges related to information sharing and risk mitigation, and the strategies they employ to manage such risks consistently marginalize some poor individuals in favor of others.

MISSION DRIFT, OUTREACH AND POVERTY REDUCTION

Although many policy makers and industry practitioners have frequently argued that MFIs can focus on profit maximization without causing mission drift, rigorous analyses of outcomes over a long period of time suggest otherwise. Recent academic studies have shown that several strategies associated with financial sustainability and profit maximization reduce poverty outreach. Such results indicate that there is frequently a trade-off related to outreach and financial sustainability, and that such a trade-off often involves an MFI pushing the very poor out of the market in favor of the moderately poor.

Cull et al. (2007) surveyed more than 120 MFIs on the above concerns. Regarding profitability and outreach, they found that an institution's lending method was a deterministic variable. Individual-based lenders, rather than solidarity-based lenders and village banks, 'that charge high interest rates are more profitable than others, but only up to a point'. When interest rates exceed a threshold, delinquency rates increase and demand for credit falls. Furthermore, the authors find no significant association between profitability and average loan size. Importantly, they find that 'larger loan sizes are associated with lower average costs for both individual-based lenders and solidarity group lenders', which provides a disincentive, due to personnel expenses, for MFIs to maintain a high depth of outreach (p. 131).

When analyzing the impact that increased regulation has on outreach outcomes, Cull et al. (2011) find that an MFI's funding sources plays an important role. Looking at the income statements of 245 MFIs, the authors argue that MFIs that receive savings deposits are more likely to have higher average loan sizes and lend less to women, due to the fact that they are subject to more on-site regulatory supervision than MFIs that do not receive savings. These results are consistent with the authors' idea that 'profit-oriented MFIs that have to comply with prudential supervision respond by curtailing their outreach to segments of the population that are costlier to serve' (p. 961). In contrast, MFIs who rely on donations rather than deposits as a funding source are more likely not to adjust their average loan size and to maintain consistent lending patterns to women.

Hermese et al. (2011) identify a similar pattern in which gains in efficiency negatively affect outreach. After observing more than 1300 MFIs, the authors argue that an institution that has a lower average loan size is more likely to be less efficient. They also find that MFIs with more female borrowers are also more likely to be less efficient. Overall, these conclusions indicate that 'improving efficiency may only be achieved if MFIs focus less on the poor' (p. 945). Adding a caveat, the authors state that efficiency-seeking MFIs may contribute to broader macro-level gains, which can produce spillover effects and contribute to poverty reduction.

One important efficiency-seeking strategy has been information sharing. Many MFIs have contributed to new and innovative ways of reducing asymmetric information, especially through solidarity lending and credit bureaus. Still, such a strategy has a trade-off related to outreach and efficiency. Karlan (2007) explores how solidarity group lending uses social connections to improve information sharing. The author finds that 'monitoring and enforcement activities do improve group lending outcomes, and that social connections, broadly defined, facilitate the monitoring and enforcement of joint liability loan contracts' (p. 78). The data show direct evidence of peer-to-peer monitoring, particularly involving default status and its causes, as well as a deterioration of relationships in the case of a bad outcome. Results also illustrate that loan outcomes are the most positive when group members are geographically concentrated and culturally similar.

In discussing increasingly competitive markets, McIntosh and Wydick (2005) suggest that 'the onus for the inclusiveness of the market passes from the practitioners of microfinance to the donors'. They argue that both subsidized MFIs and non-subsidized MFIs can perform in the same competitive market, but that effective subsidy targeting must occur in order to prevent unfair competition and to ensure that subsidies reach the poorest borrowers. The authors recommend that credit bureaus, or internet-based central risk management systems, be used in order to 'monitor borrower quality and indebtedness', as well as improve lending targeting (p. 292).

De Janvry et al. (2010) further explore credit bureaus. The authors find that the introduction of credit bureaus reduces asymmetric information and has an impact on both borrowers and lenders. When lenders can observe new information about borrowers, those with lower repayment rates are ejected, there is an improvement in the repayment performance of new clients, there is an increase in employment efficiency through higher loans made without decreasing portfolio performance, and solidarity group sizes decrease. Likewise, when borrowers become aware that lenders can see information about their repayment behavior, repayment rates improve, particularly among solidarity group lending, which reinforces the theory that group lending can reduce asymmetric information. Losers in this new scenario include borrowers who were screened out and borrowers who lose insurance opportunities associated with a decrease in solidarity group sizes. Such results follow the pattern outlined by Hermes et al. (2011): increases in efficiency reduce the depth of outreach.

Overall, it is important to recognize the innovative contributions that microfinance practitioners have made to credit markets in poor populations.

But it is also imperative to acknowledge that many of the new developments and gains in efficiency have outcomes that involve trade-offs. Although mission drift may not simply involve rising average loan balances, the implementation of efficiency-seeking strategies, at times related to profit maximization, frequently marginalizes the poorest in favor of the less poor, and women in favor of men. Moreover, efficiency-seeking strategies have adverse effects on providing adequate access to formal credit in rural markets, as the next section explains.

LAND TITLING AND INCOMPLETE RURAL CREDIT MARKETS

One of the most salient tenets of neoliberal philosophy has been the promotion of private property rights. World Bank President Robert Zoellick has said that 'land titling is at the heart of a strategy to overcome poverty and spread the benefits of a growing economy' (World Bank 2007). Proponents of institutionalizing private property rights, such as de Soto (2000), have suggested that asset collateralization facilitates access to formal credit, which permits the activation of land markets. Woodruff summarizes de Soto:

> the lack of formal titles prevents them from using the land as collateral, prevents the 'unlocking' of capital from the assets. Although entrepreneurs in the United States routinely start new businesses with capital raised from second mortgages on their houses, entrepreneurs in the developing world are unable to do so. No small sum is involved. Extrapolating from the five cities he examined to all of the developing world [*sic*], de Soto concludes that there are $9.34 trillion in informally owned assets. (Woodruff 2001, p. 2116)

Since the 1990s many governments in developing countries have embarked on land titling projects, often working in collaboration with and using financial support from multilateral development banks. For instance, the World Bank and the Mexican government have worked in conjunction on PROCEDE (Program for Certification of Rights to Ejido Lands), which began under the Salinas administration in the early 1990s and sought to achieve three major objectives: (1) surveying and certifying parcels; (2) certifying rights to common use lands; and (3) titling urban plots for individuals. Each farmer receives a certificate that does not confer actual ownership until the land is transferred after the farmer dies, at which time the new holder can apply for an actual title. Henceforth, the parcel can be sold or used as collateral on a loan ('Mexico Indigena').

However, in an empirical analysis of how land titling programs in Nicaragua and Honduras have impacted access to formal credit, Boucher et al. (2005) demonstrate that a collection of persistent market imperfections, on both the supply and demand sides, prevent the true activation of markets through asset collateralization. Regarding credit markets, the authors suggest that banks may be unwilling to lend due to high transaction costs and the low value of the collateralized landholding, while small landholders may engage in 'risk-rationing' and be unwilling to borrow because inadequate insurance coverage would leave them vulnerable in the case of a bad outcome with the transaction. Land rental markets also would remain stagnant and based primarily on 'intra-class', rather than 'inter-class', exchanges due to the fact that liquidity restraints, related to the aforementioned credit market imperfections, would prevent land-poor households from engaging in land transactions with land-rich households. Furthermore, land ownership markets may result in a bias in favor of land-rich households, given the likely existence of a 'wealth threshold' which would prevent land-poor households, even with land titles, from using 'credit markets to finance fixed investment or purchase additional land', leaving land-rich households in the best position to utilize credit for land accumulation.

Household surveys in Nicaragua and Honduras, carried out in 2000 and 2001, revealed that land titling programs throughout the 1980s and 1990s did not produce the desired results, in spite of increased title holdings. The authors illustrate that the only statistically significant increase in credit market participation, in either country, has been for rural households in Nicaragua with more than 150 manzanas.[3] In Honduras, those households with the smallest land parcels remain the most likely to be excluded from possessing a formal title. In fact, the poorest 40 percent of the sample, those with 3 manzanas or less, had lower formal credit market participation at the time of the survey in 2000 than before the land titling project's acceleration in 1993. Given that the biggest increase in formal market participation occurs at the 45-manzana mark, it would appear that there is indeed a wealth threshold that determines whether or not a land title improves formal credit access or not. In Nicaragua the wealth threshold is even more pronounced. Regarding land rental markets and ownership patterns, operational farm sizes of the land-poor have either decreased or remained stagnant, which runs counter to the desired outcome that titling would increase land access equity. Finally, the authors conclude that 'the hoped for synergies of more productive and more egalitarian economies associated with liberalization have not occurred' (p. 123).

Expanding on these conclusions, Ahlin et al. (2011) argue that incomplete markets and national context can significantly influence an MFI's ability to produce the desired effects of microfinance activities. The authors suggest that a country's microfinance performance is heavily influenced by a country's growth, labor force participation, private credit market, income level and institutions. Additional factors include remittances, foreign direct investment, size of agricultural sector, size of manufacturing sector and inflation. The authors conclude that a country's microfinance success 'is significantly affected by the macroeconomic and macro-institutional environment in which an MFI is situated. While national context is not the whole story, its effects are non-negligible and systematic enough to be factored into rigorous MFI evaluation' (Ahlin et al. 2011, p. 119).

The prevalence of incomplete markets in developing countries poses a significant challenge for market-based development strategies, such as microfinance. In particular, the fastest-growing segment of the microfinance industry, for-profit MFIs, have yet to deeply penetrate the rural market due to geographic isolation and issues associated with land collateralization previously discussed. For these reasons, rural areas remain primarily served by not-for-profit MFIs and state-subsidized credit programs. Increases in technology have helped to lower the transaction costs associated with rural lending. However, for those MFIs that prioritize profit maximization, rural areas have yet to offer an investment environment that is as appealing as urban areas.

CONCLUDING REMARKS

One of the principal challenges for the microfinance industry today is rigorously evaluating the impact of microfinance activities at the client level, especially in relation to social performance. Although microfinance was founded as an anti-poverty tool, there is scant evidence that rigorously proves a causal relationship between microfinance and poverty reduction. Often analysts operate under the assumption that a microloan has inherently good benefits and that repayment alone is evidence of poverty reduction. For example, in the 2005 World Development Report, the World Bank writes that 'microfinance has demonstrated its success in reducing poverty', then proceeds to support its assertion by citing increasing portfolio sizes, repayment rates and number of customers served (World Bank 2005, p. 120). In fact, few peer-reviewed studies exist that show a clear relationship between microfinance activities and poverty reduction. At the time of writing in July 2012, an EBSCO search for the terms 'microfinance and poverty reduction' results in seven peer-reviewed articles. Of the seven, two concluded that microfinance programs resulted in modest decreases in poverty in the localities of interest.[4] One responded with a very cautious affirmation of the hypothesis.[5] The results of the other four ranged from firm rejections of the hypothesis to inconclusive findings.[6]

Similarly, multilateral development banks and their partners have often made the claim that microfinance produces employment due to its association with income-generating activities. For example, the International Development Association, a branch of the World Bank, 'supports job creation through microfinance initiatives' in their efforts to strengthen the private sector in developing countries (International Development Association 2012). However, there is thin evidence that convincingly demonstrates this relationship. An EBSCO search for the terms 'microfinance and employment' produces only one peer-reviewed article. In the study, the authors conclude that results are mixed, but that microfinance may bring modest benefits to the financial health of a community.[7] Grameen America has admitted that it is extremely rare for a microentrepreneur to ever hire any employees. More often than not the client uses the microloan to start a business that simply supplements the salary from another job that provides the lion's share of income (Grameen America 2010).

Indeed, there has recently been a shift in how researchers, analysts and MFIs rigorously evaluate microfinance activities at the client level, particularly in relation to issues of social performance. The Social Performance Task Force, which was founded in 2008 and has since expanded considerably, evaluates the degree to which an MFI meets its stated social goals and whether or not clients receive their proportional share of the benefits of microfinance activities. Other evaluation criteria include transparency, poverty reduction measures and financial performance of microenterprises. The Social Performance Task Force is a consortium of approximately 700 groups affiliated with universities, MFIs, investors, research centers, government regulators and consultants (Social Performance Task Force 2012). The work by the Social Performance Task Force is complemented by Microfinance Transparency, a group that works to increase transparency and public visibility of the real interest rates of microloans (Microfinance Transparency 2012). The combined efforts of each of these organizations help to shed light on microfinance's true contributions to poverty, employment and entrepreneurship, as well as reducing the potential for predatory lending. Such strategies were often needed, but absent, during the microfinance industry's period of transformation from pilot projects to a global industry.

In order for microfinance to truly fulfill its promise, microfinance activities must include several strategies that have the customer's interest in mind: rigorous evaluations of social performance at the client level, consumer protection and increased transparency. For too long the success of microfinance activities was simply measured by financial returns and illustrated by anecdotal stories of client satisfaction. Analysts and researchers could only speculate as to what was the true impact of microfinance on the poor. A growing body of peer-reviewed academic studies, based on large, randomly sampled data, deepens our understanding of what microfinance can and cannot do, how specific lending methodologies may produce distinct outcomes and how incomplete land and credit markets may influence microfinance performance. Through the accumulation of such knowledge, the microfinance industry can come to better understand its strengths and weaknesses, and MFI practitioners, policy makers and researchers can more accurately shape the industry in ways that optimize benefits for poor clientele.

NOTES

1. For example, see Drake and Rhyne (2002) and Accion International (2007).
2. For more on the commercialization debate, see Sinha (2011), Rhyne (2009), Olsen (2010) and Conning and Morduch (2011).
3. 1 manzana = 2.1 acres.
4. See Khan (2009) and Shah (2010).
5. See Khan (2009).
6. See Shaw (2004), Gurses (2009), Shetty (2010) and Li et al. (2011).
7. See Kotir and Obeng-Odoom (2009).

REFERENCES

Accion International (2007), 'Microfinance in the real world: for-profit growth will benefit the world's poor'. Available at http://accion.org (accessed 14 June 2012).
Accion International (2012), 'Compartamos Banco'. Available at http://accion.org (accessed 14 June 2012).
Ahlin, C., J. Lin and M. Maio (2011), 'Where does microfinance flourish? Microfinance institution performance in macroeconomic context', *Journal of Development Economics*, 95, 105–20.
Boucher, S., B. Barharm and M. Carter (2005), 'The impact of "market-friendly" reforms on credit and land markets in Honduras and Nicaragua', *World Development*, 33, 107–28.
Business Week (2007), 'Yunus blasts Compartamos'. Available at www.businessweek.com (accessed 1 May 2008).
Carlos, D. and C. Labarthe (2008), 'A letter to our peers'. Available at www.compartamos.com (accessed 30 June 2008).
Conning, J. and J. Morduch (2011), 'Microfinance and social investment', *Annual Review of Financial Economics*, 3, 1–28.
Consultative Group to Assist the Poor (2012), 'Why do MFIs charge high interest rates?' Available at www.cgap.org (accessed 14 June 2012).
Cull, R., A. Kunt and J. Morduch (2007), 'Financial performance and outreach: a global analysis of leading microbanks', *Economic Journal*, 117, 107–33.
Cull, R., A. Kunt and J. Morduch (2011), 'Does regulatory supervision curtail microfinance profitability and outreach?', *World Development*, 39, 949–65.

Drake, D. and E. Rhyne (eds) (2002), *The Commercialization of Microfinance: Balancing Business and Development*, West Hartford, CT: Kumarian Press.

Dutt, N. (2010), 'India's loan arrangers hit by crisis'. Available at www.bbc.co.uk (accessed 14 June 2012).

The Economist (2008), 'Poor people, rich returns'. Available at www.economist.com (accessed 1 June 2008).

Epstein, K. and G. Smith (2007), 'The ugly side of micro-lending', *Business Week*, 24, 38–44.

Grameen America (2010), 'Grameen America and the microfinance movement: past, present and future', University of Wisconsin–Madison, November 17.

Grameen Bank (1998), 'A short history of Grameen Bank'. Available at www.grameen-info.org (accessed 13 May 2008).

Grameen Bank (2011), 'Grameen at a glance'. Available at www.grameen-info.org (accessed 14 June 2012).

Gurses, D. (2009), 'Microfinance and poverty reduction in Turkey', *Perspectives on Global Development and Technology*, 8, 90–110.

Hermes, N., R. Lensink and A. Meesters (2011), 'Outreach and efficiency of microfinance institutions', *World Development*, 39, 938–48.

International Development Association (2012), 'Microfinance and private sector development'. Available at web.worldbank.org (accessed 14 June 2012).

De Janvry, A., C. McIntosh and E. Sadoulet (2010), 'The supply-and-demand-side of credit market information', *Journal of Development Economics*, 93, 173–88.

Karlan, D. (2007), 'Social connection and group banking', *Economic Journal*, 117, 52–84.

Kennedy, E. and P. Peters (1992), 'Household food security and child nutrition: the interaction of income and gender of household head', *World Development*, 20, 1077–85.

Khan, S. (2009), 'Poverty reduction efforts: does microcredit help?', *SAIS Review of International Affairs*, 29, 147–57.

Kotir, J. and F. Obeng-Odoom (2009), 'Microfinance and rural household development', *Journal of Developing Societies*, 25, 85–105.

Lewis, J. (2008), 'Microloan sharks', *Stanford Social Innovation Review*, 6, 54–9.

Li, X., C. Gan and B. Hu (2011), 'The welfare impact of microcredit on rural households in China', *Journal of Socio-Economics*, 40, 404–11.

McIntosh, C. and B. Wydick (2005), 'Competition and microfinance', *Journal of Development Economics*, 78, 271–98.

Microfinance Transparency (2012), 'About our organization'. Available at http://www.mftransparency.org/ (accessed 14 June 2012).

Morduch, J. (1999), 'The microfinance promise', *Journal of Economic Literature*, 37, 1569–1614.

Olsen, T. (2010), 'New actors in microfinance lending: the role of regulation and competition in Latin America', *Perspectives on Global Development and Technology*, 9, 500–519.

ProMujer (2008), 'Glossary'. Available at http://promujer.org (accessed 26 April 2008).

ProMujer (2012), 'Our approach'. Available at http://promujer.org (accessed 14 June 2012).

Rhyne, E. (2009), 'Microfinance for bankers and investors: understanding the opportunity at the bottom of the pyramid', Center for Financial Inclusion.

Robinson, M. (2001), *The Microfinance Revolution: Sustainable Finance for the Poor*, New York: World Bank Publications.

Shah, N. (2010), 'Microfinance and poverty reduction: evidence from a village study in Bangladesh', *Journal of Asian and African Studies*, 45, 670–83.

Shaw, J. (2004), 'Microenterprise occupation and poverty reduction in microfinance programs: evidence from Sri Lanka', *World Development*, 32, 1247–64.

Shetty, S. (2010), 'Microcredit, poverty, and empowerment: exploring the connections', *Perspectives on Global Development and Technology*, 9, 356–91.

Sinha, S. (2011), 'Initial public offerings: the field's salvation or downfall?' Available at http://www.globalmicrocreditsummit2011.org (accessed 1 March 2012).

Social Performance Task Force (2012), 'What is social performance?' Available at http://sptf.info/ (accessed 14 June 2012).

de Soto, H. (2000), *The Mystery of Capital: Why Capitalism Triumphs in the West and Fails Everywhere Else*, New York: Basic Books.

Woodruff, C. (2001), 'Review of de Soto's *The Mystery of Capital: Why Capitalism Triumphs in the West and Fails Everywhere Else*', *Journal of Economic Literature*, 39, 1215–23.

World Bank (2005), *World Development Report*, Washington, DC: World Bank.

World Bank (2007), 'Land titles give people a stake in their country'. Available at www.worldbank.org (accessed 14 June 2012).

Yunus, M. (2003), *Banker to the Poor: Micro-Lending and the Battle Against World Poverty*, New York: Public Affairs.

Yunus, M. (2007), *Creating a World Without Poverty: Social Business and the Future of Capitalism*, New York: Public Affairs.

12. The implications of corn-based ethanol production for non-metropolitan development in the North Central region of the US

W. Richard Goe and Anirban Mukherjee[1]

Over the first decade of the twenty-first century, a wave of investment in new manufacturing capacity spread throughout the North Central region of the US as ethanol factories were constructed at a rapid pace.[2] This was prompted by new energy policy initiatives of the federal government, spikes in gasoline prices, the need to reduce US dependency on foreign oil supplies, and the need to reduce the amount of environmental degradation resulting from the consumption of fossil fuels, among other concerns (Schnepf 2007). Based on information sources described below, we estimate there to have been 165 ethanol plants in operation within the region in 2010. Approximately 91 percent of these factories were constructed during or after the year 2000. Finally, 78.2 percent of these ethanol factories were located in non-metropolitan localities within the region (*Ethanol Producer Magazine* 2010; Renewable Fuels Association 2010).[3]

This wave of growth occurred within the context of a pattern of uneven development among non-metropolitan localities within the region. Many of these non-metropolitan localities have been subject to long-term population loss, economic stagnation and decline, while others have experienced population growth and economic development (see, for example, Rathge et al. 2001). One potentially important development implication of the growth of the ethanol industry is that it may change this pattern of development. Over the long term, the continued growth of the industry could ameliorate the stagnation and decline of non-metropolitan localities that serve as production locations, even potentially leading to their growth and development through the provision of new jobs, new sources of income and local tax revenues. In addition, ethanol production can provide market opportunities for other local businesses in non-metropolitan localities (for example, grain producers and distributors, trucking firms), thereby stimulating multiplier effects and further improvement of local economic conditions. The extent to which such effects are realized depends upon how value/commodity chains in ethanol production are spatially organized (Gereffi

1994; Gereffi et al. 2005; Sturgeon et al. 2008).[4] Value chains that are predominantly organized at the local level would presumably allow non-metropolitan localities to capture a greater share of the economic benefits from ethanol production.

This chapter has two primary objectives. The first is to examine the characteristics of non-metropolitan localities where ethanol factories have been constructed and put into operation and compare them to non-metropolitan localities that did not become locations for ethanol production during this rapid growth phase in the industry. The second objective will be to identify links in the value/commodity chain of ethanol production that are systematically located in proximity to ethanol plants within the North Central region. As will be described below in more detail, these objectives will provide insight into how the growth of the ethanol industry will impact the development of non-metropolitan localities within the region.

The chapter is organized as follows. The first section describes the hypothesized impacts of ethanol factories on non-metropolitan localities. The second section describes the value chain involved in ethanol production. The third section discusses factors influencing where businesses are located, how facets of the ethanol commodity chain could influence where ethanol factories are sited, and discusses reasons why ethanol factories might be sited in non-metropolitan versus metropolitan locations. The fourth section describes the research hypotheses and research methods used to meet the study objectives. The fifth section presents the research findings. Finally, the implications of the study findings are discussed.

THE HYPOTHESIZED DEVELOPMENT IMPACTS OF ETHANOL FACTORIES ON NON-METROPOLITAN LOCALITIES

The growth of the ethanol industry has been touted as a possible solution to the economic development problems faced by non-metropolitan communities and their surrounding localities. For example, former President Bill Clinton stated in a 2007 lecture given at Kansas State University: 'the greatest thing about biofuels ... is that they don't travel well ... That means no big long pipelines and every 50 or 100 or 200 miles you got to have a new production facility and a new distribution network ... we can revitalize rural America. We can bring back the small towns and the rural areas' (Clinton 2007).

The North Central region contains many non-metropolitan localities and communities that are highly dependent upon agriculture, have been unable to develop diversified economies, and have aging, dwindling populations

(Rathge et al. 2001). The lack of new employment opportunities combined with the relative lack of high-wage employment has promoted out-migration, economic stagnation and impoverishment. The impoverished population found in these communities is typically characterized by a substantial number of working poor (Anderson et al. 2007).

Past research has indicated that non-metropolitan jobs in manufacturing tend to pay higher wages compared to those in service sector industries (Gibbs et al. 2005). Thus, boosters of the ethanol industry have contended that locating ethanol plants in non-metropolitan communities will bring much-needed jobs that pay higher wages, increase local tax revenues, enhance public services, stimulate new multiplier effects in the local economy, and attract and retain new population (Hipple et al. 2007). These projected impacts are typical of community development projects where proponents portray growth as a public good in order to gain the support of community citizens and the local government (Logan and Molotch 1987).

It is important to note that the rapid growth of ethanol factories in the North Central region has not been without controversy. Conflict has erupted in some non-metropolitan communities over proposals to locate an ethanol factory in the community (see, for example, Barrett 2007; Sanders 2007). Members of opposition groups have perceived ethanol factories as posing risks to the health and safety of community residents, increasing air pollution through emitting a malodorous stench and releasing airborne particles and other potentially dangerous organic compounds, and increasing heavy truck traffic and congestion. Some anecdotal evidence suggests that opposition groups have been organized by recent in-migrants who moved to the rural community for certain quality-of-life attributes that they feel are threatened by the establishment of an ethanol factory (Barrett 2007). In turn, this pits their quality-of-life interests against local agricultural producers and other community residents whose economic interests would be advanced by the ethanol factory.

Further controversy has been generated in some cases where local tax breaks have been provided to companies producing ethanol as part of the economic development package aimed at attracting the construction of the factory (see, for example, Bain 2011). In this case, the projected impact of the ethanol factory in increasing local tax revenues is greatly reduced and delayed until the tax break expires. While the spending of wages by workers employed by the ethanol factory in the local economy may benefit local businesses and generate some local tax revenue, the provision of a tax break to the ethanol factory itself serves to limit the impact of the factory in generating additional local tax revenue that could be used to support and enhance local public services.

The extent to which these impacts are realized in non-metropolitan localities where ethanol factories are located remains to be seen. Moreover, the full extent of these impacts may not be realized for many years until ethanol is more extensively used in the production of fuel for motor transportation. One issue that can be examined at this juncture in time is to compare the characteristics and conditions of non-metropolitan localities where ethanol factories have been constructed and put into operation, with those where ethanol factories have not been constructed. This will provide insight into how the growth of the ethanol industry may influence the pattern of uneven development within the region as well as the types of localities that are experiencing the development impacts associated with such factories. The extent to which the purported economic benefits of an ethanol factory are realized within the locality in which the factory is located will be highly influenced by how value chains in ethanol production are spatially organized.

THE VALUE CHAIN IN ETHANOL PRODUCTION

A 'commodity chain' or 'value chain' (Gereffi 1994; Gereffi et al. 2005; Sturgeon et al. 2008) refers to the sequence of interlinked economic activities involved in the production, marketing and distribution of a single product or commodity. A value chain is characterized by an organizational form. At one extreme, individual firms engage in only one activity with exchange between firms in the chain being coordinated through markets (in other words, the value chain is completely organized via the social division of labor). At the other extreme is complete vertical integration in which all activities in the chain occur within the organizational hierarchy of a single firm (in other words, the value chain is completely organized within the technical division of labor of a firm). In between these extremes are organizational forms consisting of a combination of market contracting (or outsourcing) and vertical integration.

The division of labor in a value chain has a spatial dimension in that the economic activities comprising the chain may or may not take place in the same location. With the phenomenon of globalization, the value chains for a growing number of commodities extend across international boundaries (Gereffi 1994; Gereffi et al. 2005; Sturgeon et al. 2008). In addition, the set of economic activities that comprise a value chain may be distinguished in terms of the amount of value added to the finished commodity, with some activities adding more value than others. Moreover, firms participating in a value chain may vary on the basis of their extent of power to set the terms of exchange and/or control the actions of other firms participating in the chain (assuming the chain involves market contracting between firms).

In applying these concepts, the economic activities comprising the value chain in ethanol production may be described through a sequence of both 'upstream' and 'downstream' linkages in the production of ethanol. At the upstream end, a key link in the chain is the production of a 'bio-crop'. In broad terms, a bio-crop is any plant or plant-based substance that is fermentable. This includes food crops such as corn (maize), milo (sorghum) and sugar cane; non-food plants such as switchgrass and jatropha; and waste resulting from processing food products such as wheat gluten, beer, cheese and potato products (Moll 2007; US Environmental Protection Agency 2007). Of these, corn is by far the most extensively used bio-crop in the US ethanol industry as nearly 95 percent of the ethanol supply is produced from corn (Williams 2004). As such, ethanol factories typically contract with grain producers, grain wholesale firms, and/or grain elevators to provide the supply of corn or other grain needed to produce ethanol. However, vertical integration is also used in that some ethanol factories are owned by farmer co-operatives or agribusiness corporations (for example, Archer Daniels Midland Co., Cargill Inc.).

Other upstream linkages in the value chain include manufacturers and suppliers of inputs required to construct and operate an ethanol factory. In addition to land on which to construct an ethanol factory, other key inputs include storage facilities, distillation equipment and other industrial machinery (for example, milling equipment for grain, drying equipment for distillers' grain), and storage tanks for the processed ethanol. Ethanol production also requires access to an adequate water supply. It has been estimated that 4.2 gallons of water are required to produce a gallon of ethanol (Keeney and Muller 2006). Finally, another critical input is labor to staff the factory. At White Energy's ethanol factory in Russell, Kansas, for example, 24 workers were used to staff a factory with a production capacity of 45 million gallons of ethanol per year. This includes workers needed to staff and maintain the production line, factory managers, and laboratory workers engaged in monitoring and testing to ensure product quality and workplace safety (White Energy 2007).

When used as an input, grain is typically trucked into an ethanol factory on a just-in-time basis that ensures a steady stream of trucks moving in and out of a facility. In the process of converting it to ethanol, the grain is milled, mashed, cooked, saccharified, cooled and fermented.[5] It then undergoes distillation as the liquid ethanol is separated from the solid residue of the bio-crop (known as stillage). Once the distillation process is completed, the ethanol is moved to storage tanks to await shipping. Because of its corrosiveness, ethanol cannot be transported through a pipeline. Therefore, it is typically transported by train or by truck. Using it again as a case example, White Energy's ethanol plant in Russell, Kansas reports that 100 trucks and five rail cars per day move grains in and ethanol out of the factory (White Energy 2007). Thus, proximate access to infrastructure for truck and rail transportation is essential.

On the downstream end of the value chain, the primary market for ethanol is for use as a fuel additive, where petroleum refineries purchase it as an input to be mixed with gasoline. Much smaller markets also exist for the use of ethanol as an industrial solvent (predominantly in the manufacture of chemicals and paints), and as an ingredient in cosmetics, medicines and beverages (Meiller 2005; Sriroth et al. 2003). An important byproduct of the stillage that is separated from the ethanol in the distillation process is distillers' grains. These are used as an additive to enhance the nutritional value of cattle and other animal feeds. As such, distillers' grains provide an additional revenue stream for ethanol producers. Potential markets for distillers' grains include animal feed manufacturers, cattle feedlots (whether independent or integrated into meat packing firms), and independent cattle and livestock producers.

BUSINESS LOCATION THEORY AND THE SELECTION OF SITES FOR ETHANOL FACTORIES

Social scientists examining the spatial structure of economic activity have long noted the tendency of related economic activities to be clustered in the same location (see, for example, Marshall 1900; Storper and Walker 1989; Tornqvist 1968). This occurs because spatial proximity allows the realization of economic benefits (for example, agglomeration economies, lower transaction costs, spillovers of technological knowledge), facilitates economic transactions with high contact requirements, and allows the realization of benefits from participation in local business and social networks (see, for example, Goe et al. 2000; Kenney and Patton 2005; Storper and Walker 1989). As related economic activities cluster together in space, industrial complexes are formed as firms locate business establishments in proximity to each other (Scott 1988).

The formation of industrial complexes is characteristic of large metropolitan areas where firms have access to larger markets, larger pools of labor and larger numbers of suppliers, among other factors (Storper and Walker 1989). Although this does not preclude the formation of small-scale industrial clusters in non-metropolitan localities (see, for example, Goe 2002), as will be demonstrated below, the ethanol industry is not highly concentrated within the metropolitan areas of the North Central region at this juncture in time. The majority of operating factories are located in non-metropolitan localities. Moreover, very few of these localities contain more than one factory.

One potential explanation for this pattern of spatial development relates to the rapid growth and relative immaturity of the ethanol industry. Scott and Storper (1987) contend that early stages of development in an industry that involve rapid growth are characterized by windows of locational opportunity in which firms have greater freedom in where to locate due to not yet being pinned down by enormous investments in physical facilities and industrial complexes. At the same time, however, firms still have locational specifications that are necessary to remain in business; that is, they must be located in a place where they are able to obtain the inputs required to produce a product and transfer the product to the customers that purchase it. The concept of locational capabilities refers to a firm's level of ability to accomplish this at a specific location (Storper and Walker 1989, pp. 73–4).

As noted above, the ethanol industry is in a relatively early stage of development and has undergone rapid growth over the past decade. While some large agribusiness and/or energy corporations (for example, Archer Daniels Midland Co., Cargill, Poet Biorefining LLC, Valero Renewable Fuels LLC) have entered the ethanol industry and operate multiple ethanol factories, market competition within the industry has yet to unfold to the point where the structure of the industry is characterized by an oligopoly. At this juncture, the industry is characterized by a substantial number of smaller, start-up firms that operate a single ethanol factory (see *Ethanol Producer Magazine* 2010; Renewable Fuels Association 2010). Moreover, the formation of large industrial complexes in the ethanol industry has yet to occur. As will be demonstrated below, the locational structure of the industry within the North Central region is spatially diffused outside of metropolitan areas with the majority of factories located in peripheral areas (in other words, non-metropolitan counties). Further, only a few of these counties contain more than one ethanol factory.

The location of industry in peripheral areas has been attributed to the need to: (1) realize lower factor costs of production (for example, labor costs, taxes) in order to improve profit margins; (2) be in close proximity to and/or ensure a stable supply of important inputs; (3) be in closer proximity to important markets in general; or (4) be better able to develop less lucrative market segments in peripheral areas as part of a broader growth strategy (Storper and Walker 1989). All of these reasons would potentially be applicable to the location of ethanol factories in non-metropolitan localities in the North Central region.

A second key objective of this research is to determine whether there are any economic activities in the organization of value chains in ethanol production to which ethanol factories have been systematically located in spatial proximity. This will provide insight into whether there is a systematic pattern to the locational specifications of ethanol factories within the North Central region and identify links in the value chain of ethanol production most likely to generate multiplier effects within the local economies of non-metropolitan localities. Finally, this analysis will provide insight into the reasons why ethanol factories have predominantly located in non-metropolitan localities.

It is important to point out that several other studies have addressed this issue (see Haddad et al. 2010; Lambert et al. 2008). This research may be distinguished from these earlier analyses in several important ways. First, this research employs commodity/value chain analysis as an overarching theoretical framework guiding the specification of a locational model for ethanol factories (see model description below). The previous analyses were either an empirically based exercise focused on identifying correlates of ethanol factory location without reference to a developed body of social theory, or analyzed a smaller set of locational determinants. Second, this analysis focuses on the entire North Central region (a 12-state region), which represents the core regional location of the ethanol industry and accounts for the vast majority of ethanol factories in the US. In contrast, Lambert et al. (2008) analyzed the US as a whole while Haddad et al. (2010) limited their analysis to four states within the North Central region. Finally, both of these previous studies were concerned with a seven-year time frame from 2000 to 2007. This research extends these analyses by examining a longer time period from 2000 to 2010.

RESEARCH METHODS

In order to meet the research objectives, we constructed a panel data set for the 1055 counties comprising the 12 states in the North Central region using secondary sources. The data set contained indicators of whether an operating ethanol factory (or factories) was located in the county, local economic and social conditions, and the presence of economic activities and infrastructure comprising or essential to the value chain in ethanol production.

Identification of Counties with an Ethanol Factory in Operation

Data on ethanol factories in operation within the North Central region were compiled from multiple sources. First, data were collected from the Renewable Fuels Association (RFA). The RFA maintains an online database on ethanol factories currently in operation across the US that includes the name of the company operating the factory, the factory location, primary bio-crop (or feedstock) used to produce ethanol, and the production capacity of the factory.[6] Second, data were also collected from *Ethanol Producer Magazine*, which also maintains an online database on US ethanol factories currently in operation. This database contains the same data as the RFA database with the addition of the date on which the factory began operation.[7] Finally, data were also collected on the location of operating ethanol factories from trade associations in each state that promote the ethanol industry.[8] Ethanol factories that were identified as being in operation within the region from these sources were then cross-referenced and verified for accuracy.

Table 12.1 displays a contingency table cross-tabulating the number of ethanol factories in operation in 2010 by the spatial location of a county. In total, there were 165 ethanol factories in operation that were located in 152 out of the 1055 counties in the 12-state region. Of the 152 counties with an operating ethanol factory, 139 contained one operating factory while 13 counties contained two operating factories. Further, 129 of the ethanol factories (78.2 percent) were located in non-metropolitan counties while 36 (21.8 percent) were located in metropolitan counties. These data indicate that the estimated odds are slightly less than 4:1 that an operating ethanol factory will be located in a non-metropolitan county compared to a county that is part of a metropolitan area. In effect, the ethanol industry is largely a non-metropolitan industry. Figure 12.1 maps the counties within the North Central region that contain at least one operating ethanol factory. This map reveals that while the ethanol industry is predominantly centered in the 'corn belt' states of Iowa and Nebraska, it is spatially diffused across non-metropolitan counties of the other states that comprise the region.

Table 12.1   Number of ethanol plants per county by spatial location within the North Central region

Number of ethanol plants in operation 10/2009	Metropolitan county	Non-metropolitan county	Total
0	253	650	903 (85.6%)
1	28	111	139 (13.2%)
2	4	9	13 (1.2%)
Total	285 (27.0%)	770 (73.0%)	1055

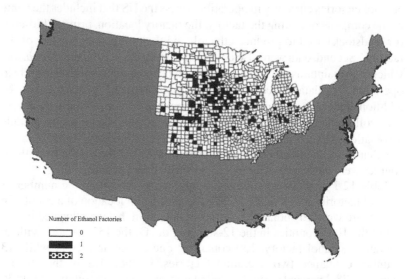

Figure 12.1   Ethanol factories in the North Central region

Analyzing Socio-Economic Conditions in Counties with Ethanol Factories

Counties in which an ethanol plant was constructed and put in operation in the year 2000 or beyond were compared with counties that did not have an ethanol factory on a range of indicators measuring social and economic conditions.[9] The conditions examined included impoverishment, the growth and distribution of income, employment and population characteristics. Indicators of impoverishment included: (1) the poverty rate in 2000; (2) size of the impoverished population in 2000; (3) change in the size of the impoverished population 1990–2000; (4) the percentage of households that were working poor in 2000;[10] and (5) change in the number of households that were working poor between 1990 and 2000.

Indicators of the growth and distribution of income that were analyzed included: (1) aggregate income in 1999; (2) change in real aggregate income between 1989 and 1999 (in 1999 constant dollars); (3) median household income in 1999; (4) change in real median household income between 1989 and 1999 (in 1999 constant dollars); (5) the Gini coefficient in 1999; and (6) change in the Gini coefficient between 1989 and 1999.

Indicators of employment that were examined included: (1) total employment in 2000; (2) change in total employment between 1990 and 2000; (3) the unemployment rate in 2000; (4) number of unemployed persons in

2000; and (5) change in the number of unemployed persons between 1990 and 2000. Finally, population characteristics that were examined included: (1) total population in 2000; (2) change in total population between 1990 and 2000; (3) percent urban population in 2000; (4) change in urban population between 1990 and 2000; and (5) change in rural population between 1990 and 2000.

A difference-of-means test was used to identify significant differences on these indicators between counties that had an ethanol plant constructed and put into operation in the year 2000 or beyond versus counties that did not have an ethanol plant in operation.[11] Given that the majority of ethanol factories are located in non-metropolitan counties, this analysis was conducted using both metropolitan and non-metropolitan counties, with a separate analysis conducted for non-metropolitan counties only.

Identifying Local Dimensions of the Ethanol Value Chain Correlated with Plant Location

The identification of local dimensions in the value chain of ethanol production that were systematically associated with ethanol plant location was accomplished through the use of logistic regression analysis. A binary variable was created measuring whether or not a county had at least one ethanol plant in operation. This was treated as a dependent variable that was regressed on a set of independent variables measuring the local presence of activities and characteristics central to the value chain in ethanol production. The measures and data sources used for the dependent variable and independent variables are listed in Table 12.2.

Table 12.2   Data sources and measurement of variables for the logistic regression model

Variable	Data source
Dependent variable	
Does county have an ethanol plant in operation? 1 = Yes, 0 = No	Renewable Fuels Association; State Corn and Grain Commissions; *Ethanol Producer*
Independent variables	
Indicators of upstream value chain linkages	
1. % acres of cropland planted with corn	*US Census of Agriculture* (2002)
2. % acres of cropland planted with sorghum	*US Census of Agriculture* (2002)

Table 12.2   Continued

Variable	Data source
3. Does county have a business establishment manufacturing distilling equipment? 1 = Yes, 0 = No	*County Business Patterns* (2000)
4. Does county have a business establishment manufacturing metal storage tanks? 1 = Yes, 0 = No	*County Business Patterns* (2000)
5. Does county have a grain elevator?[1] 1 = Yes, 0 = No	*County Business Patterns* (2000)
6. Does county have a business establishment engaged in wholesale trade of grain? 1 = Yes, 0 = No	*County Business Patterns* (2000)
7. % employed labor force accounted for by workers in working-class occupations[2]	*US Census of Population & Housing* (2000)
8. % employed labor force accounted for by workers in managerial occupations	*US Census of Population & Housing* (2000)
9. % employed labor force accounted for by life & physical scientists & lab technicians	*US Census of Population & Housing* (2000)
Indicators of downstream value chain linkages	
10. Does county have a business establishment engaged in specialized freight trucking? 1 = Yes, 0 = No	*County Business Patterns* (2000)
11. Does county have workers employed in rail transportation? 1 = Yes, 0 = No	*US Census of Population & Housing* (2000)
12. Does county have a business establishment engaged in petroleum refining? 1 = Yes, 0 = No	*County Business Patterns* (2000)
13. Does county have a business establishment manufacturing animal feed? 1 = Yes, 0 = No	*County Business Patterns* (2000)
14. Does county have a business establishment engaged in animal slaughtering & processing? 1 = Yes, 0 = No	*County Business Patterns* (2000)

Variable	Data source
15. Total number of cattle on feed in county	*US Census of Agriculture* (2002)
Control variables	
16. Is county non-metropolitan and adjacent USDA, Economic Research Service, to a metropolitan area? 1 = Yes, 0 = No	Beale Code, 2003
17. Is county non-metropolitan and not adjacent USDA, Economic Research Service, to a metropolitan area? 1 = Yes, 0 = No	Beale Code, 2003
18. Does county have an interstate within it? 1 = Yes, 0 = No	*Rand McNally Road Atlas*
19. % urban population	*US Census of Population & Housing* (2000)
20. % households that are working poor	*US Census of Population & Housing* (2000)
21. Average earnings per employed worker	*US Census of Population & Housing* (2000)
22. % population 25 years & older with a college degree	*US Census of Population & Housing* (2000)

Notes:

1. Grain elevators are classified under farm product warehousing (49313) using the North American Industrial Classification System (NAICS).
2. Following Florida (2002, p. 328) working-class occupations include production occupations, construction and extraction occupations, installation, maintenance and repair occupations, and transportation and material moving occupations.

One set of independent variables included indicators of the local presence of upstream linkages in the ethanol value chain. This included indicators of the local production of key bio-crops within the North Central region (corn, sorghum), the local presence of business establishments that manufacture relevant industrial equipment (distilling equipment, storage tanks and equipment), the local presence of business establishments that distribute grain (grain wholesale firms and grain elevators) and the local presence of workers with occupational skills relevant to ethanol production (production and related workers, managers, lab scientists and technicians) (see Table 12.2). Assuming that proximity to these upstream inputs in the ethanol value chain is beneficial to ethanol factories, we hypothesize that counties with a more extensive local presence of these factors will be more likely to serve as locations for operating ethanol factories.

Another set of independent variables included indicators of the local presence of downstream linkages in the ethanol value chain. This included indicators of the local presence of relevant transportation industries (trucking, rail), petroleum refineries, animal feed manufacturers, animal slaughtering and processing (in other words, meat packing), and other organizations with cattle on feed (see Table 12.2).[12] Assuming that proximity to these downstream linkages in the value chain is beneficial to ethanol factories, we hypothesize that counties with a more extensive local presence of these factors will be more likely to serve as locations for operating ethanol plants.

Finally, a set of control variables was specified in the logistic regression model to statistically control for spatial context, wage rates and human capital. Four indicators of spatial context were included as control variables. The first two indicators included: (1) whether or not a county was non-metropolitan, and adjacent to a metropolitan area; and (2) whether or not a county was non-metropolitan and not adjacent to a metropolitan area. These indicators were included in the logistic regression model to control for the spatial dispersion of the industry and other characteristics of non-metropolitan localities not directly measured and incorporated into the model (for example, production of bio-crops other than corn and sorghum). In addition, adjacent non-metropolitan counties were distinguished from those not adjacent in order to control for non-metropolitan spillover effects not measured by variables in the model (for example, greater market demand for gasoline blended with ethanol). The third indicator was whether or not a county had an interstate highway running through it. This was used to control for immediate access to the primary US transportation arteries for motor vehicles. We hypothesize that counties with immediate access to interstate highways will be more likely to serve as a location for an operating ethanol factory.

The fourth indicator of spatial context was the percentage of the total population living in an urban area. This was specified as a control variable to account for other benefits of having an urban location not directly measured in the model such as differences in infrastructure (for example, utilities) and the availability of some urban amenities for workers and residents. We hypothesize that counties with a greater percentage of urban population are more likely to serve as a location for an operating ethanol factory.

Two indicators of wage rates were included as control variables. The first indicator was the average earnings per employed worker. As a more direct measure of the prevalence of low wage employment, the second indicator was the percentage of households that were working poor. Assuming that ethanol firms have an incentive to pay lower wages and enhance their profitability, we hypothesize that counties with lower average earnings per worker and those with a higher percentage of working poor households will be more likely to serve as a location for an operating ethanol factory.

Human capital was measured by one indicator: the percentage of the population, 25 years and older, that has earned a college degree. This was used to control for the educational credentials of local workers, independent of their employment experience and occupational skills. Assuming that ethanol factories would be more likely to hire college graduates compared to workers with lower educational credentials, we hypothesize that counties with a higher percentage of people with a college degree will be more likely to serve as a location for an operating ethanol factory.

Specified in this way, the logistic regression model identifies linkages and conditions in the value chain of ethanol production that are systematically present in counties that serve as a location for an operating ethanol factory, compared to counties without such a factory. In turn, the estimated model provides insight into whether there is a systematic pattern of locational specifications in the counties where firms in the ethanol industry have chosen to locate their factories. Moreover, it provides insight into the nature of local multiplier effects emanating from ethanol factories. The logistic regression analysis employed a block model approach so the effects of independent variables measuring the upstream and downstream value chain linkages and the control variables could be analyzed separately and in combination. Further, following the protocol proposed by Menard (1995, pp. 77–80), diagnostics were performed on each logistic regression model. The level of multicollinearity among independent variables was assessed through the tolerance statistic and examining bivariate correlations. The Box–Tidwell test was used to test for non-linear relationships. Finally, studentized residuals were used to identify outliers and assess the validity of their scores on variables.

FINDINGS

Including both metropolitan and non-metropolitan counties in the North Central region, the difference-of-means tests revealed that counties that became locations for ethanol factories in the post-2000 period exhibited significant differences from counties that did not on the following indicators: (1) poverty rate, 2000; (2) change in number of working poor households, 1990–2000; (3) change in real aggregate income, 1989–1999; (4) Gini coefficient, 1999; (5) total employment, 2000; (6) change in employment, 1990–2000; (7) unemployment rate, 2000; (8) change in total population, 1990–2000; (9) percentage urban population, 2000; and (10) change in urban population, 1990–2000 (see Table 12.3).

Table 12.3   *Comparison of means for indicators of social and economic well-being between counties within the North Central region that became locations for ethanol plants following the year 2000 vs. counties that did not*

	All counties in region		Non-metropolitan counties only	
	Counties with an ethanol plant (n =137)	Counties without an ethanol plant (n = 903)	Counties with an ethanol plant (n = 107)	Counties without an ethanol plant (n = 650)
Indicators of poverty				
Poverty rate, 2000	9.81***	11.41	10.12***	12.47
Size of impoverished population, 2000	3973.57	6408.10	2272.01	2133.72
Change in impoverished population, 1990–2000	–593.52	–577.06	–418.34	–418.74
% households that are working poor, 2000	8.34	9.11	8.51**	9.79
Change in number of working poor households, 1990–2000	–60.66**	68.63	–78.35*	–39.92
Indicators of income growth & distribution				
Aggregate income, 1999[1]	811 264.74	1 375 151.74	424 812.54*	333 831.40
Change in real aggregate income, 1989–1999[1,2]	153 217.19*	275 590.51	73 631.64	67 658.89
Median household income, 1999	37 155.30	36 359.48	35 839.50***	33 450.46
Change in real median household income, 1989–1999[2]	3994.57	4131.34	3898.74	4101.33
Gini coefficient, 1999	0.3782*	0.3845	0.3801***	0.3902
Change in Gini coefficient, 1989–1999	–0.0086	–0.0092	–0.0083	–0.0010
Indicators of employment				
Total employment, 2000	20 926.78*	31 162.31	11 780.63***	9101.74
Change in employment, 1990–2000	2160.31*	3197.41	1018.42	1088.74
Unemployment rate, 2000	4.20***	4.95	4.12***	5.13
Number of unemployed, 2000	1026.33	1692.32	546.29	508.18
Change in number of unemployed, 1990–2000	–94.97	–181.17	–34.54	–56.81

	All counties in region		Non-metropolitan counties only	
	Counties with an ethanol plant (n=137)	Counties without an ethanol plant (n = 903)	Counties with an ethanol plant (n = 107)	Counties without an ethanol plant (n = 650)
Indicators of population				
Total population, 2000	42739.04	64423.10	24151.88*	19586.75
Change in total population, 1990–2000	2459.77**	4847.81	804.81	1065.83
% urban population, 2000	44.68***	34.73	39.89***	25.89
Change in urban population, 1990–2000	2923.98*	5437.75	1037.38	1108.20
Change in rural population, 1990–2000	−464.21	−589.94	−232.57	−42.37

Notes:

1: in thousands of dollars; 2: in 1999 constant dollars
t test indicated significant difference of means *** $p < 0.001$; ** $p < 0.01$; * $p < 0.05$.

Source: *US Census of Population and Housing* (1993, 2003).

In regard to the indicators of poverty, the results of the difference in means test revealed that counties that became locations for ethanol factories in the post-2000 period (hereafter termed location counties) had lower poverty rates in 2000 compared to those that did not. Further, location counties experienced a significant decline in the number of working poor households during 1990–2000 while non-location counties experienced an increase. In terms of the income distribution, location counties had a significantly lower level of income inequality in 1999 as measured by the Gini coefficient. Further, location counties had significantly lower unemployment rates in 2000 and were relatively more urbanized compared to non-location counties as measured by the percentage of urban population in 2000.

Contrary to this pattern, however, location counties were found to have experienced smaller increases in real aggregate income during 1989–1999 compared to non-location counties. Further, location counties had significantly smaller levels of total employment in 2000 and employment growth during 1990–2000. Finally, location counties also experienced smaller increases in total population and urban population during 1990–2000 compared to non-location counties. We interpret these findings to indicate that ethanol factories tended to be located in counties within the region with smaller cities and smaller economies. However, these counties also had relatively less poverty, fewer working poor, lower unemployment and less income inequality. Limiting this analysis to the non-metropolitan counties in the region supports this interpretation and provides additional insights.

The difference in means tests for the non-metropolitan counties indicated that non-metropolitan counties that became locations for ethanol factories in the post-2000 period exhibited significant differences from non-metropolitan counties that did not on the following indicators: (1) poverty rate, 2000; (2) percentage of households that were working poor, 2000; (3) change in number of working poor households, 1990–2000; (4) aggregate income, 1999; (5) median household income, 1999; (6) Gini coefficient, 1999; (7) total employment, 2000; (8) unemployment rate, 2000; (9) total population, 2000; and (10) percentage urban population, 2000 (see Table 12.3).

The difference-of-means tests reveal that on all of these dimensions, ethanol factories tended to locate in non-metropolitan counties within the region that were larger, more urbanized and possessed more highly developed, local economies. Non-metropolitan location counties had significantly lower poverty rates and lower rates of working poor in 2000, and experienced significantly larger declines in the number of working poor households during 1990–2000 compared to non-metropolitan counties that did not get ethanol factories in the post-2000 period. Further, non-metropolitan location counties had significantly larger levels of aggregate income in 1999, greater median household incomes in 1999, and lower levels of income inequality in 1999 as measured by the Gini coefficient. Non-metropolitan location counties had significantly larger numbers of jobs and significantly lower unemployment rates in 2000. Finally, non-metropolitan location counties had significantly larger populations and were relatively more urbanized in 2000 compared to non-metropolitan counties in the region that did not get ethanol plants. In sum, non-metropolitan counties that became locations for ethanol factories in the post-2000 period were less impoverished, more prosperous, had larger economies and larger, relatively more urbanized populations at the beginning of the decade compared to non-metropolitan counties that did not get ethanol plants.

Results of the Logistic Regression Analysis

The results of the logistic regression analysis are displayed in Table 12.4. Model 1 examines the effects for the independent variables measuring upstream linkages in the ethanol value chain without taking into account the effects of the independent variables measuring downstream linkages and the control variables. The model chi-square test indicates that this model fits the data with a moderate goodness-of-fit (Nagelkerke r^2 = 0.215). The significance tests for the logistic regression coefficients indicate that within the North Central region, ethanol factories tend to be located in counties with a higher percentage of planted acreage devoted to corn production, and counties that had at least one business establishment engaged in wholesale trade of grain. Further, the direction of these relationships (positive) supports the research hypotheses. The standardized coefficients indicate that percentage of crop acreage planted with corn was the strongest predictor of ethanol plant location in Model 1.

Contrary to the research hypotheses, it was found that having a larger percentage of acreage dedicated to sorghum production, having local business establishments manufacturing distilling equipment and storage tanks, having a local grain elevator, and having a larger percentage of local labor with relevant occupational skills, were not associated with where ethanol factories were located. Taken together, these findings suggest that having proximate access to a sufficient corn or grain supply is an important factor influencing ethanol factory location.

Model 2 examines the effects for the independent variables measuring downstream linkages in the ethanol value chain without taking into account the effects of the independent variables measuring upstream linkages and the control variables. The model chi-square test indicates that this model also fits the data, although with a weaker goodness-of-fit (Nagelkerke r^2 = 0.101). The significance tests for the logistic regression coefficients indicate that ethanol factories tend to be located within the region in counties that have at least one business establishment that manufactures animal feed, at least one business establishment that engages in meat packing, and also have a larger number of cattle on feed (in other words, larger feedlots). The direction of all these relationships (positive) supports the research hypotheses. The standardized coefficients indicate that presence of a local business that manufactures animal feed is a stronger predictor of ethanol plant location than the number of cattle on feed and the presence of a meat packing plant (see Table 12.4).

Contrary to the research hypotheses, having a local business establishment engaging in specialized freight trucking, having local employment in rail transport, and having a local business establishment engaged in petroleum refining, were not associated with where ethanol factories are located. Taken together, these findings suggest that when not taking into account the effects of the upstream linkages in the value chain and the control variables, ethanol factories tend to provide one dimension of an industrial cluster in the North Central region; that is, they tend to co-locate in counties that also have a local presence of animal feed manufacturing, meat packing and feedlots. These findings suggest that being in proximity to the market for distillers' grains represents an important locational consideration for ethanol factories.

Table 12.4   *Unstandardized and standardized logistic coefficients for regression of ethanol plant location on selected independent variables (n = 1055)[1]*

Independent variable	Model 1	Model 2	Model 3	Model 4	Model 5
Upstream value chain linkages					
1. % acres cropland planted with corn	0.055***	……	0.047***	……	0.046***
	(0.257)		(0.229)		(0.228)
2. % acres cropland planted with sorghum	0.042	……	0.014	……	0.002
	(0.046)		(0.016)		(0.002)
3. County has a business establishment manufacturing distilling equipment	−0.320	……	−0.530	……	−0.321
	(−0.033)		(−0.057)		(−0.034)
4. County has a business establishment manufacturing metal storage tanks	−0.279	……	−0.420	……	−0.365
	(−0.022)		(−0.035)		(−0.030)
5. County has a grain elevator	0.539	……	0.546	……	0.563
	(0.038)		(0.040)		(0.042)
6. County has a business establishment engaged in wholesale trade of grain	1.458**	……	1.419**	……	1.195*
	(0.163)		(0.166)		(0.139)
7. % employed labor force accounted for by workers in working-class occupations	−0.008	……	−0.0001	……	0.053
	(−0.010)		(−0.0001)		(0.075)
8. % employed labor force accounted for by workers in management occupations	0.003	……	0.012	……	0.047
	(0.005)		(0.016)		(0.067)

9. % employed labor force accounted for by life & physical scientists and lab technicians				
-0.067	......	0.068	......	0.313
(-0.006)		(0.007)		(0.030)
Downstream value chain linkages				
10. County has a business establishment engaged in specialized freight trucking				
......	-0.109	-0.617	......	-0.839
			(-0.045)	
11. County has workers employed in rail transportation				
...... 0.483	(-0.033) 0.377	......	0.463	......
(0.061)	(0.033)		(0.040)	
12. County has a business establishment engaged in petroleum refining				
......	-0.370	-0.189	......	-0.089
(-0.025)	(-0.009)		(-0.004)	
13. County has a business establishment manufacturing animal feed				
(0.159) (0.090)	0.840***	0.685***	......	0.620**
		(0.082)		
14. County has a business establishment in animal slaughtering & processing				
......	0.451*	0.372	...... 0.283	
		(0.039)		
15. Total number of cattle on feed				
(0.088) (0.051)	0.002***	0.001*	......	0.0007
	(0.049)	(0.039)	(0.038)	
Control variables				
16. Non-metropolitan adjacent county				
......	......	...... 0.444	0.265	
		(0.064)	(0.034)	

Independent variable	Model 1	Model 2	Model 3	Model 4	Model 5
17. Non-metropolitan non-adjacent county	......	......	......0.488	0.452	
			(0.075)	(0.061)	
18. County has interstate access	......	......	......0.132	0.183	
			(0.019)	(0.024)	
19. % urban population	......	......	......0.027***	0.020***	
				(0.245)	(0.164)
20. % households that are working poor	......	......	......	−0.181***	−0.080
				(−0.238)	(−0.093)
21. Average earnings per employed worker	......	......	......	−0.0002***	−0.0002***
				(−0.294)	(−0.250)
22. % population (≥25 yrs) with a college degree	......	......	0.057*	0.056	
				(0.072)	(0.063)
Intercept	−4.718***	−2.912***	−5.075**	3.197*	−2.927
−2 log-likelihood	735.095	808.560	709.127	798.978	678.631
Chi-squared	134.845***	61.380***	160.813***	70.962***	191.309***
Nagelkerke r-squared	0.215	0.101	0.252	0.116	0.295

Notes:

* $p < 0.05$; ** $p < 0.01$; *** $p < 0.001$

[1] Standardized logistic regression coefficients were computed following the formula proposed by Menard (1995, p. 46) and are listed in parentheses.

Model 3 examines the effects of variables measuring both upstream and downstream linkages in the value chain. The model chi-square test indicates that this model also fits the data with a slight improvement in goodness-of-fit (Nagelkerke r^2 = 0.252). Statistically controlling for both types of linkages, the results of the significance tests for the logistic regression coefficients are largely the same as for models 1 and 2; that is, percentage crop acreage planted with corn, having a local business establishment engaged in wholesale grain trade, having a local business establishment engaged in manufacturing animal feed, and having a larger number of cattle on feed, were positively associated with ethanol plant location (see Table 12.4).

The standardized coefficients indicate that the percentage of crop acreage planted with corn and the presence of a local grain wholesaler were the strongest predictors of ethanol plant location, when statistically controlling for both upstream and downstream linkages, respectively, in the ethanol value chain. These findings suggest that proximity to a sufficient corn supply is a more important locational consideration for ethanol factories than proximity to the secondary market for distillers' grains.

The key difference in the results of Model 3 was that statistically controlling for upstream linkages in the ethanol value chain, the effect of having a local business establishment engaged in meat packing became insignificant (see Table 12.4). Further analysis revealed that the inclusion of percentage of crop acreage planted with corn, or having a business establishment engaged in wholesale grain trade, into the logistic regression model rendered this relationship insignificant.[13] In effect, there is a tendency for meat packing establishments to be located in counties within the region where corn is more extensively cultivated, and which contain grain wholesale establishments. However, the latter two variables are more strongly prevalent in counties that contain ethanol factories compared to meat packing.

Model 4 examines the effects of the control variables without statistically controlling for the effects of the variables measuring upstream and downstream linkages in the ethanol value chain. The model chi-square test indicates that this model also fits the data with a decline in goodness-of-fit (Nagelkerke r^2 = 0.116). Consistent with the research hypotheses, the tests of significance for the logistic regression coefficients indicate that counties within the North Central region where ethanol factories were located were more likely to have a higher percentage of urban population, a higher percentage of adult population with college degrees, a lower rate of working poor, and lower average earnings per worker. The standardized coefficients indicate that the average earnings per employed worker and percentage of urban population were the strongest predictors of ethanol plant location in Model 4.

Contrary to the research hypotheses, being in a non-metropolitan location and having immediate interstate access were not associated with where ethanol factories are located when taking into account the other control variables. Further, the percentage of households that are working poor was found to be negatively associated with ethanol plant location (see Table 12.4). Thus, when only the control variables were considered, ethanol plants tended to locate in counties with smaller rates of working poor households. This relationship is ostensibly contradictory to the negative relationship found for average earnings per worker. One possible explanation is that ethanol plants tend to be located in counties where jobs provide lower average earnings compared to non-location counties, but wages are not so low that working poor households are highly prevalent.

Model 5 includes all three sets of independent variables. The model chi-square test indicates that this model also fits the data with a stronger goodness-of-fit compared to Models 1–4 (Nagelkerke $r^2 = 0.295$). The significance tests for the logistic regression coefficients for the full model predominantly replicate and support the findings from the previous block models, with one key exception: that is, when the control variables were introduced into the logistic regression model, the positive relationship found between ethanol plant location and number of cattle on feed became statistically insignificant (see Table 12.4).

Further analysis revealed that this was attributable to the inclusion of the two non-metropolitan location variables and average earnings per employed worker in the logistic regression model.[14] Thus, there is a tendency for counties within the region with a large number of cattle on feed to be in non-metropolitan locations and have lower earnings per worker. This suggests, in turn, that ethanol factories are more prevalent in non-metropolitan counties with lower average earnings per worker compared to those that also have a large number of cattle on feed. The standardized logistic regression coefficients indicates that average earnings per employed worker was the strongest predictor of ethanol plant location, followed by percentage of crop acreage planted with corn, percentage of urban population, the local presence of a grain wholesale establishment, and the local presence of an animal feed manufacturer (see Table 12.4).

DISCUSSION

The findings from this study indicate that from 2000 to 2010, only one of every five ethanol factories constructed and put into operation within the

North Central region were located in counties that are part of the metropolitan areas of the region (in other words, those areas that possess the largest populations and local economies). In contrast, four out of every five factories were located in non-metropolitan counties within the region. However, such factories did not tend to be located in those non-metropolitan counties with smaller populations and less developed economies that have faced population decline and economic stagnation. Instead, they tended to be located in non-metropolitan counties that are more highly urbanized, with larger populations and more highly developed local economies. These local economies tended to be characterized by lower levels of poverty, more income, less income inequality and lower unemployment rates at the beginning of the decade.

This locational pattern has several implications for the spatial pattern of uneven development within the region. First, the growth of the ethanol industry within the region is serving to lessen the degree of uneven development between metropolitan and non-metropolitan localities. However, within the non-metropolitan portion of the region, the growth of the ethanol industry is serving to reinforce the structural advantage of larger, non-metropolitan localities with stronger positions in the urban hierarchy. Thus, unless this pattern changes, the growth of the ethanol industry is likely to contribute toward exacerbating the pattern of uneven development within the non-metropolitan portion of the region, while contributing little toward stemming the decline of those non-metropolitan localities that have experienced population loss and economic stagnation.

The findings from the logistic regression analysis suggest that within the context of the ethanol value chain, ethanol factories within the North Central region tend to have been located in counties characterized by lower-wage labor markets. Having a relatively larger presence of local workers with occupational skills that are broadly required to staff and run an ethanol factory was not found to be systematically related to ethanol factory location. The cost of labor, however, appears to have been an important factor in this locational calculus. Ethanol factories were found to have been systematically located in counties characterized by lower earnings per employed worker. Further, this variable was the strongest predictor of ethanol factory location within the region.

The findings also suggest that having proximate access to a sufficient corn or grain supply is also an important consideration influencing the location of ethanol factories within the region. Ethanol factories were systematically located in counties within the region that devoted a higher percentage of crop acreage to corn cultivation and had a grain wholesale establishment located within the county. The percentage of crop acreage planted with corn was found to be the second-strongest predictor of ethanol location. The importance of this variable replicates a key finding from both the national-level analysis of ethanol factory location by Lambert et al. (2008) and the four-state analysis of Haddad et al. (2010). Finally, the findings from the logistic regression model suggest that having proximate access to an important downstream consumer of distillers' grains – animal feed manufacturers – is also an important consideration influencing the location of ethanol factories within the region.

Taken together, these findings suggest that proximate access to a sufficient corn or grain supply and markets for distillers' grains are important locational specifications that influence where ethanol factories have been sited within the region. A caveat must be attached to these conclusions because they may be subject to the ecological fallacy: that is, the data do not provide evidence of actual economic transactions between local corn producers, grain wholesalers, ethanol factories, and manufacturers of animal feed and other businesses that purchase distillers' grains. Rather, the data only show that these economic activities in the ethanol value chain tend to co-locate in the same counties. Nonetheless, it does seem likely that such transactional linkages exist since corn is transported on a just-in-time basis to ethanol factories, and non-metropolitan counties have economies that are relatively small in size with fewer market opportunities. Assuming that such transactions do occur, the predominant, systematic multiplier effect related to ethanol production in localities with ethanol factories across the region involve corn producers, grain distributors, ethanol factories and animal feed manufacturers.

Interestingly, proximity to the primary downstream consumers of ethanol – petroleum refineries –was not associated with the location of ethanol factories within the region. This suggests that proximity to refineries is not an important locational specification for ethanol factories. One possible reason for this locational pattern is the involvement of the federal and state governments in subsidizing the industry. During the period examined in this study, the Federal Renewable Fuel Standard mandated that every gallon of gasoline produced in the US must contain 10 percent ethanol. Further, gasoline refiners were provided with a federal tax credit of 45 cents for each gallon blended. In addition, many of the states within the North Central region implemented state policies that either provided further incentives to produce ethanol or encouraged ethanol consumption (for example, requiring 'greener' vehicles in state vehicle fleets). Taken together, these policies not only sustained demand for ethanol, but also may have reduced the need for ethanol factories to be located in close proximity to refineries, since the tax credit reduces the urgency of minimizing the cost of transporting ethanol.

Not taking into account the extensiveness of corn cultivation and the local presence of grain wholesale firms, this research provides evidence of an industrial cluster found within counties across the North Central region consisting of ethanol factories, animal feed manufacturers, meat packing firms and large feedlots. However, the findings indicate that this cluster is not consistently found across all counties within the region where an ethanol factory is located, particularly those where corn is extensively cultivated and grain wholesale firms are located.

In closing, the long-term stability of the ethanol production complex within the North Central region will depend not only upon the continued use of ethanol as an alternative fuel, but also upon the maintenance of corn as the primary bio-crop in ethanol production. While the creation of path dependency on corn-based ethanol production in the US will likely make it more difficult (Carolan 2009), a shift to alternative bio-crops (for example, jatropha, switchgrass) and/or cellulosic ethanol over the long term could provide windows of opportunity to restructure the spatial organization of ethanol value chains. The status of the North Central region as the core location of the ethanol industry could be threatened if alternative bio-crops allow ethanol to be produced at a lower cost and prove not to be amenable to regional soils and climatic conditions. In turn, the economic development benefits presently accruing to non-metropolitan localities within the North Central region from ethanol production would be lost, re-exacerbating the problem of creating jobs and additional sources of income and tax revenue in face of declining populations and farm numbers.

NOTES

1. Funding for this research was provided by the Kansas State Agricultural Experiment Station, Multi-State Research Project NC-1100, and the United States Department of Energy, Biological and Environmental Research, Life and Medical Science Division, grant #ER64476.
2. The North Central region consists of the 12-state area of Illinois, Indiana, Iowa, Kansas, Michigan, Minnesota, Missouri, Nebraska, North Dakota, Ohio, South Dakota and Wisconsin.
3. For the purposes of this research we use the term 'non-metropolitan' as synonymous with 'rural'. We use the term 'locality' to refer to a non-metropolitan community and its surrounding territory that encompasses the local labor market and trade area. Depending on the pattern of development and spatial organization, a locality could encompass more than one community.
4. Gereffi (1994) and Gereffi et al. (2004) have used the concepts 'commodity chain' and 'value chain' to refer to the set of labor activities involved in the production and circulation of a specific commodity. Both examine the division of labor involved in this process as it is manifested within and between firms and across geographic space. The concept of a value chain adds an additional dimension by contending that the activities comprising the chain vary according to the value added to the finished commodity. As

applied to agricultural commodities, these concepts correspond to Friedland et al.'s (1981) concept of a commodity system.

5. In the mashing process, water and enzymes are added to the grain. After cooking the mash, saccharification involves adding further enzymes to convert the starch in the mash to sucrose. Once cooled, yeast is added to ferment the mixture.

6. See http://www.ethanolrfa.org/industry/locations/.

7. See http://ethanolproducer.com/plant-list.jsp?country = USA&view = .

8. Some states had state-level renewable fuels associations (for example, Iowa) while others provided information on their ethanol industry through commodity associations. For example, a database on Kansas ethanol factories is provided by the Kansas Corn Commission, the Kansas Corn Growers Association and the Kansas Grain Sorghum Producers Association.

9. Only counties in which an ethanol factory had been constructed and put into operation in the year 2000 and beyond were included in this phase of the analysis to ensure the proper temporal ordering of processes – that is, ethanol factories were subsequently located in counties with specific baseline conditions in the year 2000. Factories constructed prior to 2000 would likely have an impact on the socio-economic conditions within a county in the year 2000.

10. A household was considered working poor if at least one person was employed and the household income was below the poverty threshold.

11. Power transformations were used on highly skewed variables to reduce asymmetries and better approximate a normal distribution. An F-test was used to test the equality of variances between the two groups of counties. In cases where variances were equal, a pooled t-test was used. In cases where the variances were unequal, Satterthwaite's t-test for unequal variances was used.

12. The US Department of Agriculture (2002) defines cattle on feed as cattle and calves that were fed a ration of grain or other concentrates that will be shipped directly from the feedlot to the slaughter market and are expected to produce a carcass that will grade 'select' or better. This category excludes cattle that were pastured only, background feeder cattle and veal calves. Non-disclosed intervals for the number of cattle on feed in a county were estimated by multiplying the state average number of cattle on feed for a particular size class, times the number of farms in the county in that size class. The detailed methodology for this can be obtained from the author.

13. In Model 2, the probability (significance level) that having a meat packing establishment had no effect on ethanol plant location was 0.026. Introducing the percentage of acres of cropland planted with corn into Model 2 increased this probability to 0.166. Introducing whether a county had a grain wholesale establishment increased this probability to 0.065. No other upstream linkage variable rendered the effect statistically insignificant. In Model 3, the significance level for having a meat packing establishment was 0.084.

14. In Model 3 the probability (significance level) that the number of cattle on feed had no effect on ethanol plant location was 0.023. Introducing non-metropolitan location into Model 3 increased this probability to 0.0633. Introducing average earnings per worker increased this probability to 0.0544. Introducing both variables increased the probability to 0.068. Including the remaining control variables in Model 5 increased the significance level for the number of cattle on feed to 0.101.

REFERENCES

Anderson, Cynthia D., W. Richard Goe and Chih-YuanWeng (2007), 'A multi-method research strategy for understanding change in the rate of working poor in the North Central region of the United States', *Review of Regional Studies*, 37, 367–91.

Bain, Carmen (2011), 'Local ownership of ethanol plants: what are the effects on communities?', *Biomass and Bioenergy*, 35, 1400–1407.

Barrett, Joe (2007), 'Ethanol reaps a backlash in small Midwestern towns', *Wall Street Journal*, March 23, A1, A8.

Clinton, William J. (2007), Landon Lecture, presented at Kansas State University, March 2.

Ethanol Producer Magazine (2010), 'Plant list – producing'. Available at http://ethanolproducer.com/plant-list.jsp?country = USA&view = (accessed February 13, 2010).

Florida, Richard (2002), *The Rise of the Creative Class*, New York: Basic Books.

Friedland, William H., Amy E. Barton and Robert J. Thomas (1981), *Manufacturing Green Gold: Capital, Labor and Technology in the Lettuce Industry*, New York: Cambridge University Press.

Gereffi, Gary (1994), 'The international economy and economic development', in Neil J. Smelser and Richard Swedberg (eds), *The Handbook of Economic Sociology*, Princeton, NJ: Princeton University Press, pp. 206–33.

Gereffi, Gary, John Humphrey and Timothy Sturgeon (2005), 'The governance of global value chains', *Review of International Political Economy*, 12, 78–104.

Gibbs, Robert, Lorin Kusmin, and John Cromartie (2005), 'Low-skill employment and the changing economy of rural America', Economic Research Report No. (ERR10), US Department of Agriculture, Economic Research Service, October.

Goe, W. Richard (2002), 'Factors associated with the development of non-metropolitan growth nodes in producer services industries, 1980–1990', *Rural Sociology*, 67, 416–41.

Goe, W. Richard, Barry Lentnek, Alan MacPherson and David Phillips (2000), 'The role of contact requirements in producer services location', *Environment and Planning A*, 32, 131–45.

Haddad, Mônica A., Gary Taylor and Francis Owusu (2010), 'Locational choices of the ethanol industry in the Midwest Corn Belt', *Economic Development Quarterly*, 24, 74–86.

Hipple, Patricia, Jill Auburn and Rob Hedberg (2007), 'The human and social dimensions of a bioeconomy: implications for rural people and place', US Department of Agriculture, Cooperative State Research Education and Extension Service, Social Science Working Group Discussion Paper, March 29.

Keeney, Dennis and Mark Muller (2006), 'Water use by ethanol plants: potential challenges', Institute for Agriculture and Trade Policy, Minneapolis, MN, October.

Kenney, Martin and Donald Patton (2005), 'Entrepreneurial geographies: support networks in three high technology industries', *Economic Geography*, 81, 201–28.

Lambert, D.M., M. Wilcox, A. English and L. Stewart (2008), 'Ethanol plant location determinants and county comparative advantage', *Journal of Agricultural and Applied Economics*, 40, 117–35.

Logan, John and Harvey Molotch (1987), *Urban Fortunes: The Political Economy of Place*, Berkeley, CA: University of California Press.

Marshall, Alfred (1900), *Elements of Economics of Industry*, New York: Macmillan.

Meiller, Renee (2005), 'Ethanol treatment may be instrumental in fighting-IV based infections', *Medical News Today*, August 10. Available at: http://www.medicalnewstoday.com/articles/28975.php (accessed October 14, 2009).

Menard, Scott (1995), *Applied Logistic Regression Analysis*, Quantitative Applications in the Social Sciences, No. 106, Thousand Oaks, CA: Sage Publications.

Moll, Arthur P.J. (2007), 'Boundless biofuels? Between vulnerability and environmental sustainability', *Sociologia Ruralis*, 47, 297–315.

Rathge, Richard, Karen Olsen, Romona Danielson and Mary Clemenson (2001), 'Demographic chartbook: profiling change in the Great Plains', North Dakota State Data Center, North Dakota State University, October.

Renewable Fuels Association (2010), 'Biorefinery locations'. Available at http://www.ethanolrfa.org/ industry/locations/ (accessed 13 February 2010).

Sanders, Matt (2007), 'Opposition forms to Scott County plant', *Southeast Missourian*, April 9. Available at http://www.semissourian.com/story /1197369.html (accessed 26 October 2009).

Schnepf, Randy (2007), 'Agriculture-based renewable energy production', Congressional Research Service, CRS Report for Congress, March 7.

Scott, Alan and Michael Storper (1987), 'High technology industry and regional development: a theoretical critique and reconstruction', *International Social Science Journal*, 39, 215–32.

Sriroth K., K. Piyachomkwan, K. Amornitikul, N. Termvejsayanon and I. Buranares (2003), 'A study of directions for the development of the ethanol industry in Thailand', Cassava and Starch Technology Research Unit, National Center for Genetic Engineering and Biotechnology, Bangkok, Thailand. Available at http://www.cassava.org/2007/images/stories/document /study003.pdf (accessed 26 October 2009).

Storper, Michael and Richard Walker (1989), *The Capitalist Imperative: Territory, Technology and Industrial Growth*, New York: Basil Blackwell.

Sturgeon, Timothy, Johaness Van Biesebroeck and Garry Gereffi (2008), 'Value chains, networks and clusters: reframing the global automotive industry', *Journal of Economic Geography*, 8, 297–321.

Tornqvist, Gunnar (1968), 'Flows of information and the location of economic activities', *Geografiska Analer B*, 50, 99–107.

US Bureau of the Census (1993), *Census of Population and Housing, 1990*, Summary Tape File 4 (machine-readable data files), prepared by the Bureau of the Census, Washington, DC.

US Bureau of the Census (2000), *County Business Patterns*, (machine-readable data files), prepared by the Bureau of the Census, Washington, DC.

US Bureau of the Census (2003), *Census of Population and Housing, 2000*, Summary Tape File 4 (machine-readable data files), prepared by the Bureau of the Census, Washington, DC.

US Department of Agriculture (2002), *2002 Census of Agriculture*, (machine-readable data files), prepared by the National Agricultural Statistics Service, USDA, Washington, DC. Available at http://www.agcensus.usda.gov/Publications/2002/Volume_1. Chapter_2_County _Level/index.asp (accessed 13 October 2009).

US Environmental Protection Agency (2007), 'Regulatory impact analysis: renewable fuel standard program', Assessment and Standards Division, Office of Transportation and Air Quality', #EPA420-R-07-004, April. Available at http://www.epa,gov/otaq/renewable fuels /420r07004.pdf (accessed 13 October 2009).

White Energy (2007), 'Fact sheet', brochure prepared by White Energy Ethanol Plant, Russell, KS.

Williams, Jessica (2004), 'Beyond corn', *Ethanol Producer Magazine*, July. Available at http://www.ethanolproducer,com/article,jsp?article _id = 1004&q = &page = 1 (accessed October 26, 2009).

PART III

REGIONAL

13. Land grabbing in the name of development
Elisa Da Vià

INTRODUCTION

In the Makeni area of central Sierra Leone, a land dispute has flared up after Addax Bioenergy, a division of the Swiss-based energy corporation Addax & Oryx Group, won a 50-year lease for around 20 000 hectares to produce ethanol for export to the European Union (EU) market. When they signed away their land with thumb prints in villages of mud huts without electricity or running water, local farmers were told that the Addax project would not affect the seasonally waterlogged 'bolilands' where most subsistence rice production takes place because the sugarcane was to be planted in drier areas (Akam 2010). From the outset, the firm committed to create 2000 jobs, train and support farmers with inputs and agricultural equipment, bring infrastructural development, and generate further employment opportunities for local businesses and outgrowers.[1] Since 2008, however, Addax has employed only 50 local men to work in its sugarcane nursery, paying them the equivalent of a mere US$2.50 a day on a casual basis (Daniel and Mittal 2010). In the meantime, irrigation channels dug up by the company have drained some of the bolilands, thus damaging the rice fields, while other food crops such as cassava and wild palm trees used for cooking oil were razed when the land was leased (Akam 2010). Local pastoralists and land tenants are being displaced to make way for the sugar plantation, and the large-scale use of chemical pesticides and fertilizers for agrofuel production is threatening the groundwater and food harvests in surrounding lands (Baxter 2010).[2]

By the same token, as a result of legislative reforms recommended by the World Bank's International Finance Corporation (IFC), Addax benefits from a broad set of incentives, exemptions and protections afforded to foreign agribusiness investors in Sierra Leone.[3] These include: attractive tax rates, with complete exemption from corporate income tax up to 2020; complete exemption from import duty on farm machinery, agro-processing equipment, agrochemicals and other key inputs; a three-year exemption from import duty on any other plant and equipment; a 125 percent tax deduction for expenses on research and development, training and export promotion; and full repatriation of profits, dividends and royalties (SLIEPA 2009). Furthermore, the Addax project is protected under the World Bank's Multilateral Investment Guarantee Agency (MIGA) and African Trade Insurance Agency (ATI) accords, and benefits from the technical assistance and advisory services provided by the Sierra Leone Investment and Export Promotion Agency (SLIEPA) in partnership with the World Bank's IFC, and the United Kingdom's Department for International Development (DFID).[4] Within this framework, the development and growth of corporate-based markets, export revenues and land rights is prioritized at the social, environmental and economic expense of local communities.

Far from representing an isolated or singular case, this plantation project in Sierra Leone is part of a much wider, global process. Characterized by a severe lack of transparency, high levels of speculative activity and extremely limited public consultation, the rush to purchase or lease vast tracts of arable land across the global South has indeed reached enormous proportions in the midst of the deepening food, fuel, finance and climate crises of the past few years. In this respect, the World Bank estimates that about 45 million hectares of farmland have been subject to negotiations or transactions since 2008, compared to an average annual expansion of agricultural land of less than 4 million hectares before 2008 (World Bank 2010, p. vi). Specifically, the World Bank (2010, p. 35) reports that a quarter of all projects involve more than 200 000 ha, and only a quarter consist of less than 10 000 hectares – a scale which is disproportionate in size in comparison to average landholdings in the affected regions.[5]

At a time of heightened market volatility, this ongoing and dramatic rise in the volume of cross-border land grabs is driven by a complex combination of mechanisms of accumulation. National governments in a number of 'finance-rich, resource-poor' countries have started to invest in offshore farming projects through government agencies, sovereign wealth funds, public and parastatal enterprises, in order to guarantee their access to productive lands and water resources as part of a long-term strategy for food and energy security (Daniel and Mittal 2009, p. 3; Borras and Franco 2011, p. 14). Correspondingly, increasing investment opportunities in the fuel and food sectors, combined with a general decrease in trade and investment barriers, have prompted a surge in land acquisitions by corporate players pursuing vertical integration strategies and seeking 'to build, maintain, or extend large-scale extractive and agro-industrial enterprises' (Borras and Franco 2010a, p. 508; Taylor and Bending 2009, p. 9). In particular, private investors have been encouraged to acquire land for agrofuel production by public policies that make it mandatory to include a percentage of biodiesel and ethanol in transportation fuels, or that grant subsidies and tax exemptions to processing companies (Meinzen-Dick and Markelova 2009, p. 70).[6]

The emergence of new markets for carbon credits and payments for biomass conservation within the context of cap-and-trade programs and Reducing Emissions from Deforestation and Degradation (REDD) initiatives has further contributed to the rush to control agricultural and forest lands all over Africa, Asia and Latin America (AGTER 2010, p. 16).

In a parallel development, many private sector financiers are turning towards land and agriculture as strategic assets poised to produce significant returns in an otherwise shaky financial climate. Seeking to capitalize financially on the food and energy crises, and convinced that the price of arable land will continue to rise in the future, private investors have unleashed a wave of newly created investment structures and financial instruments over the past few years, raising capital to acquire land overseas and invest across the entire agricultural value chain (Graham et al. 2010; GRAIN 2009). In their pursuit of double-digit revenue gains, hedge funds, investment banks, private equity funds and the like are treating not only land but also food security as an increasingly globalized commodity that 'provides a hedge against inflation, contributes to portfolio diversification', and could even be traded in futures markets (Blumenthal 2009, 58).[7] By the same token, the recent, aggressive inflow of capital into farmland and agribusiness transactions has attracted a significant volume of funds from a large number of multilateral development organizations and development financial institutions (DFIs) such as the World Bank's IFC, the European Investment Bank (EIB) and the African Development Bank (ADB), as well as single-country development agencies. Financed by public investors (in other words, member states), these institutions are working to provide a war chest of financial, advisory, technical, legal and infrastructural tools through which corporate agendas can be sustained and pushed forward.

Fuelling new waves of massive land enclosures by foreign investors, along with the conversion of local land uses into monoculture-based, export-oriented enterprises, this global rush for farmland poses a direct threat to rural economies and livelihoods, land reform agendas and international food security. To be sure, the case studies included in the World Bank's 2010 publication *Rising Global Interest in Farmland* document clearly that these deals are disproportionately benefiting corporate players at the expense of rural livelihoods and environments. Focusing on large land transfers in 14 different countries during 2004–2009, the report underscores how most projects: (1) ignored the proper legal procedures for land acquisitions; (2) displaced local people without compensation; (3) encroached on areas not transferred to the investor; (4) had strong negative gender effects; (5) were environmentally destructive; (6) created far fewer jobs than promised; (7) leased land for free or well below its value; and (8) excluded pastoralists and internally displaced people from consultations (World

Bank 2010, pp. xxii, 50). Accordingly, the overall conclusion of the report is that 'many investments ... failed to live up to expectations and, instead of generating sustainable benefits, contributed to asset loss and left local people worse off than they would have been without the investment' (World Bank 2010, p. 51). In fact, 'even though an effort was made to cover a wide spectrum of situations, case studies confirm that in many cases benefits were lower than anticipated or did not materialize at all' (World Bank 2010, p. 51).

And yet, rather than calling for a moratorium on large-scale land alloca-tions, the World Bank claims that we should not get alarmed, for these 'immense risks' and 'real dangers' can be turned into 'equally large opportunities'. Specifically, the World Bank (2010, p. ix) insistently points out that 'new investments in agriculture could help create the preconditions for sustained, broad-based development' by allowing 'land abundant coun-tries to gain access to better technology and more jobs for poor farmers and other rural citizens' while increasing 'productivity and effectiveness' in the utilization of large areas of uncultivated or low-yield land. Similarly, several research institutions and international governance agencies, including the Food and Agriculture Organization (FAO), have proposed ways to make the land grab phenomenon a 'win–win' situation for both investors and host countries, whereby profit-seeking endeavors can be reconciled with broader development goals.[8] In this respect, the International Food Policy Research Institute (IFPRI) believes that investment projects can 'provide key resources for agriculture' and benefit smallholders involved in contract farming and outgrower schemes (Von Braun and Meinzen-Dick 2009). Following this view, the International Fund for Agricultural Development (IFAD) portrays massive foreign investments in rural areas as an opportun-ity for agriculture-led development, poverty reduction and economic growth. Indeed, while recognizing that 'landlessness and land fragmen-tation are growing worldwide', and that large-scale acquisitions have led to increased land concentration, forced evictions and 'land-use changes to the detriment of food security, bio-diversity and the environment' (2009, pp. 5, 7), IFAD goes on to argue that 'increased investments in food and agro-fuel production flowing to rural areas of developing countries could present important benefits and opportunities for poor rural communities' (2009, p. 8). These include: the development of processing industries; increased agricultural productivity through the provision of improved seed varieties, know-how, financial services and new technologies; livelihood diversifica-tion and employment generation through contract farming and outgrower schemes; and increased access to reliable markets (2009, p. 8).

Arguably, the institutional framing of land grabs as win–win develop-ment outcomes is premised upon a number of assumptions that need to be overcome when considering adequate responses to this global phenomenon. On the one hand, the claim that large-scale investments can improve global food and energy security by increasing production in low-yield areas of land-abundant countries reflects the reductionism of mainstream, capital-centric projects of agrarian transformation and provides no account of actual land uses, resource rights and land reform agendas. On the other hand, the argument that land acquisitions contribute to rural development by enabling smallholders to gain access to inputs, technologies and markets through contract farming and other 'partnership' arrangements fails to locate the expansion of commercially oriented farming within global agro-food and agrofuel commodity chains controlled by the monopoly power of corporate capital.

As a whole, the institutional legitimization of land grabs is rooted in a model of agricultural development that is fomenting rural displacement and dispossession while exacerbating environmental problems on a global scale. Such an approach, as Borras and Franco (2010a, p. 515) put it, 'a priori dismisses the possibility of other development pathway options and ignores the clamor of those who believe that other pathways are possible – and better – and are either working toward or attempting to actualize them'. Correspondingly, it is precisely in the name of 'development' that public investors are becoming increasingly complicit in and directly engaged in processes of land grabbing, thus deepening the fundamental causes of the global food, energy and climate crises.

YIELD GAPS, SATELLITE IMAGERY AND CORPORATE ENCLOSURES

There's no other place in the world where there's as much acreage that is low productivity as in Africa. Well, you just need to help these farmers get their productivity up. Many of those land deals are beneficial, and it would be too bad if some were held back because of Western groups' ways of looking at things. (Bill Gates interviewed by Tami Hultman, AllAfrica, February 9, 2011)

In 2008, agricultural commodity prices on world markets reached their highest levels in 30 years: global wheat prices rose 130 percent, rice 74 percent, with similar spiraling costs of corn, soybeans, cooking oil and other major foodstuffs. As a result, a cascade of food riots erupted in more than 40 countries around the globe, from Haiti to Cameroon to Indonesia, where people took the streets in anger at being unable to afford the food they need. At the same time, bringing together different factors (weather problems, the diversion of crops into agrofuels, oil price hikes, speculative trade and growing meat consumption) into a 'perfect storm scenario' (McMichael

2009) of dwindling supplies and rising demand, much of the official discourse called for the formulation of production-oriented, market-based responses to the surge in food prices. Correspondingly, global development institutions such as the World Bank were quick to reframe the food crisis as an opportunity to reverse a long period of declining investment in agriculture, bring more land into production, increase productivity by means of agribusiness technologies and enhance trade liberalization (cf. McMichael and Schneider 2011, p. 121). This 'narrow economistic conceptualization' (Scoones 2010) of the crisis is in turn directly related to the characterization of large-scale investments in farmland as a win–win situation whereby development is achieved through mechanized farming and higher yields.

The argument that land grabs constitute a development opportunity insofar as they are aimed at boosting crop production is part of an ongoing effort to promote the role of the corporate sector in the global provisioning of food and energy supplies. During the height of the 2008 agflation, for example, the World Bank launched a New Deal on Global Food Policy, which pushed for a vast expansion in agricultural production through increased lending to agribusiness and the agroindustry. The number of the IFC's investments across the agribusiness value chain has also grown exponentially since 2008, with special emphasis on the increased incorporation of large tracts of fertile land into productive use. In particular, in February 2009, the IFC teamed up with Altima Partners to create the $625 million One World Agricultural Development Fund aimed at investing in farm production, high-input technologies and agricultural land in 'emerging market countries' (IFC 2009a). Similarly, the African Union's New Partnership for Africa's Development (NEPAD) recently established a Comprehensive Africa Agriculture Development Program (CAADP) with the aim to 'raise the capacity of private entrepreneurs' as a key plank in the quest to boost agricultural productivity (CAADP 2009, p. 5). Within this framework, the rhetoric of the global food crisis is deployed as a legitimizing device for land grabs, prioritizing an approach to development that reflects the agribusiness model of productivity increase and is geared toward deepened private sector control.[9]

This model is further reproduced by the assumption that large-scale investments could rehabilitate idle, marginal or underutilized agricultural land and therefore be beneficial for local communities and environments in the host nations. Premised on such an assumption, the World Bank's 2010 report puts forward a global assessment of the amount of land 'where investor interest may actually materialize', by classifying countries according to the availability of 'uncultivated' but 'agronomically suitable' land as well as the 'share of potential output achieved on areas currently cultivated (the yield gap)' (World Bank 2010, pp. x, xvi). Using geographically referenced data, satellite imagery and agro-ecological simulations[10] to quantify the gap between actual and potential yields by current producers, the report classifies much of sub-Saharan Africa as a Type 4 region (with suitable land available, high yield gap) where, it argues, rainfed cultivation could be massively intensified. In a similar vein, the promotion materials issued by both the IFC and its country-specific agencies such as SLIEPA in Sierra Leone encourage investors to take advantage of acquiring idle or unused land in developing countries, while providing detailed information about its availability (Daniel and Mittal 2010; IFC 2009a; SLIEPA 2009).

By the same token, far from being coerced into these land deals, many developing-country governments are welcoming them – and even lobbying aggressively for them – by declaring the land for sale or lease as idle land. In Ethiopia, for example, all land allocations recorded at the national investment promotion agency are classified as involving 'wastelands' with no pre-existing users (Cotula and Vermeulen 2009, p. 2). The strategy is being replicated all over the global South, where governments such as those of Mozambique, Tanzania, Indonesia and the Philippines are engaged in the attempt to quantify the amount of reserve land available within their borders in order to attract investors (ILC 2009, p. 7; Kugelman 2009, p. 10). As such, 'the very notion of "reserve" more or less automatically renders such land, by definition, "available", amenable to and appropriate for transformation into global granaries or new oil wells' (Borras and Franco 2010a, p. 516), at the expense of local livelihood practices that do not fit this top-down classificatory grid.

Although no large-scale land allocations can take place without displacing or affecting local populations, existing land uses and claims are made 'illegible' by the politics of satellite maps, yield gap analyses and government inventories. In many countries, the category of marginal land is applied to areas that are officially catalogued as 'public' or state-owned, but in fact provide livelihoods to millions of cultivators, pastoralists and forest users 'under a variety of unofficial and semi-official or "customary", individual or collective, tenurial relationships' (White and Dasgupta 2010, p. 600). Top-down calculations of land availability are drawn from official census data about land use and land property relations that recognize only those rights awarded by the state and therefore facilitate central state regulation and administration (Borras and Franco 2010b, p. 516). The livelihood practices of unrepresented and marginalized groups are particularly affected by nation-state classifications that seek to entice investors while developing tightened forms of territorial rule. Indeed, by targeting countries with a poor track record of protecting the land rights of their citizens, the current investment rush is riding a tide of state-sponsored grabbing of resources that directly interferes with social justice and land redistribution agendas.

On the other hand, when drawn from satellite images and projections that are not rooted in on-the-ground understanding of land-based practices, the notion of marginal land reflects a capital-centric assessment of the productivity rather than existence of resource uses. In the World Bank report, for example, the terms 'suitable', 'available' and 'uncultivated' are applied not to unoccupied lands, but to lands used in ways that are not perceived as productive (Cotula et al. 2009, p. 100). In this respect, the World Bank focuses on low productivity and yield gaps, 'as a justification for a procedural approach to regulating land deals in such a way as to facilitate transfer of land rights from less to more efficient producers', following the same logic that underlies its market-based land and agricultural reforms over the past two decades (Hall 2010, p. 6). As a result, the politics of land grabbing gets absorbed into a technocratic definition of productivity that portrays the expansion of large-scale, industrialized, capitalist agriculture as the only viable strategy to achieve tangible development outcomes (Borras and Franco 2010b).

CONTRACT FARMING, ADVERSE INCORPORATION AND ACCUMULATION BY DISPOSSESSION

> Basically, millions of smallholder farmers have to go through a transformation from being subsistence to commercial producers, and by doing so, help maintain Africa's march toward economic growth. (Kurt Hoffman, Director of TransFarm Africa, quoted in Gillam 2010)

According to win–win narratives on land grabs, farmland investments work particularly well as a rural development strategy when they create the conditions for new contractual arrangements between smallholders and agribusinesses. Notably, all development agencies are calling for the formulation of contract farming schemes as an alternative to outright purchases or leasing of land that can provide farmers with access to credit and technological improvements, a ready market and increased cash earnings (Von Braun and Meinzen-Dick 2009), while allowing corporations to acquire a secured supply of produce at no risk (IFAD 2009, pp. 8–9). The expectation is that the private sector will drive 'the organization of value chains that bring the market to smallholders and commercial farms', thereby fostering the growth of what the World Bank calls a 'new agriculture' for development (World Bank 2008, p. 8). The characterization of contractual partnerships as a 'development tool' has in turn been integrated in the discursive strategies of international investment funds promoting commercial land deals and agroindustrial projects across the global South. In particular, while engaged in the attempt to incorporate smallholders into commercial food chains, both institutional and private land grabbers are increasingly portraying their initiatives as 'impact investing' for the growth of 'transformative' agriculture and 'mutually profitable partnerships' in the developing world (Gillam 2010; Chen 2010). Put differently, to demonstrate that farmland investments have a 'social impact' in addition to being commercially viable, the private sector has reframed contract farming as a new business model that can 'transform' traditional farming systems into dynamic and opportunistic enterprises to the benefit of both small farmers and agroindustries (McLaren 2010; Chen 2010; SAGCOT 2011).

To be sure, contract farming historically emerged – and currently operates – as a mechanism to eliminate intermediaries, bypass competition and structure the operation of markets to the advantage of dominant agents in increasingly globalized agrofood commodity chains.[11] More specifically, contract farming entails relations that 'substitute for open-market exchanges by linking nominally independent family farmers with a central processing, export, or purchasing unit that regulates prices, production practices, product quality and credit arranged in advance under contract' (Watts 1992, p. 69). As a means to introduce new on-farm technologies and distinctive work routines, the contract circumscribes 'what one might call the social space of autonomy and subordination that the grower occupies in relation to the labor process' (Watts 1992, p. 70). As such, contracting represents a 'recomposition of peasant producers' in which peasants are increasingly captured by, and incorporated into, new social relations and patterns of accumulation (Hall 2010; Watts 1992, p. 75).

The controversial nature of contract farming schemes in Africa has been extensively analyzed by Watts (1992), who points to the widespread manipulation of contracts and the growing household tensions generated by this externally induced change parallel to the rise of flexible accumulation in advanced capitalist industrial organization. In a similar vein, focusing on the very weak position of contract growers in relation to agribusiness, White (1997) argues that contract farming in Indonesia has trapped peasants in debt and forced them to gradually degrade their position from landowners to laborers while allowing the processing industries to exploit unpaid rents and family labor. More recent research by Sawit Watch and the Forest Peoples Programme into the conditions of some of Indonesia's 4–4.5 million oil palm smallholders has revealed that as a result of contractual agreements that force them to sell to a particular company, they often receive below-market prices and suffer from practices such as questionable product grading and late payment (Taylor and Bending 2009, p. 16). This analysis corresponds to what has been observed in the industrial tomato sector of the

Dominican Republic, where contract growers, faced with rising costs generated by the compulsory introduction of increased chemical inputs and mechanical cultivation, have become tied to their processors via their debts (Raynolds 2000).

The role of debt and the distribution of risks in contract farming make the contract relationship significantly more complicated than the employer–worker relation. On the one hand, most growers require credit to finance their sowing and harvesting operations because the crops purchased by agroindustrial processors entail higher production costs. Yet, unlike state-owned or even commercial banks, agro-processors can: (1) extract a grower's debt directly from the crop revenue before the grower receives his payment; (2) obtain raw agricultural product at below-market prices, in exchange for credit (Key and Runsten 1999, p. 384); and (3) oblige indebted growers to renew their contracts the next season, with high percentages of resulting profits going to debt repayment (Raynolds 2000). On the other hand, many studies have shown that contract agreements protect agrofood companies from all and even unforeseen obligations, shifting responsibility for assembling labor, assuring work performance and dealing with crop failure from the contractors to the growers. Specifically, in most contracts the farmers are bound to sell to the company only and are penalized for default, whereas there is no specified company liability for the failure to buy the farm produce (Singh 2002, p. 1633).

In a growing trend, agribusinesses are pursuing contract production as a strategy to avoid both labor and environment-related costs. In the Philippines, for example, contract growing has become more popular in recent years as it 'enables firms to reduce their employee-related costs and obligations, to subvert the power of unions, and to acquire the flexibility to reduce their workforce without having to worry about retrenchment and retirement costs' (Montemayor 2009, p. 105). Within this context, contract farming does lead to gender inequalities in both the quantity and the quality of work for women (and children) who not only end up working longer hours in the fields (Collins 1993), but also carry the burden of off-farm work (White 1997). Correspondingly, as contract farmers are often selected on the basis of their land suitability, assured irrigation, financial position and ability to adopt new technologies, the development of these arrangements has caused deepened regional and socio-economic differentiation among producers (Singh 2002). At the same time, the growth of contract farming leading to industrialized, export-oriented agriculture typically results in the overexploitation of groundwater, salination of soils, soil fertility decline and pollution (Siddiqui 1998). The cost of these 'environmental externalities' is nonetheless avoided by firms that tend to move on to new growers and lands after exhausting the potential of productive resources in a given area.

Whatever its origins, contract farming constitutes a particular form of rural proletarianization, premised on the 'adverse incorporation'[12] of smallholders into new value chains dominated by corporate capital. Put differently, the establishment of contract and outgrower schemes becomes a vehicle for deepened rural dispossession precisely because small producers are institutionally captured into, rather than excluded from, global food and agricultural markets (Akram-Lodhi 2009). This insertion is inevitably based on the subordination of smallholders to the power of firms with monopoly or oligopoly control over inputs (such as seed varieties and agrochemicals) as well as firms with monopsony or oligopsony control of processing facilities or market access. Indeed, as White (1997, p. 105) puts it:

> In all food commodity chains ... the setting of prices at the various points in the production, processing and marketing chain is not a matter of 'real' value added or of supply–demand interactions, but reflects more the relative social/political bargaining strength of the parties involved. Contract farming, through institutionalizing monopoly/monopsony relations between farm and agribusiness, can reflect this property of 'real' markets in exaggerated ways.

And yet, other than promoting the formulation of contractual partnerships within win–win agroinvestment scenarios, development institutions make no recommendations for tackling the monopoly or monopsony power of capital in these markets (Akram-Lodhi 2008, p. 1159).

More to the point, the characterization of contract farming as a 'development opportunity' is rooted in the obsessive tendency of win–win approaches to 'naturalize' unequal social relations and 'to represent that inequality as just' (Clapp 1994, p. 92). In this respect, instead of addressing the root causes of rural poverty from a politico-economic perspective, the rhetoric of win–win scenarios reflects the attempt 'to neglect, silence, or misrepresent power struggles and unequal and conflictual relations, which are pervasive among participants in global value chains, and clearly intrinsic to the structure of relations of production and surplus extraction in contemporary capitalism' (Oya 2009, p. 598). As a result, these discursive formulations further reproduce and entrench the mechanisms – the contracts and monopolies – that act as 'conduits' to extract value from producers which are increasingly subsumed in real and formal terms to capital (Akram-Lodhi 2008, p. 1159; Watts 1992, p. 75).

BEYOND CODES OF CONDUCT: PUBLIC INVESTORS' INVOLVEMENT IN LAND GRABS

> IFC is implementing a market-driven and private sector-led strategy to increase global food production ... and is providing $75 million, its largest equity investment in agribusiness, to help set up a fund that will invest in world-class farm operators to increase the global food supply. (IFC 2009b)

Over the past few years, the development apparatus has become increasingly involved in land grabs well beyond the formulation of legitimizing narratives. In fact, while putting forward a facade of proposals for monitoring land deals through voluntary guidelines and codes of conduct, development institutions from the World Bank to UN, regional and single-country agencies have unleashed an array of resources aimed at: (1) financing profit-seeking enterprises through investment funds; (2) providing information, consultancy and infrastructure to private investors; (3) changing laws to create investment-friendly environments in target countries; and (4) implementing investment protection treaties.

On a first level, the presence of multilateral and development financial institutions as cornerstone or anchor investors in a range of international investment funds has played a crucial role in attracting private capital for land grabs. Most privately run financial vehicles that are leading the rush for the world's farmland with 'an out-and-out mission to generate above-market returns' have in other words been created through the direct engagement of public development money (Miller et al. 2010, p. 7). The Africa Enterprise Challenge Fund (AECF), for example, constitutes a special partnership initiative of the Alliance for a Green Revolution in Africa (AGRA) also funded by the Australian Government Aid Program, the UK Department for International Development (DFID), the International Fund for Agricultural Development (IFAD) and the Netherlands Ministry of Foreign Affairs (NMFA). Focusing on agribusinesses as key drivers of agricultural growth, the fund provides for-profit private sector companies looking to work in Africa with kick-start grants of between $150 000 and $2.5 million, and has so far committed more than $30 million to 40 business deals, leveraging about $150 million from the private sector (DFID 2010). In a similar vein, IFAD, the African Development Bank (ADB), the French development agency (Agence Française de Développement), the Spanish Agency for International Development and Cooperation (AECID), AGRA and the West African Development Bank have partnered with the private equity and corporate finance advisory firm Phatisa Group to create the African Agriculture Fund (AAF). The fund, whose total size exceeds $300 million, is aimed at 'backing private-sector companies that implement strategies to increase and diversify food production and distribution in

Africa' (Hansen and Oshry 2011).[13] Overall, the involvement of United Nations (UN) agencies, European DFIs, as well as the IFC, ADB and EIB, encompasses a whole host of investment programs geared toward the development of agribusiness value chains across the global South (see Table 13.1).

On a second level, the World Bank and other multilateral organizations are fueling the global land grab through the provision of technical assistance and advisory services aimed at improving the investment climate of foreign markets. Specifically, both the IFC and the Foreign Investment Advisory Service (FIAS) of the World Bank have devised a wide range of products to assist countries in opening their land markets to foreign investors,[14] developing domestic investment promotion agencies, and cutting down on administrative and institutional barriers that 'inhibit business growth' (Daniel and Mittal 2010). Within this framework, teams of consultants are constantly being parachuted all around Africa, Asia and Latin America 'to rewrite laws, register titles and set up satellite mapping and cadastral systems to smooth the way for foreign investors to acquire farmland' (GRAIN 2010c). FIAS for instance helped Sudan modify six investment laws in 2008, and various land deals have occurred since then allocating over 1 million hectares of land (PANAP 2010, p. 24). Correspondingly, FIAS has worked to create or bolster Investment Promotion Agencies in Sierra Leone, Cape Verde, Senegal and Tanzania, among others, in the attempt to streamline the process through which foreign investors must go through in order to acquire land (Daniel and Mittal 2010, p. 11). At the same time, the IFC has set up or improved leasing legislation and regulations in 60 countries, and has provided advisory services to leasing facilities in Ghana, Tanzania, Rwanda, Madagascar, Senegal, Cameroon, the Democratic Republic of the Congo (DRC), Mali and Ethiopia (Daniel and Mittal 2010, p. 19).

On a third level, land deals are facilitated by the enabling environment provided by an array of bilateral and multilateral trade and investment treaties – collectively known as the international investment protection regime. As part of broader bundles of non-financial assistance and development aid, bilateral investment treaties (BITs) provide legal protection to cross-border investments against 'adverse host state action' such as expropriation and arbitrary treatment (Cotula et al. 2009). More specifically, investment treaties typically include provisions on profit repatriation and currency convertibility; they require host governments to treat the foreign investor exactly like domestic investors; and they strengthen the legal value of individual contracts by making their violation a breach of international

Table 13.1 Development institutions' involvement in investment funds

	Investment sector		Type of investment	Development institutions involved
	Agribusiness	Smallholders		
Actis Africa Agribusiness Fund	X		Private equity investments in agro-infrastructure, agro-processing and the biofuel subsectors.	Commonwealth Development Company (CDC)/ British government
Africa Enterprise Challenge Fund	X		Special partnership initiative of AGRA to encourage private sector investment	Australian Government Aid Program, the UK Department for International Development (DFID), IFAD and the Netherlands Ministry of Foreign Affairs (NMFA)
African Agriculture Fund	X		Private sector companies with strategies to increase and diversify food production and distribution	IFAD, AfDB, the French and Spanish Agencies for International Development Cooperation, AGRA – core funding from the UK's Department for International Development (DFID)
Africa Seed Development Fund	X		Seed companies	AGRA
Emerging Capital Partners Africa Fund	X		Equity and quasi-equity investments such as convertible debt focusing on high-growth agribusinesses	AfDB, IFC, OPIC (US government's development finance institution) and CDC
Africa Agribusiness Investment Fund (Agri-Vie)	X		Agribusiness value chain	ADB, Industrial Development Corp. (using money from EIB)

Fanisi Venture Capital Fund	X	Agribusiness, retail, financial services	Proparco (DFI majority owned by the French government), Finnfund (Finnish government's development finance agency), IFC
Aventura Rural Enterprise Fund	X	Agribusiness value chain and rural services	EIB, FMO (The Netherlands' Entrepreneurial Development Bank), CDC and Finn Fund
India Agribusiness Fund	X	Agribusiness, agro-infrastructure	IFC, FMO, CDC, DEG (German Development Bank)
Atlantic Coast Capital Fund (ACRF)	X	Agribusiness, transportation and logistics, financial services, mining and manufacturing	AfDB, CDC, EIB, FinnFund and IFC
AfricInvest Fund	X	Agribusiness companies	IFC, AfDB and EIB
Altima One World Agriculture Development Fund	X	Agribusiness production	IFC

Sources: FAO (2009) and Mullin (2010).

law (Spiedloch and Murphy 2009, p. 44). Although state-to-state agreements, BITs pave the way to investor-to-state claims, by giving investors direct access to international arbitration in case of disputes with the host government, even when specific investment contracts are silent on this (Graham et al. 2010, p. 56).

The past two decades have witnessed a boom in the number of bilateral investment treaties. In 2008 only, African governments signed 12 new BITs, eight of them with European countries (UNCTAD 2009, p. 32). Significantly, although host states enter into such agreements to attract foreign direct investment (FDI) as a tool of economic development, most BITs include provisions that strengthen the legal power of the foreign investor vis-à-vis the position and rights of local communities. In particular, through the clause of 'national treatment' and the prohibition of using 'performance requirements', these treaties give investors the right to avoid any linkages with the local community (such as local employment or local input use) in addition to exporting all or almost all of what is produced (Graham et al. 2010, p. 57). Moreover, most BITs allow host countries to limit exports in the midst of a financial crisis but not necessarily in times of food shortages, and allow foreign investors to sue host governments for any lost profits (Spiedloch and Murphy 2009, p. 44). Coupled with the direct involvement of development agencies in for-profit investment funds, and the creation of business-enabling environments in recipient countries, this special international regime of investment protection is directly shaping social and economic outcomes that affect local livelihoods and food security. In fact, by promoting enhanced rights and protections for private investors, the combination of these policies is leading to the broader development outcome of increased land grabbing and rural dispossession on a global scale.

CONCLUSION

Despite evidence of the 'immense risks' and 'real dangers' (World Bank 2010) associated with the global rush to grab land, the development apparatus has been actively involved in the formulation of policies and financial mechanisms that indiscriminately support the large-scale acquisition of land or land-related rights and resources by corporate entities. In this respect, the politics of win–win narratives on land grabs reflects the attempt to relegitimize a specific model of agricultural development characterized by the concentration of corporate power in the food system, the expansion of 'value chains', the commodification of land and labor, and the removal of public interventions in support of small producers. As illustrated by the current articulation of food, climate, energy and financial crises at the global level, this development model is increasing rural vulnerability and undermining the ecological sustainability of local land and water resources with profound and long-term implications for the economic and social structures of rural societies.

These trends are further exacerbated by current attempts to regulate large-scale land deals as if these were inevitable or even desirable under certain conditions. Reflecting an agribusiness-oriented vision for agriculture, such a presupposition draws attention away from the promotion of alternative forms of investment that are both more equitable and more environmentally sustainable. In this context, as argued by UN Rapporteur on the Right to Food Olivier de Schutter (2011, pp. 250, 263), 'the most pressing issue regarding investment in agriculture is not how much, but how … what we need is to put forward an alternative programme' protecting tenure security, promoting agrarian reform, and supporting small-scale farming through comprehensive rural development policies.

A substantively different formulation of alternatives to the structural meltdown of the corporate food regime stems from the promotion of smallholders' equitable access to their means of reproduction, the development of diverse markets and effective venues of political participation, the collective engagement of producers in participatory research and knowledge exchange, and the reorientation of agricultural systems towards agro-ecological modes of production within the comprehensive human rights approach to land and food expounded by civil society groups and peasant movements on a transnational scale.

NOTES

1. See Addax Bioenergy website, available at: http://www.addax-oryx.com/Addax Bioenergy/Addax-Bioenergy Questions&Answers.pdf.
2. Given that the Addax project is supported by European Development Finance Institutions and the African Development Bank, it has been geared to meet 'Performance Standards' on local consultation and social sustainability laid down by the World Bank. Accordingly, the company claims to have established a 'formal grievance mechanism' based on working committees as well as letter boxes installed throughout the project area, in order to inform local communities about the project. The efficacy of suggestion boxes as a means to obtain informed consent is nonetheless highly questionable in a context where the majority of local inhabitants cannot read or write (Addax Bioenergy website, Baxter 2010, MADAM press conference 8/6/2010, available at: http://www.madam-sl.org/ ?Projects:Right_to_Food).
3. The International Finance Corporation (IFC) is part of the World Bank's private sector arm. Its primary activity is private sector financing, as well as the provision of investment lending and advisory services to both investors and state governments. It also carries out technical cooperation projects in many countries to make their 'legislative environment' more attractive to foreign investors. These activities are often aimed at promoting investment climate reforms such as cutting down on administrative and institutional barriers, developing investment promotion agencies (for example, SLIEPA in Sierra

Leone), and advising governments on changes to tax, customs and land laws. See Daniel and Mittal (2010).

4. As a member of the World Bank Group, the Multilateral Investment Guarantee Agency (MIGA) was established to promote foreign direct investment (FDI) in developing countries by insuring investors against political risk, advising governments on attracting investment, sharing information through online investment information services, and mediating disputes between investors and governments. See http://www.miga.org/about/index_sv.cfm?stid=1736.

5. According to the World Bank (2010, p. xiv) more than 75 percent of these deals involve African land. Strikingly, in a continent where most smallholdings consist of no more than 2- or 3-hectare plots (Kugelman 2009, p. 1), land transfers amounted to 2.7 million ha in Mozambique, 4 million in Sudan, 1.6 million in Liberia and 1.2 million in Ethiopia.

6. Specifically, the US Renewable Fuel Standard aims to increase ethanol use by 3.5 billion gallons between 2005 and 2012, and the EU aims to increase the proportion of agrofuels used in land transport to 10 percent by 2020. Not surprisingly, as Franco et al. (2010, p. 664) underscore, most members of the European Biofuel Technology Platform (EBFTP) – the EU consultative body which has highly influenced the formation and implementation of EU agrofuel policies – come from the oil, auto, biotech, biofuels and forest products industries, as well as from the industrial farmers' organization COPA-COGECA. Within this framework, Borras and Franco (2011, p. 28) argue, 'biofuels policy will be aggressively pursued based on calculations about corporate profit, rather than on official discourses around GHG [greenhouse gas] savings or livelihood gener-ation in producing countries'. Indeed, as reported by Friends of the Earth Africa and Friends of the Earth Europe (2010), European companies figure prominently in the recent surge of land grabbing for agrofuels in Africa. For example, the UK company Sun Biofuels has acquired land in Ethiopia (80 000 ha), Tanzania (8000 ha) and Mozambique (5000 ha) to grow jatropha; the UK-based CAMS Group bought 45 000 ha in Tanzania to produce ethanol from sweet sorghum; and the German company Flora Eco Power has spent $77 million in land purchases in Ethiopia for biofuel production using contract farming.

7. In this respect, while Soros Economic Development Fund President Stewart Paperin maintains that 'food security will become the next tradable commodity' in what can be considered as 'the decade of agriculture in Africa' (Gillam 2010), new proposals for 'alternative food security investments' have recently emerged within the finance industry. These include the creation of 'farmland futures contracts' to be traded by investors, hedgers and speculators in addition to current financial assets like equity, debt and commodity derivatives (Kanitra 2011).

8. As early as September 2008, Director-General of the FAO Jacques Diouf expressed his support for the increase in farmland investments from oil-rich Middle Eastern states, arguing that 'if the deals are constructed properly, they have the potential to transform developing economies by providing jobs both in agriculture and other supporting industries like transportation and warehousing' (Coker 2008).

9. Not surprisingly, as Holt-Gimenez and Shattuck (2011) among others underscore, 'the global food crisis of 2008 ushered in record levels of hunger for the world's poor at a time of record global harvests as well as record profits for the world's major agrifoods corporations'. With more than enough food in the world to feed everyone (FAO 2009), the confluence of factors that led to the dramatic surge in world prices highlights an underlying structural crisis of the global food system brought about by decades of agricultural restructuring under capitalist relations of value extraction. Within this context, increasing food production does not necessarily lead to increased food security – nor does it implement the right to food – unless it takes place on the fields of small-scale producers who do so in ecologically and socially sustainable ways (Graham et al. 2010).

10. In order to assess potential yields that can be achieved on a given plot, the Bank uses the agro-ecological zoning (AEZ) methodology developed by the International Institute for Applied Systems Analysis (IISA) for five main rainfed crops. This predicts potential yields based on simulation of plant growth – which depends on agro-ecological factors, such as soil, temperature, precipitation, elevation and other terrain factors – together with assumptions on management and input intensity. The potential revenue from cultivation is then assessed by applying a price vector (using 2005 prices) and identifying the highest value of output (World Bank 2010, pp. 53–4).

11. The contracts under study could be of three types: (a) market specification contracts are pre-harvest agreements that bind the firm and grower to a particular set of conditions governing the sale of the crop (such as price, quantity and timing); (b) resource-providing contracts include the provision of crop inputs, extension or credit in exchange for a marketing agreement; and (c) production management contracts bind the farmer to follow a particular production method or input regimen. In all cases, there is a systematic link between product and factor markets as contracts require definite quality of produce and, therefore, specific inputs (Key and Runsten 1999; Little and Watts 1994).

12. The concept of 'adverse incorporation' embodies a critique of neoliberal agricultural policies and mainstream development narratives which fail to account for the risks and disadvantages associated with the inclusion and participation of smallholders in global value chains, by positing a 'level playing field' whereby new entrants are assumed to compete in the same way, and in the same markets as their large–industrial, corporate equivalents (Hickey and DuToit 2007; Borras and Franco 2011).

13. Specifically, IFAD will manage the Technical Assistance Facility of the AAF for which core funding has been committed by the European Commission with the contribution of AGRA and the Italian Cooperation.

14. In this respect, FIAS has developed a 'Land Market' product aimed at 'designing and implementing effective policies and procedures for making land available for new and expansion investment' as well as 'developing simple and transparent procedures for investors to acquire and secure land property rights (or land use rights), at reasonable costs' (FIAS 2008).

REFERENCES

AGTER (2010), 'Large scale land appropriations: analysis of the phenomenon and proposed guidelines for future action'. http://www.agter.asso.fr/IMG/pdf/appropriation_en_web-finale.pdf (accessed on February 24, 2011).

Akam, S. (2010), 'Africa mulls biofuels as land grab fears grow', *Reuters*, November 30. http://www.reuters.com/article/2010/11/30/us-africa-biofuels-idUSTRE6AT3ZE201011 30 (accessed on February 13, 2011).

Akram-Lodhi, A.H. (2008), '(Re)imagining agrarian relations? The *World Development Report 2008: Agriculture for Development*', *Development and Change*, 39, 1145–61.

Akram-Lodhi, A.H. (2009), 'Modernizing subordination? A South Asian perspective on the *World Development Report 2008: Agriculture for Development*', *Journal of Peasant Studies*, 36, 611–19.

Baxter, J. (2010), 'Africa's land and family farms – up for grabs?' *GRAIN, Seedling Magazine*, 15, 13–16.

Blumenthal, G. (2009), 'Investors' perspectives on farmland', in M. Kugelman and S.L. Levenstein (eds), *Land Grab? The Race for the World's Farmland*, Princeton, NJ: Woodrow Wilson International Center for Scholars, pp. 55–68.

Borras, S., Jr and J.C. Franco (2010a), 'From threat to opportunity? Problems with the idea of a "code of conduct" for land-grabbing', *Yale Human Rights and Development Law Journal*, 13, 507–23.

Borras, S., Jr and J. Franco (2010b), 'Towards a broader view of the politics of global land grab: rethinking land issues, reframing resistance', *ICAS Working Paper Series*, 1, 1–39.

Borras, S., Jr and J. Franco (2011), *Political Dynamics of Land Grabbing in Southeast Asia: Understanding Europe's Role*, Amsterdam: Transnational Institute.

CAADP (2009), 'Framework for the improvement of rural infrastructure and trade-related capacities for market access'. http://www.nepad-caadp.net/pdf/%28FINAL%29_CAADP_Brochure-Area_A_%281-21-09%29.pdf (accessed on February 7, 2010).

Chen, L. (2010), *Promoting Integration and Food Security in Africa*. Washington, DC: NEPAD Business Foundation.

Clapp, R.A.J. (1994), 'The moral economy of the contract', in P. Little and M. Watts (eds), *Living Under Contract: Contract Farming and Agrarian Transformation in Sub-Saharan Africa*, Madison, WI: University of Wisconsin Press, pp. 78–96.

Coker, M. (2008), 'UN food chief warns on buying farms'. *Wall Street Journal*, September 10. http://online.wsj.com/article/SB122098802643115897.html?mod=googlenews_wsj (accessed on January 7, 2011).

Collins, J.L. (1993), 'Gender, contracts and wage work: agricultural restructuring in Brazil's Sao Francisco Valley', *Development and Change*, 24, 53–82.

Cotula, L. and S. Vermeulen (2009), *'Land Grabs' in Africa: Can the Deals Work for Development?* London: IIED.

Cotula, L., S. Vermeulen, R. Leonard and J. Keeley (2009), *Land Grab or Development Opportunity? Agricultural Investments and International Land Deals in Africa*, London: IIED.

Daniel, S. and A. Mittal (2009), *The Great Land Grab: Rush for the World's Farmland Threatens Food Security For The Poor*, Oakland, CA: Oakland Institute.

Daniel, S. and A. Mittal (2010), *Mis(Investment) in Agriculture: The Role of the International Finance Corporation in Global Land Grabs*, Oakland, CA: Oakland Institute.

De Schutter, O. (2011), 'How not to think of land grabbing: three critiques of large-scale investments in farmland', *Journal of Peasant Studies*, 38, 249–79.

Department for International Development (DFID) (2010), *The Africa Enterprise Challenge Fund*. http://www.dfid.gov.uk/Working-with-DFID/Funding-opportunities/Countries-and-regions/AECF/ (accessed on January 28, 2011).

FIAS (2008), 'Facilitating the land market for investment'. http://www.fias.net/uploads/LandMarket.pdf (accessed on February 6, 2011).

Food and Agriculture Organization (FAO) (2009), '1.02 billion people hungry', FAO Media Center. http://www.fao.org/news/story/en/item/20568/icode/ (accessed on January 14, 2011).

Franco, J., L. Levidow, D. Fig, L. Goldfarb, M. Hönicke and M.L. Mendonça (2010), 'Assumptions in the European Union biofuels policy: frictions with experiences in Germany, Brazil and Mozambique', *Journal of Peasant Studies*, 37, 661–98.

Friends of the Earth Africa and Friends of the Earth Europe (2010), 'Africa: up for grabs: the scale and impact of land-grabbing for agrofuels'. http://www.foeeurope.org/agrofuels/FoEE_Africa_up_for_grabs_2010.pdf (accessed on February 17, 2011).

Gillam, C. (2010), 'Investors try new tactic with African agriculture', *Reuters*, December 1. http://www.reuters.com/article/2010/12/01/us-transfarm-feature-idUSTRE6B06BN20101201 (accessed on January 29, 2011).

Graham, Alison, Sylvain Aubry, Rolf Kunnemann and Sofia Monsalve Suarez (2010), 'Advancing African Agriculture (AAA): the impact of Europe's policies and practices on African agriculture and food security: land grab study', Foodfirst Information and Action

Network (FIAN), CSO Monitoring 2009–2010. http://www.fian.org/resources/documents/others/report-on-land-grabbing/pdf (accessed on February 10, 2011).

GRAIN (2009), 'The new farm owners: corporate investors lead the rush for control over overseas farmland'. http://www.grain.org/articles_files/atg-22-en.pdf (accessed on February 4, 2011).

Hall, R. (2010), 'The many faces of the investor rush in Southern Africa: towards a typology of commercial land deals', Working Paper No 2, Institute for Critical Agrarian Studies (ICAS) and Land Deal Politics Initiative (LDPI) Working Paper series, The Hague: Institute of Social Studies.

Hansen, A. and N. Oshry (2011), 'Agribusiness funds: harvesting promise'. *AfricaInvestor*, 66. http://www.phatisa.co.za/images/file/Harvesting%20promise%20%28small%29.pdf (accessed on February 7, 2011).

Hickey, S. and A. Du Toit (2007), 'Adverse incorporation, social exclusion and chronic poverty', Working Paper No. 81. CPRC (Chronic Poverty Research Centre).

Holt-Gimenez, E. and A. Shattuck (2011), 'Food crises, food regimes and food movements: rumblings of reform or tides of transformation?', *Journal of Peasant Studies*, 38, 109–44.

International Fund for Agricultural Development (IFAD) (2009), *The Growing Demand for Land: Risks and Opportunities for Smallholder Farmers*, Rome: IFAD Governing Council.

IFC (2009a), 'IFC's largest equity investment in agribusiness to increase global food supply', IFC News, February 12. http://ifcext.ifc.org/ifcext/media.nsf/content/SelectedPress Release?OpenDocument&UNID=ADFC6E67913A542A8525755B004BA7BA (accessed on February 14, 2011).

IFC (2009b), *IFC and Agribusiness*, August 2009. http://www.ifc.org/ifcext/media.nsf/AttachmentsByTitle/AM09_Agribusiness/$FILE/AM09_Agribusiness.pdf (accessed on February 19, 2011).

International Land Coalition (ILC) (2009), *Commercial Pressures on Land Worldwide: Issues and Conceptual Framework*. http://www.landcoalition.org/pdf/09_05_Conceptual_framework_ENG.pdf (accessed on February 14, 2011).

Kanitra, Paul (2011), 'Visionary alternatives to boost food security'. http://farmlandgrab.org/post/view/18125.

Key, N. and D. Runsten (1999), 'Contract farming, smallholders, and rural development in Latin America: the organization of agroprocessing firms and the scale of outgrower production', *World Development*, 27, 381–401.

Kugelman, M. (2009), 'Introduction', in M. Kugelman and S.L. Levenstein (eds), *Land Grab? The Race for the World's Farmland*, Princeton, NJ: Woodrow Wilson International Center for Scholars, pp. 1–23.

Little, P. and M. Watts (1994), 'Introduction', in P. Little and M. Watts (eds), *Living Under Contract: Contract Farming and Agrarian Transformation in Sub-Saharan Africa*, Madison, WI: University of Wisconsin Press, pp. 3-20.

McLaren, H. (2010), 'Transfarm Africa: routes to prosperity. Executive summary', NEPAD Business Foundation. http://www.thenbf.co.za/pmo/289-transfarm-africa-routes-to-prosperity.html?date=2011-01-01 (accessed on February 7, 2011).

McMichael, P. (2009), 'A food regime genealogy of the global food crisis', *Journal of Peasant Studies*, 36, 139–69.

McMichael, P. and M. Schneider (2011), 'Food security policy and the Millennium Development Goals', *Third World Quarterly*, 32, 119–39.

Meinzen-Dick, R. and H. Merkelova (2009), 'Necessary nuance: toward a code of conduct in foreign land deals', in M. Kugelman and S.L. Levenstein (eds), *Land Grab? The Race for the World's Farmland*, Princeton, NJ: Woodrow Wilson International Center for Scholars, pp. 69–81.

Miller, K., S. Richter, P. McNellis and N. Mhlanga (2010), *Agricultural Investment Funds for Developing Countries*, Rome: FAO.

Montemayor, R. (2009), 'Overseas farmland investments – boon or bane for farmers in Asia?' in M. Kugelman and S.L. Levenstein (eds), *Land Grab? The Race for the World's Farmland*, Princeton, NJ: Woodrow Wilson International Center for Scholars, pp. 95–107.

Mullin, K. (2010), 'African agricultural finance under the spotlight', *Reuters*, August 24. http://blogs.reuters.com/africanews/2010/08/24/african-agricultural-finance-under-the-spotlight (accessed on February 12, 2011).

Oya, C. (2009), 'The *World Development Report 2008*: inconsistencies, silences, and the myth of "win–win" scenarios', *Journal of Peasant Studies*, 36, 593–601.

Pesticide Action Network Asia and the Pacific (PANAP) (2010), 'Global land grabbing, eroding food sovereignty', *Turning Point*, 1, 1–44. http://www.panap.net/sites/default/files/TurningPoint_GlobalLandGrabbing.pdf (accessed on February 6, 2011).

Raynolds, L. (2000), 'Negotiating contract farming in the Dominican Republic', *Human Organization*, 59, 441–51.

Scoones, I. (2010), 'Investing in land: a commentary on the World Bank Report', Transnational Institute, September. http://www.tni.org/article/investing-land-commentary-world-bank-report (accessed on February 5, 2011).

Siddiqui, K. (1998), 'Agricultural exports, poverty and ecological crisis – case study of Central American countries', *Economic and Political Weekly*, 33, A128–A136.

Sierra Leone Investment and Export Promotion Agency (SLIEPA) (2009), 'Sierra Leone: it's time to think again'. http://www.sliepa.org/sites/default/files/documents/Country%20Presentation.pdf (accessed on February 4, 2011).

Singh, S. (2002), 'Contracting out solutions: political economy of contract farming in the Indian Punjab', *World Development*, 30, 1621–38.

Southern Agricultural Growth Corridor of Tanzania (SAGCOT) (2011), 'Investment blueprint'. http://www.agdevco.com/images/stories/pdf/TANZANIA/invest-blueprint-sagcot.pdf (accessed on February 24, 2011).

Spieldoch, A. and S. Murphy (2009), 'Agricultural land acquisitions: implications for food security and poverty alleviation', in M. Kugelman and S.L. Levenstein (eds), *Land Grab? The Race for the World's Farmland*, Princeton, NJ: Woodrow Wilson International Center for Scholars, pp. 39–53.

Taylor, M. and T. Bending (2009), *Increasing Commercial Pressures on Land: Building a Coordinated Response*, Rome: International Land Coalition.

UNCTAD (2009), *World Investment Report: Transnational Corporations, Agricultural Production and Development*. http://www.unctad.org/en/docs/wir2009_en.pdf (accessed on February 12, 2011).

Von Braun, J. and R. Meinzen-Dick (2009), '"Land grabbing" by foreign investors in developing countries: risks and opportunities', IFPRI Policy Brief 13, Washington, DC: IFPRI.

Watts, M. (1992), 'Living under contract: work, production politics, and the manufacture of discontent in a peasant society', in A. Pred and M. Watts (eds), *Reworking Modernity. Capitalisms and Symbolic Discontents*, New Brunswick, NJ: Rutgers University Press, pp. 65–105.

White, B. (1997), 'Agroindustry and contract farmers in upland West Java', *Journal of Peasant Studies*, 24, 100–136.

White, B. and A. Dasgupta (2010), 'Agrofuels capitalism: a view from political economy', *Journal of Peasant Studies*, 37, 593–607.

Wolford, W. (2009), 'Book Review of *Land, Poverty and Livelihoods in an Era of Globalization: Perspectives from Developing and Transition Countries*, A.H. Akram-Lodhi, S.M. Borras Jr and C. Kay (eds), London, Routledge. 2006', *Journal of Agrarian Change*, 9, 291–313.

World Bank (2008), *World Development Report 2008: Agriculture for Development*, Washington, DC: World Bank.

World Bank (2010), *Rising Global Interest in Farmland: Can It Yield Sustainable and Equitable Benefits?* Washington, DC: World Bank.

14. Rural development in sub-Saharan Africa
David Kraybill

INTRODUCTION

Africa has the highest poverty rate of any continent in the world and, after Asia, the second-largest number of people living in poverty. Within the African continent, poverty rates are far higher in the 49 countries that comprise sub-Saharan Africa (SSA) than in the six countries of North Africa.[1] Three-fourths of persons living on less than $1.25 per day in SSA are located in rural areas (IFAD 2010). The rural population of SSA has been the focus of more than five decades of rural development policies and programs. Despite these efforts, the rural poverty rate worsened over the 20-year period, 1988–2008 (IFAD 2010). In 1988, East Asia and South Asia had higher rural poverty rates than SSA, based on the $1.25/day poverty line. However, over the subsequent 20 years, the ranking reversed and, by 2008, SSA was far behind East and South Asia and all other world regions in rural poverty rates. In 2008, the estimated rural poverty rate in SSA was 62 percent based on the $1.25/day poverty line and 87 percent based on the $2.00/day poverty line. Moreover, the rural share of poverty has grown in SSA from 72 percent in 1988 to 75 percent in 2008.

Rural residents of SSA, like people in rural areas in many parts of the developing world, have limited livelihood opportunities, limited access to public services and limited voice in national governance. Remoteness imposes severe constraints on rural development, and the deterrent it represents to income generation and democratic participation cannot readily be overcome by getting market prices or citizen participation 'right'. While rural areas abound in land and natural resources, other forms of capital (human, financial, physical, and perhaps even social) are typically much scarcer in rural areas than in urban areas (Wiggins and Proctor 2001). Settlement-size agglomeration economies, a driving force behind urban growth, are non-existent or weak in rural areas, creating vast gaps in markets and social networks. Rural areas, however, are diverse and development prospects vary according to location, resource endowment, climate and population characteristics, though the effects of these factors are modulated by economic, political and social institutions.

A distinguishing feature of the national economies of SSA is the enduring primacy of a single city, or at most two or three, and the slow emergence of economically vibrant secondary cities and towns to provide a range of modern goods and services to rural areas. While the urban population is growing at a rapid rate in many countries, the growth is often concentrated disproportionately in the political or commercial capital city. The lack of transport infrastructure to link urban and rural areas is an important factor in lagging rural economic conditions. Rural transport infrastructure is much poorer in SSA than in Asia or Latin America. Head loading, usually by women, and bicycles remain the major modes of rural commodity transport in much of SSA (Porter 2002).

Though Africa lags behind the rest of the world on key development indicators, there is growing optimism about its economic development prospects (*The Economist* 2011), including prospects for agricultural and rural development (Binswanger-Mkhize and McCalla 2010; Diao 2007). Reasons for optimism include rapid growth of domestic urban demand for rural commodities, an increase in the number of countries ruled by democratic institutions and elected leaders, a decline in civil wars, availability of new food production technologies, a renewed emphasis by African governments and foreign donors on agriculture as an engine of economic growth, the remarkable penetration of mobile phone networks into the remotest corners of the continent, and increased investment in roads and transport infrastructure (World Bank 2008a).

The new-founded optimism is based in part on relatively high growth rates of gross domestic product (GDP) in many African countries in the first decade of the twenty-first century, despite a global recession. Africa's growth, however, is characterized by a highly uneven distribution across regions, sectors of the economy and segments of the population. Though much of the recent growth is based on rural resources, especially minerals, many challenges remain in delivering the benefits of economic growth to rural residents.

APPROACHES TO RURAL DEVELOPMENT IN AFRICA

Rural development efforts aimed at improving the material well-being of rural residents increased greatly with the transition to independence in Africa, which dominated the period from 1957 to 1965. Over the subsequent 50 years, a variety of rural development approaches were adopted on the continent. These approaches, for the most part, were not unique to Africa but reflected worldwide thinking about rural development. While it is impossible, and probably fruitless, to attempt to assign paradigms to particular time periods, Ellis and Biggs (2001) identify an overlapping sequence of rural development approaches over the period 1950–2000: community development; small farm growth; integrated rural development;

market liberalization; process, participation and empowerment; and poverty reduction. These emphases involved differing views about whether rural development initiatives should be top-down or bottom-up, the role of the state versus the market, and the roles of productive sectors versus social sectors. By approximately year 2000, rural development efforts had gravitated towards a view that both markets and the state are important, as well as that both productive and social sectors are important (Ashley and Maxwell 2001).

Attempting to move beyond technocratic solutions, many rural development writers in the late 1970s and early 1980s advocated integrated rural development (IRD). This approach emphasized participatory processes of development in which intended beneficiaries collaboratively identified priority problems and participated in implementing solutions (Johnston and Clark 1982). IRD aimed to empower beneficiaries to control their assets and their futures. Participatory-process and empowerment initiatives focused on a wide range of activities, including formation of rural organizations, rural non-farm income generation, small-scale rural industries, natural resource conservation, rural road building, rural water supplies, village health care delivery and other activities.

From a sector standpoint, small-scale agriculture is a common theme throughout the literature on rural development in Africa, reflecting the relative importance of the sector in national economies and in household livelihoods (Ellis and Biggs 2001). Since farming is the major livelihood, it is difficult to imagine significant reduction in rural poverty without a major emphasis on agriculture. Agriculture, however, has been a disappointing generator of economic well-being in SSA, with persistently low rates of growth of productivity. A technocratic approach to rural development, however, that focused predominantly on improving agricultural productivity, would fail to improve food security and reduce poverty. An array of other rural development factors, including transportation, education, health care, nutrition, rural finance, governance and climate change also affect rural economic and social well-being, and must be addressed to sustainably improve agricultural productivity.

The broad, multisectoral vision behind IRD was attractive and persuasive to many writers and practitioners but the approach eventually proved to be unsustainable (USAID/Armenia 2005). IRD-inspired projects were largely funded by foreign aid organizations and heavily staffed by expatriates, and technical assistance was a major budgetary component in IRD projects. The large infusion of outside money and personnel failed to create local ownership and empowerment. Donor-funded IRD initiatives in Africa often created their own management units parallel to national and local government agencies. At the end of many IRD projects, funds were no longer available to continue development activities, and government agencies and community organizations had not gained the capacity needed to sustain them. Ruttan (1984) criticized IRD projects for failing to focus on specific technologies and for failing to emphasize productivity increases.

Partnership and empowerment are complex processes. Harrison (2002) identifies gaps between the ideal and the actual in many participatory projects in which the participation agenda was controlled by development experts rather than by the intended beneficiaries. The language of participation, popular in development circles, often obscures the strong hand of donors and their contractors in the design and implementation of rural development projects. In the context of natural resource management initiatives in Ethiopia, Harrison points out that agencies implementing 'participatory' projects often fail to appreciate the heterogeneity of localities and ignore local constraints and solutions that a truly participatory process would accommodate.

Another rural development approach adopted in Africa attempts to get participation 'right', beginning with the formative stages of a project. Participatory rural appraisal (PRA) involves rural development beneficiaries in participatory research in which beneficiaries work side by side with development researchers and practitioners to influence the process of discovery and problem identification. Tools of PRA include village mapping, transect walks, seasonal calendars, analysis of trends and subjective ranking of wealth and well-being (Chambers 1994). Another angle on participation emphasizes conflict and negotiation as inevitable and perhaps even essential elements of development decision making (Leeuwis 2000).

Writings by Amartya Sen in the early 1980s on the origin of famines had a profound impact on conceptualization and practice in rural development in Africa (Sen 1981). In a series of papers and books, Sen argued that famines in East Africa, the Horn of Africa, India and other locations occurred during periods of surplus food production within the affected regions or nations. What matters is command over resources, both of which can be attenuated by natural, political, social and economic shocks. Sen's writings inspired subsequent researchers to focus on why some famines lead to widespread malnutrition and starvation while others do not.

The sustainable rural livelihoods approach, promoted especially by Britain's Department for International Development (DFID) beginning in the late 1990s, expanded upon Sen's concern with household command over resources. This approach focuses on the livelihood-generating assets available to households, threats to secure command over those assets, institutions that mediate household access to assets, strategies households adopt to cope with adversity, and livelihood outcomes (Ashley and Carney 1999; Farrington et al. 1999). Livelihood assets include physical, human, social, financial and natural capital; while livelihood outcomes include food security, income, health, reduced vulnerability to shocks and investment.

Since the mid-1990s, interest in African rural development has gained force through renewed focus on poverty alleviation. Following nearly two decades of Structural Adjustment Programmes (SAPs) mandated by the International Monetary Fund (IMF) and the World Bank and supported by some donor countries as a condition for developing countries to receive loans and grants, the so-called 'Washington Consensus' began to fall apart. SAPs required governments to reduce public employment and expenditures and to promote market liberalization, especially privatization and deregulation. By the mid-1990s, it was apparent that this policy prescription resulted in too few public expenditures and investments in SSA to extend the benefits of growth to poor households (Killick 1995). Critics questioned whether SAPs contributed to growth at all (Easterly 2005; Schatz 1994). Beginning in 2002, the IMF and World Bank have required each country participating in the Heavily Indebted Poor Country (HIPC) initiative to prepare a Poverty Reduction Strategy Paper (PSRP) that sets country targets for poverty alleviation as well as for market liberalization and other reforms. Thirty-three of the 39 HIPC countries are in Africa. The renewed focus on lifting households out of poverty has led to new attention to rural development since the majority of the poor live in rural areas.

MAJOR TRENDS UNDERLYING RURAL DEVELOPMENT IN AFRICA

Demographics

Population growth rates in Africa are high compared to other parts of the world. Over the period 1950–2011, the population growth rate of Africa has remained relatively constant, averaging 2.5 percent annually (United Nations, Department of Economic and Social Affairs 2012). At this growth rate, it takes a mere 29 years for population to double.

Fertility rates, measured as births per woman, are higher in Africa than in any other world region. In 2010, the fertility rate in SSA was 4.9, nearly double the next highest world-region fertility rate of 2.7 in South Asia (World Bank 2012). The result is a population pyramid with a very wide base, implying that the working-age population supports a relatively large population of young dependents. The trend in the fertility rate in SSA is downward from a record high of 6.7 but the speed of decline is slow.

A significant spatial redistribution of population from rural to urban areas is occurring on the African continent. In 1988, the urban population share in

SSA was 27 percent; by 2008, it had increased to 36 percent (IFAD 2010). The growing urbanization and rising incomes in urban areas create increased demand for rural goods and services. By 2040, more than half of the population of SSA is projected to live in urban areas, according to the United Nations, Department of Economic and Social Affairs (2012).

Ninety percent of the population in Africa is concentrated on 21 percent of the surface area (Linard et al. 2012). The bulk of the population is located in the most agriculturally productive rural areas. A smaller, but rapidly growing share of the population is located in urban areas. In many rural areas, access to urban areas is limited by poor roads and inadequate transportation systems. In Africa as a whole, the average travel time to settlements of more than 50 000 persons is 3.5 hours (Linard et al. 2012).

Economy

The GDP of the 48 countries of SSA, excluding Somalia, grew over the period 2001–2011 at an average annual rate of 4.9 percent, higher than the average annual country growth of 4 percent in the rest of the world (World Bank 2012). Over the same period, the GDP growth rate in SSA was over 3 percent per anum in 35 countries, over 5 percent in 20 countries, and over 7 percent in nine countries.

Markets affecting the inflow and outflow of goods from rural areas have changed markedly over the past two decades. Between the time of independence and the early 1980s in many African countries, marketing of agricultural inputs and outputs had become dominated by monopolistic parastatal enterprises. Parastatals seldom attained the efficiency required for financial self-sustainability but, instead, taxed their intended beneficiaries heavily (for example, by paying farmers less – often far less – than the world market price for commodities). Furthermore, many parastatals received subsidies from the national treasury (Binswanger-Mkhize and McCalla 2010). Structural Adjustment Programs of the IMF and World Bank resulted in privatizing of most marketing parastatals by 1990. Subsequently, national governments and donors developed policies intended to stimulate the private sector, including both firms and agricultural producer organizations, to handle marketing functions.

Agriculture continues to dominate the rural economy in SSA as a source of food, employment and income. Most rural dwellers are directly involved in agricultural production as either laborers or as managers of laborers and land. Traditional export crops (for example, coffee, tea, cocoa, cotton, sisal) are no longer the sole cash crops, as many farm households also sell a portion of their food crop harvest for cash. Farm size remains relatively small, typically between 1 and 5 acres, large enough to provide for the subsistence food needs of the household, but not large enough to provide the incomes to which many households aspire. The dominance of the agricultural sector in rural SSA is due largely to the fact that it is the default repository for resources, especially human resources, not because it has been a dynamic sector. Over the 1971–2000 period, agricultural value added in SSA grew at the relatively slow rate of 2.5 percent per year, slower than any other major world region (World Bank 2012). Agricultural value added grew more slowly during this period than population, raising serious concerns about food security. In the decade of the 1990s, the agricultural value added growth rate increased slightly to 2.8 percent. In the first decade of the twenty-first century, the rate increased to 3.4 percent, exceeding the population growth rate. While agricultural value added grew, most of the increase arose from expanded acreage rather than from increases in yields. Cereal yields remained relatively flat for SSA as a whole from 1960 to 2005 (World Bank 2008a); in contrast, cereal yields grew substantially in all other parts of the developing world over this period.

Non-farm sectors also provide income and essential goods and services for rural residents. Among major world regions, however, Africa has diversified away from agriculture the least, measured in terms of sectoral share of total national value added (IFAD 2010). The non-farm sector in rural areas consists largely of small-scale enterprises in which the only employees are family members engaged in activities such as charcoal making, beverage brewing, small-scale milling, tailoring, furniture making, repair work of various kinds, and retailing of basic household and farm supplies. Rudimentary agricultural and natural resource processing also provides employment in rural enterprises that seldom exceed 10 to 20 workers. For SSA as a whole, including both urban and rural areas, manufacturing grew slowly with a nearly constant average value added growth rate of 3 percent per annum over the period 2001–2010. Though rural manufacturing statistics are not generally available for SSA, it is quite certain that the rural manufacturing growth rate has been much lower than the overall 3 percent rate.

Climate

Consistent with global trends, the climate of Africa is changing and is expected to continue to change. Northern and southern Africa are predicted to get hotter and drier, while eastern and central Africa will get wetter, according to climate scientists affiliated with the Intergovernmental Panel on Climate Change (2007). The frequency of extreme weather events such as torrential downpours, flooding and drought is expected to increase. Apart from these broad patterns, much remains uncertain about climate change in Africa.

Climate change is expected to affect agriculture to a greater extent than other sectors of the rural economy in Africa. In most of SSA, crop production is rain-fed, so if rains start late or taper off during the growing season, the probability of widespread malnutrition and hunger is high. Climate change is expected to reduce the length of the growing season and cause agricultural yield reductions of up to 50 percent in some African countries by 2020 (Boko et al. 2007). The increased temperatures will cause physiological stress in plants and are expected to create a net reduction in crop yields in Africa (Warren et al. 2006). Yield reductions are expected particularly in maize, a crop that is relatively intolerant of high temperatures and drought. Maize is a staple crop in many parts of eastern and southern Africa.

Increased ambient temperatures are also expected to affect agriculture indirectly through soil fertility and the quantity and quality of water in Africa. The proportion of the African land surface that is arid and semi-arid is predicted to increase 5–8 percent by 2080, according to the Inter-governmental Protocol on Climate Change (Boko et al. 2007). De Wit and Stankiewicz (2006) simulated river basin drainage in Africa and concluded that 25 percent of the continent will be subject to reduced drainage and water supply by 2100.

Transportation

Poor transportation infrastructure in Africa hinders growth of markets for private goods and services, and raises costs of producing public goods and services. According to Teravaninthorn and Raballand (2009), transport costs in Africa are higher than in any other global region. The quality of transport, in terms of predictability and reliability, is lower in Africa than the rest of the world. The poor transportation infrastructure in Africa is the major cause of its poor trade performance, according to Limao and Venables (2001). For rural residents, the high costs imposed by transport infrastructure deficiencies are a daily reality. Over 70 percent of the continent's rural residents live more than 2 kilometers from all-weather roads, making the cost of transporting goods and people high and even prohibitive (Teravaninthorn and Raballand 2009). In addition to costly internal transportation, SSA has high costs of obtaining goods from the global market. The World Bank (2012) estimates that the average cost of importing a shipping container to SSA is $2567, much higher than the rates of $1736 in South Asia, $1612 in Latin America and the Caribbean, $1240 in the Middle East and North Africa, and $950 in East Asia and the Pacific. Similarly for exports, SSA has a much higher cost per shipping container than other major world regions.

Communications

A truly remarkable feature of Africa's recent economic development has been the rapid growth of mobile phone usage (Aker and Mbiti 2010). Mobile phone towers are now visible even in many relatively remote villages. In 2011, an estimated 62 percent of Africans lived in localities served by mobile phone networks (Phillips et al. 2011). In SSA, by 2011, there were 53 mobile phone subscriptions for every 100 persons (World Bank 2012). This is a 21-fold increase since 2001 and a fourfold increase since 2005. In contrast, land lines, which are used primarily in urban areas, have remained relatively constant at around 1.4 lines per 100 persons over the past ten years.

Gender

Women produce up to 80 percent of the household food supply in many parts of rural sub-Saharan Africa and provide 45–80 percent of agricultural labor (Gladwin 2002). The role of women in particular agricultural activities, such as land preparation, tillage, planting, weeding, watering and irrigation, pest management and harvesting, varies according to local cultural traditions. In general, women are heavily involved in the production of food crops but somewhat less involved in cash crops.

Gender is an important factor in understanding every aspect of rural development. Men and women have distinctly different economic and social roles in many rural African societies. Women invest large amounts of time in both productive and reproductive activities, and both types of activities make an economic contribution (Holmes and Slater 2008). Over the past 25 years, greater attention has been paid to women's roles in rural development, but still deeper understanding of gender is required for increasing agricultural productivity, reducing malnutrition, raising education levels and improving general material well-being. A focus on gender is important for reasons of justice for women, overall economic efficiency and socio-economic well-being of the entire population.

The literature on intra-household economics makes important departures from the neoclassical view that the household operates as a single cooperative unit (Folbre 1986). Rather, allowance is made for possible divergence of husbands' and wives' preferences regarding consumption, including the desired number of children and the amount of income and time allocated to childbearing and rearing and child-related goods and services. Couples bargain with each other over consumption decisions but bargaining power is not equal, influenced by the individual income-earning opportunities of husband and wife. Empirical studies provide evidence that men and women, indeed, have different preferences and that women are more inclined than men to allocate money and time to the next generation (Haddad et al. 1997; Quisumbing and Maluccio 2000; Thomas 1990).

Women's productive activities are constrained by limited access to land, financial capital, education and other resources. Given the major role that women play in the rural economy, inequality in access to resources results in economic inefficiency and loss of growth of income of households and communities (Holmes and Slater 2008). Low productivity in African agriculture may be due in part to women's limited access to agricultural inputs, a result of circumscribed land rights and limited opportunities for earning cash income or obtaining credit. Evidence of gender constraints on agricultural productivity can be found by comparing the conditional marginal productivity of resources controlled by men and women. Udry (1996), for example, found that household agricultural output in Burkina Faso could be increased 10–20 percent by reallocating fertilizer, manure and labor from men to women within households. Gender equality also has important effects on investment. For example, women's lack of land rights and barriers to entry in rural labor markets limit the investments women can make in enhancing the fertility of the soil they till (Gladwin 2002).

Health and nutrition

SSA has registered significant improvements in health and nutrition since the independence era. Life expectancy at birth rose from 44 years in 1971 to 54 in 2010, and maternal mortality is estimated to have dropped from 850 per 100 000 live births in 1990 to 500 in 2010 (World Bank 2012). The latter is a significant decrease, though the rate is still very high compared to other parts of the world. While some health indicators have improved, the rate of change has been slow, and other indicators have not improved at all. According to a report by the African Union (2012), SSA is unlikely to meet 2015 targets for all three Millennium Development Goals focused on health and for the one goal that focuses on hunger.

Infant mortality (deaths before age one per 1000 live births) declined in SSA from 136 in 1970 to 71 in 2010 (World Bank 2012). Authors of a recent study of six countries in West and Central Africa estimated the rural infant mortality rate to be 141 compared to an urban rate of 96 (Poel et al. 2009).

They attributed two-thirds of the rural–urban gap to differences in household characteristics, such as absence of potable water and electricity, quality of housing materials, and unobserved heterogeneity of households. In Kenya, researchers concluded that 58 percent of the decline in infant mortality over the period 2003–2008 can be attributed to the use of insecticide-treated bed nets (Demombynes and Trommlerová 2012).

Improvement in mortality rates in SSA has been curbed over the last quarter century by AIDS and HIV. As a percentage of the population aged 15–49, HIV incidence rose from 2.5 percent in 1990 to 6.3 percent in 1999 and then declined to 5.0 percent in 2009 (World Bank 2012). Life expectancy of persons living with AIDS and HIV has been partially restored by the use of antiretroviral (ARV) medication. ARV therapy coverage, measured as a percentage of people with advanced HIV infection, was 41 percent in 2009 (World Bank 2012).

Nutrition plays a major role in human health and economic productivity. Malnutrition in SSA remains high, particularly for children. The average stunting rate in SSA from 2000–2010 was 41 percent of the under-five population, underweight was 21 percent, and wasting was 10 percent (UNDP 2012). For the population as a whole, malnutrition, measured in terms of calorie deficiency, decreased from 34 percent in 1991 to 24 percent in 2011 in SSA (World Bank 2012). Though this drop is considerable, the malnutrition rate is still considerably higher than the rates of 18 percent in South Asia, 11 percent in East Asia, and 9 percent in Latin America in 2011.

The most successful health initiative in SSA in the past decade has been immunization against childhood diseases, and many countries have undertaken immunization campaigns (Clements et al. 2008). The rate of immunization against diphtheria, pertussis and tetanus (DPT) in the population of children of age 12–23 months in SSA increased from 52 percent in 2000 to 74 percent in 2010 (World Bank 2012). Nearly identical rates were registered for measles in 2000 and 2010. Though separate immunization rates are not available for subnational geographies in SSA, immunization rates are undoubtedly lower in rural areas than in urban areas (WHO 2010). For example, in Nigeria, a recent study reported a rural immunization rate of 33 percent compared to an urban rate of 57 percent for DPT, and 28 percent in rural areas versus 47 percent in urban areas for measles (Antai 2011).

Health care personnel and facilities remain scarce in SSA. The number of physicians per 1000 people has changed from 0.13 in 1990 to 0.16 in 2010 (World Bank 2012). Births attended by skilled health staff increased only slightly from 43 percent in 2000 to 46 percent in 2010. Pregnant women receiving prenatal care increased from 66 percent in 2000 to 74 percent in 2010.

Sanitation and potable water are vital for good health. The percentage of the rural population of SSA with access to improved sanitation facilities was only 23 percent in 2010, up just four percentage points from 19 percent in 1990 (World Bank 2012). The percentage of the rural population with access to improved water sources increased from 35 percent in 1990 to 49 percent in 2010.

Education

Relatively low levels of educational human capital in SSA reflect inadequate investment during the colonial era and continuing low levels of investment in the post-colonial. In 2010, the estimated literacy rate in SSA was 63 percent (World Bank 2012). Since the independence era, impressive advances have been made in school enrollment rates. The net primary school enrollment rate as a percentage of primary school age children has increased from 39 percent in 1972 to 76 percent in 2011 (World Bank 2012). At the secondary school level, the gross enrollment rate rose from 12 percent in 1972 to 40 percent in 2011.

The gender gap in primary school enrollment rates, relatively large at the time of independence in most SSA countries, has nearly disappeared (World Bank 2012). At secondary and tertiary levels of education, the gender gap has narrowed but remains substantial. In 2011, the ratio of female to male enrollment was 82 percent at the secondary level and 63 percent at the tertiary level.

Although elementary school enrollment rates are relatively high at the entry level, many pupils drop out for economic and social reasons. In 2011, the primary school dropout rate as a percentage of the relevant age group was 30 percent (World Bank 2012). Though this figure is down from 56 percent in 1972, it is still high compared to all other major world regions.

Government budgets for education have not kept up with the growing population and enrollment. Consequently, many schools in SSA are under-equipped and understaffed. In 1972, 22 percent of primary school teachers were not trained as teachers (World Bank 2012). Stark evidence of the resource gap in education is provided by the fact that by 2011, the percentage of primary school teachers without training had increased to 28 percent. The poor quality of teaching staff, facilities and teaching materials is well understood by many parents, and enrollment in private schools is growing for those who can afford it, though the high cost of private tuition surpasses the financial capability of the majority of households. In 2011, 16 percent of primary school students in SSA attended private schools, up from 11 percent in 1994 (World Bank 2012).

Unfortunately, a rural–urban breakdown of education data is not available for most SSA countries. However, in general, educational opportunities are much more limited in rural than in urban areas, and school enrollment and completion rates are almost surely much lower in rural areas (IFAD 2010). For rural residents who are able to obtain a diploma or degree, relatively few employment opportunities exist in rural areas, and therefore the rural-to-urban brain drain is large.

INSTITUTIONAL ARRANGEMENTS FOR RURAL DELIVERY OF GOODS AND SERVICES

The state has a relatively shallow footprint in much of rural SSA. Government offices in rural areas, whether local branches of national ministries or headquarters of subnational levels of government, often lack the technical and managerial expertise and material inputs required for effective delivery of public services to the populations they nominally serve. Budgets for rural public services tend to be small relative to the level of public demand and often vary enormously from one budget cycle to the next. Compounding the financial resource problem is a human resource problem: well-educated, career-focused public servants are generally unwilling to accept assignments to rural posts. Given the shortage of financial and human resources and weak mechanisms of accountability, rural services in many parts of SSA fall far short of international norms in terms of quantity and quality.

Governmental decentralization has been adopted in a number of SSA countries on the grounds that when government is close to the people, the supply of public services is better matched to local demand (Crook 2003).[2] In principle, public sector accountability improves when decision makers and service providers are within reach of the target population. Decentralization could be a vehicle for increasing rural voice and empowerment in public sector decision making that otherwise would take place primarily in the capital city. In practice, decentralization of responsibility for provision of public services in SSA has seldom been accompanied by devolution of revenue-raising powers (Olowu et al. 2004). Even if local governments are given taxing authority, the weak economies of many rural areas provide a shallow tax base for collection of revenue.

Village and community organizations often play the role of de facto local governments in rural development in SSA (Olowu et al. 2004). A study in Senegal and Burkina Faso found that a high percentage of households belong to village organizations, some of them performing community-oriented activities and others performing market-oriented activities (Bernard et al. 2008). The authors concluded, however, that most of the village organizations in their sample were relatively ineffective in delivering services because of limited managerial capacity and limited financial resources. These are similar to the limitations of national and local governments in the provision of rural services. Non-governmental organizations (NGOs) of both local and international origin also play direct and indirect roles in rural service provision (Bratton 1990). NGOs often participate in policy dialogue with national governments, foreign aid donors and other civil society organizations and, in many cases, they provide direct services to constituents.

Markets, themselves, are institutions that interact with other institutions (for example, the legal system) and with technology in the production and delivery of rural goods and services (Kydd and Dorward 2004). Whether or not market forces lead to broad-based increases in economic efficiency and greater equity depends on the legal, financial, social and political underpinnings of the market. Without requisite supporting and complementary institutions, markets are subject to development-impeding failures, especially coordination failures and low-level equilibrium traps (Hoff 2000). Markets for many goods and services are thin or missing (that is, non-existent) in rural areas of SSA (de Janvry et al. 2006). The failure or absence of one type of market, such as the credit market, limits the growth of other types of markets, such as the market for agricultural inputs. Kydd and Dorward (2004) make a convincing argument that without substantial government investment in roads, irrigation systems, research, extension and land reform, market liberalization has little effect on agricultural growth and rural development.

AGRICULTURAL DEVELOPMENT

The role of agriculture in rural overall economic development has been controversial. An influential paper in 1961 by Johnston and Mellor argued that agriculture is particularly important in the early stages of economic development and can serve as an 'engine of growth' for the entire economy. Schultz (1964) argued that small-scale farmers in developing countries are poor but rational. This view transformed the thinking of many rural development experts and provided a rationale for focusing investments on smallholders in an effort to alleviate rural poverty and transform national economies.

During the first decade of the twenty-first century, an apparent consensus has emerged in the mainstream development community that agriculture is central to economic development in low-income regions and especially in Africa (Binswanger-Mkhize and McCalla 2010). In 2008, the World Bank devoted its World Development Report entirely to the role of agriculture in economic development for the first time in 25 years.

The rate of adoption of improved agricultural technology has remained markedly low in SSA. Kydd and Dorward (2004) point to coordination failure as a reason that fertilizer usage rates declined in SSA during the 1980s and 1990s while increasing in other parts of the developing world. The kilograms of fertilizer used per hectare of arable land in SSA is just one-seventh of the amount used per hectare in the next-lowest major world region, the Middle East and North Africa. Rates of adoption of improved seeds are low in SSA; for example, Langyintuo et al. (2008) estimated that improved seed was planted on 33 percent of maize acreage in Eastern Africa and 38 percent in Southern Africa in 2006–2007. Use of irrigation also lags in SSA; irrigated land as a percentage of arable land was 2.2 percent in SSA in 2008, compared to 35.7 percent in Asia and the Pacific (IFAD 2010).

The Green Revolution of the late 1960s and 1970s largely bypassed Africa. Improved crop varieties that registered large yield gains in Asia and to a lesser extent in Latin America were introduced in SSA but overall adoption rates were low. In the first decade of the twenty-first century, international organizations have made large investments in an attempt to stimulate a Green Revolution in Africa. The Alliance for a Green Revolution in Africa (AGRA), funded by the Bill and Melinda Gates Foundation and the Rockefeller Foundation, launched a four-pillar effort in SSA in 2006 focused on improved seeds, soil health, market access and improved agricultural policies. Factors affecting the likelihood of a successful Green Revolution in Africa include human resource capacity (de Janvry and Sadoulet 2010), technology and technology policy (Otsuka and Kijima 2010), property rights for biological technology and market power of international corporations involved in technology transfer (Oyejide 2010), and climate change (Hassan 2010).

Gradual commercialization of African agriculture is occurring through an increase in market participation by smallholder farmers and the growth of medium-sized and large farms (Barrett 2008; Poulton et al. 2008). Producing an increasing marketable surplus is an important element in alleviating poverty in smallholder agriculture. Given the growth in marketable surplus in SSA and the inevitable expansion of the middle segment of the size distribution of farms in countries throughout the world during the course of economic development, it is surprising that many rural development experts and foreign donor organizations continue to promote smallholder agriculture exclusively in SSA (Wiggins 2009). Although a strong case can be made that support to smallholders is essential for poverty alleviation, it does not follow from this proposition that agricultural policies should focus exclusively on smallholders. Collier and Dercon (2009) argue that the vibrancy of agriculture in SSA has suffered from a lack of policies and program supports for medium-sized and large farms. Indeed, farms of different sizes can achieve mutual benefits through coordination and collaboration, providing a rationale for policies that encourage both small and large farms. For example, out-grower schemes operated by large farms provide contract opportunities for smallholders to receive purchased inputs, credit, technical training and output marketing services. Furthermore, mid-sized and large farms can play an important role in gaining the political support for funding required to build rural infrastructure, such as roads.

Land tenure is an important and complex factor in African agriculture. In much of SSA, aside from a handful of former settler colonies, most rural land is regulated by customary land rights rather than by formal land titles. Since independence, some African countries have experimented with land registration and titling on the grounds that it promotes efficient allocation of land and provides collateral for lending (Deininger and Feder 2009). In general, however, the new land titling systems have not delivered the expected increases in agricultural productivity. Moreover, land titling can worsen access to land for vulnerable populations, including women, who often obtain access to land through social arrangements such as marriage (Meinzen-Dick and Mwangi 2009; Moore 2012). Without reform in social and financial institutions that hinder the empowerment of women and other vulnerable populations, land titling hastens the reallocation of land and may cause them to lose access to the little they have. Other institutional arrangements, such as civil liberties, credit markets and agricultural input markets, must be in place for land titling to improve efficiency and equity in agriculture.

Compared to other world regions, Africa has a relative abundance of arable land that is not used intensively, though availability varies greatly across the continent. Consequently, a number of African countries have attracted international investors, especially since the 2007–2008 global food price spike. Since 2000, some African governments have leased large tracts of land to foreign private investors and many other large land deals have been reported, stirring international concern about the potentially negative effect of 'land grabs' on local residents and national food security (Cotula 2009).

THE RURAL NON-FARM ECONOMY

The non-farm economy is an important source of income, goods and services in rural areas in Africa. In 33 studies on African rural labor markets,

Reardon found the share of non-farm income ranged from 22 percent to 93 percent (Reardon 1997). The simple average across the studies was 45 percent. The non-farm economy plays an important role in affording households the opportunity to diversify sources of income. In the absence of financial markets, households can self-insure against consumption reductions tied to agriculture by engaging in non-farm employment and self-employment (Barrett et al. 2001).

In reviews of non-farm income studies in Africa, Reardon (1997) and Barret et al. (2001) find the share of non-farm income positively related to the level of household income. This implies that while non-farm income reduces the risk faced by better-off agricultural households, it has limited potential to alleviate the poverty of marginalized households, since their non-farm earnings are relatively small.

NATURAL RESOURCES AND CLIMATE CHANGE

Africa has vast natural resources in the form of minerals, water, timber, wildlife and other natural assets. Outside agriculture, natural resource exploitation is the major alternative livelihood option in many rural areas.

The institutional framework for harnessing natural resources for national development is weak in many countries and, when high-value resources are concentrated in particular locations, local residents often receive relatively little benefit. Mineral extraction, in particular, often brings the 'curse of natural resources' upon local communities. This occurs as land is expropriated by national governments; prices of local services (including housing) increase; streams and rivers are contaminated by runoff from mining operations; conflicts with in-migrating laborers and business persons arise; overall levels of corruption increase; and general social conditions deteriorate due to crime, illegal trade, violence and prostitution.

Natural resource management plays an important role in adaptation to climate change in SSA (Nhemachena and Hassan 2007). More than half of 800 Ethiopian farmers who perceived that the climate had changed over the previous 20 years had adopted measures to cope with the change (Deressa et al. 2009). By declining order of adoption rate, the responses were tree planting, soil conservation techniques, a change in crop varieties planted, planting either early or late, and irrigation.

High temperatures tend to reduce soil moisture and speed up the breakdown of organic matter in the soil. By altering the volume of organic content and structure of the soil, conservation practices increase moisture retention and the availability of soil nutrients. Soil moisture can be retained through minimum tillage, mulching, green manure and perpetual use of cover crops to avoid exposing bare soil (Lal 2000). Without rapid replenishment of soil carbon through biomass input and management, soil fertility declines rapidly, particularly in the tropics where temperatures are relatively high.

Water harvesting has been used for many centuries in Africa to cope with weather variations (Ngigi et al. 2005). In semi-arid areas of SSA, water harvesting makes it possible to irrigate crops and lengthen the growing season (Pandey et al. 2003). In regions with normally high rainfall, water harvesting has potential to reduce the adverse effects of drought if rainfall patterns become more erratic.

Conservation agriculture (CA) has been introduced in many African countries in recent years. CA is defined as 'any cropping system which results in conservation of natural or other resources, and sustainable agriculture as the use of agricultural practices which conserve water and soil and are environmentally non-degrading, technically appropriate, economically viable and socially acceptable' (Fowler and Rockstrom 2001). The primary motivation for its introduction appears to be a general concern about soil degradation, yet it serves potentially as an adaptive response to climate change. CA aims to improve soil structure, increase soil moisture retention and increase soil fertility. Some CA proponents are opposed to the use of inorganic fertilizer, while others advocate using a mix of organic and inorganic fertilizers (Giller et al. 2009; Hobbs 2007). Currently, CA adaptation rates are low in most Africa countries (Giller et al. 2009). Pockets of adoption are found in southern Africa, where drought is a frequent occurrence. Reasons cited for the low rate of adoption of CA include increased labor requirements during weeding, insecure property rights and a gender division of labor that assigns field tasks disproportionately to women in SSA (Ajayi 2007; Giller et al. 2009).

Carbon payments are a new potential source of rural income in Africa. Soil management practices can create ideal conditions for the capture of soil carbon that would otherwise be released into the atmosphere (Lal and Bruce 1999). Capturing carbon in the soil, known as carbon sequestration, represents a valuable ecosystem service to the global community. Markets for activities that remove 'bads', such as atmospheric carbon dioxide, have emerged and, in recent years, there have been various proposals for tree planting or replanting and other activities that sequester carbon. Given the abundance of land and biomass in Africa, carbon sequestration payments could play a significant role in poverty reduction on the continent and in improving soil fertility (Wunder 2008).

The Clean Development Mechanism (CDM), created under the Kyoto Protocol on climate change, is the largest of several institutional arrangements through which carbon payments from industrialized countries are channeled to carbon-reducing projects in developing countries. The World Bank estimates that the worldwide value of project-based carbon trading in 2007 was $13.4 billion, of which CDM accounted for 91 percent (World Bank 2008b). Only 5 percent of CDM transactions went to projects in Africa. A major reason is the exclusion of agriculture from CDM eligibility. In 2008, a group of 25 African countries launched the African Climate Solution (ACS) to seek funding for soil carbon sequestration from CDM, as well as from other sources.

A recent study of carbon sequestration in two African countries, Kenya and Senegal, concluded that carbon payments could turn unsustainable agricultural systems into systems that are sustainable from both an ecological and a financial perspective (Antle and Stoorvogel 2008). The carbon contracts in the study required farmers to return crop residues to the soil and to apply organic and mineral fertilizers at specified rates.

CONCLUSION

So far in the twenty-first century, the economies of many countries in sub-Saharan Africa have grown rapidly. The widespread political instability that characterized the region during much of the twentieth century has given way to governments in which democracy in various forms has begun to take shape. A vibrant civil society is emerging in many countries and communities. School enrollment is up across the continent and infant mortality is down.

Poverty is still unacceptably high in rural areas and continues to lag behind that of urban areas. Strengthening economic linkages between urban and rural areas is key to the transformation that will eventually make rural areas dynamic. Those linkages remain weak despite the widespread rapid growth of mobile telecommunications. Phones, radio, television and the internet connect rural communities with domestic urban areas and the outside world, increasing information flows and reducing some of the high costs of transactions in rural areas. Still, large barriers impede the flow of goods and people. Massive rural investment is needed to create more and better roads, greater dispersion of economic activity from one or two primary cities to secondary cities and towns, greater productivity in agriculture, wider spread of rural banking and financial markets, and new and sustainable tax revenue streams to finance local government services.

Getting national policies right in terms of the appropriate mix of public and private sectors, as well as the mix of productive versus social sectors, is important but not enough. Spatially targeted public investments in transportation corridors among subnational regions and between countries, in secondary cities and small towns serving rural hinterlands, and in rural feeder roads, rural schools and rural health clinics, are essential for stimulating greater private sector investment in agriculture, rural manufacturing and services.

In addition to rural development programs that aim to improve the livelihoods of smallholders and national investment agency programs that focus on attracting large-scale investors, there is also need for rural development programs that aim to fill out the 'missing middle' in the agricultural, natural resource and manufacturing sectors. Markets for many goods and services in rural areas remain non-existent or thin. An emphasis only on smallholders is likely to doom rural communities in SSA to more decades of slow rural growth and high rates of out-migration to urban areas. As cities in SSA grow rapidly, they will continue to draw economic vitality from rural areas unless the sources of growth are themselves located outside the largest urban areas. Expanding the middle range of agricultural producers, natural resource extractors and processors and manufacturers, and doing so in a geographically dispersed way, is essential for spreading economic growth and its benefits to rural areas.

This chapter addresses broad trends, average conditions and common issues in sub-Saharan Africa without paying much attention to variations across countries and regions. Yet, SSA is characterized by enormous economic, social, climatic and ecological diversity. Across countries of the region, there is a wide range of statistical values of the indicators reported in this chapter. For example, the rural population as a percentage of total national population ranges from 16 percent to 90 percent. Averaged over the period 2001–2010, country GDP growth rates range from -4.5 percent to 18 percent, poverty (headcount) rates range from 0.25 percent to 87 percent, literacy rates range from 31 percent to 94 percent, and stunting rate of under-five children ranges from 20 percent to 63 percent. Although not addressed here, Africa's enormous heterogeneity and its implications for individual country policy and for the future of rural Africa is an important topic.

NOTES

1.   There is no universally accepted definition of North Africa and sub-Saharan Africa. In this chapter, North Africa is defined as consisting of Algeria, Egypt, Libya, Morocco, Tunisia and Western Sahara. Sub-Saharan Africa is defined as consisting of Angola, Benin, Botswana, Burkina Faso, Burundi, Cameroon, Cape Verde, Central African Republic, Chad, Comoros, Côte d'Ivoire, Democratic Republic of the Congo, Djibouti, Equatorial Guinea, Eritrea, Ethiopia, Gabon, Gambia, Ghana, Guinea, Guinea-Bissau, Kenya, Lesotho, Liberia, Madagascar, Malawi, Mali, Mauritania, Mauritius, Mozambique, Namibia, Niger, Nigeria, Republic of the Congo, Rwanda, São Tomé and Príncipe,

Senegal, Seychelles, Sierra Leone, Somalia, South Africa, South Sudan, Sudan, Swaziland, Tanzania, Togo, Uganda, Zambia and Zimbabwe.
2. Widely documented cases of decentralization in Africa include Côte d'Ivoire, Ghana, Kenya, Nigeria, Tanzania, and Uganda (Crook 2003).

REFERENCES

African Union (2012), *MDG Report 2012: Assessing Progress in Africa Toward the Millennium Development Goals*, Addis Ababa: African Union Commission.
Ajayi, O.C. (2007), 'User acceptability of sustainable soil fertility technologies: Lessons from farmers' knowledge, attitude and practice in southern Africa', *Journal of Sustainable Agriculture*, 30, 21–40.
Aker, Jenny C. and Isaac M. Mbiti (2010), 'Mobile phones and economic development in Africa', *Journal of Economic Perspectives*, 24, 207–32.
Antai, D. (2011), 'Rural–urban inequities in childhood immunisation in Nigeria: the role of community contexts', *African Journal of Primary Health Care and Family Medicine*, 3(1). Available at http://www.phcfm.org (accessed January 15, 2013).
Antle, John M. and Jetse J. Stoorvogel (2008), 'Agricultural carbon sequestration, poverty, and sustainability', *Environment and Development Economics*, 13, 327–52.
Ashley, Caroline and Diana Carney (1999), *Sustainable Livelihoods: Lessons from Early Experience*, London: Department for International Development.
Ashley, Caroline and Simon Maxwell (2001), 'Rethinking rural development', *Development Policy Review*, 19, 395–425.
Barrett, Christopher B. (2008), 'Smallholder market participation: concepts and evidence from eastern and southern Africa', *Food Policy*, 33, 299–317.
Barrett, Christopher B., Thomas Reardon and Patrick Webb (2001), 'Nonfarm income diversification and household livelihood strategies in rural Africa: concepts, dynamics, and policy implications', *Food Policy*, 26, 315–31.
Bernard, Tanguy, Marie-Hélène Collion, Alain de Janvry, Pierre Rondot and Elisabeth Sadoulet (2008), 'Do village organizations make a difference in African rural development? A study for Senegal and Burkina Faso', *World Development*, 36, 2188–204.
Binswanger-Mkhize, Hans and Alex F. McCalla (2010), 'The changing context and prospects for agricultural and rural development in Africa', *Handbook of Agricultural Economics*, 4, 3571–3712.
Boko, M., I. Niang, A. Nyong, C. Vogel, A. Githeko, M. Medany, B. Osman-Elasha, R. Tabo and P. Yanda (2007), 'Africa in climate change 2007: impacts, adaptation and vulnerability', contribution of Working Group II to M.L. Parry, O.F. Canziani, J.P. Palutikof, P.J. van der Linden and C.E. Hanson (eds), *Fourth Assessment Report of the Intergovernmental Panel on Climate Change*, Cambridge: Cambridge University Press, pp. 433–67.
Bratton, Michael (1990), 'Non-governmental organizations in Africa: can they influence public policy?', *Development and Change*, 21, 87–118.
Chambers, Robert (1994), 'The origins and practice of participatory rural appraisal', *World Development*, 22, 953–69.
Clements, C. John, Deo Nshimirimanda and Alex Gasasira (2008), 'Using immunization delivery strategies to accelerate progress in Africa towards achieving the Millennium Development Goals', *Vaccine*, 26, 1926–33.
Collier, Paul and Stefan Dercon (2009), 'African agriculture in 50 years: smallholders in a rapidly changing world', in *Proceedings of the Expert Meeting on How to Feed the World in 2050*, Rome: Food and Agriculture Organization.
Cotula, L. (2009), *Land Grab or Development Opportunity? Agricultural Investment and International Land Deals in Africa*, London, UK and Rome, Italy: FAO/IIED/IFAD.

Crook, Richard C. (2003), 'Decentralisation and poverty reduction in Africa: the politics of local–central relations', *Public Administration and Development*, 23, 77–88.

Deininger, Klaus and Gershon Feder (2009), 'Land registration, governance, and development: evidence and implications for policy', *World Bank Research Observer*, 24, 233–66.

Demombynes, Gabriel and S.K. Trommlerová (2012), 'What has driven the decline of infant mortality in Kenya?', World Bank Policy Research Working Paper 6057, Washington, DC.

Deressa, Temesgen Tadesse, Rashid M. Hassan, Claudia Ringler, Tekie Alemu and Mahmud Yesuf (2009), 'Determinants of farmers' choice of adaptation methods to climate change in the Nile Basin of Ethiopia', *Global Environmental Change*, 19, 248–55.

Diao, X. (2007), *The Role of Agriculture in Development: Implications for Sub-Saharan Africa*, Washington, DC: International Food Policy Research Institute.

Easterly, William (2005), 'What did structural adjustment adjust?', *Journal of Development Economics*, 76, 1–22.

The Economist (2011), 'The sun shines bright: the continent's impressive growth looks likely to continue', December 3.

Ellis, Frank and Stephen Biggs (2001), 'Evolving themes in rural development 1950s–2000s', *Development Policy Review*, 19, 437–48.

Farrington, J., D. Carney, C. Ashley and C. Turton (1999), 'Sustainable livelihhods in practice: early applications of concepts in rural areas', *Natural Resource Perspectives*, 42, 1–14.

Folbre, Nancy (1986), 'Hearts and spades: paradigms of household economics', *World Development*, 14, 245–55.

Fowler, Richard and Johan Rockstrom (2001), 'Conservation tillage for sustainable agriculture: an agrarian revolution gathers momentum in Africa', *Soil and Tillage Research*, 61, 93–108.

Giller, Ken E., Ernst Witter, Marc Corbeels and Pablo Tittonell (2009), 'Field crops research conservation agriculture and smallholder farming in Africa: the heretics' view', *Food Crops Research*, 114, 23–34.

Gladwin, Christina H. (2002), 'Gender and soil fertility in Africa: introduction', *African Studies Quarterly*, (1–2), 1–26.

Haddad, L., J. Hoddinott and H. Alderman (1997), *Intrahousehold Resource Allocation in Developing Countries: Models, Methods, and Policy*, Washington, DC: International Food Policy Research Institute.

Harrison, Elizabeth (2002), '"The problem with the locals": partnership and participation in Ethiopia', *Development and Change*, 33, 587–610.

Hassan, Rashid M. (2010), 'Implications of climate change for agricultural sector performance in Africa: policy challenges and research agenda', *Journal of African Economies*, 19 (Suppl. 2), 77–105.

Hobbs, P.R. (2007), 'Conservation agriculture: what is it and why is it important for future sustainable food production?', *Journal of Agricultural Science*, 145, 127–37.

Hoff, Karla (2000), 'Beyond Rosenstein–Rodan: the modern theory of coordination problems in development', in *Proceedings of the Annual World Bank Conference on Development Economics*, Washington, DC: World Bank.

Holmes, Rebecca and Rachel Slater (2008), 'Measuring progress on gender and agriculture in the 1982 and 2008 World Development Reports', *Gender and Development*, 16, 27–40.

IFAD (2010), *Rural Poverty Report 2011*, Rome: International Fund for Agricultural Development.

Intergovernmental Panel on Climate Change (IPCC) (2007), *Working Group I Report: The Physical Science Basis, Fourth Assessment Report: Climate Change 2007*, Geneva: Intergovernmental Panel on Climate Change.

De Janvry, Alain and Elisabeth Sadoulet (2010), 'Agriculture for development in Africa: business-as-usual or new departures?', *Journal of African Economies*, 19(Suppl. 2), ii7–ii39.

De Janvry, Alain, Marcel Fafchamps and Elisabeth Sadoulet (2006), 'Peasant household behaviour with missing markets: some paradoxes explained', *Economic Journal*, 101, 1400–1417.

Johnston, B. F. and W. C. Clark (1982), *Redesigning Rural Development: A Strategic Perspective*, Baltimore: Johns Hopkins University Press.

Johnston, Bruce F. and John W. Mellor (1961), 'The role of agriculture in economic development', *American Economic Review*, 51, 566-93.

Killick, Tony (1995), 'Structural adjustment and poverty alleviation: an interpretative survey', *Development and Change*, 26, 305–30.

Kydd, Jonathan and Andrew Dorward (2004), 'Implications of market and coordination failures for rural development in least developed countries', *Journal of International Development*, 16, 951–70.

Lal, Rattan (2000), 'Physical management of soils of the tropics: priorities for the 21st century', *Soil Science*, 165, 197-207.

Lal, R. and J.P. Bruce (1999), 'The potential of world cropland soils to sequester C and mitigate the greenhouse effect', *Environmental Science and Policy*, 2, 177–85.

Langyintuo, A.S., W. Mwangi, A.O. Diallo, J. MacRobert, J. Dixon and M. Banzinger (2008), *An Analysis of the Bottlenecks Affecting the Production and Deployment of Maize Seed in Eastern and Southern Africa*, Harare: CIMMYT.

Leeuwis, Cees (2000), 'Reconceptualizing participation for sustainable rural development: towards a negotiation approach', *Development and Change*, 31, 931–59.

Limao, Nuno and Anthony J. Venables (2001), 'Infrastructure, geographical disadvantage, transport costs, and trade', *World Bank Development Review*, 15, 451–79.

Linard, Catherine, Marius Gilbert, Robert W. Snow, Abdisalan M. Noor and Andrew J. Tatem (2012), 'Population distribution, settlement patterns and accessibility across Africa in 2010', *PloS One*, 7, 31743.

Meinzen-Dick, Ruth and Esther Mwangi (2009), 'Cutting the web of interests: pitfalls of formalizing property rights', *Land Use Policy*, 26, 36–43.

Moore, Charity M.T. (2012), 'Formal land rights , plot management, and income diversification in Tigray region, Ethiopia', Dissertation, Ohio State University, Columbus, OH.

Ngigi, Stephen N., Hubert H.G. Savenije, Johan Rockström and Charles K. Gachene (2005), 'Hydro-economic evaluation of rainwater harvesting and management technologies: farmers' investment options and risks in semi-arid Laikipia district of Kenya', *Physics and Chemistry of the Earth*, 30, 772–82.

Nhemachena, C. and R. Hassan (2007), *Micro-Level Analysis of Farmers Adaption to Climate Change in Southern Africa*, Washington, DC: International Food Policy Research Institute.

Olowu, Dele, James Stevenson Wunsch and Joseph R.A. Ayee (2004), *Local Governance in Africa: The Challenges of Democratic Decentralization*, Boulder, CO: Lynne Rienner Publishers.

Otsuka, K. and Y. Kijima (2010), 'Technology policies for a Green Revolution and agricultural transformation in Africa', *Journal of African Economies*, 19(Suppl. 2), ii60–ii76.

Oyejide, T. Ademola (2010), 'World trade order and agricultural transformation in Africa', *Journal of African Economies*, 19(Suppl. 2), 40–59.

Pandey, D. N., A. K. Gupta, and D. M. Anderson (2003), 'Rainwater harvesting as an adaptation to climate change', *Current Science*, 85, 46–59.

Phillips, Tom, Peter Lyons, A.T. Kearney, Mark Page, Laurent Viviez, Maria Molina and Tim Ensor (2011), *African Mobile Observatory 2011*, London: GSM Association.

Poel, Ellen Van De, Owen O. Donnell and Eddy Van Doorslaer (2009), 'Infant mortality: household or community characteristics?', *Demography*, 46, 827–50.

Porter, Gina (2002), 'Living in a walking world: rural mobility and social equity issues in sub-Saharan Africa', *World Development*, 30, 285–300.

Poulton, Colin, Geoff Tyler, Peter Hazell, Andrew Dorward, Jonathan Kydd and Mike Stockbridge (2008), *Commercial Agriculture in Sub-Saharan Africa: Lessons from Success and Failure*, London: School of Oriental and African Studies.

Quisumbing, Agnes R. and John A. Maluccio (2000), *Intra-household Allocation and Gender Relations: New Empirical Evidence from Poor Developing Countries*, Washington, DC: International Food Policy Research Institute.

Reardon, T. (1997), 'Using evidence of household income diversification to inform study of the rural nonfarm labor market in Africa', *World Development*, 25, 735–47.

Ruttan, Vernon W. (1984), 'Integrated rural development programmes: a historical perspective', *World Development*, 12, 393–401.

Schatz, Sayre P. (1994), 'Structural adjustment in Africa: a failing grade so far', *Journal of Modern African Studies*, 32, 679–692.

Schultz, T.W. (1964), *Transforming Traditional Agriculture*, Chicago, IL: University of Chicago Press.

Sen, Amartya (1981), 'Ingredients of famine analysis: availability and entitlements', *Quarterly Journal of Economics*, 96, 433–64.

Teravaninthorn, S. and G. Raballand (2009), *Transport Prices and Costs in Africa: A Review of the Main International Corridors*, Washington, DC: World Bank.

Thomas, D. (1990), 'Intra-household resource allocation: an inferential approach', *Journal of Human Resources*, 25, 635–64.

Udry, Christopher (1996), 'Gender, agricultural production, and the theory of the household', *Journal of Political Economy*, 104, 1010–46.

UNDP (2012), *Human Development Report 2012 Africa Human Development Report 2012 Towards a Food Secure Future*, New York: United Nations Development Programme.

United Nations, Department of Economic and Social Affairs (2012), 'World urbanization prospects'. Available at http://esa.un.org/unpd/wup/index.htm (accessed January 20, 2013).

USAID/Armenia (2005), *Integrated Rural Development Lessons Learned*, Yerevan, Armenia: USAID.

Warren, R., N. Arnell, R. Nicholls, P. Levy and J. Price (2006), 'Understanding the regional impacts of climate change', research report prepared for the Stern Review on the Economics of Climate Change, Tyndall Centre for Climate Change Research, University of East Anglia, UK.

Wiggins, Steve (2009), 'Can the smallholder model deliver poverty reduction and food security for a rapidly growing population in Africa?', *Proceedings of the Expert Meeting on How to Feed the World in 2050*, Rome: Food and Agriculture Organization.

Wiggins, Steve and Sharon Proctor (2001), 'How special are rural areas? the economic implications of location for rural development', *Development Policy Review*, 19, 427–36.

de Wit, Maarten and Jacek Stankiewicz (2006), 'Changes in surface water supply across Africa with predicted climate change', *Science*, 311, 1917–21.

World Bank (2008a), *World Development Report 2008: Agriculture for Development*, Washington, DC: World Bank.

World Bank (2008b), *State and Trends of the Carbon Market 2008*, Washington, DC: World Bank.

World Bank (2012), 'World Development Indicators'. Available at http://databank.world bank.org.

World Health Organization (2010), *State of the World's Vaccines and Immunization*, 3rd edition, Geneva: World Health Organization.

Wunder, Sven (2008), 'Payments for environmental services and the poor: concepts and preliminary evidence', *Environment and Development Economics*, 13, 279–97.

15. Urbanization, farm dependence and population change in China[1]

Li Zhang

INTRODUCTION AND OVERVIEW

As the most populous country, China has 20 percent of the world's population, which is four times the US population. Geographically, China occupies 7 percent of the world's land area with the third-biggest landmass, following only Russia and Canada. The majority (94 percent) of the population in China lives in the eastern half of the country, divided by a line drawn from the town of Aihui in the Northeast province of Heilongjiang to Tengchong in the Southwest province of Yunnan. About 41 percent of the population lives in the coastal provinces and only about 6 percent of the population lives in the mountainous west where 55 ethnic minority groups reside.

Currently, China has 31 province-level administrative units, comprising 22 provinces, five autonomous regions and four municipalities. The 22 provinces are Hebei, Shanxi, Gansu, Liaoning, Jilin, Heilongjiang, Jiangsu, Zhejiang, Anhui, Fujian, Jiangxi, Shandong, Henan, Hubei, Hunan, Guangdong, Hainan, Sichuan, Guizhou, Yunnan, Shaanxi and Qinghai. The five autonomous regions are Guangxi, Inner Mongolia (Nei Menggu), Ningxia, Tibet (Xizang), and Xinjiang. And the four central administrative municipalities are Beijing (the capital of China), Tianjin, Shanghai and Chongqing. The five autonomous regions and the four municipalities are governmental equivalents of provinces, and are referred to and treated as provinces in this chapter. In addition to these administrative units, there are two special autonomous regions (SARs) of China: Hong Kong (since 1997) and Macau (since 1999).

The 31 administrative units are classified into six regions: Northeast, North, Northwest, East, Southwest, and Central and South. North China is perhaps the most important region in China due to its size and location. The national capital, Beijing, along with the Tianjin metropolis, forms the urban center of North China. The North China Plain, as part of the North region, is the largest flat area in China, which contains a little over one-quarter of China's total farmland and slightly over one-quarter of the total population. The Plain is predominantly rural and many of the areas in the Plain are not irrigated. The primary staple crop in the North China Plain is wheat, although economic crops such as cotton and peanuts are also produced in some areas (Naughton 2007). According to Naughton (2007), the import-ance of the North China region also lies in the fact that the region accounts for 27 percent of the national population and produces 30 percent of the national industrial output and for 31 percent of the national crop output.

The East region, centered by Shanghai metropolis, is the most developed region in China. The urbanization level and living standards in the region are also significantly higher than most other areas in China. With industri-alization, many areas in the East region that are traditionally classified as rural have now rapidly changed to urban. The East region covers the Yangtze River Delta (YRD), which is about 50 000 square kilometers. The YRD is considered as one of the greatest river deltas in the world. The delta comprises 7 percent of China's arable land but produces 10 percent of crop output (Naughton 2007).

The Northeast region has rich reserves of iron ore, coal and petroleum, which made the region the center of China's heavy industry. About 9 percent of China's population lives in the Northeast region and the region cultivates 17 percent of China's arable land (Naughton 2007). The agricul-tural mechanization level in this region is also relatively higher than most of the other regions, which made it an exporter of food grains and soybeans to other parts of China. The Northwest region, comprising Shannxi, Qinghai, Gansu, Ningxia and Xinjiang, is primarily rural and is the least developed region in China.

The Southwest region of China is composed of the Chongqing metropo-lis, Sichuan, Guizhou, Yunnan provinces and Tibet. Provinces in this region are traditionally agricultural and they share about 15 percent of China's population and produce 8.5 percent of national gross domestic product (GDP) (Naughton 2007). Compared to most other regions, the regional overall income in the Southwest is relatively low.

The Central and South region is along the southeast coast, which covers the fertile Pearl River Delta, the heart of Guangdong province. Diversified agriculture and dense population may well characterize the Central and South region. Since the late 1970s, the region has experienced a drastic transformation due to China's economic reforms. Four special economic zones (SEZs), Shenzhen, Zhuhai, Shantou and Chaozhou, were established in 1979–1980 in this region to attract foreign investment. The four SEZs link Fujian, Guangdong, Hong Kong and Taiwan together and transform the entire eastern delta into an integrated economic zone. The urbanization pace of the Central and South region is also fast since the economic reforms.

Overall, even though China was historically an agriculturally-based society, China has more land that is inhospitable than arable. Only 15 percent of land is arable and there is very little land that is 'potentially suited for cultivation but not already exploited' (Naughton 2007, p. 20). As compared to the United States, the largest plains in China are only a fraction of the central plain of the American Midwest. According to Naughton (2007), on average, per capita arable land in China is only one-tenth of a hectare or one-quarter of an acre. As a result, agriculture in China has long been labor-intensive due to land scarcity, which yields more total food grain than other countries.

Given that China is a traditionally agricultural society, how it has transformed into a nation with 50 percent of its population living in cities nowadays has long been a fascinating topic to scholars studying contemporary China. This chapter will focus on discussing the urbanization process in China as well as how population has been redistributed due to such an urbanization process. In addition, the chapter also discusses the association between population change and farm dependence in the unique context of China.

URBANIZATION AND RURAL–URBAN POPULATION REDISTRIBUTION IN CHINA

Urbanization in China started rather late. The urbanization pattern in China is also unique. It has not followed the urbanization trends in other developed or less developed countries because the urbanization process in China has been determined primarily by government policies that, until recently, have tightly constrained the scope for individual choices. For most developed countries, it is clear that the main driving force of urbanization is natural increase. When the importance of urban natural increase gradually declined, rural-to-urban migration became a leading factor for urban growth (Liang et al. 2008). As to less developed countries, Preston (1979) found that urbanization in most less developed countries has also been driven by urban natural increase instead of rural-to-urban migration that is regulated by government policies. In this chapter, I demonstrate that urbanization in China has been a product of government policies; rural-to-urban migration regulated by government policies has been the major driving force for urban growth. I classify the urbanization process in China into several stages, which falls in line with Chan's (1992) discussion. I show the way in which the urbanization process is highly responsive to policy changes.

Before discussing the urbanization process in China, it is necessary to clarify the definition of 'urban' population. The urban population in China has not been well defined since 1949 in large part due to the various definitions of urban places and urban population that have been used. Urban population in China has sometimes been defined as a combination of where people live and how they make a living (Goldstein and Goldstein 1990). Chan (1992) argued that three major factors – the urban designation, the urban boundary and the household registration classification – have been affecting the calculations of the size of urban population in China. Among the three, household registration status seems to be the main one that has been used to define the urban population. Under such a circumstance, individuals who moved into an urban location but had not changed their registration continued to be classified as agricultural even if they were engaged in non-agricultural activities. In a similar vein, people who were commune members, but located in city boundaries, were defined as 'agricultural' since they obtained their grain from communes. In partial recognition of these anomalies, the Chinese censuses made some adjustments. For instance, the 1982 census defined the urban population as all persons who registered in the designated urban places, regardless of the source of their grain ration (Goldstein and Goldstein 1990). It needs to be noted that the definition of urban population, even in censuses, is not consistent. The Chinese dual system of agricultural/non-agricultural classification based on household registration and urban/rural classification by residence results in a classification of the population into four groups: urban agricultural, rural agricultural, urban non-agricultural and rural non-agricultural. It has been suggested that the Chinese authorities need to remedy the situation of an unclear definition of urban population. In this chapter, I echo Chan's (1992) discussion and classify China's urbanization process into the following stages.

Period 1: 1949–1957

This period is considered as one of rapid population growth. The average population growth rate was 7.2 percent per year, which coincides with the economic revival of the Recovering Period (1945–1952) after the civil war and under the first Five Year Plan (1953–1957). The Chinese population was encouraged to migrate to cities to help in industrial construction. As a result, the urban population consistently increased. The higher living standards as well as better medical care in cities also led to a high in-migration rate of cities. Overall, the urban population growth trend resembled that in many rapidly industrialized nations.

In rural areas, changes have occurred as well. Private property in land was abandoned in 1955. Land in each village was pooled together and became a property of the village as a whole. Collective ownership became the predominant form of ownership. The collectives were supposed to manage agricultural labor and deliver grain to the government (Naughton 2007).

Although the peasants contributed grain to the government, they were completely ruled out from the social welfare system of China. In urban areas, on the other hand, the urban work units, *Danwei*, received government investments. Urban workers were fully covered by the social welfare system of China. The roots of a dualistic system began to emerge in this period.

Period 2: 1958–1960

This period represents a drastic urban inflow of population. The Chinese government launched the Great Leap Forward (GLF) movement in 1958, which encouraged rural residents to move to cities to accelerate industrialization. Many farmers migrated to cities to take up better-paying jobs and the in-migration rate to cities remained high through the GLF years. Mao considered iron and steel production as the key pillars of the economy. In 1959 alone, Mao drew 15 million rural people to cities to work on heavy industry. As a result, the percentage of urban population in China rose from 16.2 percent in 1958 to 19.7 percent in 1959 (Chan 1992).

Period 3: 1961–1965

In contrast to the previous two periods, this era shows significant urban outflow. The drastic shift of rural to urban labor during the GLF movement soon triggered labor shortages on farms. The government continued to extract food from the countryside and eventually there was no more to take. Urban dwellers continued to enjoy the huge privilege that they could still receive at least some of their grain rations. The GLF collapsed after a few years of practice. Combined with natural calamities and a shortage of labor on farms, a nationwide famine occurred. It is estimated that about 20 million people starved to death (Ashton et al. 1984). The Chinese government realized that with the shortage of labor on farms, China's grain production capacity was not able to sustain the large amount of urban industrial population. Thus, the government decided to move 20 million residents who relocated from rural to urban setting back to their home villages during 1961–1963. As a result, an outflow of urban population occurred. Since the early 1960s, the Chinese government began to strictly control the rural–urban population flow. The system of household registration that was initially created to divide the urban–rural domains began to serve as an internal passport in China and play a crucial role in controlling population mobility, particularly from rural to urban areas.

Period 4: 1966–1977

This period can be characterized by two-way movements. During the Cultural Revolution (1966–1976), Mao Zedong launched the 'sending down' policy, which required urban youth and intellectuals to go to mountains and villages to be educated by the peasants. In the meantime, a large number of rural residents also moved to urban sectors. It is estimated that roughly 30 to 50 million moved either into or out of cities during this time frame. Some workers were also moved from big cities to western China to build factories. Shanghai, for instance, experienced an out-migration stream of 1.86 million during 1955–1976 (Naughton 2007).

Period 5: 1978–1982

After the Cultural Revolution, urban youth and intellectuals began to return to cities. Rural reforms also took place in the late 1970s when the government decided to reduce the pressure on farmers. Since 1949, farmers in China had been under the pressure of increasing productivity. Procurement targets had been kept high and procurement prices were low. Part of the rural reforms was that the government allowed contracting of individual pieces of land to farm households. Each farm household took over management of a specific piece of land, subject to a contractual agreement that the household turned over a certain amount of procurement (low price) and tax (zero price) grain after the harvest and the rest was released to the market. Under such a policy, the rural collective began to play a role as a landlord. Contracting land to households soon spread rapidly in rural China and became almost universal by 1983 (Naughton 2007). Agricultural production began to surge in the following years. Consequently, large numbers of surplus labor arose on farms, which provided a background for rural-to-urban migration in later years.

Starting in 1978, the reforms also ended extreme forms of population control. Though the household registration system still existed in China, the government became less restrictive towards population mobility to smaller cities. The policies were more restrictive in terms of limiting the growth of megacities. Such policies allowed a large number of surplus labor to move to medium-sized or small cities, which led to a rapid urban population growth. It is worth mentioning that even with in-migration to cities, the urbanization level in China was still low. By 1978, China's urbanization rate was only 17.9 percent, compared with a developing-country average of 31 percent (Naughton 2007).

Period 6: 1983–1999

This period experienced rapid urban growth. In the 1980s, the Chinese reformers extended the reform approaches in rural sectors to industrial and commercial areas. China began to experience a transition from a planned economy to a market-oriented economy. Perhaps China's transition has led to major changes in the way in which cities operate. One noticeable change is that peasants no longer needed to obtain urban household registration status to stay and work in cities. The 'open door' policy initiated by Deng Xiaoping allowed foreign companies and the non-government-owned sectors to start their businesses in many cities in China. The booming private businesses, service sectors as well as joint enterprises, particularly in the coastal areas, created a constant demand for labor. A large number of peasants therefore moved to cities in response to the job opportunities. These migrants could be hired by non-state-owned sectors, which made the household registration status in the destination places no longer a prerequisite for migrants to survive. As a result, rural-to-urban migration in China accelerated in the 1980s. During the 1980s and 1990s, there was a significant increase of 'floaters' (people who did not have the household registration status in the destination places) moving to cities. By 2000, a quarter of the population in Guangdong was migrants (Liang 2001).

Liang et al. (2008) emphasized that the rapid urbanization trend was largely due to the gap between average rural and urban incomes. Net urban income per capita was over three times as high as rural income. Farmers moved to cities for better job opportunities, educational systems and higher living standards. Prior research has also documented that though two-way migration occurred, urban in-migrants largely outnumbered out-migrants during this period (Yang 1994). It needs to be noted that a tremendous regional variation in the pace of urbanization is observed as well. The coastal region in general had a faster urbanization pace than the other regions. For instance, from 1990 to 1995, the urbanization level in Shanghai increased from 66.1 percent to 83.8 percent (Naughton 2007). This pace of urbanization is not observed in many inland cities.

As compared to migration, the influence of fertility on urbanization is much less important. China adopted its 'one-child policy' in the late 1970s, which had a tremendous impact on the fertility decline in China. For instance, the total fertility rate (TFR) dropped to 1.2 in cities, 1.5 for towns and 1.8–2.0 in rural areas for the period of 1990 to 1995 (Liang et al. 2008). Such a low level of fertility is less likely to have a profound influence on urban population growth. The number of 'floating population', in contrast, increased drastically. It is estimated that the cross-country floating population increased from 22 million in 1990 to more than double in 1995 in

China (Liang et al. 2008), and the majority of them poured into cities. Therefore, fertility in urban China has contributed very little to urban growth compared to migration.

Period 7: 2000–present

This is a period with a steady increase of urban population. The post-2003 Hu Jintao-Wen Jiabao administration placed their emphasis on rural areas and regions behind the development process. The government reduced the tax rate in rural areas and some extra burdens that rural-to-urban migrants experience in cities. The more recent urbanization policies are less restrictive as compared to previous years, particularly for small and medium-sized cities. Nevertheless, strict control still remains when it comes to in-migration to large cities. According to Vermeer (2006), since 2000, the annual urbanization rate has been well above 1 percent and it is expected that there will be 300 million people who move to cities between 2000 and 2020. The existing literature shows that the number of rural-to-urban migrants has declined since 2000 due to higher migration costs, including management fees, train tickets, restrictions on urban labor markets and so on. But the number increased again during 2002 to 2004 to an estimated 140 million people (Vermeer 2006).

Vermeer (2006) pointed out that there are three main determinants of the pace of urbanization in China: (1) future levels of productivity of farming, industry and services; (2) changes in the socio-economic function of the collective village; and (3) the migration policies. The capability of small towns to absorb surplus labor on farm through generating local job opportunities may slow down the urbanization pace in China. In the next 20 years, however, the urban population is expected to grow continuously, particularly among small and medium-sized cities.

FARM DEPENDENCE AND POPULATION CHANGE

Thus far, the chapter has focused on the urbanization trends in China and shown how urbanization has been highly influenced by government policies through controlling internal migration. In the this section, the chapter moves to a discussion of another important factor – farm dependence – and addresses how government policies have influenced rural–urban population distribution through farm dependence.

Farm dependence has been considered as an important factor that influences the size of rural population. Farm dependence is defined as the extent to which population in an area depends on agricultural activities. A negative relationship between farm dependence and population change has been well documented in the literature based on studying Western countries, especially during the post-mechanization era (Albrecht 1993, 1986; White 2008). The literature shows that in the US, for instance, it coincided with farm mechanization and industrialization. Regions with high farm dependence have generally experienced more population loss and lower population growth rates than low-farm-dependent regions. Below, I review major theoretical explanations of farm dependence and population change based on the context of Western countries and then move to a discussion of the case in the Chinese society. The classical theories to be reviewed are the farming–manufacturing thesis, mechanization and technological innovation theory, and the human ecological approach.

Farming–Manufacturing Complex Thesis

The first theory to be discussed here is the farming–manufacturing complex thesis. The main argument of this theory is that alternative employment opportunities in the industrial sector moderate the influence of farm dependence on population change. Friedman's (1978) research provided a good example of how competitive production has reduced family labor on farms in the United States and Great Britain. Page and Walker (1991) also observed the mutually interdependent and competing nature between agriculture and manufacturing in the United States. White (2008) further proposed two scenarios explaining the mechanism of farm dependence and population change when non-farm economic alternative exists. First, farm dependence is influenced by wage labor markets. When family farms are able to reproduce themselves 'at a rate on par with wage labor', then the industrial sector is less likely to draw labor away from farms (White 2008, p. 366). However, when farm income is less than wage labor, people are more likely to switch to the industrial sector though the total population may remain stable. Second, the mutual dependency between agriculture and manufacturing leads to population growth on farms due to the contribution of manufacturing to household income. In this situation, population growth is maintained and is positively moderated by manufacturing. White (2008) argued that the positive association between farm dependence and population change should occur prior to mechanization, and the negative relationship turns out to be the case after mechanization.

In the case of China, it is believed that rural industrialization was first put forward in the late 1950s following the establishment of the people's commune system and the Great Leap Forward (GLF) movement (Zhang 1999). With the GLF turning out to be a failure in the early 1960s, most rural industries were shut down so that communes could devote their effort to farming. By the end of 1960s and the early 1970s, rural enterprises operated by people's communes and production brigades began to be revived. The revival of commune and brigade enterprises (CBEs) was in response to the government's call for agricultural mechanization and modernization to raise agricultural productivity. The promotion of rural enterprises was then plagued during the Cultural Revolution when production and exchange of commodities by non-state enterprises were largely banned. It was not until the late 1970s when township and village enterprises began to develop again. A gradual shift of agricultural processing from urban state-owned enterprises to rural CBEs was encouraged. Zhang (1999) argued that the success of agricultural reforms in the late 1970s and the early 1980s in fact acted as a precursor to the development of rural industry. Since then, rural enterprises have become 'a new force suddenly coming to the force' of China's roaring economy (Zhang 1999, p. 86). Among many regions that had booming farm enterprises, Jiangsu province served as an example of a rapid growth of rural enterprises in China. The regional disparity has always been associated with rural industrialization. Due to the lack of infrastructure and fertile farm land, rural enterprise development in China's hinterland has long been lagging behind the coastal region (Naughton 2007).

Regarding the association between manufacturing and farm population change, one body of research highlighted a negative association between the existence of industrial sectors outside of agriculture and rural population growth (Chan and Zhang 1999; Leeming 1985; Meisner 1999). It is observed that as part of the first Five-Year Plan (1953–1957), millions of peasants were recruited by burgeoning state industrial enterprises in urban areas. Many rural people moved without restriction to look for jobs in urban areas, which caused a rural population loss (Meisner 1999). To restrain this rapid population flux, the household registration (*hukou*) system was established in 1955 to divide the population into agricultural and non-agricultural as a basis for restricting further rural-to-urban migration and for returning rural migrants to the countryside (Wu and Treiman 2004). The *hukou* regulations became even more stringent in the aftermath of the Great Leap Forward (1958–1960). As a result, a return migration of 18 million people to villages occurred between 1961 and 1963 (Chan 1994). China's *hukou* system was able initially to control rural-to-urban migration. Since the economic reform started in the late 1970s, informal migration (change of residence without a change in *hukou* status) became somewhat easier. More and more private- or foreign-owned industrial sectors emerged in China. Those industrial sectors do not require the *hukou* status of employees at the destination places, which boosted population movement from countryside to urban areas (Liang and White 1996). The lax administrative control resulted in a large floating population of urban migrants who lack the entitlements of permanent residents, which has caused a population loss in rural areas (Solinger 1999).

Another group of studies focuses on examining the influence of rural enterprises and industries inside of farms on farm population change. The most well-known case is the study conducted by Xiaotong Fei, a pioneer researcher on rural small town development. He conducted research on Jiangchun village in Jiangsu province (Fei 1989) and showed that industrial enterprises in rural areas created job opportunities on farms, which absorbed surplus farm laborers. Thus, rural enterprises positively influence population growth in the countryside in China and have prevented over-population in large and medium-sized cities. Goldstein et al.'s (1991) research corroborated Fei's research. They studied rural industrialization and migration in Hubei province and found that rural enterprises had the effect of gradually creating a non-agricultural labor force, which retards to some extent the flow of rural laborers into the cities. Results of some more recent studies seemed to challenge Fei's argument of a positive association between industrial enterprises and farm population growth. For instance, Yang's (1996) research on several rural regions in Zhejiang province demonstrated that regions with well-developed rural enterprises in fact experienced the most out-migration, which resulted in a rural population loss. Liang and White's (1997) research cast further doubt on the efficiency of rural enterprises absorbing peasants on farms. They found that China's rural enterprises are in fact likely to increase interprovincial migration though they tend to reduce intraprovincial migration. Liang and White contended that rural enterprises seem to absorb only those who have moving potential within rather than between provinces in China. If this is the case, then rural enterprises will not be effective in absorbing migrants who intend to move between provinces. A piece by Liang et al. (2002) examined the impact of rural industrialization on migration using data from the 1990 China Population Census. They found that rural industrialization does not have a statistically significant impact on the probability of either intraprovincial or interprovincial migration.

In sum, it seems to be the case that the existence of industrial enterprises outside farms results in a rural population loss. However, mixed findings are documented in terms of the influence of rural industrialization on rural population change. Such a relationship tends to change over time and vary by region. These results imply that the mechanism behind Chinese rural industrialization and population change may not be as simple as the scenarios proposed by Western scholars.

Mechanization and Technological Innovation Theory

The second theory is the mechanization and technological innovation theory. This theory explains the relationship between agriculture and population dynamics from the changing pattern of technology during the 'pre-mechanization' and 'post-mechanization' periods. According to the mechanization thesis, population growth on farms during the pre-mechanization period in Western countries, including in the US, was due to a booming agricultural industry (farming industry) promoted by technological innovations. This booming farming industry due to farm mechanization increased the demand for labor, which led to a population growth on farms. During the post-mechanization period, mechanization and technological innovations again played a role in shaping population distribution. During this period, however, new technological innovations resulted in less demand for farm labor, which eventually caused the farm population to decrease.

Although farm mechanization in the United States is believed to have begun far before 1940 (Cochrane 1993), this year is often considered as the landmark of post-mechanization because rapid improvements and adoption of machines occurred after this year. A decline of farm population has been observed in the US since 1940, which is caused partly by farm mechanization and technological innovations. For example, Albrecht's (1986, 1993) research on population change in the Great Plains in the US showed a consistent negative association between the percentage of population employed in farming and county population growth in the Great Plains after World War II. He demonstrated that this negative relationship continued even during the considerable population turnaround of the 1970s. Although White's (2008) recent research slightly altered the mechanization thesis, her results to a large extent echoed Albrecht's findings. Researchers also showed that in the United States, non-metropolitan areas with a higher level of farm dependence are likely to experience a lower population growth rate (Johnson 1989; Johnson and Fuguitt 2000). These findings provided evidence to support the argument of the mechanization and technological innovation theory that during the post-mechanization period, farm population has declined partially due to new technological innovations that reduced demand for farm labor.

In China, farming has long been considered as a labor-intensive activity and has been largely based on traditional technology. According to Tam (1985), China's agricultural mechanization did not start until the early 1950s after the land reform movement. Hsu (1979) has proposed several phases to describe agricultural mechanization in China. The first phase started in the early 1950s, Mao and Liu Shaoqi were influenced by the

Soviet experience of collectivization and believed that big tractors were a symbol of modern agriculture. Although they attempted to improve agricultural mechanization, total agricultural output did not increase significantly due to the absence of new agricultural inputs, such as chemical fertilizer and better seeds. In the mid-1950s, state economic planner Bo-I-bo began to emphasize improving traditional farm implements. Bo argued that mechanization was not practical because mechanization frees labor, which was abundant in China. Bo contended that taking measures to increase crop yields per unit of land was more appropriate. The farm implement program, nevertheless, did not completely succeed due to the fact that the much-publicized double-wheel double-share plows were unsuitable for use in the south (Kang 1970). The next phase began when the GLF movement was launched in 1958. Farm labor poured into water conservation projects and backyard furnaces, which created widespread labor shortages on farms. As a consequence, the progress of agricultural mechanization was 'slower than expected' (Hsu 1979, p. 438). The failure of the GLP had further hindered the progress of agricultural mechanization. Many tractors were transferred from the communes to the tractor stations. The shortage of steel, electric power, coal and gasoline also handicapped agricultural mechanization. During 1964 to 1965, the emphasis on mechanization shifted to small walking tractors (in other words, power tiller or hand-guided tractors). This emphasis was carried on to the period from 1966 to 1976. Tam (1985) stated that though a large-scale adoption of modern farm technology (big tractors and adopting walking tractors) appeared in China, it was not until the convention of China's Fourth National People's Congress in 1975 that the mechanization of agriculture became the focus of China's agricultural development, and it made rapid progress since then. Beginning in 1977, under the leadership of Deng Xiaoping, agricultural mechanization was given high priority as the basis of agricultural modernization. From the late 1970s until now, agricultural mechanization has experienced fast progress. Advanced mechanized production methods are replacing the traditional manual, backward modes of production. The central government allocated 13 billion yuan (about $2 billion) in subsidies for agricultural machinery purchases in 2009. Various policies have also been launched to advance agricultural mechanization.

With regard to the association between farm mechanization and population change, Butler (1978, p. 14) indicated that like other Western countries, mechanization in China did increase 'labor power and frees it for other uses'. This may have caused population changes in rural China. The effect of mechanization on population dynamics in China, however, is believed to be less significant as compared to the effect of political forces. As stated earlier, the shortages of farm labor during the Great Leap Forward movement in the early 1950s was more responsive to Mao's political policies than to farm mechanization (Chan 1992). During the Cultural Revolution (1966–1976) and the early 1980s, the political influence on population change was also greater than that of farm mechanization. A large number of college students and intellectuals were sent down to rural China during the Cultural Revolution. The subsequent return migration of students and intellectuals to their original urban residences was a consequence of policy modification as well. Thus, during the 1950s to the early 1980s, the role of farm mechanization in shaping Chinese population change was largely surpassed by political forces.

Since the mid-1980s, Chinese population trends have begun to be more responsive to market needs than to policy regulations. This shift was due to a couple of reasons. First, farm mechanization had created a large amount of surplus rural labor in China in the 1980s (Chan and Zhang 1999; Ma and Lin 1993; Wu 1994; Zhao 1999). Second, China experienced a dramatic social system transition from a planned economy to a market-oriented economy. The social system transition and the less restrictive control of the *Hukou* registration system allowed the rural population to move more 'freely' than before. Consequently, a significant amount of the rural population composed a huge migration stream moving from the countryside to towns and cities as a response to market needs, which causes a population loss in high-farm-dependent areas.

Overall, findings of previous research regarding farm mechanization and Chinese population change can be summarized as follows. From the 1950s and the early 1980s, political forces have significantly influenced the distribution of population in China. The effect of political force outweighs the effect of farm mechanization on farm population change. Thus, farm mechanization did not show a strong effect on population change in China as it did in Western industrialized countries. Since the mid-1980s, a positive correlation between farm mechanization and out-migration has occurred in the Chinese society, which leads to a potential farm population loss. Such a fact generally supports the mechanization thesis that technological innovation causes a rural population decline. In recent years, consolidation of village farmland has occurred in many coastal areas. Meanwhile, some rural regions in coastal areas have also imported labor from outside the areas, including outside the province, to farm the land. However, rural out-migration still surpasses in-migration by importing labor elsewhere in most rural areas.

Human Ecological Approach

The third theoretical approach is the human ecological theory. Mechanization theory can be considered as drawn from human ecological theory because technological development is one of the four rubrics of the human ecological approach. Human ecological theory argues that there are four dimensions (rubrics) of the ecosystem: population, organization, environment and technology (POET). From the perspective of sociological human ecology, population change is the major mechanism of social change and adaptability for human populations. Human populations redistribute themselves so to approach an equilibrium between their overall size and the surrounding ecosystem which includes environment, organization and technology. These factors determine the life chances available to population. Among the four rubrics of the human ecological system, migration is viewed as the principal mechanism for effecting this adjustment (Poston and Frisbie 2005).

The interrelationships among and between these four dimensions inform one's understanding of population change patterns, as follows: all populations must necessarily adapt to their environments, and these adaptations vary among populations on the basis of their social and sustenance organization, their technology, and the size, composition and distribution of their population. The environment is comprised of both social and physical factors that tend to set constraints on the population and the form and characteristics of its organization. The technology that the population has at its disposal sets the boundaries for the form and type of environmental adaptation the population may assume. These may well change, however, as new and/or different technologies are introduced, allowing its relationship with the environment to change, and resulting also in changes or adjustments in the population's organization, and in its population size (Hawley 1950).

The efficiency of the human ecological theory in explaining population change in the US has been supported by multiple empirical studies (Micklin and Poston 1997; Poston et al. 2009; Sly and Tayman 1977). Environment and organization have been proved to play decisive roles in determining population sizes. Research on the Great Plains and the twentieth-century agricultural transition concentrates primarily on technological innovations, accompanied with organizational changes in shaping farm population growth. Friedman's (1978) research implies a negative impact of technology on farm population growth. He claims that the adoption of farm technology by the family farm is a central source for successful competition. Mechanization characterized by adopting new technology makes competitive production possible for family farms by reducing labor input but at the same time maintaining acreage expansion. In this sense, new technology affects farm population growth negatively.

In the case of China, prior research has shown the power of human ecological theory in explaining population mobility. For instance, through exploring the influence of human ecological factors on population change in the form of migration streams among 31 provinces during 1995 to 2000, Poston and Zhang (2008) showed that the human ecological model has a strong capability for explaining population mobility in China. The population, organizational, environmental as well as technological factors all played a role in determining migration. Particularly, coastal provinces with relatively lower percentages of farm population and greater foreign investments attracted a considerable number of migrants from provinces in the North and the West with higher levels of farm dependence. These findings suggest that high farm dependence may result in a lower population growth rate due to out-migration.

In sum, theories presented in most previous analyses are largely based on the social context of Western industrialized countries. The association between farm dependence and population change in less developed regions, such as China, has rarely been explored. Most studies that examine population change in China have focused mainly on rural-to-urban migration (Li 1996; Liang and White 1997; Wu 1994; Yang 1996). The dynamic between farm dependence and overall population change in highly farm-dependent areas remains overlooked. The capacity of existing theories in explaining population change in high-farm-dependent areas in less industrialized regions, such as China, has also largely eluded researchers. In order to fill such voids, Zhang (2011) studied the association between farm dependence and rural population change in 31 provinces from 1953 to 2000 and in over 500 counties of selected provinces (Shandong, Henan, Hunan, Sichuan, Guizhou and Shaanxi) from 2000 to 2005. These provinces were selected because they are considered as major agricultural provinces in China. Zhang's (2011) research showed that by year 2000, the national level of agricultural population was 75.3 percent. The percentages of population engaged in agriculture in year 2000 in the selected provinces were 79.1 percent, 83.1 percent, 80.4 percent, 81.6 percent, 85.2 percent and 77.9 percent, respectively. In Zhang's (2011) study, 'rural population' was defined as people who live in or have characteristics of farming or country life. 'Agricultural population' refers to people who are related to promoting agriculture or farming (http://wordnetweb.princeton.edu/perl/webwn?s= agricultural). The definition of 'rural population' is largely based on the residence of the population who reside on farms, whereas the definition of 'agricultural population' is according to the agricultural occupation of the population. Zhang's (2011) research demonstrated that at the provincial level, the Chinese population had a dramatic increase during the 1953–1964 and 1964–1982 periods. On average, the 31 provinces had a total population increase rate of 37.1 percent and 47.7 percent, respectively, during the two time frames. It is equivalent to an average annual increase rate of 3.4 percent and 6.0 percent, respectively. From 1953 to 1964, the fastest population growth occurred in large cities, especially Beijing, Shanghai and Tianjin. Beijing had the highest population growth rate of 173.4 percent and Anhui had the lowest population growth rate of 3.0 percent. From 1964 to 1982, the population growth pattern seemed to be reversed. Provinces in the North and the West with higher levels of farm dependence showed faster population growth rates than those more urbanized provinces. Shanghai, one of the most urbanized subregions in China, experienced the lowest population growth rate of 9.6 percent. According to Zhang (2011), such a reverse pattern could be due to Mao's 'sending down' policy that encouraged youths and intellectuals to move to rural areas. Since 1982, provincial population growth rates slowed down considerably with less variation among provinces. Municipalities and coastal provinces again experienced faster population growth than other provinces, with Beijing showing the highest population growth rate (13.4 percent) during 2000–2005 among the 31 provinces. Since 1982, population growth has slowed down with an average annual increase rate below 2 percent.

In terms of the percentage of rural population among provinces of China, Zhang (2011) found that, on average, provinces in China generally have had high levels of farm dependence. In 1953, 86.7 percent of the Chinese population was rural. The percentage of rural population remained high until the year 2000 when about 75 percent of China's population resided on farms. The year 2005 seems to represent a milestone of Chinese urban–rural population distribution: for the first time, around 50 percent of the whole nation's population resided in cities. Zhang's (2011) study also examined 589 counties that are considered as counties with high levels of farm dependence. Zhang claimed that the general trends of population growth in the counties she studied were either growing or remaining stable during the 1995–2000 period. As far as the distribution of farm population in 589 counties studied is concerned, 87.6 percent of county population resided on farms by the year 2000. This percentage is higher than the average national percentage of 71.9 percent mainly because the counties studied are chosen from several primary agricultural provinces that contain higher percentages of rural population.

By operationalizing the three major theories explaining farm population change to various variables predicting population change, Zhang (2011) found that those theories were not supported by the empirical evidence from China. A great deal of regional variation was shown in the dynamics between farm dependence and population change as well as the association between mechanization, industrial alternatives, human ecological factors and population change. In general, change in farm dependence rather than level of farm dependence tended to be a much better predictor of county population growth during the studied period. This suggested that if the demographic theory on farm dependence and population change can be modified to consider change in farm dependence rather than level of farm dependence, the theory would work better when predicting Chinese population change. The findings also provided evidence that the existing sociological theories on population change need to be revised when being applied to less developed countries, such as China.

CONCLUSION

This chapter has focused on discussing the urbanization process in China during Mao and post-Mao eras and how overall population change is influenced by farm dependence at both provincial and county levels. The chapter emphasizes that urbanization in China has been heavily influenced by policies of the central government and the household registration system that has served as an internal passport regulating population mobility inside of China. As a consequence, the urbanization process in China is considered as a unique model that is significantly different from other industrialized or less developed nations.

Regarding rural population change and farm dependence, the chapter has reviewed the existing theories and empirical analyses on farm dependence and population change and pointed out that farm dependence can be an important factor that determines rural population change and the distribution of rural and urban population. In the social context of China, a negative correlation between farm dependence and population change suggested by previous literature is overly simplistic and requires re-examination. Before the year 2000, political forces may well explain provincial population change in China. Since the year 2000, rural population change in China is more 'free' of political influences. Though farm dependence plays a role in determining rural population change, results from prior literature (for instance, Zhang's research) only showed a negative influence of farm dependence on population change in the Central and Southern counties. In Eastern and Southwestern provinces, high farm dependence was found to lead to a faster population growth. The Northwestern provinces did not demonstrate any statistically significant correlation between farm dependence and population change. These findings suggest that urbanization in China could either positively or negatively influence population growth depending upon regional variation. In addition, traditional demographic theory of urbanization explains the effect of urbanization on population change by relying on considering the effects of the three demographic processes. Zhang's (2011) research, however, has challenged this statement by showing the effect of urbanization on population change remains significant even after the three demographic processes are controlled. This finding implies that urbanization itself may have a significant influence on population size, which is independent of the three demographic processes.

Regional variation needs to be considered when understanding population change caused by farm dependence. The existing theories on farm population change need to be revised when they are applied to less developed countries, such as China. The chapter highlights the regional variation and differentials in the Chinese society. Kueh (1989) has argued that the disparity between coastal and interior regions already existed in the 1950s. Though Mao stressed the need to correct industry's coastal bias and was in favor of the interior areas, the uneven development pattern remained and became more significant in the post-Mao era. Yang (1990) initiated the 'uneven development strategy' to describe the pattern of China's regional development (Yang 1990, p. 230). This chapter echoes Kueh and Yang's statements and suggests that the uneven development pattern of Chinese regions may be the key that explains the urbanization process as well as population change in China.

NOTE

1.   Part of the information in this chapter is drawn from Zhang (2011).

REFERENCES

Albrecht, D.E. (1986), 'Agricultural dependence and the population turnaround: evidence from the Great Plains', *Journal of the Community Development Society*, 17, 1–15.
Albrecht, D.E. (1993), 'The renewal of population loss in the nonmetropolitan Great Plains', *Rural Sociology*, 58, 233–46.
Ashton, B., K. Hill, A. Piazza and R. Zeitz (1984), 'Famine in China: 1958–61', *Population and Development Review*, 10, 613–45.
Butler, Steven (1978), *Agricultural Mechanization in China: the Administrative Impact*, New York: Columbia University Press.
Chan, K.W. (1992), 'Post-1949 urbanization trends and policies: an overview', in G.E. Guldin (ed.), *Urbanizing China*, New York: Greenwood Press, pp. 41–65.
Chan, K.W. (1994), *Cities with Invisible Walls*, Hong Kong: Oxford University Press.
Chan, K.W. and L. Zhang (1999), 'The *Hukou* system and rural–urban migration in China: processes and changes', *China Quarterly*, 160, 818–55.
Cochrane, W.W. (1993), *The Development of American Agriculture: A Historical Analysis*, Minneapolis, MN: University of Minnesota Press.

Fei, Xiaotong (1989), *Rural Development in China: Prospect and Retrospect*. Chicago, IL: University of Chicago Press.

Friedman, H. (1978), 'World market, state, and family farm: social bases of household production in the era of wage labor', *Comparative Studies in Society and History*, 20, 545–86.

Goldstein, Sidney and Alice Goldstein (1990), 'Town and city: new directions in Chinese urbanization', in R. Kwok, W.L. Yin-Wang, A. Parish, Gar-On Yeh and X. Xu (eds), *Chinese Urban Reform*, London: M.E. Sharpe, pp. 17–44.

Goldstein, Alice, Sidney Goldstein and Shengzu Gu (1991), 'Rural industrialization and migration in the People's Republic of China', *Social Science History*, 15, 289–314.

Hawley, A.H. (1950), *Human Ecology: A Theory of Community Structure*, New York: Ronald Press.

Hsu, Robert C. (1979), 'Agricultural mechanization in China: policies, problems, and prospects', *Asian Survey*, 19, 436–49.

Johnson, K.M. (1989), 'Recent population redistribution trends in nonmetropolitan America', *Rural Sociology*, 54, 301–26.

Johnson, K.M. and G.V. Fuguitt (2000), 'Continuity and change in rural migration patterns, 1950–1995', *Rural Sociology*, 65, 27–49.

Kueh, Y.Y. (1989), 'The Maoist legacy and China's new industrialization strategy', *China Quarterly*, 119, 420–47.

Leeming, Frank (1985), 'Chinese industry-management systems and regional structures', *Transactions of the Institute of British Geographers*, 10, 413–26.

Li, Cheng (1996), 'Surplus rural laborers and internal migration in China: current status and future prospects', *Asian Survey*, 36, 1122–45.

Liang, Z. and M.J. White (1996), 'Internal migration in China, 1950–1988', *Demography*, 33, 375–84.

Liang, Z. and M.J. White (1997), 'Market transition, government policies, and interprovincial migration in China: 1983–88', *Economic Development and Cultural Change*, 45, 321–39.

Liang, Zai (2001), 'The age of migration in China', *Population and Development Review*, 27, 499–524.

Liang, Zai, Yiu Por Chen and Yanmin Gu (2002), 'Rural industrialization and internal migration in China', *Rural Industrialization and Migration*, 39, 2175–87.

Liang, Zai, Hy Van Luong and Yiu Por (Vincent) Chen (2008), 'Urbanization in China in the 1990s: patterns and regional variations', in J.R. Logan (ed.), *Urban China in Transition*, New York: Blackwell Publishing, pp. 203–25.

Ma, Laurence J.C. and Chusheng Lin (1993), 'Development of towns in China: a case study of Guangdong Province', *Population and Development Review*, 19, 583–606.

Meisner, M. (1999), *Mao's China and After: A History of the People's Republic*, New York: Free Press.

Micklin, Michael and Dudley L. Poston (eds) (1997), *Continuities in Sociological Human Ecology*, New York: Plenum Press.

Naughton, Barry (2007), *The Chinese Economy: Transitions and Growth*, Cambridge, MA: MIT Press.

Page, B and R. Walker (1991), 'From settlement to Fordism: the agro-industrial revolution in the American Midwest', *Economic Geography*, 67, 281–315.

Poston, D.L. and W.P. Frisbie (2005), 'Ecological demography', in D.L. Poston and M. Micklin (eds), *Handbook of Population*, New York: Springer Publishers, pp. 601–24.

Poston, D.L. and Li Zhang (2008), 'Ecological analyses of permanent and temporary migration streams in China in the 1990s', *Population Research and Policy Review*, 27, 689–712.

Poston, Dudley L. Jr., Li Zhang, David Gotcher and Yuan Gu (2009), 'The effect of climate on migration: United States, 1995–2000', *Social Science Research*, 38, 743–53.

Preston, Samuel H. (1979), 'Urban growth in developing countries: a demographic appraisal', *Population and Development Review*, 5, 195–216.

Sly, David and Jeff Tayman (1977), 'Ecological approach to migration reexamined', *American Sociological Review*, 42, 783–95.

Solinger, D.J. (1999), *Contesting Citizenship in Urban China: Peasant Migrants, the State, and the Logic of Market*, Berkeley, CA: University of California Press.

Tam, On Kit (1985), *China's Agricultural Modernization: the Socialist Mechanization Scheme*, Sydney: Croom Helm.

Vermeer, Eduard B. (2006), 'Demographic dimensions of China's development', *Population and Development Review*, 32, 115–44.

White, Katherine J. Curtis (2008), 'Population change and farm dependence: temporal and spatial variation in the U.S. Great Plains, 1900–2000', *Demography*, 45, 363–86.

Wu, Harry Xiaoying (1994), 'Rural to urban migration in the People's Republic of China', *China Quarterly*, 139, 669–98.

Wu, Xiaogang and Donald J. Treiman (2004), 'The household registration system and social stratification in China: 1955–1996', *Demography*, 41, 363–84.

Yang, Dali (1990), 'Patterns of China's regional development strategy', *China Quarterly*, 122, 230–57.

Yang, Xiushi (1994), 'Urban temporary out-migration under economic reforms: who moves and for what reasons?' *Population Research and Policy Review*, 13, 83–100.

Yang, Xiushi (1996), 'Economic reforms and spatial mobility', in A. Goldstein and F. Wang (eds), *China: The Many Facets of Demographic Change*, Boulder, CO: Westview Press, pp. 167–85.

Zhang, Li (2011), 'Farm dependence and population change in China', *Population Research and Policy Review*, 30, 751–79.

Zhang, Zhihong (1999), 'Rural industrialization in China: from backyard furnaces to township and village enterprises', *East Asia*, 17, 61–89.

Zhao, Yaohui (1999), 'Leaving the countryside: rural-to-urban migration decisions in China', *American Economic Review*, 89, 281–6.

16. Work, mobility and livelihoods in a changing rural Latin America
Michael L. Dougherty[1]

INTRODUCTION

Rural Latin America is made up of a diverse set of places, but global economic forces have generated a great deal of convergence among rural places in Latin America over the past two decades. The traditional Latin American peasantry – smallholder farmers engaged in agriculture for subsistence and limited marketization – is giving way to a savvy proletariat with increasingly diverse sources of income and complex linkages to national, regional and transnational economic and social networks. The transformation of the Latin American peasantry is taking place in three principal arenas. The first of these is the influx of investment capital in extractive industries since 1990 and the economic development and social resistance that this has engendered. The second is the growth in both South–South and South–North migration and the increasing importance of remittance income for rural livelihoods. Third, deepening transnational social linkages have facilitated the emergence of hybrid social movements that mobilize identity politics and the international legal system to defend rural livelihoods in new ways. Agriculture remains important for rural livelihoods in Latin America, but mobility and growing economic dynamism are bringing about transformations in the rural landscape that have implications for rural livelihoods. This chapter examines these trends and engages with two important questions: (1) Are rural peoples in Latin America experiencing improved quality of life as a result of these transformations? and (2) What are the policy implications and lessons of these trends?

In Latin America, despite increasing urbanization, rural development issues remain salient. In contrast to the United States, where approximately 20 percent of the population resides in rural regions, in Latin America the majority of citizens continue to live in rural areas. That said, Latin America is rapidly urbanizing, and the World Bank projects that by 2020 the continent will be predominantly urban (World Bank 2008). Reversing long-standing trends, in recent years, poverty has been increasing more quickly in urban areas than in rural areas in Latin America (World Bank

2008). However, this has more to do with unchecked urban expansion than with meaningful poverty alleviation in rural regions. Despite these shifts, residents of rural regions continue to have lower development indicators such as per capita income and educational attainment than their urban counterparts. Further, by virtue of the relative isolation of rural places, rural residents lack the access to the resources of upward mobility that urban citizens possess. Finally, the rural landscape – in both physical and social terms – has been transformed over the past two decades by rapid and expansive urban growth. On the one hand, urban growth has driven metropolitan areas outward into previously rural zones, thus transforming the landscape. On the other hand, urbanization serves as a draw for emigration from rural areas into urban environments, conferring a 'brain drain' on rural areas but also generating significant remittance income for rural communities. In sum, economic and demographic trends have shifted the focus of development studies from rural to urban environments; yet rural underdevelopment remains an urgent issue.

RURAL LIFE AND RURAL LIVELIHOODS IN LATIN AMERICA

This chapter examines the transformations in the social landscape of rural Latin America from a livelihoods perspective. That is, this chapter is predominantly concerned with what these changes mean for the quality of life and the sources of livelihood available to residents of rural areas.

Latin America became deeply integrated into the global economy over the decade of the 1990s. Globalization led to economic development in many urban areas, but rural people have been largely left out of these gains from market expansion. Further, government social programs are more difficult and more expensive to execute in remote hinterlands, leaving many rural communities out of the state social safety net. For these reasons, many poor rural families must assemble a living from piecemeal, often informal, strategies that are rooted in local social networks and moral economy effects. These creative approaches to survival are referred to as livelihood strategies, and many scholars find that a livelihood strategies framework is a useful way of conceptualizing rural development.

In contrast to the conventional economic understanding of rural development in which development is a function of per capita income, the livelihoods framework is a broader, more holistic way to conceptualize rural development. The livelihoods framework favors a greater focus on the social aspects of development over the economic aspects, and attributes the agency and power of survival to rural citizens themselves (Bebbington

1999). Livelihoods themselves include a diverse portfolio of assets – both individual and collective – including natural resources, social networks, legal rights, cultural knowledge and a variety of other resources that complement cash income (Blaikie et al. 1994; Zoomers 2001). Livelihood strategies refer to the activities undertaken to secure access to these assets, secure well-being and cope with shocks (Hernandez-Juarez 2009; Valdivia and Gilles 2001).

As the notion of sustainability and sustainable development became the predominant environmental discourse in the 1990s, rural development scholars began to integrate discussions of livelihood strategies and sustainability into the concept of sustainable livelihoods. The concept of 'sustainable livelihoods' is often mobilized as an alternative to 'sustainable development', which is seen as being uncritical of economic growth (Lahiri-Dutt 2011). A livelihood is considered sustainable when it is resilient in the face of economic shocks, and individuals can increase their asset pools without drawing down the natural resource base disproportionately (Carney 1998).

Because the livelihood strategies framework gives equal weight to domestic activities and cash income-generating activities, it has been lauded for its holism and for largely doing away with gender hierarchies by treating men's and women's work equally. However, the livelihood strategies framework has also received criticism for reproducing neoliberal tendencies to exonerate the state from its responsibility to its rural citizens. In sum, conceiving of rural development as an arrangement of assets and a bundle of livelihood strategies highlights the fact that development is much more than the expansion of market opportunities and per capita income.

In Latin America, rural citizens have historically been peasant farmers that derive the majority, if not the entirety, of their livelihoods from agricultural production for household consumption. Over the past several decades, and more intensively since the 1990s, this familiar pattern has undergone major shifts. Today's rural citizens are no longer peasants. Rather, they form a semi-proletarian class in which peasant agriculture remains important, but constitutes a minority of their sources of livelihood (Brass 2003; Kay 2000; Moyo and Yeros 2005). Instead, contract agriculture on large, foreign-owned plantations for minimum wage, together with contract work in petroleum fields and gold mines, form the basis of the rural economy. Land for peasant agriculture has become increasingly scarce and threatened, which has led to the formation of massive and vociferous social movements in rural Latin America. Finally, these transformations have led many rural residents to emigrate away from their homelands toward cities in their own and other countries to work, and the money sent back – remittance income – has become a centerpiece of rural livelihoods in the new rural Latin America. The following sections will deal with these trends in greater detail.

EXTRACTIVE INDUSTRIES IN RURAL LATIN AMERICA: IMPLICATIONS FOR RURAL LIVELIHOODS

Can I tell you a story that, may he rest in peace, my father used to tell? One time, in Chiapas, it was said that they totally ran out of corn, and there was just nothing. The men that owned the plantation, it was said they had a huge package of money. So one finquero said to the other, money we have, but hunger is a fire. What do you make of that?

This evocative statement, 'hunger is a fire', comes from a Mexican saying, 'hunger is a fire but food is fresh,' meaning that only food – not currency – can satiate hunger. This quotation, from a peasant woman in the Western Highlands of Guatemala, was in response to my questioning about her reasons for opposing mineral development in her community. She was making the point that the cash income from mineral development will mean very little if it has a negative effect on agricultural productivity through the conversion of agricultural land, contaminating water sources or diminishing soil quality. This sense of the trade-offs that come from mineral development – increased cash income but diminished agricultural productivity – embodies the current debate in rural Latin America regarding the changing relevance of peasant agriculture in rural community development (Moyo and Yeros 2005).

Some scholars in the Marxian tradition see the entry of multinational extractive firms into agrarian zones of Latin America over the past decade as a potentially fruitful way to incorporate peasant agrarian communities into the circuit of capital as long as trade unionism and strong state regulation are in place – the conversion of peasants into a rural proletariat. In contrast, other leftist scholars, coming primarily from liberal traditions of identity politics and human rights, favor the re-peasantization of rural residents. They argue, as has the peasant woman quoted above, that there is a dignity and quality of life in peasant livelihoods and any economic relationship with outside capitalists will be inherently exploitative. This is a simplification. Rural peoples in Latin America have been semi-proletarianized for several decades at least, but the dramatic increase in extractive activity in rural Latin America over the past 20 years has intensified the more obvious, in situ forms of consolidating the rural proletariat. The exponential growth of mining and energy extraction has come to dominate discussions around rural livelihoods in Latin America since the early 2000s.

Starting in the 1970s, but ramping up dramatically in the 1990s, investment capital in mining began to move out of the few, select national economies that traditionally produced the majority of the world's industrial and precious metals – the United States, Canada, Australia and South Africa – and began to find its way into previously unmined regions of the developing world (Bridge 2004). Since the 1990s, along with sub-Saharan Africa, South East Asia and Central Asia, Latin America has become a major recipient of mining investment. Many countries of Latin America have experienced an uptick in mining activity over the past two decades. Chile, Argentina, Brazil, Colombia, Ecuador and Guyana have all hosted new mineral concessions. However, a great deal of this investment has been in Central America and the Andes – some of the poorest, most vulnerable and most heavily indigenous regions of the continent. In these marginal areas, significant social mobilization against mining and in defense of indigenous rights and land access has emerged in recent years.

Four chief factors help to explain this movement of mineral capital away from traditional mining countries and into the developing world. Firstly, technological innovations in extraction and milling of metallic ores have allowed mining companies to mine lower-grade deposits more profitably. This has effectively opened up vast new mineral frontiers to mining that had once been considered uneconomic, allowing exploration to cover a much larger swathe of the globe. Secondly, many of the industrial-scale metal deposits in the traditional mining economies have past their peak production levels, and returns to production in these places diminish further every year. Miners and investors have seen the writing on the wall with respect to peak reserves, and this recognition has fed a lot of the innovation driving the expanded geographic scope of exploration. Relatedly, the politics of scarcity has driven state–private alliances to seek geostrategic ownership of mineral and fuel reserves in developing countries (Bunker and Ciccantell 2005; Donnelly and Ford 2008). Thirdly, since the 1990s most countries in the developing world have sought to increase their economic integration with the global economy. They have done this largely through policies that facilitate trade with other countries and incentivize foreign direct investment in their economies. Policies of this nature – what has come to be labeled 'neoliberalism' – have created more welcoming political environments for mining companies to set up shop in these countries. Finally, significant urban growth over the past two decades in Brazil, Russia, India, China and elsewhere has increased demand for industrial metals and fossil fuels, further incentivizing these industries to locate new, profitable zones of mineralization.

All of these trends taken together have brought about a shift in the global mining industry toward investment in the developing world and practices that increasingly elicit resistance from host community residents (Dougherty 2011). The result has been that mining investment in Latin America has tripled since the year 2000, and in specific target countries such as Guatemala, investment has increased by as much as 1000 percent. All of this has had a significant impact on rural livelihoods in Latin America. The proliferation of mining activity in rural Latin America has transformed the economic, social and biophysical landscape in host communities in significant ways.

Mining has transformed historically agrarian regions of rural Latin America into extractive communities, providing sharp spikes of cash income for the thousands of short-term contract workers hired from surrounding hamlets. In the long run, however, the cash income and the learning spillovers that mining generates do not contribute meaningfully to economic development in these places. Further, the episodic influxes of income to mine contractors can create social divisions that inhibit social capital formation and have deleterious long-term social and economic impacts (Bury 2004). Additionally, royalties and taxes that mineral firms pay into municipal coffers can allow local governments to finance development programs, but also have the effect of inundating municipal governments with more income than they have the capacity to process (Arellano Yanguas 2008). Further, because extractive projects are, by definition, finite, they do not provide sustained employment and income in host communities. Most contemporary mining projects have a time horizon of 10 to 20 years. Contemporary mining, much of which is technologically intensive surface mining, employs a fraction of the workers that mining of previous generations employed. For these and other reasons, mining can contribute to economic development but these are short-term gains which weaken social capital and reinforce social divisions.

This debate around mining for economic development in rural Latin America is embodied in the following two divergent quotes from peasant residents of the same mining region of Western Guatemala:

> What they [foreign mining firms] are doing here is making money. They're taking, taking the fortunes, the riches of Guatemala to other countries. That's what they're doing. We know this very well. Guatemala is rich but they take it to other countries, and what they leave us with is just a piece of candy.

> Here in Sipacapa there is no other source of work, and we, when the mine here began, well, we had a bit of work and now I think the mine has 2000 people that work there now. And these people have improved. Before the people from these communities only lived to get drunk. They would go to the coast [as seasonal harvesters at large plantations] to get money. But when the mine arrived, the situation got better, we got better. Before we didn't even have a horse. Now we have cars and motorcycles.

In addition to the economic risks, mining can transform the social landscape in host communities. Rural Latin America is relatively population dense, which means that often the mineralization that firms wish to develop is often underneath or adjacent to human settlements. This can generate social conflicts between locals over whether or not to support mineral development, and it can also generate deep tensions between locals and mining companies over the efficacy and appropriateness of mining as a rural development tool. These conflicts are referred to in the literature as ecological distribution conflicts. This is the notion that environmental conflicts are motivated by contests for control of access to natural resources, which emerge from different social understandings of nature (Martinez-Alier 2001). The 'boom town' effect of large-scale mineral development in remote rural areas also brings about social change (Gaventa 1980; Tauxe 1993). Often, industrial scale mines attract large numbers of prospective workers, and prostitution, petty crime and alcoholism increase with such population growth (Laite 2009).

Finally, the mining boom in rural Latin America has taken a severe toll on the biophysical environment in host communities and beyond, which presents further challenges for rural livelihood strategies. Although the right technology and safeguards can mitigate some, but not all, of the environmental threats that mining represents, many mining companies, particularly the numerous smaller 'junior' firms, elect to save money on operating costs by not implementing state-of-the-art safeguards (Dougherty 2011). The principal ways through which extractive projects negatively impact the environment include the removal of the forest cover and overburden, acid mine drainage and tailings disposal. With surface mining, to access the orebody, the company must excavate many tons of surface vegetation and tons of rock, soil and other matter. This generates large quantities of dust, promotes desertification, disrupts ecosystems and renders landscapes more vulnerable to erosion. Additionally, the excavation of these massive craters is aesthetically unappealing and permanently modifies rural peoples' patrimonial landscapes. Beyond the removal of the overburden, acid mine drainage and tailings disposal represent serious environmental threats.

Acid mine drainage takes place when ore that is high in sulfide is extracted from deep beneath the Earth's surface. Exposing the sulfide minerals to the oxygen and the iron-oxidizing bacteria at the surface allows for the release of heavy metals and sulfuric acid. These toxins can then be washed into surface water systems and leach into the soil and subterranean aquifers. Tailings refer to the waste material that is a byproduct of milling metallic ores. In many instances the chemicals used to separate ore from rock can be toxic, which make the tailings toxic as well. This separation process is known as leaching. Tailings usually take the form of a slurry containing pulverized waste rock, acid mine drainage and toxic leaching chemicals (such as cyanide in the case of gold mining).

The storage, treatment and reclamation of tailings is one of the costliest aspects of mining operations and also one of the aspects of mining that poses the greatest environmental risk. Therefore, unfortunately, many mineral firms elect to employ cost-efficient designs which could amplify the risk of systemic failure of the tailings enclosure. Although tailings enclosures are highly engineered systems, they can fail. Over the past century, hundreds of dams have failed, often resulting in significant environmental disasters.

These transformations in the economic, social and physical landscape of rural Latin America have, unsurprisingly, transformed rural livelihoods. The new extractive economy has intensified resource tenure vulnerabilities while providing new, albeit limited, opportunities for cash income and skill acquisition. This concern with resource tenure vulnerability is reflected in the following quotation from a Guatemalan peasant woman:

> Our water comes from those mountains [where the mine is proposed to be built]. So I think about the future, the children. What are they going to drink? What will they live off of? It's true that maybe the [mining] company could be here and give them some money, but the water, things that are nature? Where will they go to build that again?

In addition to direct concerns about resource tenure vulnerability, there can also be a sense of connection between environmental and resource concerns, sense of place, and the community social ties that mining threatens. The following quotation evidences this concern:

> We don't use anything else here to cook with [other than firewood] ... So we take care of what belongs to the people, what belongs to the people is ours. So if we propose to all take care of a thing, well we're all going to take care of a thing. Because it serves us. Because we live off of it. We live very far from the capital, very far. But we live happy here contemplating the nature that God left us.

These changes in social divisions and physical landscape that characterize the new mineral economy of rural Latin America have further proletarianized the peasantry and stoked social movements to protect traditional livelihoods. Mining has become a significant economic activity in rural Latin America over the past two decades, and the social and environmental risks of mining are high compared to the potential economic gains. Therefore, mining has become a symbolic touchstone for peasant and transnational activist resistance to the neoliberalization of rural Latin America. The following section will explore some of the social dynamics around new peasant social movements in rural Latin America over the past decade.

Understanding these movements – their claims, their strategies and the resources they mobilize – is key to understanding the changing nature of the Latin American peasantry and the configuration of rural livelihoods.

LAND STRUGGLES, TRANSNATIONAL LINKAGES AND THE RURAL PROLETARIAT IN LATIN AMERICA

Contemporary social movements in rural Latin America are very different from movements of previous decades. One of the principal characteristics that distinguish today's movements from those of earlier decades is their size and density. Today's rural movements are generally denser and incorporate a larger swathe of rural residents into the goals and actions than rural movements of previous generations. In part this is the case because the threats to rural livelihoods from today's sprawling industrial agriculture and mining are perceived as more acute and as affecting greater percentages of rural citizens. This is because, as discussed in the previous section, these industries today consume more land and produce greater environmental degradation without contributing correspondingly to economic development. Additionally, as mentioned above, economic integration and state social programming overwhelmingly bypass hinterland residents for the more readily accessible urban poor. Further, contemporary movements are larger because direct state repression of peasants, indigenous peoples and other marginal groups has diminished with the deepening of democracy, economic development and the global spread of instant media, all of which gives peasants more room to air their grievances (Brockett 2005). Finally, the proliferation of transnational activist networks and solidarity organizations, beginning in the 1990s, has helped galvanize and underwrite new rural movements, allowing them to flourish (Keck and Sikkink 1998).

A second way in which contemporary social movements in Latin America differ from those of previous decades regards the semi-proletarian character of rural communities and their social movements (Moyo and Yeros 2005). Historically, rural movements in Latin America had been peasant movements in which movement actors were unified by their position in the world-division of labor as smallholder farmers. In this context, movement claims emerged from agrarian culture, and the primary objective was the pursuit of land reform. As capitalism worked its way into the rural Latin American landscape, beginning in the 1950s, peasants began a process of proletarianization, and their movements began to reflect this changing character (Mintz 1974; Paige 1983). Proleterianization refers to the transition from family-owned smallholder farming for subsistence, to working for wage labor in mines and large-scale corporate farms. With increasing proletarianization, rural movements became politicized, abandoned land and agrarian reform as principal movement objectives in favor of the collective bargaining of trade unionism, and began to identify with the urban proletariat, assuming a character of class struggle. These were the rural movements that played significant roles in the guerrilla insurgencies of the 1970s and 1980s across Central America, Peru and the Southern Cone. The Communist Revolution in Cuba of the 1950s was instrumental in fostering this identity shift from peasantry to rural proletariat.

Contemporary rural social movements in Latin America no longer prioritize class-based grievances and electoral politics. Today's rural movements, according to some scholars, have experienced a re-peasantization, where land reform, territorial sovereignty, environmental issues and identity politics galvanize social organization and rural activism. The unifying force of contemporary rural Latin American movements is the individualizing language of human and indigenous rights rather than the collectivizing language of class struggle (Becker 2012). Today, Latin America's rural citizens are largely semi-proletarian – supplementing family farm income with rural off-farm work such as artisanal mining, seasonal migration, remittance income and participation in the informal economy (Kay 2000).

Beginning in the 1990s, this emphasis on rights and identity came to characterize what many social scientists have referred to as 'new social movements' in contrast to so-called 'old social movements' which were embedded in trade unionism, left-wing political parties and class-based guerrilla insurgencies (Escobar and Alvarez 1992). After Latin America's 'lost decade' of the 1980s, returns to workers in rural industry decreased dramatically, reducing worker leverage and trade union density. At the same time, international conventions, regional agreements and national constitutions began to open up space for indigenous rights and multicultural nationalism, allowing for the ascendancy of the global human rights and indigenous rights regimes (Barelli 2010). These shifts help account for the diminishing of old social movements and the emergence of new ones. Advocates of the local appropriation of legal practices, known as juridification, which have characterized rural social movements in Latin America since 2005, see promise in international legal instruments and their local interpretation (Sieder 2010). In contrast, critics of the legal basis for these actions describe this practice as 'neoliberal multiculturalism', deriding new social movements for their stylized and simplistic, and ultimately disempowering, reconstructions of indigenous identity as *indio permitido* (Hale 2002, 2005). Neo-Marxist scholars are critical of new social movements in Latin America as synchronizing with neoliberal efforts to exclude some social groups from the benefits of the circuit of capital by preventing peasants from engaging with the structures of capital accumulation (Brass 2002).

Since the 1980s, international legal instruments such as the International Labour Organization's Convention 169 on the Rights of Indigenous and Tribal Peoples in Independent Countries, and the United Nations Declaration on the Rights of Indigenous Peoples, have institutionalized the right of free, prior and informed consent for indigenous peoples facing mining projects. According to this international norm, indigenous peoples must be substantively consulted and grant their consent before any large-scale external project (such as a mine or hydroelectric dam) can begin in indigenous territory. The right to grant or withhold consent is not the same as the right to reject a mining project outright. Rather, indigenous groups have the right to shape the project, within reason, to maximize benefits and minimize adverse impacts for the host community. Increasingly, international institutions such as the International Council for Mining of Metals and the World Bank are conceding to some level of consultation of indigenous peoples, but in most cases this falls short of the standards for free, prior and informed consent established in international law.

In one recent case, the gold mining company Manhattan Minerals sought to locate a mine on top of the large town of Tambo Grande in northern Peru. In 2002, the inhabitants of the town, facing displacement, organized a municipal referendum to decide whether or not to allow mining in their territory. Ninety-four percent of participants voted to prohibit mining. This model has been duplicated in other places, most notably in Guatemala, where since 2005 nearly 700 000 people in 61 municipalities have voted to prohibit mining in their territory. These votes are not legally binding, however, since the government usually owns subsoil rights and mining is considered to be in the national interest. Nevertheless, they give a sense of the growing resistance to large-scale, high-tech mining in Latin America.

In addition to the ascendancy of the global human rights discourse, a shift in the structures of capital accumulation from accumulation by exploitation to accumulation by dispossession has fortified the re-peasantization of rural Latin America and the emergence of new social movements (Harvey 2005). Extractive industries and commercial agriculture in rural areas have dramatically reduced their need for unskilled labor, which translates into a significant diminishment of employment opportunities for rural residents around mine sites. In previous generations, foreign firms maximized profit by pushing against acceptable labor standards and seeking to exploit their large local labor forces. Movements, therefore, turned on improving standards for workers. Today these firms, rather than viewing rural residents as a flexible and exploitable labor force, tend to see them as in the way, and profits turn on expropriating peasant land rather than exploiting peasant labor. This shift in the way extractive companies perceive local populations has been described as a shift from accumulation by exploitation to accumulation by dispossession (Bebbington et al. 2008).

This shift serves as both cause and effect for the re-peasantization – the transformation from worker back to peasant – of the Latin American rural population as well as the shift from old to new social movements. The shift in the way locals have reacted to mining projects in Guatemala from the 1970s to the 2000s exemplifies this transformation. In late 1977 Mario Mujía Córdoba, leader of the Mines Union of Ixtahuacán and the National Workers Center (Central Nacional de Trabajadores), today affiliated with the International Trade Union Confederation, helped to organize a strike of mine workers in a tungsten mine in San Idelfonso Ixtahuacán, Huehuetenango. The mine workers, predominantly of the Maya Mam ethnolinguistic group, struck for improved working conditions and wages. The continued ignorance of worker demands by management led workers to organize a foot-march from Huehuetenango to Guatemala City (roughly 150 kilometers over extremely mountainous terrain). As they marched, sympathizers fed and housed them, and hundreds joined in. Upon their arrival in Guatemala City thousands of sympathizers received them (Hurtado Paz y Paz 2009, p. 13). This march became an important symbol of the struggle for justice in Guatemala and had far-reaching historical impacts. It helped to solidify the guerrilla insurgency in the Sierra de los Cuchumatanes, and it helped to give birth to the Campesino Unity Committee (CUC), a clandestine political organization operating on behalf of peasants and workers. Rather than seeking to critically engage mineral capital to extract a more equitable share of the rents, the indigenous and land rights model of resistance rejects all mining activity categorically on the basis of the globally recognized indigenous right to free, prior and informed consent. Today mine workers, far from being the symbols of righteous proletarian struggle that they were in the 1970s, are seen as traitors to the cause.

Bebbington et al. (2008a, p. 901) recognize this same shift in the Andean context and suggest that the change reflects a hopeful and potentially transformative shift to struggles 'over the meaning of development rather than simply the distribution of rent'. These authors contend that contemporary anti-mining movements challenge neoliberal orthodoxy by opposing 'development oriented towards economic growth' in favor of 'development as a process that fosters more inclusive economies ... and allows for the co-existence of cultures and localized forms of territorial governance' (Bebbington et al. 2008a, p. 901). Similarly, although writing from the other end of this same historical process in reference to tin miners in Bolivia in the 1970s, Michael T. Taussig (1980, p. 153), laments 'the proletarianization of Indians, associated with a strange fetishization of commodities and the unnatural economy of wage work'. Yet as Jeffery Paige (1983) argues, it was the very proletarianization of the Maya that empowered Mayan peasants in the Western Highlands of Guatemala in the late 1970s to become politically active, as the Ixtahuacán miners' strike exemplifies.

New social movements in rural Latin America are characterized, in part, by the drive to defend and enforce human rights, including the right to territorial sovereignty. This idea dovetails with the multicultural and individualistic character of new social movements. More recently, the idea of sovereignty has been adapted from a strict territorial interpretation, tied up with indigenous peoples' nationalism, to an application to food and environmental stewardship through the visibility of La Via Campesina and the recent food sovereignty movement. The term 'food sovereignty' emerged in the late 1990s but developed momentum in 2003 as a critique of and an alternative to the notion of food security. Food security promised access to sufficient and nutritious food but failed to challenge the global, corporate, industrial food complex's emphasis on techno-scientific food production where yield is the most important metric. Food sovereignty – a formulation that emerged from Latin America's re-peasantized agrarian movements – emphasized local control of food production and distribution as well as more conventional emphases on cultural appropriateness and nutrition. La Via Campesina is a coalition of over 148 organizations from 69 countries, which has become the most powerful and widely recognized voice for food sovereignty across Latin America and beyond (Wittman et al. 2010).

The changing goals and composition of rural social movements in Latin America are intimately tied to asset bundles and livelihood strategies. Livelihoods are becoming both less secure and more varied as agriculture diminishes in importance while migration and remittances become the centerpiece of rural income. This insecurity drives a retrenchment of community sovereignty and well-founded mistrust of outsiders. Also in the current climate, social and affective ties to land and territory have intensified even as the dependence on agriculture has diminished. Finally, natural resources – land, water, timber and minerals – are at the center of the current ecological distribution conflicts between rural citizens, extractive companies and the state. New rural social movements are responding to this environment of insecurity and mistrust. The growing predominance of migration and income remittance as a livelihood strategy in rural Latin America has complex and contradictory impacts on these rural movements. On the one hand, the additional income allows rural residents the economic space to organize and struggle. On the other hand, it diminishes the urgency of their claims to resource tenure and sovereignty. In the next section, I turn to the role of migration and remittance income in forging livelihoods in the new rural Latin America.

MIGRATION, WORK AND REMITTANCE INCOME

As the scope of economic opportunities in rural Latin America becomes increasingly limited – as land for family farming becomes increasingly scarce, returns to rural labor stagnate and inflation increases economic pressures on families – many rural workers seek to migrate to other regions, and indeed other countries, to seek employment. Once employed, these migrants often remit a portion of their income to their family members who remained in source communities. This remittance income, as it is called, can comprise a significant percentage of income for family members remaining behind. Indeed remittance income from citizens working abroad can form a large percentage of certain source countries' gross domestic product and foreign exchange.

Latin America is among the largest remittance-receiving regions across the globe. In 2006, for example, Latin America received more than $50 billion in remittances, the largest relative quantity of any world region. Remittances to Latin America represent 70 percent of direct flows of US dollars to the region and are more than eight times larger than income from overseas development assistance to the region. Within Latin America there is a great deal of unevenness between countries in terms of remittance receipts. Mexico receives the largest gross amount of remittance income, almost exclusively from immigrants working in the United States. The Caribbean is also a significant recipient of remittance income. In Haiti, remittances constitute approximately 50 percent of gross domestic product, and the Dominican Republic also receives large remittance inflows (Fajnzylber and Lopez 2008).

There are three principal types of migration for employment. These are categorized by their geographic patterns. South–North migration refers to emigration from the poorer countries of Latin America to the wealthier countries of North America. Mexican and Central American emigration to the United States is the emblematic case of South–North migration. There is also significant South–South migration from poorer countries of Latin America to wealthier neighboring nations. Bolivian, Ecuadorian and Peruvian migration to Chile and Argentina represent this particular pattern. Finally, there is a great deal of internal migration from rural areas to urban areas within the same countries.

South–North migration is the archetypal emigration from Latin America to the United States and Canada. In large stretches of Mesoamerica – Mexico and Northern Central America – migration to the United States has become a pillar of the rural economy. Northern Mesoamerica sources a disproportionate amount of immigrant workers from Latin America to the United States simply because of the push/pull of proximity and need. Further, formal government programs, such as the United States' Bracero Program, which imported Mexican agricultural guest workers from the 1940s until the 1960s, helped develop social networks that continue to facilitate emigration, both legal and illegal, from Mexico today. Dollarization, the adoption of the US dollar as the official currency in countries other than the United States, is intended to facilitate foreign direct investment, but also has the effect of encouraging South–North migration. Both Ecuador and El Salvador have dollarized their economies in recent years, which has led to increased emigration to the United States. As a result of dollarization combined with acute need and proximity to the United States, remittance income accounts for nearly 20 percent of gross domestic product in El Salvador.

South–South migration is the term used to describe emigration from one developing country to another developing country. South–South migration from rural Latin America is nearly as common as South–North migration. The vast bulk of South–South migration occurs across adjacent or nearby countries with common languages, and, like rural to urban migration, often consists of off-season migration of agricultural wage workers. In this way, South–South migration reinforces the semi-proletarian nature of rural residents in contemporary Latin America. Although the returns to work are often much smaller in South–South versus South–North movement, the transaction costs are many fewer. There is generally less distance to travel, a smaller cultural and linguistic divide to overcome, and easier and less costly border crossings. The reduced transaction costs often outweigh the promise of greater incomes in North America. For this reason, nearly half of Latin American migrants reside in other developing countries in Latin America, and scholars estimate between 10 and 30 percent of remittance income flows into Latin America come from South–South migrants (Ratha and Shaw 2007).

The economic sectors in which South–South migrants work are similar to those of South–North migrants – domestic service, retail service and agriculture – although the distribution of migrant labor across these sectors differs. South–South migrants are mostly women and are concentrated in domestic service, while migrants to the United States are mostly male and are concentrated in agriculture, retail service and agroindustry. The case of Chile exemplifies the growth of South–South migration in Latin America. Over the past decade, emigration from Ecuador and Peru to Chile has grown by nearly 300 percent (*Revista Capital* 2008). Well over half of Peruvian emigrants to Chile are female (Gonzáles 2006).

The final category of rural out-migration in contemporary Latin America is rural-to-urban migration within national boundaries. In this case, economic pressures drive out-migration from rural areas to outer-ring urban settlements in search of work. This process, which accounts for the vast majority of urban population growth over the past 30 years, is driven by the processes of de-peasantization discussed above. Agricultural deregulation and fiscal austerity imposed on the governments of Latin America throughout the 1980s and 1990s as part of the World Bank and International Monetary Fund structural adjustment policies had the dual squeezing effects on the Latin American peasantry of modernizing and mechanizing agriculture, thus diminishing the number of jobs in this sector and rolling back social safety nets and infrastructural development in hinterland regions (Davis 2006).

These trends forced billions of peasants to migrate to urban centers in Latin America, less as a function of opportunities associated with urban economic growth, and more as a function of the untenable bleakness of rural regions (Davis 2006). The effect has been the generation of megalopolises and urban corridors choked with informal slums. Since 1960, Latin America has urbanized by over 1000 percent. Sao Paulo, Brazil and Mexico City have grown by 17 and 19 million people, respectively, while Rio de Janeiro and Buenos Aires have both added 8 million residents. Lima, Peru and Bogotá, Colombia have both added over 7 million. This has dramatically deepened the gap between the poor and the middle class in urban Latin America. Worse, city governments lack the capacity to plan, accommodate and integrate the slums that house most of these rural migrants into municipal service provision, creating sprawling, informal slums. In Brazil, ringing Rio de Janeiro, these areas are famously known as *favelas*. Outside of Lima, Peru, these communities are referred to as *Pueblos Jovenes*; in Guatemala City, they are *asentamientos*. Across Latin America, they are dirty, ad hoc, dangerous places where the newly urbanized and the semi-proletarian former farmers seek wage work in an effort to improve their livelihoods and those of their families.

These patterns of movement (South–North migration, South–South migration, and rural-to-urban migration) across Latin America, and the significant remittance income that results, has a series of contradictory impacts on rural livelihoods in sending regions. Remittance flows can enhance human and built capital and help alleviate poverty, but the out-migration that necessarily prefigures remittance income drains human capital, transforms social structures and can create dependencies that rob rural residents of agency and power.

Remittances in many parts of rural Latin America represent the considerable majority of cash income. For this reason, as remittance flows increase, poverty decreases because recipient families have more disposable income with which to purchase staples. Further, remittance flows are positively correlated with educational attainment and public health indicators on the community level (Fajnzylber and Lopez 2008). The additional income allows families to purchase more and better-quality education and health care for children. Remittance income can also serve to insulate agrarian communities against exogenous shocks such as drought, inflation, commodity price volatility, crop disease and natural disaster. Remittance income allows semi-proletarianized rural citizens to live less precariously and manage in times of austerity or crisis. Further, on the national scale, remittance flows are associated with higher rates of economic growth and investment (Fajnzylber and Lopez 2008). In short, remittances represent meaningful and important short-term economic development on the community and national levels for countries that receive significant remittance income.

Despite clear short-term gains, the longer-term effects are more dubious. In particular, the selection effect embedded in the phenomenon of rural migration transforms demographic and social structures in problematic ways. Not all rural residents are equally likely to migrate. Out-migrants from rural Latin America, particularly within the dominant South–North paradigm, are positively selected for educational and income levels, which means families with individuals that emigrate from rural Mesoamerica to the United States are generally better educated and better off financially than those families who do not source migrants. This generates a phenomenon known as 'brain drain' in which the better-educated, more entrepreneurial and less risk-averse residents – in other words those who contribute most substantially to local economic development – are disproportionately absent. Some migrant source countries have lost significant percentages of their college-educated population (Fajnzylber and Lopez 2008). In addition to the education and income selection effects, emigration from Latin America in general and Mesoamerica in particular is positively selected for younger males. In general, men on the lower end of working age – men in their teens, twenties and thirties – tend to migrate most often. This leaves source communities disproportionately populated by females, older individuals and individuals with lower relative education and incomes, all of which greatly skews community development and livelihood strategies for source communities (Hanson 2006).

In addition to selection effects, out-migration from rural Latin America can fall short of its economic development potential in two key ways. First, it can generate additional expenses for sending families which can neutralize some of the added income that remittances provide. Second, the net profits from remittances are often 'misspent'.

Out-migration of young men can represent significant expenses for sending families. Not only do families have the expense of the migration itself, but female-headed households often have to hire expensive day laborers – *jornaleros* – to help with the planting and the harvest rather than depend on family labor. These added expenses, in years when commodity prices are low, often make the harvest uneconomical, leaving many acres of crops to rot in the fields. These additional costs absorb much of the remittance income, rendering the ultimate economic impact on households relatively modest.

While remittance income on the national level is correlated with higher rates of investment, on the community level such income is often culturally earmarked for non-productive destinations such as house construction and the purchase of consumer durables such as modern household appliances and automobiles. This is the case because, as Douglas M. Massey (2005) suggests, rural Mexicans are often unable to receive financing for home purchases in Mexico, and remittance income is a way to overcome this market failure. Because much remittance income becomes destined for bricks and mortar rather than investment in entrepreneurship, these flows fall short of their local development potential.

In addition to the fairly modest short-term economic gains and questionable impact on equitable and sustainable long-term economic development, migration for remittances creates social change in rural source communities. First off, the remittance phenomenon can intensify class disparities between remittance recipient and non-recipient families. Since the poorest households lack the financial flexibility to emigrate, remittance flows accrue to better-off households and bypass the poorest segments of the population (Fajnzylber and Lopez 2008). This exacerbates inequality and social conflict as well as limiting the equitability of economic development. As mentioned above, sending communities are disproportionately populated by women, children and the elderly. One positive effect of migration is the way in which women who remain behind when their partners and children migrate become more emotionally and financially independent, assume more leadership and take over a greater amount of financial as well as familial decision making. These changes also reconfigure the division of labor by expanding the range of responsibilities women confront and the amount and types of work they are called upon to perform. Remaining parents must administer the household, the finances and participate in educational and civic activities. One solution to this problem, which is in use in Southern Mexico, is referred to as clustering. Clustering occurs when multiple households band together to share workloads and for social protection in the absence of the male members of the household (Hernandez-Juarez 2009).

Also in Southern Mexico, local governance often takes place through a hybrid public–private system in which community members, particularly adult men, perform essentially voluntary roles in local committees, state-run social programming, and community police and fire brigades. The exodus of out-migrants from these areas has weakened local governance structures and diminished direct citizen participation in governance (Hernandez-Juarez 2009). Further, not only does the disproportionate absence of working-age men impact social organization in sending communities, but where remittance income is invested in sending children away from the community for high school and college education, migration creates a feedback loop in which young people become effectively too educated to remain in the community. Because economic opportunities appropriate for their educational level are unavailable at home, this new generation, educated on remittance income, is forging new lives in the cities, further exacerbating the brain drain in rural areas.

In sum, remittance impacts on rural livelihoods are most pronounced in the case of South–North emigration, but are present also among the other geographic patterns. Remittances do promote economic development and should be encouraged, but the economic impacts are modest and the social transformations significant.

SUMMARY, DISCUSSION AND POLICY IMPLICATIONS

In sum, rural Latin America has undergone a series of major changes over the past three decades. These include the further disappearance of peasant farming due to the volatility of commodity prices, the large-scale land acquisitions of agroindustrial firms, and the failure of states to implement land reform. Further, Latin America's remote landscapes have been inundated with large-scale metal mining and energy projects, including hydro-electric dams, which flood the countryside and displace communities. The entrenchment of the semi-proletarian lifestyle for rural residents – together with the proliferation of transnational activist networks – has catalyzed forceful social movements on behalf of rural peoples. Finally, many families have responded to this squeezing of their traditional sources of livelihoods by emigrating from rural areas in search of work in cities or other countries.

In light of these changes to rural landscapes, economic opportunities and social structures, are rural people in Latin America experiencing improved quality of life? Under this semi-proletarian regime, characterized by remittance income and short-term contract work, many households are experiencing higher levels of income and more economic flexibility than they experienced as peasant farmers in previous decades. Yet, they also experience the stress of the volatility and uncertainty of these sources of livelihoods in contrast to the secure austerity of peasant subsistence. Further, many households are unable to capitalize on these changes and experience even greater insecurity vis-à-vis their sources of clean water for drinking, washing and irrigation, their ownership of arable land for agriculture and their capacity to provide health care and education to their children. In short, some households have benefitted greatly while others are marginally better off or remain largely unchanged economically, but social and political shifts elevate the level of uncertainty regarding the future as livelihoods become less related to natural resource tenure and more related to short-term contract work and remittance income.

The transformations discussed above have had the effect of exacerbating social divisions in rural Latin America, which is problematic on two fronts. First, it disrupts the traditional mechanisms of social organization and control and can cause problems in the community such as resentment, violence, crime and drug and alcohol abuse. Second, by creating or emphasizing class divisions in rural societies that are traditionally relatively egalitarian, these changes diminish the multiplier effect of economic development. The multiplier effect occurs when increased income leads to increased local spending that in turn bolsters income for other sectors of the local economy and creates a beneficent upward spiral of local economic development. However, this effect is predicated on the availability of desired goods and services within the local economy and the willingness of those households receiving additional income to spend that income rather than save it. When local elites capture the majority of new income flows, as is happening in rural Latin America, that additional income is often spent on consumer durables, which are not available locally, or it is put into savings. These actions limit the multiplier effect, and therefore prevent the new sources of income from contributing to meaningful and equitable local economic development in which everyone experiences improved quality of life.

Another crucial consideration regarding changes to rural livelihoods in Latin America is environmental degradation. The onslaught of extractive projects across rural Latin America has not only complicated access to land and water resources, but in certain sites has reduced water quality and soil fertility through acid mine drainage and the release of tailings into the environment. In addition, industrial agriculture, while not necessarily more chemical-intensive than peasant agriculture, is certainly larger scale. Because of the sheer expanse of industrial agriculture, it is responsible for introducing a great deal of insecticide into the environment and choking riverine ecosystems with aquatic plants fed from fertilizer runoff. Moreover, industrial-scale livestock operations produce large quantities of effluent, which can further contaminate water sources. This point-source variety of environmental pollution is more concentrated in specific areas than in others and tends to disproportionately impact rural peoples living near the sources, who depend on the water and land resources being degraded.

Finally, we must consider whether shifts in livelihood bundles and strategies taking place in rural Latin America constitute improvement in quality of life. This is a difficult assessment because quality of life is subjective and challenging to measure. Per capita income has largely grown for rural residents over the past decade, although inflation and the rising cost of food and fuel may mitigate a good deal of these gains. Yet, surely life quality is more than just income. Despite the wealth of qualitative attention paid to the complexities of poverty and life quality, orthodox development studies continue to evaluate these phenomena with simplistic measures such as income and consumption, and ignore social relations (Green and Hulme 2005). As Green and Zinda remind readers in Chapter 1 of this volume, growth and development are not synonymous. Rather, there are a host of social and political considerations external to economic growth that matter in evaluating development. Similarly, quality of life is more than income. It includes easily measurable variables such as educational attainment and public health outcomes, but it also includes nebulous and elusive variables such as affective ties, civic strength, women's empowerment and social equity.

Recent shifts in rural livelihoods in Latin America have had complex impacts on these phenomena. Social equity has diminished and class divisions are underscored, but women's empowerment has improved as females take over a range of traditionally male responsibilities while men migrate internationally for work. Changes to affective ties and mental health are more difficult to evaluate, but as resource tenure security is challenged, it seems likely that acquiring and sustaining livelihoods has become more stressful. Ultimately, the semi-proletarianization of rural Latin America over the past two decades has had ambiguous impacts on rural life quality. It has clearly improved some aspects while complicating others.

The lessons of these trends and their implications are fourfold. Communities and states must: (1) mitigate the ills and capitalize on the strengths of migration and remittances; (2) fortify workers' rights and bargaining positions; (3) strengthen rural civil society; and (4) diversify the rural–industrial mix.

Both the state and local civil society should develop programs to mitigate some of the most adverse impacts of migration while capitalizing on the income flows that result. Microcredit and micro-insurance programs should be expanded to encourage small business development in areas losing their risk-tolerant and well-educated to emigration. Further, programs should work to channel remittance income into productive destinations rather than into imported consumer durables. In other words, remittance-receiving households must learn to treat that income as capital rather than as profit.

Regarding the changing nature of rural work in Latin America, from smallholder agriculture to contract extractive work, states must develop the capacity and the willingness to shore up the rights and the bargaining positions of rural workers in mining and plantation agriculture. This should be done through legislation, regulation, effective monitoring and an independent judiciary. The new rural work contains promise, but so far, returns to workers have fallen far short of compensating for the new land tenure insecurities and environmental risks these industries portend.

Social organization has been upset in rural Latin America by these recent changes, and some aspects of civil society have been weakened as a result while others have been strengthened. Inequality and social conflict are greater today than in the past. Yet, the intensity of threats to traditional livelihoods has galvanized rural social movements around collective identities and goals. Rural communities must work to strengthen the local social ties necessary to distribute gains from economic development more evenly, thus enhancing the multiplier effect.

Finally, while rural work has diversified in recent years, it has done so from outside the community. Rural Latin America itself must make an effort to further diversity its industry mix, including a rehabilitated small-scale agriculture aimed at niche export markets rather than subsistence, value-added processing of agricultural products and careful, locally driven ecotourism. In short, rural livelihoods are at a crossroads. If rural civil society and the state in Latin America are able to harness these new income opportunities to enhance local decision making, industrial diversity and equity, the new economic landscape could become a boon to development in rural Latin America.

NOTE

1.   I appreciate the input of Annabel Ipsen.

REFERENCES

Arellano Yanguas, Javier (2008), 'A thoroughly modern resource curse? The new natural resource policy agenda and the mining revival in Peru', IDS Working paper 300, Institute for Development Studies.

Barelli, M. (2010), 'The interplay between global and regional human rights systems in the construction of the indigenous rights regime', *Human Rights Quarterly*, 34, 951–79.

Bebbington, A. (1999), 'Capitals and capabilities: a framework for analyzing peasant viability, rural livelihoods and poverty', *World Development*, 27, 2021–44.

Bebbington, A., L. Hinojosa, D.H. Bebbington, M.L. Burneo, and X. Warnaars (2008), 'Contention and ambiguity: mining and the possibilities of development', *Development and Change*, 39, 887–914.

Bebbington, A., D. Humphreys Bebbington, J. Bury, J. Lingan, J.P. Muñoz and M. Scurrah (2008), 'Mining and social movements: struggles over livelihood and rural territorial development in the Andes', *World Development*, 36, 2888–2905.

Becker, M. (2012), 'Social movements', in S.G. Beavis, M.L. Dougherty and T. Gonzalez (eds), *Encyclopedia of Sustainability Volume 8: The Americas and Oceania: Assessing Sustainability*, Great Barrington, MA: Berkshire Publishing.

Blaikie, P.T., T. Cannon, I. Davis, and B. Wisner (1994), *At Risk: Natural Hazards, People's Vulnerability and Disasters*, London: Routledge.

Brass, T. (2002), 'On which side of what barricade? Subaltern resistance in Latin America and elsewhere', *Journal of Peasant Studies*, 29, 336–99.

Brass, T. (2003), 'Latin American peasants – new paradigms for old?', in T. Brass (ed.), *Latin American Peasants*, London: Frank Cass, pp. 1–42.

Bridge, G. (2004), 'Mapping the bonanza: geographies of mining investment in an era of neoliberal reform', *Professional Geographer*, 56, 406–21.

Brockett, C.D. (2005), *Political Movements and Violence in Central America*, Cambridge: Cambridge University Press.

Bunker, S.G. and P.S. Ciccantell (2005), *Globalization and the Race for Resources*, Baltimore, MD: Johns Hopkins University Press.

Bury, J. (2004), 'Livelihoods in transition: transnational gold mining operations and local change in Cajamarca, Peru', *Geographical Journal*, 170, 78–91.

Carney, D. (1998), 'Implementing the sustainable livelihoods approach', in D. Carney (ed.), *Sustainable Rural Livelihoods: What Contributions Can We Make?* Nottingham: Russell Press, pp. 2–27.

Davis, M. (2006), *Planet of Slums*, New York: Verso.

Donnelly, R. and B. Ford (2008), 'Into Africa: how the resource boom is making sub-Saharan Africa more important to Australia', Lowy Institute for International Policy, Lowy Institute Paper 24.

Dougherty, M.L. (2011), 'The global gold mining industry, junior firms, and civil society resistance in Guatemala', *Bulletin of Latin American Research*, 30, 403–18.

Escobar, A. and S. Alvarez (1992), 'Introduction: theory and protest in Latin America today', in A. Escobar and S.E. Alvarez (eds), *The Making of Social Movements in Latin America: Identity, Strategy and Democracy*. Boulder, CO: Westview Press, pp. 1–18.

Fajnzylber, P. and J.H. Lopez (2008), 'The development impact of remittances in Latin America', in Fajnzylber, P. and J.H. Lopez (eds), *Remittances and Development: Lessons from Latin America*, Washington, DC: World Bank, pp. 1–20.

Gaventa, J. (1980), *Power and Powerlessness: Quiescence and Rebellion in an Appalachian Valley*, Urbana, IL: University of Illinois Press.

González, F. (2006), 'Derechos humanos de las personas inmigrantes', in *Informe Anual sobre Derechos Humanos en Chile*. Available at http://www.bcn.cl/carpeta_temas/temas_

portada.2006-05-16.1264867506/documentos_pdf.2006-05-16.5645522940/archivos_
pdf.2006-05-16.1875964063/archivo1 (accessed June 11, 2012).

Green, M. and D. Hulme (2005), 'From correlates and characteristics to causes: thinking about poverty from a chronic poverty perspective', *World Development*, 33, 867–79.

Hale, C.R. (2002), 'Does multiculturalism menace? Governance, cultural rights and the politics of identity in Guatemala', *Journal of Latin American Studies*, 34, 485–524.

Hale, C.R. (2005), 'Neoliberal multiculturalism: the remaking of cultural rights and racial dominance in Central America', *PoLAR: Political and Legal Anthropology Review*, 28, 10–28.

Hanson, G.H. (2006), 'Illegal migration from Mexico to the US', *Journal of Economic Literature*, 44, 869–924.

Harvey, D. (2005), *The New Imperialism*, Oxford: Blackwell.

Hernandez-Juarez, M. (2009), *Changing Livelihoods among Low-Income and Rural Households in Oaxaca, Mexico*, unpublished PhD dissertation, Madison, WI: University of Wisconsin–Madison.

Hurtado Paz y Paz, M. (2009), 'Organización y lucha rural, campesina e indígena: Huehuetenango, Guatemala, 1981', Guatemala City: FLACSO.

Kay, C. (2000), 'Latin America's agrarian transformation, peasantization and proletarianization', in D.F. Bryceson, C. Kay and J. Mooij (eds), *Disappearing Peasantries? Rural Labour in Africa, Asia and Latin America*, London: Intermediate Technology Publications, pp. 123–38.

Keck, M.E. and K. Sikkink (1998), *Activists beyond Borders: Advocacy Networks in International Politics*, Ithaca, NY: Cornell University Press.

Lahiri-Dutt, K. (2011), 'Gendering the masculine field of mining for sustainable community livelihoods', in K. Lahiri-Dutt (ed.), *Gendering the Field: Towards Sustainable Livelihoods for Mining Communities*, Canberra: ANU Press, pp. 1–21.

Laite, J.A. (2009), 'Historical perspectives on industrial development, mining, and prostitution', *Historical Journal*, 52, 739–761.

Martinez-Alier, J. (2001), 'Mining conflicts, environmental justice, and valuation', *Journal of Hazardous Material*, 86, 153–70.

Massey, D. (2005), 'Five myths about immigration: common misconceptions underlying US border-enforcement policy', *Immigration Policy in Focus*, 4, 1–12.

Mintz, S.W. (1974), 'The rural proletarian and the problem of rural proletarian consciousness', *Journal of Peasant Studies*, 1, 291–325.

Moyo, S. and P. Yeros (2005), 'The resurgence of rural movements under neoliberalism', in S. Moyo and P. Yeros (eds), *Reclaiming the Land: The Resurgence of Rural Movements in Africa, Asia and Latin America*, London, UK and New York, USA: Zed Books, pp. 8–66.

Paige, J.M. (1983), 'Social theory and peasant revolution in Vietnam and Guatemala', *Theory and Society*, 12, 699–736.

Ratha, D. and W. Shaw (2007), 'South–South migration and remittances', World Bank Working Paper No. 102.

Revista Capital (2008), 'Marea Extranjera', N. 220, Dec. 07–Jan 08. http://www.capital.cl/reportajes-y-entrevistas/marea-extranjera-3.html (accessed June 21, 2012).

Sieder, R. (2010), 'Legal cultures in the (un)rule of law: indigenous rights and juridification in Guatemala', in Couso, J., A. Hunneus and R. Sieder (eds), *Cultures of Legality: Judicialization and Political Activism in Latin America*, New York: Cambridge University Press, pp. 161–81.

Taussig, M.T. (1980), *The Devil and Commodity Fetishism in South America*, Chapel Hill, NC: University of North Carolina Press.

Tauxe, C. (1993), *Farms, Mines and Main Streets: Uneven Development in a Dakota County*, Philadephia, PA: Temple University Press.

Valdivia, C. and J. Gilles (2001), 'Gender and resource management: households and groups, strategies and transitions', *Agriculture and Human Values*, 18, 5–9.

Wittman, H., A. Desmarais and N. Wiebe (2010), 'The origins and potential of food sovereignty', in H. Wittman, A. Desmarais and N. Wiebe (eds), *Food Sovereignty: Reconnecting Food, Nature and Community*, Winnepeg, CA: Fernwood Publishing, pp. 1–14.

World Bank (2008), *World Development Report: Agriculture for Development*, Washington, DC: World Bank.

Zoomers, A. (2001), 'Linking land to livelihoods', in A. Zoomers (ed.), *Land and Sustainable Livelihood in Latin America*, Amsterdam, KIT Publishers.

Index